EPI

Rule the Rules of
Workplace
Wellness
Programs

BARBARA J. ZABAWA, JD, MPH

JOANN M. EICKHOFF-SHEMEK, PHD

Employer Services

Kristina Jan Beale
senior compliance consultant
t: 415.356.3998
c: 415.710.1428
f: 415.284.9954
kbeale@edgewoodins.com

AMERICAN BAR ASSOCIATION
Health Law Section

Cover design by Mary Ane Kulchawik/ABA Design

Printed in the United States of America.

21 20 19 18 17   5 4 3 2 1

ISBN: 978-1-63425-778-7
e-ISBN: 978-1-63425-779-4

Library of Congress Cataloging-in-Publication Data

Names: Zabawa, Barbara J., author. | Eickhoff-Shemek, JoAnn M., author.
Title: Rule the rules of workplace wellness programs / Barbara J. Zabawa and JoAnn Eickhoff-Shemek, Authors.
Description: Chicago : American Bar Association, 2017. | Includes index.
Identifiers: LCCN 2016058983 (print) | LCCN 2016059741 (ebook) | ISBN 9781634257787 (softcover : alk. paper) | ISBN 9781634257794 (ebook)
Subjects: LCSH: Employee health promotion—Law and legislation—United States. | Employee fringe benefits—Law and legislation—United States. | Labor laws and legislation—United States. | Employees—Health risk assessment.
Classification: LCC KF3515 .Z33 2017 (print) | LCC KF3515 (ebook) | DDC 344.7301/2554—dc23
LC record available at https://lccn.loc.gov/2016058983

Discounts are available for books ordered in bulk. Special consideration is given to state bars, CLE programs, and other bar-related organizations. Inquire at Book Publishing, ABA Publishing, American Bar Association, 321 N. Clark Street, Chicago, Illinois 60654-7598.

www.shopABA.org

This book is dedicated to my family, who is always there for me: my husband, Branden; my children, Patrick and Vivian; and my parents, Gerald and Avila.

—Barbara J. Zabawa, JD, MPH

This book is dedicated to my husband, Patrick. I am truly grateful for his love, support, humor, and patience throughout this academic endeavor and many others.

—JoAnn M. Eickhoff-Shemek, PhD

Contents

Acknowledgments

Barbara's Acknowledgments

I have learned that contributions to a book come in many forms. There are those who inspire you to write a book, those who encourage you to keep writing even when the finished product seems impossible, those who offer ideas to improve your book, those who offer support (financial or otherwise), those who offer to help with research or writing, those who agree to publish your book, and those who just help remind you why you are writing the book in the first place. I have many people to thank in each of those categories and I am certain that I won't be able to call out everyone by name. The names that come to mind, however, are my husband, Branden Zimmerman, who has the honor of helping in most of the categories listed above; my children, Patrick and Vivian, who sacrificed a lot of time without their mom so I could finish this project; the Wisconsin Chiropractic Association, and its Executive Director John Murray, as well as Turville Bay MRI and its Executive Director Barb Thiermann, for giving me the opportunity to dive into wellness law on my own; my co-author, JoAnn Eickhoff-Shemek, for offering to help and contributing some really fantastic ideas to the book; my wellness colleagues Amy Williams, Michelle Spehr, Patricia Lenius, Lisa Elsinger, Marybeth Herbst-Flagstad, Michaela Conley, and Carrie Aiken for their encouragement and validation on the need for the book; Joe Forward, for being eager to learn about wellness law and help the cause; the board members for Health Promotion Advocates, and Michael O'Donnell in particular, for providing me insight into the health promotion field; the University of Wisconsin Law School and the University of Michigan School of Public Health for teaching me the skills that form the foundation of this book; the Watson Foundation and Lawrence University, for offering me the once-in-a-lifetime opportunity to travel abroad after my undergraduate term to study workplace wellness; and finally, my all-time favorite mentor, Louise G. Trubek, for always believing in my academic abilities and teaching me how to change the legal landscape through the written word.

JoAnn's Acknowledgments

Given a 40-plus-year career as a fitness and wellness professional, there are many individuals who have helped and influenced me with academic endeavors such as this book, but I can only name a few here. First is Barbara Zabawa, a gifted writer who invited me to be her co-author for this groundbreaking book. I am so grateful for this opportunity and everything I learned from her about federal laws and wellness law while working with her throughout this effort. Second are those who have contributed to my legal education throughout my career, such as my PhD committee members at the University of Nebraska-Lincoln (UN-L), Drs. John Scheer, Charles Ansorge, Kris Berg, and Frank Forbes. With their guidance, they allowed me to design my doctoral program of study, which included completing law classes in the UN-L College of Law and a dissertation in the legal/risk management area. This wonderful educational experience led to many opportunities to learn from and collaborate with legal scholars such as Betty van der Smissen, JD; David Herbert, JD; and Drs. Dan Connaughton and Doyice Cotten; and being invited by Drs. Larry Golding and Ed Howley, EICs of the *ACSM's Health & Fitness Journal*, to serve as the legal columnist for this journal. Also, in the legal area, I'd like to thank Patrick Keyser, Dean of the Law College at La Trobe University in Melbourne, Australia, who invited me to travel to Australia and contribute to the Australia Fitness Industry Risk Management (AFIRM) research project—an amazing learning experience. Third are the many pioneers in worksite wellness, such as Drs. Bill Baun, Paul Couzelis, and Nicholas Pronk, from whom I have learned so much by having the opportunity to work with them on several projects over the years. Finally, I would like to recognize my husband, Patrick Shemek, who continually encourages me; and my parents, Ralph and Hilda Eickhoff, who instilled in my brothers and me a strong work ethic and taught us, by example, the importance of living a balanced life and serving others. My parents were the epitome of wellness and they reaped the culmination of its many benefits—a long, happy, and healthy life.

Preface

This book attempts to tackle most of the major federal laws that affect workplace wellness programs. The book touches on some state-based laws, such as workers' compensation, as well. However, covering each and every state law that may impact workplace wellness programs would take numerous volumes. As a result, readers of this book should be aware that, although this book aims to be comprehensive in its coverage of federal law, it does not tell the whole legal story because the book does not address most state laws.

Nevertheless, those who yearn for an in-depth examination of workplace wellness program compliance should find this book useful. The book refers to this audience frequently as "workplace wellness professionals and organizations." *Workplace wellness professionals* include human resource professionals, corporate executives, and health promotion professionals, including health educators, fitness professionals, diet and nutrition professionals, health coaches, and traditional and alternative healthcare providers such as physicians, nurses, occupational therapists, chiropractors, massage therapists, acupuncturists, and naturopathic physicians, to name a few. These professionals may work for a "workplace wellness organization," which may be a company that sponsors a workplace wellness program, a vendor or health insurer that offers workplace wellness program products or services, or a company that might be developing innovative tools for the workplace wellness industry. Entrepreneurs and technology professionals specifically may value the chapters on data privacy, mHealth, and FDA regulation of medical devices. Health and employee benefits attorneys who advise clients on workplace wellness program compliance may also find that this book serves as a valuable resource for their law practice. In addition, academicians who teach courses in health promotion, workplace wellness, or health law may want to adopt this book as a text for their courses.

The approach of this book is to inform the reader of the "what," "why," and "how" of workplace wellness program laws: (1) what laws are important for workplace wellness program compliance; (2) why those laws exist and why they are important for workplace wellness program design and implementation; and (3) how workplace wellness professionals and organizations can apply workplace wellness laws effectively. The diagram in Figure FM.1 outlines this approach.

The chapters of this book are organized by legal issue, such as offering incentives or screening services, with a discussion of the applicable laws pertinent to each of those legal issues. There is a list of learning

Figure FM.1 Workplace Wellness Laws: Linking the What, Why, and How

objectives at the beginning of each chapter to help prepare the reader for the different concepts and ideas discussed in the chapter. At the end of each chapter is a list of Key Points or Case Scenarios and then a list of Study Questions to help the reader achieve the "how" to apply the law, as shown in Figure FM.1. For those interested in more structured study of the topics in this book, a training curriculum is available. For more information about the training curriculum, visit www.wellnesslaw.com.

Following is a brief description of each chapter:

Introduction—Both authors offer their own perspectives on workplace wellness and the role of law in the workplace wellness field.

Chapter 1: Understanding the U.S. Legal System—This chapter provides background on the legal system in the United States. It covers the different sources of law and the three branches of government to give the reader a strong knowledge base regarding legal concepts. This knowledge base will be very useful when reading subsequent chapters.

Chapter 2: A Solid Foundation—Like the first chapter, the second chapter also seeks to provide the reader with a foundation of knowledge, but this time in regard to the book's legal approach. The chapter discusses the concepts of preventive law and therapeutic jurisprudence and why it makes sense to apply these concepts to workplace wellness programming.

Chapter 3: To Plan or Not to Plan: A Historical Look at the Employer-Employee Relationship and the Birth of Employee Benefits—This chapter explores the importance of determining whether a wellness program is part of a group health plan, how to determine group health plan status, and what group health plan status means from a legal perspective. The chapter also covers the history of labor and employment laws, as well as employee benefit laws to help the reader appreciate their existence.

Chapter 4: The Law of Wellness Incentives and Screening—This chapter looks at the laws that govern workplace wellness program incentives, including HIPAA/ACA, ADA, and GINA. The chapter reviews the history of each of these laws, explains what they say about workplace wellness programs, and offers the reader opportunities to apply concepts from the incentive laws. Because some of the incentive laws depend upon a screening component in a wellness program (such as a health risk assessment or biometric screen), the chapter also addresses the federal CLIA law, some state screening laws, and pre-activity screening standards and guidelines.

Chapter 5: The Taxing Truth—After a short exploration of the history and purpose of the United States' income tax, the chapter examines the medical care expense deduction. This deduction is at the heart of whether wellness incentives are taxable or not taxable as income. The chapter provides examples of wellness incentives that qualify as tax exempt or are subject to tax.

Chapter 6: Are They Qualified to Do That?—This chapter covers the different types of credentialing available in the workplace wellness field, such as accreditation, licensure, and certification. It also reviews the legal concept of "scope of practice" and applies that concept to the different professionals in the workplace wellness industry, emphasizing the consequences of wandering outside one's scope of practice. Finally, the chapter offers some risk management strategies to ensure that only those who are competent and qualified provide workplace wellness services.

Chapter 7: Is That Part of Their Workday?—Many workplace wellness programs take place during working hours. This chapter explores the importance of laws that govern compensable employee activities, such as the Fair Labor Standards Act and state worker compensation laws. The chapter offers case examples to illustrate how workplace wellness programs can be affected by when, how, or why workers participate in wellness activities.

Chapter 8: What About Stress?—Because work-related stress has effects on employee well-being, this chapter provides insight into what causes work-related stress and what authorities like the World Health Organization recommend to minimize it. The chapter advocates for a wellness program that addresses stress inducers comprehensively, and uses various laws, such as workers' compensation, OSHA, mental health parity laws, and civil rights laws, as a basis for implementing such comprehensive programs.

Chapter 9: Data Privacy: The Web We Have Weaved—As workplace wellness programs become more digital, such as through wearable technology and online tools, data privacy and security becomes a more prominent issue. This chapter studies the numerous federal laws that could govern data privacy and security for workplace wellness programs. It also gives the reader an appreciation of the massive amounts of data that are shared and disclosed on a daily basis, and the industry that has sprouted around data collection and sharing. The chapter offers readers best practices to minimize data privacy and security concerns of wellness program participants.

Chapter 10: Moving Wellness to eHealth: A World of Heavier (FDA) Regulation—This chapter recognizes the interest by some in the workplace wellness industry in moving from outside the workplace into the clinical world, particularly by those who are creating new technologies to help improve the health of patients. The purpose of this chapter is to introduce those interested in moving into the clinical world to the FDA regulation of medical devices. The chapter offers decision tools to help readers determine whether a wellness technology is or could be subject to FDA regulation.

Chapter 11: What's Next for Workplace Wellness?—In this final chapter, the authors offer their insight into where workplace wellness is going … or at least should be going. The authors describe a trend by workplace wellness professionals and organizations to move into the broader community, particularly the healthcare community. The chapter offers ideas on how certain current Affordable Care Act provisions can facilitate that effort. The authors also see a benefit from applying "Precision Medicine" concepts to wellness and how that could lead to less discrimination and more diversity in the field. Finally, the authors advocate for more compliance training, standards, and guidance in workplace wellness as a way to boost the field's effectiveness and reputation.

Afterword—Author Barbara J. Zabawa gives her thoughts on how this book came to be.

Disclaimer

This publication is written and published to provide accurate and authoritative information relevant to the subject matter presented. It is published and sold with the understanding that the authors and publisher are not engaged in rendering legal, medical, or other professional services by reason of their authorship or publication of this work. If legal, medical, or other expert assistance is required, the services of competent professional persons should be obtained by those in need of such services. Moreover, in the field of workplace wellness, the services of such competent professionals must be obtained.

Adapted from the Declaration of Principles of the American Bar Association and a committee of publishers and associations.

About the Authors

Barbara J. Zabawa, JD, MPH

Barbara J. Zabawa owns the Center for Health and Wellness Law, LLC, a law firm dedicated to improving legal access and compliance for the health and wellness industries. She is also Clinical Assistant Professor in the Department of Health Informatics and Administration at the University of Wisconsin, Milwaukee (UWM) Before graduating with honors from the University of Wisconsin Law School, she obtained an MPH degree from the University of Michigan. Immediately prior to starting her own firm, she was Associate General Counsel and HIPAA Privacy Officer for a large health insurer, where she advised on Affordable Care Act matters. She was also a shareholder and Health Law Team Leader at a large Wisconsin law firm. In 2011, Barbara was named a Wisconsin Up and Coming Lawyer.

She serves health and wellness professionals and organizations across the country as an advocate, a transactional lawyer, and/or a compliance resource. Barbara is a frequent writer and speaker on health and wellness law topics, having presented for national organizations such as WELCOA, National Wellness Institute, HPLive, and HERO. She teaches health law and compliance for the UWM Masters in Health Administration program as well as the UWM undergraduate program in Health Adminstration.

Barbara's commitment to improving health and wellness is also demonstrated through her community service. Barbara sits on the Board of Directors for Health Promotion Advocates, a national nonprofit organization created to integrate health promotion into the national agenda. Wisconsin's Insurance Commissioner appointed Barbara to serve on Wisconsin's

Oversight and Advisory Council, which oversees the distribution of millions of dollars in grant funding to population health improvement projects in Wisconsin. She also is a board member for the Rogers Memorial Hospital Foundation, a healthcare organization that specializes in treating mental illness, and the State Bar of Wisconsin Health Law Section.

Barbara is licensed to practice law in both Wisconsin and New York.

JoAnn Eickhoff-Shemek, PhD, FACSM, FAWHP

Dr. Eickhoff-Shemek is a professor in the Exercise Science program at the University of South Florida (USF). She served as the founding coordinator of this program from 2003–2012. Dr. Eickhoff-Shemek also developed and coordinated a master's degree in Fitness and Wellness Management at her former institution, the University of Nebraska at Omaha (UNOmaha).

Dr. Eickhoff-Shemek has taught undergraduate and graduate courses in fitness law/risk management and worksite wellness for more than 20 years. Nominated by her students, she received outstanding teaching awards at both USF and UNOmaha.

Dr. Eickhoff-Shemek is an internationally known researcher, author, and speaker in the area of legal liability, risk management, and fitness safety. She has authored or co-authored more than 80 journal articles, as well as several book chapters. In addition, Dr. Eickhoff-Shemek is the lead author of a comprehensive textbook entitled *Risk Management for Health/ Fitness Professionals: Legal Issues and Strategies* and a contributor/ co-author of *The Australian Fitness Industry Risk Management Manual*.

To further pursue her passion to educate fitness/wellness professionals, she formed the Fitness Law Academy, a company devoted to enhancing fitness safety and minimizing legal liability.

Dr. Eickhoff-Shemek has served in a variety of elected and appointed leadership positions for professional organizations such as the American College of Sports Medicine (ACSM) and the Association for Worksite Health Promotion (AWHP). She served as the legal columnist for the *ACSM's Health & Fitness Journal* and as the Vice-President of Education on the International Board of Directors of AWHP. Dr. Eickhoff-Shemek was awarded the status of Fellow of ACSM in 1997 and of AWHP in 1990.

Prior to becoming a full-time academician in 1994, Dr. Eickhoff-Shemek worked as a health/fitness manager in various settings for nearly 20 years. During her 40-plus year career, she held several professional certifications in fitness, wellness, and health education. Dr. Eickhoff-Shemek received her PhD from the University of Nebraska-Lincoln in 1995.

Introduction

In this introduction, each author provides her personal perspective and experience to help establish the need for and purpose of this textbook. In addition, they describe some historical background and general information related to workplace wellness to help provide a foundation for understanding and applying the many workplace wellness laws.

Barbara's Perspective

Shocking. That is the word I use to describe my discovery that the wellness industry had scarce resources regarding—and paid even less attention to—how the law affects workplace wellness program design. Plenty of federal and state laws impact workplace wellness programs, but the industry is not discussing those laws at wellness education programs. My mission is now to solve that problem.

I am a lawyer and public health professional committed to making the law more accessible to the wellness industry. This book aims to serve as a guide for those interested in developing legally healthy wellness programs in the workplace. It does not, however, give legal advice. Honestly, I can't give you legal advice because you, as my reader, are not my client. Also, I am not licensed to practice law in all 50 states (only Wisconsin and New York). Nevertheless, all of you who grapple with designing or supporting legally compliant wellness programs, or those of you who do not know what legal issues might even exist: This book is for you.

Because of the dearth of wellness law resources, many in the wellness industry feel confused, lost, neglected, and scared when it comes to applying or even considering the law in their wellness program design. My message to you is "Don't be scared!" You are not alone in your quest to make the United States population healthier through workplace wellness. You are not alone in wanting to do the right thing by the law and by employee health. Most of all, you are not alone in feeling lost, confused, unappreciated, or neglected when it comes to legal compliance in the wellness industry. More on that in a moment. Before we get too far ahead of ourselves, however, let's take a step back and examine the wellness industry.

According to a 2010 study, the wellness industry represents a market of nearly $2 trillion globally.[1] It is made up of numerous clusters, such as spas, complementary and alternative medicine, healthy eating/nutrition and weight loss, preventive/personalized health, medical and wellness tourism, fitness, and mind-body, beauty and anti-aging, and workplace wellness.[2] Future books may address these other clusters. However, this first edition of *Rule the Rules* focuses on the workplace wellness component of the wellness industry. Workplace wellness makes up approximately $40 billion of the total $2 trillion global wellness industry.[3]

Interest in workplace wellness in the United States is growing.[4] A 2013 survey of about 900 large employers in 15 countries found that 84 percent planned to increase their investment in wellness programs over the following two years.[5] In addition, according to a 2013 report, annual revenue growth in employee wellness was 5.6 percent between 2008 and 2013, and that growth was projected to grow an average of 9.4 percent annually over the next four years.[6] The number of wellness vendors now totals more than 8,000.[7]

The Affordable Care Act, passed in 2010, has helped spur workplace wellness growth, in part because of its emphasis on prevention and lowering health costs, as well as the looming 40 percent excise tax starting in 2018 on high-cost plans. Nevertheless, workplace wellness was popular even before 2010. For example, in the mid-1980s, nearly two-thirds of U.S. worksites with 50 or more employees offered at least one health promotion activity.[8] It is because of this enduring popularity that

1 Global Spa Summit and SRI International, *Spas and the Global Wellness Market: Synergies and Opportunities* (May 2010): iii, http://www.sri.com/sites/default/files/publications/gss_sri_spasandwellnessreport_rev_82010.pdf.
2 *Id.* at 24.
3 *Id.*
4 Soeren Mattke et al., *Workplace Wellness Programs Study* (Final Report), RAND Health (2013): 1, http://www.rand.org/content/dam/rand/pubs/research_reports/RR200/RR254/RAND_RR254.pdf.
5 *Id.*; *see also* Steven Ross Johnson, "Firms Revamping Employee Wellness Programs," *Modern Healthcare* (May 24, 2014): 2, http://www.modernhealthcare.com/article/20140524/MAGAZINE/305249980.
6 Steven Ross Johnson, "Firms Revamping Employee Wellness Programs," *Modern Healthcare* (May 24, 2014): 4, http://www.modernhealthcare.com/article/20140524/MAGAZINE/305249980.
7 *Id.*
8 Ken Warner, "Wellness at the Worksite," *Health Affairs* 9, no. 2 (1990): 63–79.

I believe workplace wellness efforts will continue despite the fate of the Affordable Care Act in 2017 and beyond.

The popularity of workplace wellness programs offers a chance to shift America's paradigm from sickness care to well-being care. Indeed, a primary distinction between the wellness industry and conventional medicine (or, as some call it, "sickness care") is that the wellness industry is proactive, whereas the sickness industry is reactive.[9] See Figure FM.2. Specifically, the wellness industry provides products and services to people with the goal of making them feel healthier and look better, slowing the effects of aging, and/or preventing sickness from developing. People often become customers of the wellness industry voluntarily.[10]

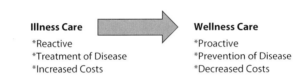

Illness Care
*Reactive
*Treatment of Disease
*Increased Costs

Wellness Care
*Proactive
*Prevention of Disease
*Decreased Costs

**Figure FM.2 Paradigm Shift from an Illness Care Model
to a Wellness Care Model**

In contrast, the sickness industry provides products and services to people to treat the symptoms of or eliminate disease. People become customers of the sickness industry by necessity, not choice.[11] Yet, conventional medicine is failing us. People who are asked to name the most important problems they and their families face generally rank concerns about health a close second behind financial issues.[12] Despite this concern, global cumulative health spending is increasing.[13] In other words, the exorbitant amount we are spending on sickness care is not addressing our most pressing concerns. In response

9 Global Spa Summit and SRI International, *Spas and the Global Wellness Market: Synergies and Opportunities* (May 2010): 18, http://www.sri.com/sites/default/files/publications/gss_sri_spasandwellnessreport_rev_82010.pdf (citing Paul Zane Pilzer, *The New Wellness Revolution*, Hoboken, NJ: John Wiley & Sons, 2007, pp. 4–5).

10 *Id.*

11 *Id.*

12 *Id.* at 14.

13 *Id.* at 14 (stating that in 2002, the cumulative health spending of 24 OECD countries was $2.7 trillion and that this amount is expected to more than triple to $10 trillion by 2020).

to the failing healthcare system, many people are maintaining their own health and investigating alternative forms of health care.[14]

Shifting from a sickness care to a wellness care model is far more important to the overall economy than it is to short-term cost-savings gains for individual companies—but the shift is also important to the employer's bottom line. Studies show that workplace wellness programs provide a number of benefits, including reduced health benefit costs. One often-cited study by Baicker, Cutler, and Song from 2010 states that medical costs fall about $3.27 for every dollar spent on wellness programs, and absentee day costs fall by about $2.73 for every dollar spent.[15] This study's authors also acknowledge many other likely benefits from workplace wellness programs, such as improved health, reduced turnover, and lower costs for public programs such as disability insurance and Medicare.[16] Meta-analyses of quality studies conducted by Aldana and Chapman also have shown similar results.[17] Some dispute the cost savings, however, or at least question the magnitude of the financial benefit.[18]

Regardless, employers in the United States provide 58.4 percent of non-elderly Americans' healthcare coverage.[19] This translates to approximately 149 million non-elderly people who receive health insurance through employment in the United States.[20] Because employees are a

---

14 *Id.* at 15.

15 Katherine Baicker, David Cutler, and Zirui Song, "Workplace Wellness Programs Can Generate Savings," *Health Affairs* 29, no. 2 (Feb. 2010).

16 *Id.*

17 Michael P. O'Donnell, ed., *Health Promotion at the Workplace,* 4th ed. (Troy, MI: American Journal of Health Promotion, 2014).

18 Steven Ross Johnson, "Firms Revamping Employee Wellness Programs," *Modern Healthcare* 2 (May 24, 2014): 2, http://www.modernhealthcare.com/article/20140524/MAGAZINE/305249980 (citing the 2013 RAND study, *supra* note 4, which found that the overall return on every dollar invested in a wellness program was $1.50 and that there were significant savings from the disease-management component of these programs, with savings up to $3.80 for every dollar spent, including a 30 percent reduction in hospital admissions); *see also* Al Lewis and Vik Khanna, *Surviving Workplace Wellness with Your Dignity, Finances and Major Organs Intact* (The Health Care Blog, San Francisco, CA: 2014) (noting that Professor Baicker, author of the *Health Affairs* study that found a 3.27 to 1 ratio of cost savings, recanted the figure and changed her story to say it is too early to tell if there are cost savings in workplace wellness programs and instead proposed that CEOs experiment on their employees to see if anything works).

19 *Employer-Sponsored Health Insurance: Recent Trends and Future Directions,* National Institute for Health Care Management Foundation Data Brief (October 2013): 2, http://www.nihcm.org/pdf/Employer-Sponsored-Health-Insurance-v2-data-brief.pdf.

20 Kaiser Family Foundation, *2014 Employer Health Benefits Survey, Summary of Findings,* 1, http://files.kff.org/attachment/ehbs-2014-abstract-summary-of-findings.

"captive audience" and exhibit a relatively high prevalence of modifiable risk factors, such as inactivity, poor nutrition, tobacco use, and frequent alcohol consumption, there is significant potential for a substantial health impact.[21]

You may ask why U.S. employers would take on a global task of improving the health and well-being of their employees and community if the immediate financial benefits may be minimal to none. Here are three reasons:

First, overall, the medical community has failed in wellness. It is not entirely their fault, however. The current public and private insurance system does not financially reward wellness, although that is slowly changing, as discussed in Chapter 11 of this book.

Second, the investment in wellness is not an isolated investment. It is tied to human resources, marketing, leadership, and research and development. Investing in employee wellness, when done right,[22] can catapult a company's most valuable asset, its employees, to unimaginable levels. Indeed, according to the Centers for Disease Control and Prevention, 40 percent of employees report feeling stressed at work.[23] Stress plays an important role in several types of chronic health problems, especially cardiovascular disease, musculoskeletal disorders, and psychological disorders.[24] The wellness way of thinking can allay stress and increase an employee's productivity. Employees who have a sense of well-being are more productive, happier, and perform their jobs better.[25]

---

21 Ken Warner, "Wellness at the Worksite," *Health Affairs* 9, no. 2 (1990): 63–79. Specifically, the worksite can offer peer support in encouraging compliance with difficult behavior-change regimens, as well as reduce time, financial, and travel barriers to wellness program participation. *Id.* at 65. Modifiable risk factors or "unhealthy lifestyles" drive up the prevalence of chronic disease, such as diabetes, heart disease, and chronic pulmonary conditions. Soeren Mattke et al., *Workplace Wellness Programs Study* (Final Report), RAND Health (2013): 1, http://www.rand.org/content/dam/rand/pubs/research_reports/ RR200/RR254/RAND_RR254.pdf. Treating chronic disease accounts for more than 75 percent of national health expenditures. *Id.*

22 For resources on designing a successful wellness program, such as a results-oriented wellness program, visit www.welcoa.org. It is also important to consider each individual's purpose to help them live a healthy life. For more information about the value of finding an individual's purpose, *see* Victor J. Strecher, *On Purpose* (Ann Arbor, MI:1–133, Dung Beetle Press, 2013).

23 Centers for Disease Control, *Stress at Work* (NIOSH Publication 99–101, 1999), http://www.cdc.gov/ niosh/docs/99-101/.

24 *Id.*

25 *Id.; see also* Hilary Dickinson, "Employers Have a Stake in the Urgent Need for Mental Health Care," *BizTimes Media* (March 23, 2015), https://www.biztimes.com/2015/03/23/employers-have-a-stake-in-the-urgent-need-for-mental-health-care/.

Third, over time, cumulative investment in well-being can reduce America's need for sickness care, which is currently eating 17.4 percent of our country's gross domestic product.[26] The more we spend on sickness care, the less we are able to spend on other items important to the growth of our economy, such as education, transportation, agriculture, or even space exploration. Forming wellness habits early in an individual's working years will likely translate to lower sickness care costs, because of delayed onset of disability later in life, also known as "morbidity compression." Early research suggests that people who adopt healthy lifestyles during their working years delay the onset of disability, reduce the years of disability at the end of life, and increase their quality of life.[27] Ultimately, a healthy, happy workforce helps U.S. employers stay competitive in the global marketplace.

So, how does the law play into all of this, and why should you not be scared of it? Because the law is an essential component of a well-designed workplace wellness program. You can "rule" workplace wellness "rules" by taking three steps: (1) learn about the rules; (2) be proactive about the rules; and (3) advocate for rule changes when necessary.

First, learning about which laws apply to workplace wellness, how they apply, and (arguably most importantly) why they apply helps workplace wellness program designers consider the needs and desires of the whole employee population. If one accepts the basic premise that laws exist for a reason and tries to learn about and understand that reason, the law can appear more friendly and less scary.

Second, being proactive about workplace wellness rules empowers you to use the law as a helpful tool in designing workplace wellness programs. People who view law as only a hindrance or afterthought often find themselves scrambling to defend their actions when someone complains. They may find themselves defending their actions against a boss, employee, auditor, government agency, or court. As in health care, in

---

26 Centers for Medicare and Medicaid Services, "National Health Expenditures 2015 Highlights," http://www.cms.gov/Research-Statistics-Data-and-Systems/Statistics-Trends-and-Reports/ NationalHealthExpendData/Downloads/highlights.pdf. "Health expenditures" included those for hospital care, physician and clinical services, other professional services such as physical therapy, podiatry, or chiropractic medicine, dental services, residential and personal care services, home health care, nursing care facilities, prescription drugs, durable medical equipment, and other medical instruments. *Id.*
27 Michael O'Donnell, "Compression of Morbidity: A Personal, Research, and National Fiscal Solvency Perspective," *American Journal of Health Promotion* 27, no. 2 (Nov./Dec. 2012): v.

law it is far more expensive and emotionally tumultuous to react to problems than to prevent them in the first place. The law can be your guide in designing effective workplace wellness programs by helping you design programs that are more thoughtful, comprehensive, and sensitive. Proactive use of the law ultimately reduces legal risk.

Third, with knowledge you can advocate for law changes when necessary. Do not be a passive bystander. Take control of the law. Own it. Sometimes the law becomes outdated or fails to capture all circumstances. Each of us reading this book likely possesses expertise in and valuable perspectives on workplace wellness. It is important that you voice your concerns to your legislators when you encounter a situation in which existing law does not line up with reality. You can also express your concern to others involved in wellness advocacy efforts, such as my firm, the Center for Health and Wellness Law, LLC; or Health Promotion Advocates, a nonprofit advocacy group created to integrate health promotion into national health policy.[28]

This book aims to assist you in achieving these three steps. Each chapter contains an opportunity to apply the legal concepts discussed in the chapter through questions and answers, checklists, or other learning methods. Some of the issues raised in these applications are drawn from the wellness industry itself; others raise interesting issues that are important for workplace wellness design. Whenever possible, the book attempts to explain the "why" behind the law as well as the fact of the law. Knowledge of the law often removes fear of it. Understanding the "why" behind the law can foster a deeper appreciation of the law and, we hope, boost willingness to comply (or perhaps stimulate efforts to change the law if the "why" seems outdated).

Use this book as a resource. Embrace the law and embed it into your wellness program design. The law should not be a burden, but a selling point for your wellness program. By investing in compliance on the front end of your wellness program design, you will not only reduce the chance of lawsuits and investigations, but you will also add an element of confidence to your wellness program that will ease the minds of your company,

---

28 *See* http://healthpromotionadvocates.org/.

clients, and program participants. In sum, preventive legal compliance will make your wellness program that much more enjoyable and effective.

Be well, and Rule the Rules!

JoAnn's Perspective

I was excited and honored when Barbara invited me to be a co-author of this much-needed book. I had started a similar book a few years ago and never got around to getting it done. Given Barbara's exceptional background and experience in healthcare law and public health, I was confident that with her leadership this collaborative effort would meet an important need.

Over the last 20 years as an academician, I have taught both undergraduate and graduate level courses in (a) workplace wellness (courses that focus on the design and delivery of quality workplace wellness programs) and (b) legal/risk management (courses that focus on laws applicable to health/fitness programs and risk management strategies to minimize legal liability). The graduate students I have taught over the years, who are often employed as fitness and wellness professionals in various settings (worksite, medical/clinical, government, private for-profit, community nonprofit, and university), enter my legal/risk management course with little or no prior knowledge of the law and its application to the field. These students have graduated from academic programs from across the country in disciplines such as exercise science, health education, health promotion/wellness, public health, and business. Their lack of knowledge of the law and its application to the field is quite concerning given the many legal liability exposures that exist in the field. (*Legal liability exposures* are situations that can lead to both civil lawsuits and criminal charges, as discussed in Chapter 1.) In addition to minimizing legal liability, adhering to the law leads to high-quality programs and services as well as daily operational efficiency.

To provide a little more context related to workplace wellness, this section sets out some definitions that may be helpful. In a couple of these definitions, the term *health promotion* is used. Often the terms *workplace wellness* and *workplace health promotion* are used interchangeably in the literature. We will be using *workplace wellness* because it is the term used by the government in the published federal laws that we will be describing throughout the book. Several definitions of these terms are available in the literature, but I like these the best.

Definitions

Comprehensive Health Promotion

Goetzel et al.[29] identify five key elements that define a comprehensive health promotion program: (a) health education, (b) links to related employee services, (c) supportive physical and social environments for health improvement, (d) integration of health promotion into the organization's culture, and (e) employee screenings with adequate treatment and follow-up.

Health Promotion

Michael O'Donnell's most recent definition of *health promotion* is: "Health promotion is the art and science of helping people discover the synergies between their core passions and optimal health, enhancing their motivation to strive for optimal health, and supporting them in changing this lifestyle to move toward a state of optimal health. Optimal health is a dynamic balance of physical, emotional, social, spiritual, and intellectual health. Lifestyle change can be facilitated through a combination of learning experiences that enhance awareness, increase motivation, and build skills and, most important, through the creation of opportunities that open access to environments that make positive health practices the easiest choice."[30]

Health Education

Health education is "any planned combination of learning experiences designed to predispose, enable, and reinforce voluntary behavior

---

29 Ron Z. Goetzel, David Shechter, Ronald J. Ozminkowski et al., "Promising Practices in Employer Health and Productivity Management Efforts: Findings from a Benchmarking Study," *Journal of Occupational & Environmental Medicine* 49, no. 2 (February 2007): 111–130.
30 Michael P. O'Donnell, ed., *Health Promotion at the Workplace*, 4th ed. (Troy, MI: American Journal of Health Promotion, 2014), 77.

conducive to health in individuals, groups, or communities."[31] Note that this definition, by Green and Kreuter, refers to "voluntary" behavior. This concept of voluntariness is particularly relevant to our discussion, later in the book, of the topic of wellness programs; in some instances employees felt coerced to participate by having to pay large financial disincentives if they chose not to participate.

Wellness

The National Wellness Institute (NWI) defines *wellness* as "an active process through which people become aware of, and make choices toward, a more successful existence."[32] NWI identifies six dimensions of wellness—physical, social, intellectual, spiritual, emotional, and occupational[33]—but there also can be additional wellness dimensions, such as financial and environmental. Wellness programs help people understand the interconnectedness among these dimensions and how to apply them into their lives.

By incorporating the dimensions of wellness into their design, quality workplace wellness programs focus on changing and sustaining behaviors (e.g., exercise, nutrition/weight management, tobacco cessation, stress management, injury prevention, and medical self-care) that help reduce the "need" and "demand" for medical services. Need is reduced through behavior change approaches (e.g., educating employees and their families on how to adopt a healthy lifestyle to prevent/control disease) and demand is reduced by self-management practices (e.g., educating employees and their families about how to properly access the healthcare delivery system through medical self-care programs). Health education programs should focus on both disease management strategies (e.g., helping people who are at risk for or who have chronic disease to reduce their risk factors or manage their disease to prevent further progression) and disease prevention strategies (e.g., helping healthy people stay healthy).

---

31 Lawrence W. Green and Marshall W. Kreuter, *Health Promotion Planning: An Educational and Ecological Approach,* 3rd ed. (Mountain View, CA: Mayfield, 2005): 27.
32 National Wellness Institute, "About Wellness," http://www.nationalwellness.org/?page=AboutWellness.
33 *Id.*

Health promotion is a broader concept than health education. It includes health education as well as the environment as stated in the preceding definition by O'Donnell. Environmental factors in the workplace, such as organizational, regulatory, social, and policy matters, influence human behavior and are essential in both changing and sustaining behavior change. Workplace wellness programs that implement the key elements of a "comprehensive health promotion" approach will be the most effective in improving both individual and organizational health outcomes.

Resources for Workplace Wellness Professionals

It is important for workplace wellness professionals to be engaged in the profession. This is best achieved by becoming an active member of professional organizations, attending conferences, and reading professional journals. The following are my recommendations for three professional organizations. Visit their websites to learn more about their many membership benefits.

- International Association of Worksite Health Promotion (IAWHP): www.acsm-iawhp.org
- National Wellness Institute (NWI): www.nationalwellness.org
- Wellness Councils of America (WELCOA): www.welcoa.org

In addition, the annual Art & Science of Health Promotion conference covers many workplace wellness issues and topics. That conference is sponsored by the *American Journal of Health Promotion* (http://www .healthpromotionjournal.com).

1

Understanding the U.S. Legal System

Learning Objectives

After reading this chapter, workplace wellness professionals will be able to:

1. Describe the three branches of the federal government and the major functions of each.
2. Distinguish civil law and criminal law.
3. Understand the U.S. court system, including trial courts and appellate courts.
4. Describe the three levels of fault under tort law.
5. Define negligence and the four elements the plaintiff must prove in a negligence lawsuit.
6. Describe how courts determine duty in negligence cases.
7. Understand two defenses to negligence: waivers and primary assumption of risk.
8. Distinguish injuries due to negligent conduct from those due to inherent risks.
9. Describe vicarious liability and workers' compensation under strict liability.
10. List and describe the four essential elements of a valid contract.

Yes, people need food and education. But one of the cornerstones of any society is a well-functioning legal system.

—Cherie Blair

A law is valuable not because it is law, but because there is right in it.

—Henry Ward Beecher

Introduction

All of us probably had some type of course on government, when we were in middle school or high school, where we learned about the U.S. legal system. However, many of us also may have forgotten what we learned in that course. Having a general understanding of how our legal system works is essential to fully appreciate the laws described in this book involving workplace wellness programs. This chapter provides a general overview of (1) the federal government and its three branches; (2) civil and criminal law; (3) the court system; (4) tort law, including negligence and strict liability; (5) defenses to negligence; and (6) contract law.

The Constitution and Three Branches of Government

The U.S. Constitution serves as the supreme law of the land. It created the national government and its three branches, as shown in Figure 1.1. Each state also has a constitution and the same three governmental branches, which function in a fashion similar to the federal government. The legislative branch, made up of the elected representatives of Congress, makes laws (statutes or codes), such as the Patient Protection and Affordable Care Act (ACA) that Congress passed and President Obama signed into law on March 23, 2010;[1] and the Americans with Disabilities Act (ADA) that Congress passed and President George H. W. Bush signed into law on July, 26, 1990.[2] The laws passed by the legislative branch are referred to as **statutory law.** The executive branch carries out the laws passed by Congress; this branch includes the president, vice president, and cabinet members who are the heads or secretaries of departmental agencies such as Health and Human Services (HHS), Education, Defense, and Homeland Security. The executive branch also contains regulatory agencies such as the Equal Employment Opportunity

---

1 U.S. Department of Health and Human Services, "Read the Law, The Affordable Care Act, Section by Section," (August 28, 2015), http://www.hhs.gov/healthcare/rights/law/index.html.
2 George Bush, "Statement on Signing the Americans with Disabilities Act of 1990," July 26, 1990, http://www.presidency.ucsb.edu/ws/?pid=18712.

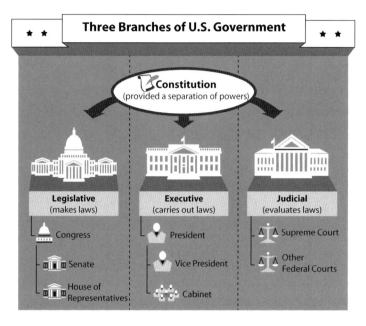

Figure 1.1   The U.S. Constitution and the Three Branches of Government
(https://www.usa.gov/branches-of-government)

Commission (EEOC), the Food and Drug Administration (FDA), the Occupational Safety and Health Administration (OSHA), and the Consumer Product Safety Commission (CPSC).

The departmental and regulatory agencies together are referred to as *administrative agencies*. Over the past several decades, both the number and staffs of these administrative agencies have grown tremendously. When individuals claim that the federal government is "too big," they are often referring to the expansion of these administrative agencies. These agencies have a great deal of power.[3] They:

- Enact rules and regulations, referred to as **administrative law**, related to the statutes passed by Congress (e.g., Health and Human Services created many of the rules and regulations related to the ACA).

---

3 Kristi L. Schoepfer Bochicchio, "The Legal System," in *Sport Law for Recreational and Sport Managers,* ed. Doyice J. Cotten and John T. Wolohan, 6th ed. (Dubuque, IA: Kendall Hunt, 2013), 2–15.

- Investigate violations of their rules/regulations and resolve disputes.
- Impose sanctions when violations are proven to have occurred. Large financial penalties have been levied as sanctions for violations of administrative agency rules and regulations, such as violations of the rules/regulations involving **protected health information (PHI)** that became effective after the Health Insurance Portability and Accountability Act (HIPAA) became law in 1996.

The following two cases demonstrate the hefty financial penalties that resulted for the failure to keep PHI private, confidential, and secure. After an investigation by the HHS Office for Civil Rights (OCR), New York Presbyterian Hospital and Columbia University paid OCR $3.3 million and $1.5 million, respectively, in a monetary settlement for a joint breach involving the disclosure of the electronic PHI of 6,800 individuals.[4] Both entities also had to agree to a substantive corrective action plan (CAP) involving a variety of steps to help ensure future compliance. Another example in which the HHS investigated HIPAA privacy violations involved a small pharmacy—Cornell Prescription Pharmacy in Denver, Colorado[5]—when paper documents containing PHI were found in an unlocked, open dumpster on the pharmacy's property. The resolution agreement resulted in the pharmacy paying $125,000 and complying with a two-year CAP. More on the HIPAA Privacy Rule can be found in Chapter 9.

The judicial branch evaluates laws and resolves disputes through the court system.[6] Legal cases begin at the **trial court** level, where either a judge or a jury renders a decision in favor of one of the parties. In a civil court, the parties are (1) the **plaintiff** (e.g., an injured fitness participant), and (2) the **defendant** (e.g., a wellness professional and/or facility). In a criminal court, the parties are (1) the defendant who is charged with

---

4 U.S. Department of Health and Human Services, HHS Press Office, "Data Breach Results in $4.8 Million HIPAA Settlements" (May 7, 2014), http://www.hhs.gov/news/press/2014pres/05/20140507b.html.
5 U.S. Department of Health and Human Services, "HIPAA Settlement Highlights the Continuing Importance of Secure Disposal of Paper Medical Records," (n.d.), http://www.hhs.gov/hipaa/for-professionals/compliance-enforcement/examples/cornell/index.html.
6 Kenneth W. Clarkson, Roger LeRoy Miller, Gaylord A. Jentz, and Frank B. Cross, *West's Business Law*, 8th ed. (St. Paul, MN: West, 2001).

violating the law and (2) the government or people (society), represented by a district attorney or attorney general. See Table 1.1 for more information that distinguishes **civil law** and **criminal law**.

	Civil Law	Criminal Law
General Description	Deals with disputes between private parties (individuals, organizations, and businesses). Party #1 (plaintiff) hires a lawyer who files a lawsuit claiming that Party #2 (defendant) failed to carry out a legal duty that resulted in some type of harm to Party #1.	Deals with crimes against society (e.g., conduct that reflects a violation of a federal or state statute) and the punishment of the crime. The government files the case against the defendant accused of committing the crime.
Examples	Negligent conduct (e.g., a fitness professional or wellness coach who provides improper instruction to a client that results in harm to the client), breach of contract, noncriminal statutory violations, and civil rights violations.	Criminal conduct such as practicing medicine or dietetics without a license (e.g., violation of a state licensing statute), theft, and sexual assault.
Standard of Proof	Preponderance of the evidence, meaning more likely than not the defendant's conduct caused the harm.	Beyond a reasonable doubt, meaning the defendant's guilt is fully demonstrated based on the evidence.
Burden of Proof	The plaintiff has the burden of proof, so must provide evidence that a legal duty existed and that the duty was breached.	The prosecution (government) must prove that the defendant was guilty; the defendant is innocent until proven guilty.
Type of Punishment	If the court rules the defendant *liable* for the harm, the defendant must compensate the plaintiff (usually financial compensation for injuries or damages) and may be ordered to stop the practice that caused the harm.	If the court rules the defendant *guilty* of the crime, the defendant is subject to fines, community service, probation, imprisonment, or any combination of these.

Table 1.1   Differences Between Civil Law and Criminal Law

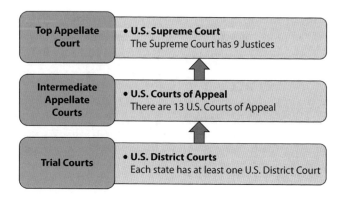

Figure 1.2 The Federal Court System; State Courts Have a Similar Hierarchy

Trial courts first obtain the facts and then determine the laws that apply to those facts.[7] Once a decision is made, either party of a civil lawsuit and only the defendant in a criminal case can appeal the decision to a higher court, such as an **appellate court**. However, there are instances in which a prosecutor can appeal.[8] The federal court system is shown in Figure 1.2. Most state court systems have a similar hierarchy. Federal courts generally rule on federal laws, but, depending on the court's jurisdiction, may also rule on state laws. State courts rule on state or federal laws. There are also many city and county courts that deal with local statutes/ordinances.

Appellate courts are made up of judges only (no juries, no witnesses, etc.), and there are always an odd number of judges so that a majority ruling will result. For example, many U.S. Supreme Court decisions are split 5–4 among the total 9 justices. The judges review the transcript and evidence from the trial court case and decide if the trial court applied the law correctly.[9] If so, they affirm (or uphold) the trial court's ruling. If they believe the trial court's ruling was incorrect, the appellate court can change (modify or reverse) the ruling or remand (send back) the case to the trial court for a new trial according to the appellate court's

---

7 Donald L. Carper and Bill W. West, *Understanding the Law,* 3rd ed. (Cincinnati, OH: West Legal Studies in Business/Thomson, 2000).

8 *See* ABA Standard 21.2 at http://www.americanbar.org/publications/criminal_justice_section_archive/crimjust_standards_crimappeals_blkold.html.

9 Bochicchio, "The Legal System," 12.

instructions. The appellate court then prepares a written opinion that is published to articulate the ruling and the rationale for it. In some cases, the court may create a new ruling or law, which is referred to as judge-made law, or **common law**.[10] These new rulings establish precedent (also referred to as *stare decisis*, a Latin phrase meaning "to stand on decided cases") and become the law (referred to as **case law**) that courts have to follow in similar future cases, especially courts within the same jurisdiction.[11] For example, the Virginia Supreme Court has ruled that waivers for personal injury are against public policy and thus are ineffective as a defense to a negligence claim/lawsuit made against a fitness facility.[12] If the enforceability of a waiver arises as an issue in a Virginia trial court or intermediate appellate court, these courts must follow the precedent or ruling established by the Virginia Supreme Court. There is more information on waivers later in this chapter and in Chapter 7.

Rulings of the Supreme Court of the United States (SCOTUS) must be followed in all U.S. jurisdictions, as demonstrated by two fairly recent rulings of the SCOTUS involving the ACA. In forming their opinion, the Justices had to evaluate the ACA law passed by Congress from various perspectives (e.g., did the law violate the Constitution, what was the intent of the law, etc.). These two cases resulted in split decisions: 5–4 in the 2012 case[13] and 6–3 in the 2015 case.[14] In split-decision cases, the dissenting minority often writes an opinion (called a *dissenting opinion*) explaining why they disagree with the majority opinion. A party that wants to appeal to the SCOTUS must first request a writ of **certiorari**— a petition asking the Court to hear the case.[15] The SCOTUS can grant or deny the request. The majority of certiorari requests are denied, and thus the lower court's ruling stands.

The major focus of this book is the many federal laws (rules and regulations or administrative laws) related to workplace wellness

---

10 Clarkson, Miller, Jentz, and Cross, *West's Business Law*, 5.
11 *Id.* at 6.
12 Doyice J. Cotton and Mary B. Cotton, *Waivers and Releases of Liability*, 9th ed. (Statesboro, GA: Sport Risk Consulting, 2016).
13 *Nat'l Fed'n of Indep. Bus. v. Sebelius*, 132 S. Ct. 2566 (2012).
14 *King v. Burwell*, 135 S. Ct. 2480 (2015).
15 Bochicchio, "The Legal System," 4.

programs. These laws are enforced, for the most part, by federal administrative agencies, as described earlier with regard to the HIPAA Privacy Rule cases. Additional cases involving workplace wellness rules and regulations are also covered in various chapters in this book. As you review these, take note of which administrative agency has the responsibility for oversight and enforcement of these rules and regulations.

In addition to being familiar with the workplace wellness rules and regulations, wellness professionals also need to be familiar with legal issues that can arise under tort and contract law. In Chapter 6, we describe some tort and contract cases that involved fitness/wellness programs and also provide **risk management** strategies (preventive measures) that can minimize legal liability exposures associated with tort and contract law. The following provides a basic overview of these two areas of law.

Tort Law

A **tort** is "an infringement (a civil wrong) by one person of the legally recognized rights of another."[16] For example, if harm occurs to a participant due to the improper conduct (wrongdoing) of a wellness professional, the participant (plaintiff) has a legal right to file a civil claim in a court of law (e.g., a negligence lawsuit) against the professional (defendant) to seek monetary damages to compensate for the harm. Tort liability can be categorized into three levels of fault (see Figure 1.3): intentional, negligent, and strictly liable.[17] The following subsections give a general description of each type.

---

16 JoAnn M. Eickhoff-Shemek, David L. Herbert, and Daniel P. Connaughton, *Risk Management for Health/Fitness Professionals: Legal Issues and Strategies* (Baltimore, MD: Lippincott Williams & Wilkins, 2009): 30.
17 W. Page Keeton, Dan B. Dobbs, Robert E. Keeton, and David G. Owen, *Prosser and Keeton on the Law of Torts*, 5th ed. (St. Paul, MN: West, 1984).

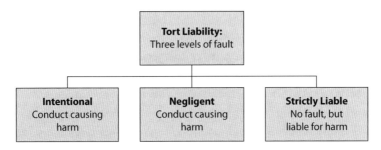

Figure 1.3   Three Levels of Tort Liability

Intentional Torts

Intentional torts include those in which the defendant "intended" to harm another, such as assault, battery, defamation, invasion of privacy, and intentional infliction of emotional distress.[18] It is beyond the scope of this book to describe all of these, but they have been briefly described elsewhere[19] and on various websites that provide all types of legal information. (See the "Website Resources" list at the end of this chapter.) The victims of these intentional torts can file a civil lawsuit against the defendant, and the government can also file criminal charges against the defendant if the defendant's conduct violated a statute. For example, a personal fitness trainer who sexually assaults a client could face both civil claims (battery, an intentional tort) and criminal charges (battery, a violation of a statute). For each intentional tort, there are certain elements that the plaintiff will have to prove in his or her civil claim. For example, to support a claim of intentional infliction of emotional distress, the victim must be able to show that the conduct was "extreme and outrageous" and caused "severe and serious" emotional distress.[20] In the workplace, this conduct could include being subjected to repeated racial slurs or severe sexual harassment that resulted in various physical symptoms of emotional distress such as depression, high blood pressure, and insomnia.

---

18 Doyice J. Cotten and John T. Wolohan, eds., *Law for Recreation and Sport Managers*, 6th ed. (Dubuque, IA: Kendall Hunt, 2013).
19 *Id.*
20 Workplace Fairness Is Everyone's Job, "Intentional Infliction of Emotional Distress," n.d., http://www.workplacefairness.org/intentional.

Negligence

Most courts consider the inherent relationship that is formed between professionals and their participants as a special relationship.[21] Because of this special relationship, wellness professionals have a general legal duty (obligation) to provide "reasonably safe" programs and facilities for their participants. Making something reasonably safe involves taking precautions, such as developing and implementing risk management strategies to help prevent "foreseeable" risks of harm. Failure to take these precautions can lead to negligence claims and lawsuits, which are quite common against fitness/wellness programs.

Negligence can be defined as failing to do something (inaction or omission) that a reasonably prudent professional would have done under the circumstances or doing something (improper action or commission) that a reasonably prudent professional would not have done under the circumstances,[22] as shown in Figure 1.4. Negligence cases against fitness/wellness professionals and facilities have included both ordinary negligence (careless, unintentional conduct) and **gross negligence** (reckless or willful/wanton conduct). Conduct that would be considered ordinary negligence includes inactions such as the failure to conduct pre-activity screening or render first aid, as well as improper actions such as improper instruction or maintenance of exercise equipment, as demonstrated in some of the negligence cases described in Chapter 6.

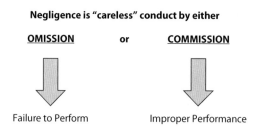

Negligence is "careless" conduct by either

OMISSION   or   **COMMISSION**

Failure to Perform   Improper Performance

Figure 1.4   Negligent Conduct: Omission and Commission

---

21 Betty van der Smissen, "Elements of Negligence," in *Law for Recreational and Sport Managers*, ed. by Doyice J. Cotten and John T. Wolohan, 4th ed. (Dubuque, IA: Kendall Hunt, 2007): 37.
22 *Id.* at 36.

Gross negligence is a more serious type of fault than ordinary negligence. The defendant usually has prior knowledge that a risk of harm or injury exists (e.g., participants have been injured due to slippery floor surfaces) but does not take any precautions to minimize the known cause(s) of the injuries, even though the risk of harm is clearly foreseeable. Ordinary negligence can result in the defendant having to pay the plaintiff **compensatory damages**, and gross negligence can result in the defendant having to pay the plaintiff punitive damages.[23] The law on punitive damages varies from state to state: some states do not allow them, and others limit the amount of the award.[24] Courts award **punitive damages** to punish the defendant for reckless conduct and to send a strong message to future defendants. For example, in *Mimms v. Ruthless Training Concepts, LLC,*[25] the plaintiff sought $350,000 in punitive damages in addition to $500,000 in compensatory damages. The case ended with Mimms, the plaintiff, being awarded $300,000 in monetary damages.

In this case, Mimms experienced severe pain and dark-colored urine two days after his first workout with a personal trainer, which included continuous strenuous leg exercises in a short period of time. He was hospitalized and diagnosed with several injuries, including rhabdomyolysis. Mimms filed a lawsuit against the trainer and the facility listing numerous negligence and gross negligence claims. Some of these included that the personal trainer (1) gave the plaintiff unreasonable and hazardous instructions, demanding that he exert extraordinary effort with no rest periods; (2) failed to refrain from exposing him to unreasonable risks of injury; and (3) failed to observe and monitor the plaintiff to guard and protect him from injury. In addition, several "failure to warn" claims were made, including that the defendants knew that this particular workout regimen caused serious risks of injuries and that the defendants failed to warn Mimms of the known risks and dangers inherent in the program.

---

23 Doyice J. Cotten, "Negligence," in *Law for Recreation and Sport Managers*, 6th ed., ed. Doyice J. Cotten and John T. Wolohan (Dubuque, IA: Kendall Hunt, 2013), 42–53.
24 *Id.*
25 *Mimms v. Ruthless Training Concepts, LLC*, Case No. 78584 (Cir. Ct. Prince William Cty., VA, 2008).

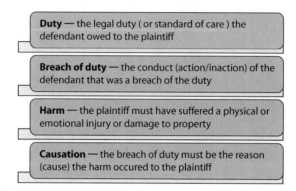

Duty — the legal duty (or standard of care) the defendant owed to the plaintiff

Breach of duty — the conduct (action/inaction) of the defendant that was a breach of the duty

Harm — the plaintiff must have suffered a physical or emotional injury or damage to property

Causation — the breach of duty must be the reason (cause) the harm occured to the plaintiff

Figure 1.5   Four Essential Elements That the Plaintiff Must Prove in a Negligence Lawsuit

In a negligence lawsuit, the plaintiff has to prove all four of the essential elements shown in Figure 1.5: **duty, breach of duty, harm,** and **causation**. It is important to understand that the courts determine duty, not the defendants, the plaintiffs, or their lawyers. The courts often allow **expert witnesses** to testify, to educate the court regarding the specific duties the defendant(s) owed to the plaintiff, given the circumstances, and whether or not the defendant(s) breached any of their duties. Expert witnesses often rely on safety standards, guidelines, and/or position papers published by professional organizations, as well as laws, rules, and regulations, to help provide evidence of the duties defendant(s) owe to plaintiffs. For example, in *Mimms*, the expert witness referred to an American College of Sports Medicine (ACSM) position stand[26] as evidence that the exercise program directed by the fitness trainer did not follow the safety recommendations set forth in the position stand. Therefore, one of the first steps in developing risk management strategies (preventive law) is for fitness/wellness professionals to become aware of these publications and to determine if they are adhering to the requirements and/or recommendations described within them. One resource for becoming familiar with many of these various published standards, guidelines, and position papers is a book by Riva Rahl, *Physical Activity*

---

26 ACSM, "ACSM Position Stand: Progression Models in Resistance Training for Healthy Adults," *Medicine & Science in Sports & Exercise* 41, no. 3 (2009): 687–708; doi:10.1249/MSS.0b013e3181915670.

and Health Guidelines.[27] For example, for the professional who is designing an exercise program for someone with Type 2 diabetes, Rahl provides a summary of guidelines published by the American Diabetes Association and the American College of Sports Medicine and citations that allow easy access to all of the published guidelines.

Fitness/wellness professionals have many legal duties and obligations to help ensure that they are providing reasonably safe programs and facilities. Many of these duties exist within the seven major areas shown in Figure 1.6. It is beyond the scope of this book to address the many duties in each of these areas, but this information can be found elsewhere,[28] along with effective risk management strategies that can be implemented to ensure adherence to these duties and therefore minimize risks of injuries and subsequent negligence claims/lawsuits. However, one of these areas, #4—Instruction and Supervision, is addressed in

Figure 1.6   Many Legal Duties Exist Within Seven Areas

27 Riva L. Rahl, *Physical Activity and Health Guidelines: Recommendations for Various Ages, Fitness Levels and Conditions from 57 Authoritative Sources* (Champaign, IL: Human Kinetics, 2010).
28 Eickhoff-Shemek, Herbert, and Connaughton, *Risk Management for Health/Fitness Professionals,* 113–347.

more detail in Chapter 6. Numerous negligence claims/lawsuits result from the improper instruction by fitness/wellness professionals: It is essential that they are not only *qualified* (possess certain credentials), but also *competent* and perform within their scope of practice.

Defenses to Negligence

When faced with negligence claims/lawsuits, defendants have several defenses they can use to refute or defend against the claims. This chapter briefly describes a couple of common defenses: **waiver** and **primary assumption of risk**. A *waiver* is a contract signed by an individual prior to participation that can absolve or protect the defendants, such as fitness/wellness staff members and the facility, from their own "ordinary" negligence; however, waivers do not provide protection for gross negligence.[29] As noted earlier, waivers are against public policy in certain states, such as Virginia, and are therefore unenforceable in those states. The *Mimms* case[30] occurred in Virginia, so a waiver would not have protected the defendants, because of the long-held ruling or precedent of the Virginia Supreme Court that waivers for personal injury are against public policy.

It is important to realize that many factors must be considered before attempting to use waivers. The law governing waivers is quite complex and is based upon individual state laws; therefore, it is essential that wellness professionals consult with a competent lawyer in their jurisdiction before using waivers. Also, legal counsel is needed to determine if having employees sign a waiver would be recommended in workplace wellness programs. Generally, if workers' compensation is applicable, the employee would not be able to sue the employer for negligence.[31] For more on the topic of workers' compensation, see Chapter 7.

Sometimes when plaintiffs file negligence lawsuits against a fitness/wellness professional and/or facility, their injury was not due to a breach of duty or to negligence, but was due to **inherent risks**. Injuries due to inherent risks just happen (they are inseparable from the activity) and

---

29 Cotton and Cotton, *Waivers and Releases of Liability.*
30 *Mimms v. Ruthless Training Concepts, LLC,* Case No. 78584 (Cir. Ct. Prince William Cty., VA, 2008).
31 82 Am. Jur. 2d *Workers' Compensation* §§ 10, 11, 12, 14 (Workers' Compensation, I. In General, B. Purposes of Workers' Compensation Acts) (2016).

they are no one's fault. Almost everyone who has participated in fitness or recreational/sport activities has experienced an injury due to inherent risks. Most of us just accept these inherent risks, and if we do get hurt, we do not blame someone else for our injury or file a legal claim against anyone. However, some individuals in our society always want to blame someone else, and therefore file a negligence claim/lawsuit to seek monetary damages.

The number of negligence claims/lawsuits has increased over the last two to three decades,[32] in what is sometimes referred to as the "litigation epidemic." Many negligence claims/lawsuits are settled out of court and never go to trial. For example, it is estimated that less than 5 percent of all cases go to trial, because they are dismissed prior to trial, settled, or defeated through various procedures such as summary judgment.[33] However, before a case is settled or goes to trial, the "primary assumption of risk" defense can be very effective to help stimulate dismissal of the case, especially if the injury was due to inherent risks. The law does not allow individuals to recover monetary damages for an injury they received when voluntarily exposing themselves to a known and appreciated danger.[34] Important in this defense is that the danger be "known" and "appreciated," meaning the plaintiff must know, understand, and appreciate the inherent risks and voluntarily assume them. Therefore, informing participants of the inherent risks (minor, major, life-threatening, and death) by describing them in a formal, signed document such as a membership agreement or informed consent can strengthen the defense of primary assumption of risk. However, courts often investigate other factors (e.g., the plaintiff's experience level and the nature of the activity) to determine if the primary assumption of risk defense will be effective or not.[35] Generally, this defense is effective for injuries due to inherent risks and the waiver is effective for injuries due to "ordinary" negligent conduct.

---

32 Eickhoff-Shemek, Herbert, and Connaughton, *Risk Management for Health/Fitness Professionals*, 6.
33 Gil B. Fried, "Introduction to Sport Law," in *Law for Recreational and Sport Managers*, 5th ed., ed. Doyice J. Cotten and John T. Wolohan (Dubuque, IA: Kendall Hunt, 2010).
34 Henry C. Black et al., *Black's Law Dictionary*, 6th ed. (St. Paul, MN: West, 1991), s.v. assumption of risk, 82.
35 Eickhoff-Shemek, Herbert, and Connaughton, *Risk Management for Health/Fitness Professionals*, 222–223.

Strict Liability

Both intentional torts and negligence are based on fault. However, **strict liability**, sometimes referred to as "no fault" liability, is based not on fault, but on public policy. *Public policy* is "a judicial determination of society's mores and views as to what is best for a civilized and enlightened community balanced against certain other constitutional interests and other basic concepts such as freedom of choice, freedom to contract."[36] Examples include **vicarious liability** and workers' compensation.

An employer can be held liable for the negligent conduct of its employees acting within their scope of employment under a legal doctrine called *respondeat superior*—an example of vicarious liability. *Jacob v. Grant Life Choices Center*[37] is an excellent case to demonstrate vicarious liability. The plaintiff in this lawsuit, Jacob, claimed that Robert Getz, an employee in a hospital-based fitness center, failed to provide him appropriate emergency medical aid in accordance with the standard of care. The plaintiff named not only Getz as a defendant in his lawsuit, but also Grant Life Choices Center (the fitness facility), Club Management, Inc. (the company that managed the fitness facility), and Grant Medical Center (the hospital where the fitness center was located). Although it was allegedly the negligent conduct of Getz that caused Jacob's injury, the other three defendants also could be held liable for Jacob's injury, even though they were not involved (they had no direct action/inaction or fault) on the day the injury occurred in the fitness center. Interestingly, in this case, the waiver signed by Jacob protected all of the defendants, so none of them was held liable. It is common, in negligent cases against fitness professionals (e.g., fitness instructors and personal trainers), for the plaintiff to sue both the professional and the employer, the manager and/or owner. An employee who was at fault may have very limited assets and/or no liability insurance, and therefore the plaintiff might not be able to recover any monetary damages for the injury if only the

---

36 *Id.* at 72.
37 *Jacob v. Grant Life Choices Ctr.*, Case No. 93 CVC-06-4353 (Franklin Cty., Ohio, Ohio Ct. Com. Pleas, 1993), cited in David L. Herbert, "Liability Insurance for Health and Fitness Facilities: Making Sure You're Covered—While Knowing What's at Stake," *Exercise Standards and Malpractice Reporter* 10, no. 3 (1996): 33, 36–38.

employee could be named as a defendant. This would not be good public policy. Therefore, based on the legal doctrine of *respondeat superior*, the plaintiff can include as a defendant the employer, which likely will have liability insurance. Because of this legal doctrine, managers of fitness/ wellness programs have a major responsibility to properly hire, train, and supervise their employees. The importance of hiring, training, and supervising employees is discussed further in Chapter 6.

Workers' compensation is another form of strict liability imposed upon the employer without fault.[38] Workers' compensation is based on state statutes that provide payment to employees for injuries occurring while the employees are on the job. Prior to passage of these statutes, employees had to sue their employers, with the hope that they could win their cases and receive monetary damages. Under the workers' compensation statutes, employees can no longer sue their employers for negligence, but instead are awarded compensation when an injury occurs while on the job. The employee receives a "fixed" compensation for medical expenses and a portion of wages while off the job due to the injury. It is a win-win for both the employee and employer: The employee is compensated for his or her injury without having to sue the employer, and the employer does not have the high costs and administrative hassles associated with a negligence lawsuit. This book covers workers' compensation in Chapter 7, with a discussion that includes case examples involving employer-sponsored fitness and wellness programs.

Contract Law

Contracts are commonly used in the workplace wellness field and therefore it is important for professionals to have at least a basic understanding of contract law. Examples include third-party contractors such as vendors, management firms, and local fitness centers. Many workplace wellness programs hire a vendor to administer health risk appraisals and biometric screenings. In addition, company-sponsored wellness programs often

---

38 Eickhoff-Shemek, Herbert, and Connaughton, *Risk Management for Health/Fitness Professionals*, 37.

contract with a management firm instead of hiring their own employees to manage the programs. In these cases, the management firm hires employees who manage and coordinate the delivery of the employee wellness program. There are pros and cons to be considered when deciding whether to contract with a management firm or hire your own employees. Third-party contracts also can include a contract with a local fitness center (e.g., YMCA, health club) to provide fitness services and programs for companies that opt not to have an in-house fitness center. Other examples of contracts include:

- Independent contractors who provide fitness/wellness services, such as personal training, group fitness instruction, flu shot administration, diet counseling, and massage therapy
- Membership contracts
- Waivers or other protective legal documents such as informed consents
- Exercise equipment purchases and lease agreements

In a contract, at least two parties exchange binding promises that can be enforceable in a court of law.[39] If one party does not fulfill the promises, the other can seek legal remedies (e.g., monetary damages) or equitable remedies (e.g., nonmonetary judgments such as specific performance or injunctions).[40] Contract law is based on court rulings or case law as well as certain statutes that may be applicable to contracts, such as laws involving employment issues, real estate transactions, and insurance policies. A contract is an **unenforceable contract** if it violates a statute or is against public policy (e.g., in Virginia, waivers are against public policy based on a ruling of the Virginia Supreme Court).[41]

For a contract to be valid, it must meet the four essential elements shown in Table 1.2.[42] If any one of the four elements is missing, it would be considered a **voidable contract** (e.g., a minor who enters into a contract does not have legal capacity and thus the contract would be voidable).[43] For contracts

39 Clarkson, Miller, Jentz, and Cross, *West's Business Law* (8th ed.), 198.
40 *Id.*
41 Cotton and Cotton, *Waivers and Releases of Liability*, 216.
42 Clarkson, Miller, Jentz, and Cross, *West's Business Law*, 199.
43 *Id.*

Element	Description
Agreement	One party must make an offer (e.g., a wellness coach offers coaching services) and the other party must accept (e.g., a client accepts the wellness coach's offer).
Consideration	Something of value that is legally bargained for by each party; the promises made by each party (e.g., money paid by the member to join a fitness facility and the programs/services provided by the facility in exchange for the money).
Contractual Capacity	Both parties must have contractual capacity; that is, both parties must be competent and of legal age (age of majority in most states is 18).
Legality	The contract must be legal (e.g., it cannot violate any statutes or be against public policy).[45]

Table 1.2   Four Essential Elements (Requirements) of a Valid Contract[44]

used in workplace wellness programs, it is recommended that they be in writing and signed by all parties. Certain contracts must be in writing according to the **Statute of Frauds**; for example, contracts for the sale of goods, such as exercise equipment, that are $500 or more must be in writing. Contract law is quite complex and it is essential that workplace wellness professionals consult with a competent lawyer before using any contract.

Website Resources

The following websites offer various legal resources that can be easily accessed, such as legal dictionaries and information explaining all types of laws.

- Legal Information Institute: www.law.cornell.edu
- FindLaw: www.findlaw.com
- Nolo Law for All: www.nolo.com

---

44 *Id.*
45 Sometimes courts will not void a contract if it violates a statute. It depends on whether the statute has a penalty or is for the protection of health and safety of the public. *See Felland v. Sauey*, 248 Wis. 2d 963, 637 N.W.2d 403 (Wis. Ct. App. 2001).

RULE THE RULES

Key Points in Chapter 1

1. It is essential that workplace wellness professionals have a good understanding of the U.S. legal system in order to properly apply the many workplace laws to the design and delivery of programs and to intelligently discuss legal matters with legal counsel.

2. There are three branches of government at the federal and state levels: (a) legislative—makes laws; (b) executive—carries out laws; and (c) judicial—evaluates laws.

3. In a civil case, the parties are the plaintiff (e.g., injured participant) and the defendant (e.g., wellness employee and facility/employer). In a criminal case, the parties are the defendant (e.g., the individual charged with violating the law) and the government (e.g., district attorney or attorney general).

4. There are three levels of courts at the federal and state levels: (a) trial courts, (b) intermediate appellate courts, and (c) top appellate courts.

5. Tort liability can be categorized into three levels of fault: (a) intentional, (b) negligence, and (c) strict liability.

6. Regarding negligence, fitness/wellness professionals have a legal duty to provide "reasonably safe" programs and facilities, which requires taking precautions to help prevent "foreseeable" risks of harm.

7. Negligence is "careless" conduct that can occur either by omission (failure to perform) or by commission (improper performance). "Gross negligence" is reckless or willful/wanton conduct.

8. In a negligence lawsuit, the plaintiff must prove four essential elements: (a) duty, (b) breach of duty, (c) harm, and (d) causation.

9. In a negligence lawsuit, the conduct of a fitness/wellness professional will likely be evaluated by expert witnesses.

10. Examples of strict liability include (a) vicarious liability (e.g., an employer can be liable for the negligent conduct of its employees based on the legal principle of *respondeat superior*), and

(b) workers' compensation (e.g., an employee can receive compensation for an injury occurring while on the job).

11. Contracts are widely used in workplace wellness programs (e.g., contracts with management companies, vendors, and independent contractors, as well as contracts that serve as protective legal documents or for the purchase/lease of equipment).

12. There are four essential elements to a valid contract: (a) agreement, (b) consideration, (c) contractual capacity, and (d) legality.

Study Questions

1. Why is it important for workplace wellness professionals to have a good understanding of the U.S. legal system?

2. Describe how statutory laws, administrative laws, and case law are formed and then give an example of a law in each category.

3. Define civil law and criminal law and then explain how each is different for the following: (a) standard of proof, (b) burden of proof, and (c) type of punishment.

4. List and describe the four essential elements that the plaintiff must prove in a negligence lawsuit.

5. Describe the difference between omission and commission and then give an example of how each occurred in the *Mimms* case.

6. How did the expert witness in the *Mimms* case show that the defendant breached his duty?

7. What is the difference between the waiver defense and the primary assumption of risk defense? Which is effective for injuries due to (a) negligence and (b) inherent risks?

8. Using the facts from the *Jacob* case, describe the legal principle of *respondeat superior* and its implications for fitness/wellness employers.

9. List five types of contracts that may be used in workplace wellness programs.

10. List and describe the four essential elements of a valid contract.

Key Terms

administrative law

appellate court

breach of duty

case law

causation

certiorari

civil law

common law

compensatory damages

criminal law

defendant

duty

expert witness

gross negligence

harm

inherent risk

intentional tort

negligence

plaintiff

primary assumption of risk

protected health information (PHI)

punitive damages

respondeat superior

risk management

stare decisis

Statute of Frauds

statutory law

strict liability

tort

trial court

unenforceable contract

vicarious liability

voidable contract

waiver

2

A Solid Foundation

Learning Objectives

After reading this chapter, workplace wellness professionals will be able to:

1. Describe the discipline of preventive law and its application to workplace wellness programs.
2. Distinguish preventive law and curative law.
3. Define therapeutic jurisprudence and its application in the design and delivery of workplace wellness programs.
4. Describe preventive law and its relevance to (a) a supportive organizational culture, (b) compliance programs, and (c) a values statement.
5. Understand the connection between workplace wellness best practices and preventive law.
6. View the law as a necessary and useful component of workplace wellness programs rather than a barrier.

Never stir up litigation . . . a worse man can never be found than one who does this.

—Abraham Lincoln[1]

---

1 Quoted in Robert Hardaway, *Preventive Law* (Cincinnati, OH: Anderson, 1997): 56.

Introduction

Now that you have an understanding of the U.S. legal system, it is important to lay the foundation for this book's legal approach, which is to understand the purpose of the law and use that purpose to design and implement better, more inclusive workplace wellness programs. By understanding the law's purpose and using that purpose as a tool in workplace wellness program design and implementation, workplace wellness professionals and organizations can "rule"—have control over—workplace wellness rules. Having control over the rules is generally less expensive and less stressful than having the rules control the wellness professional or organization. When the rules control you, you are placed in a reactive, defensive position. This book's legal approach is to educate readers about the law so that readers can be less fearful of the law and take on the legal requirements with confidence ... even if they do not wholeheartedly embrace those requirements. Control over workplace wellness rules is most effective when one adopts a workplace wellness compliance program that includes policies and procedures which address the requirements of the various workplace wellness rules discussed in this book.

To lend strength and credibility to the idea of ruling over the rules, one needs a legal framework. A framework offers a method to: (1) apply academic study; and (2) justify and legitimize an approach to solve a problem or issue, such as how best to design a workplace wellness program. Two useful frameworks that promote development and use of a workplace wellness compliance program are the concepts of preventive law and therapeutic jurisprudence. These two concepts work best in workplace cultures that support workplace wellness and well-being and that adopt workplace wellness compliance programs.

Preventive Law

The discipline of **preventive law** is one of two primary purposes that law serves. The first purpose is to protect individuals from other people who may wrong them. That kind of law is curative, or reactive, as will be discussed shortly. The second purpose is to facilitate human interaction and purpose, which is preventive.[2] Another way to describe preventive law is to compare it to preventive medicine: Just as preventive medicine tries to prevent illness and disease from occurring in the first place, preventive law tries to prevent lawsuits. Preventive law requires creative thinking, timely planning, and purposeful execution to minimize legal risks, maximize legal rights, and optimize legal outcomes of transactions (deals), relationships (disputes), and opportunities (problems).[3]

Preventive law is not, however, planning to win disputes. It is about preventing lawsuits in the first place.[4] One finds an example showing the difference in the employment context. Many attorneys advise employers to refrain from giving a discharged employee the reason for his or her dismissal for fear of revealing information that could be used against the employer in a lawsuit. If the employer provides no reason for the dismissal, it will be more difficult for the discharged employee to prove that the reason for the discharge was unlawful (such as discharge because of the employee's gender, race, disability, or workers' compensation claim).[5] While such advice may help an employer defend against a lawsuit, it will likely not prevent one. "Employees who are given no reason for their discharge will naturally (and reasonably) believe the discharge is unfair."[6] Even if an employer ultimately wins a lawsuit, the employer still loses. Average defense costs in employment law cases range from $45,000 to more than $100,000.[7]

A lawyer truly practicing preventive law would advise the employer to state the reason for the employee's discharge (assuming that the reason is not unlawful). Sharing the reason for discharge reduces the chance that the discharged employee will even consult a plaintiff's attorney or file a complaint. This phenomenon has been supported in medical malpractice studies looking at the effect of physician apologies. Interviews of patients

---

2 Thomas D. Barton and James M. Cooper, *Preventive Law and Creative Problem Solving: Multi-Dimensional Lawyering*, 15, http://preventivelawyer.com/content/pdfs/Multi_Dimensional_Lawyer.pdf.
3 David Rowley, "The Matter with Lawyers: Why Is It that People Love to Hate Lawyers? Just What Is the Matter?," www.preventivelawyer.org/content/essays/rowley.htm.
4 James Frierson, "Pre-Action Advice May Not Be Preventive Law Advice," www.preventivelawer.org/content/essays/frierson.htm.
5 *Id.*
6 *Id.*
7 *Id.*

who sued their healthcare providers reveal that these patients believe the courtroom is the only forum in which they can find out what happened.[8] Some patients also believe that the physicians were not completely honest with them about what happened.[9] One study found that 40 percent of patients who had sued regarding a preventable error would have decided against filing a lawsuit if they had received an explanation and apology from the provider.[10] Like the harmed patient, the ex-employee may not agree with the perceived "wrong" (the stated dismissal cause), but the explanation helps the employee make sense of the situation. Even if the ex-employee does see an attorney, the attorney is less likely to accept the case when the reason for discharge is given.[11]

One can compare preventive law to preventive medicine, as both try to address problems before they arise. This is in contrast to **curative law** and medicine. Curative law and medicine react to legal or medical disasters by swooping in to save the day either in court or at the hospital. With regard to curative law, both lawyers and clients see effective lawyering as developing good "fighter skills." Fighter lawyers advocate zealously with the goal of vindicating the violated rights of a client.[12] Thus, clients who view the law as curative think of consulting a lawyer only after a problem arises, and they expect the lawyer to fix it.

Preventive lawyers can help clients shift their view of law and lawyers from curative or reactive to preventive or proactive. Preventive lawyers can project an image of lawyers that reaches beyond legal experts and fighters for justice to counselors and peacemakers as well. "Peacemaking decentralizes power, encourages participation, and attempts to fashion solution systems that all the stakeholders can embrace."[13] Preventive law requires lawyers to collaborate with other professionals, to inherently understand the context in which their clients work and the dynamics of

---

8 Jennifer Robbennolt, "Apologies and Medical Error," *Clinical Orthopaedics and Related Research* 467 (2009): 376–382, http://www.ncbi.nlm.nih.gov/pmc/articles/PMC2628492/pdf/11999_2008_Article_580. pdf.
9 *Id.*
10 *Id.*
11 Frierson, "Pre-Action Advice May Not Be Preventive Law Advice."
12 Barton and Cooper, "Preventive Law and Creative Problem Solving: Multi-Dimensional Lawyering," 1, http://preventivelawyer.com/content/pdfs/Multi_Dimensional_Lawyer.pdf.
13 *Id.* at 15.

human relationships, to make the law more accessible, and to skillfully help craft environments that prevent problems from arising.[14] Preventive lawyers must also be skilled in reforming law through lobbying, legislation drafting, and working with multiple stakeholders when necessary so that communities can create sensible solutions and avoid controversy.[15]

Another way of viewing the preventive lawyer's role is that the lawyer serves as a "bridge" to the "other" individuals or issues that are often forgotten, neglected, or left behind. Lawyers who practice preventive law are well positioned to advise clients on creating and implementing compliance programs that prevent legal issues from arising in the first place.

Therapeutic Jurisprudence

In terms of workplace wellness program design, adoption of preventive law—as well as a related perspective, therapeutic jurisprudence—is helpful. One author defines **therapeutic jurisprudence** as "the use of social science to study the extent to which a legal rule or practice promotes the psychological and physical well-being of the people it affects."[16] Therapeutic jurisprudence is a method by which to analyze, learn about, and act out the law.[17]

Therapeutic jurisprudence requires us to be alert to legal measures that may not in themselves raise serious legal concerns, but may potentially cause anger, stress, hurt, and hard feelings.[18] For example, drug treatment courts may use therapeutic jurisprudence when interacting with drug offenders and trying to convince them to enter a drug diversion program instead of going to trial.[19] If the offender experiences the choice between drug diversion or trial as coerced, his or her attitude,

14 *Id.* at 21; *see also* Hardaway, *Preventive Law*, at 72 (stating that effective legal counselors provide the solvents and lubricants which reduce the frictions of our complex society and that in the role of counselor, the lawyer serves as an instrument of peace).
15 *Id.* at 33.
16 William G. Schma, "Therapeutic Jurisprudence: Recognizing Law as One of the Healing Arts," *Michigan Bar Journal* (Jan. 2003): 26, https://www.michbar.org/journal/pdf/pdf4article536.pdf.
17 *Id.*
18 David B. Wexler, "Beyond Analogy: Preventive Law as Preventive Medicine," www.preventivelawyer.org/content/essays/Wexler.htm.
19 David B. Wexler and Bruce J. Winick, "Therapeutic Jurisprudence," in *Principles of Addiction Medicine*, 4th ed. (2008). Abstract ID 1101507, http://ssrn.com/abstract=1101507.

motivation, and chances for success in the treatment program may be undermined.[20] A body of psychological work on what makes individuals feel coerced suggests that judges should strive to treat offenders with dignity and respect, to inspire their trust and confidence that the judge has their best interests at heart, to provide them a full opportunity to participate, and to listen attentively to what they have to say.[21] Judges who treat offenders in this fashion increase the likelihood that the offender will perceive treatment as a voluntary choice, will internalize the goals of treatment, and will act in ways that help to achieve those goals.

Applying therapeutic jurisprudence to workplace wellness could have benefits similar to those seen in drug treatment courts. Therapeutic jurisprudence requires the workplace wellness program designer to consider whether the wellness activity will cause discontent or discomfort among wellness program participants. This consideration is important because causing discontent or discomfort among employees or family members in wellness program design may actually defeat the whole purpose of the program. Specifically, causing anger or discomfort may not only increase the likelihood of a lawsuit, but may also cause stress in the workplace. Stress has been shown to undermine physical health.[22] As a result, practicing preventive law, mixed with a heavy dose of therapeutic jurisprudence, may constitute a powerful form of preventive medicine.[23] That is, considering legal requirements as part of the wellness program design process may actually lead employees to adopt healthier lifestyles, because they will not feel coerced.

Preventive Law Strategies

To help preventive law become more integrated into workplace wellness program design and implementation, it has to be accessible. First, increasing the number of lawyers who practice and believe in preventive law will

---

20 *Id.*
21 *Id.*
22 *See, e.g.*, Paige Bierma, "The Immune System and Stress," *Health Day* (Mar. 11, 2015), http://consumer.healthday.com/encyclopedia/stress-management-37/stress-health-news-640/the-immune-system-and-stress-645924.html.
23 Wexler, "Beyond Analogy: Preventive Law as Preventive Medicine."

facilitate the adoption of preventive law measures, such as creating meaningful compliance programs for clients. Law schools can help increase the number of preventive law practitioners by devoting more time to covering preventive law concepts, such as how to develop effective compliance programs in different industries, including health and wellness.[24] Second, the law itself must be more accessible. Those trained in the law must translate complex legal concepts into workable guidelines.[25] Not only will such translation facilitate the law's ability to deliver tangible benefits and achieve its purpose, but it will also enhance the lawyer's credibility.[26]

For preventive law to be effective, it must have a solid foundation of a **supportive organizational culture**. As mentioned earlier, preventive law often operates as part of a company's corporate **compliance program**.[27] It is often advantageous for a corporation to have a compliance program because, should the corporation ever find itself being scrutinized by the government, such programs have the potential to reduce any penalty so long as the compliance program is legally sound and followed by the corporation.[28] However, it is not enough for the company to have compliance documents, if they just sit on a shelf and collect dust. The effectiveness of a compliance program in reducing penalties and mitigating risk depends upon the cultural adoption of a formal set of values and beliefs.[29] A **values statement** heartily adopted at the highest levels of an organization forms the foundation on which a compliance or preventive law program is based.

The values statement should be in writing, be easy to read and comprehend, and be made physically available throughout the organization. The writing facilitates discussion of the beliefs by members of the

---

24 Frierson, "Pre-Action Advice May Not Be Preventive Law Advice."

25 Rowley, "The Matter with Lawyers."

26 *Id.; see also* Susan Bisom-Rapp, "Bulletproofing the Workplace: Symbol and Substance in Employment Discrimination Law Practice," *Florida State University Law Review* 26 (1999): 988 (organizations that appear attentive to employment discrimination law are less likely to provoke protest by protected classes of employees within the firm or community members who seek jobs, they are more likely to secure government resources (contracts, grants, etc.), and they are less likely to trigger audits by regulatory agencies, and if sued, such organizations can point to the structural changes as evidence of the nondiscriminatory nature of their policies and practices).

27 Gary W. Boyle, "The Foundation of Preventive Law in Corporate America," www.preventivelawyer.org/content/essays/boyle.htm.

28 *Id.*

29 *Id.*

corporation, including the manner in which the beliefs are stated, the differences of opinion regarding the beliefs, the synergy of the different beliefs, and the meaning of the beliefs in everyday business.[30] These discussions help transform the stated values into a corporate culture.[31] To reinforce that culture, it is critical that corporate leadership behave consistently with the organization's values at all times and personally and professionally commit to making the values part of the corporate culture. A company that establishes properly motivated values will by default create a preventive law program of the highest caliber.[32]

Preventive Law and Best Practices in Workplace Wellness

Fortunately, the workplace wellness community has developed a number of **best practices** in wellness program design that can be used to develop a solid corporate culture that supports preventive law practice. For example, some of the key seven benchmarks laid out by the Wellness Council of America (WELCOA) could be broadened for use as a formula for developing a preventive law program that encompasses not only employee wellness, but also compliance with laws that affect all aspects of the business. These seven benchmarks include, in general:

1. Capturing leadership support
2. Creating cohesive, diverse wellness teams
3. Collecting data to drive health efforts
4. Carefully crafting an operating plan
5. Choosing appropriate interventions
6. Creating a supportive environment
7. Carefully evaluating outcomes[33]

The first, second, fourth, and sixth benchmarks are well-suited to building a culture that supports, observes, and operates by the principles of preventive law.

---

30 *Id.*
31 *Id.*
32 *Id.*
33 WELCOA's Seven Benchmarks (n.d.), https://www.welcoa.org/services/build/welcoas-seven-benchmarks/.

As noted in the discussion about creating a supportive organizational culture for purposes of preventive law adoption, capturing leadership buy-in is key, which is the first of WELCOA's seven benchmarks. Ensuring that a cohesive, diverse team of individuals develops the values statement will mitigate the creation of an "us versus them" environment. WELCOA notes that one of the biggest mistakes organizations make when initiating wellness teams is that they only include executives from the upper echelons of the company.[34] Employees can perceive top-down initiatives as adversarial, which reduces the willingness of companies and individuals to share information (such as their personal health information) and to engage in mutually beneficial problem solving.[35] To counter the impression that the values statement is a top-down initiative, it is essential to include members from throughout the company who represent the diverse characteristics of your organization.[36]

Carefully crafting an operating plan for a workplace wellness program (WELCOA's fourth benchmark) can be part of the values statement drafting, as discussed earlier. The same diverse team of individuals that may otherwise be charged with drafting the wellness program operating plan could be tasked with creating, reviewing, or revising the company's values statement. Discussing values such as corporate integrity, employee investment, community responsibility, efficiency, cooperation, customer satisfaction,

---

34 "The 10 Secrets of Successful Worksite Wellness Teams," *WELCOA Absolute Advantage* 6, no. 3, at 6–10, https://www.welcoa.org/wp/wp-content/uploads/2014/06/02teams.pdf.

35 On Amir and Orly Lobel, "Stumble, Predict, Nudge: How Behavioral Economics Informs Law and Policy," *Columbia Law Review* 108 (2008): 2098, at 2131.

36 Barbara J. Zabawa, "Making the HIFA Waiver Work Through Collaborative Governance," *Annals of Health Law* 12 (Summer 2003), 378. This tenet of multistakeholder input into the values statement and, ultimately, wellness program design is similar to a collaborative governance model. "Collaborative governance recasts outside stakeholders as potential contributors and equal partners to the rulemaking or program creation process, rather than a threat to [governing body] ideas." *Id.* Collaborative governance has the following features: (1) a problem-solving orientation, requiring information sharing and deliberation among knowledgeable parties; (2) participation by interested and affected parties in all stages of the decision-making process, which may also facilitate effective problem solving; (3) development of temporary rules subject to revision, contingent upon the findings of continuous monitoring and evaluation; (4) replacement or supplementation of traditional oversight mechanisms with new allocations of authority because parties are interdependent and accountable to each other; and (5) the agency acting as a facilitator of multistakeholder negotiations and viewing regulatory success as contingent on the contributions of other participants. *Id.* The existence of a controversial, complex issue that is of high priority to identifiable stakeholders creates an ideal condition for the application of collaborative governance. *Id.* at 384. Certainly, one could argue that creating a values statement and wellness program in the workplace presents such an issue, and therefore an opportunity to employ collaborative governance.

long-term value of investments, creativity, and ingenuity aligns with designing effective wellness programs as well as creating a preventive law environment. Addressing workplace wellness programs through creation of a values statement for purposes of corporate compliance may face less opposition from leadership that might otherwise be hesitant to invest in a workplace wellness program.

Several of the WELCOA benchmarks also are reflected in the nine "best practice dimensions" for workplace wellness programs developed by Pronk:[37]

1. Leadership—ensuring structural support for the program
2. Relevance—engaging employees and their families
3. Partnership—integrating multiple stakeholders
4. Comprehensiveness—including elements that make up a comprehensive program
5. Implementation—ensuring a planned and coordinated execution of the program
6. Engagement—facilitating program co-ownership
7. Communication—ensuring formal communication strategies
8. Data-driven—making informed decisions through proper measurement, evaluation, reporting, and analytics
9. Compliance—meeting regulatory requirements (e.g., safeguarding individual-level data)[38]

One recent article expands on these nine dimensions and credits them for implementing a successful university employee wellness program.[39] For example, for Compliance (dimension 9), the authors[40] described how they were compliant with the HIPAA privacy rule and tax laws with regard to financial incentives.

---

37 Nico Pronk, "Best Practice Design Principles at Worksite Health and Wellness Programs," *ACSM's Health & Fitness Journal* 18, no. 1 (January/February 2014), 42–46.
38 *Id.*
39 Lisa Hoffman and Carol Kennedy-Armbruster, "Case Study Using Best Practice Design Principles for Worksite Wellness Programs," *ACSM's Health & Fitness Journal* 19, no. 3 (May/June 2015), 30–35.
40 *Id.*

Purposes of This Book

Despite their benefits, preventive law and therapeutic jurisprudence do not go far enough to explain the purpose of this book. This book not only asks the reader to support preventive law and therapeutic jurisprudence, which really relates to how a lawyer uses law, but it also asks the reader to take a broader view of the law and see it as a helpful tool rather than just a restriction on behavior. The law offers more than just commands on what to do or not do: It offers principled reasons and justifications for its existence.[41] In other words, it is a reflection of our societal values. As one author noted, "[l]egal issues aren't isolated or labeled. They're part of the warp and woof of the broader fabric of life—dreams, visions, goals and aspirations. Without the wider context, counsel is needlessly limited. Credibility is the key to the big picture."[42]

As an example of taking a broader view of the law, think of a stop sign. A stop sign is a preventive measure that helps our communities avoid accidents. You, as the driver of a vehicle, could view the stop sign as a hindrance—something that forces you to slow down and stop (especially if you are in a hurry). You can obey the stop sign begrudgingly and it will still have the desired result of preventing an accident. Your stopping is preventive law, but you may still feel annoyed by the sign. Alternatively, instead of viewing the sign as an annoyance or restriction on your behavior, you could view the sign as a helpful tool. By looking at the purpose of the sign in its larger context, which is to prevent accidents, keep traffic flowing in another direction, reduce speed in populated areas, and encourage drivers to pay attention to their surroundings because they are driving potential killing machines, you may have a greater appreciation for the sign, feel less annoyed by it, and see it as a reminder that our complex, busy society needs some structure so we can

---

41 Amir and Lobel, "Stumble, Predict, Nudge," at 2131.
42 Barton and Cooper, "Preventive Law and Creative Problem Solving: Multi-Dimensional Lawyering," 28.

all feel safe and respected. You may even work harder at leaving more time in your schedule to account for the stop sign.

The same can be said with workplace wellness laws. At first blush, such laws may seem like a hindrance to workplace wellness programs, something that comes up only after you have already expended a lot of effort on designing and implementing your wellness program. In those cases, compliance with the requirements may cause exasperation. But, because this book discusses the law's purpose and puts the law into a larger context of creating a positive culture of well-being, you may be more appreciative of workplace wellness laws. You may even be more likely to adopt a workplace wellness compliance program to serve as a roadmap for creating and implementing your workplace wellness program itself.

To help you adopt a proactive approach to compliance, each chapter in this book addresses certain aspects of workplace wellness programs and aims to help you appreciate the role the law plays in your workplace wellness design. Through learning about the purpose of the law, your view of the law may shift from seeing it only as a barrier to seeing it as a necessary and useful component of workplace wellness programs. Who knows: Perhaps your view of lawyers will also change from professionals who function as "hired guns" to experts who can be trusted partners, advisors, and members of your workplace wellness design team.

RULE THE RULES

Key Points in Chapter 2

1. There are two purposes of preventive law: (a) protect individuals from other people who may wrong them and (b) facilitate human interaction and purpose.
2. Like preventive medicine, which focuses on disease prevention, preventive law focuses on preventing lawsuits.
3. Curative law is reactive; in this paradigm, a client consults with a lawyer only after a problem arises and expects the lawyer to fix it.

4. Workplace wellness professionals who focus on compliance with workplace wellness laws in the design and delivery of their programs are being proactive by reducing legal liability for themselves and their employer.

5. Therapeutic jurisprudence is applicable to workplace wellness programs in that it promotes the psychological and physical well-bring of individuals. An example is decision making that uses a "we" approach instead of an "us versus them" approach, which will be less likely to cause anger or discontent among employees and subsequent litigation.

6. Preventive law operates as part of a company's compliance program. To be effective, it requires a solid foundation of a supportive organizational culture that is based on a formal values statement.

7. Many of the best practices associated with workplace wellness programs are applicable to preventive law strategies.

8. Workplace wellness professionals should view their efforts to comply with the law as a necessary and useful component of a well-designed and comprehensive program, rather than a barrier.

Study Questions

1. Describe the similarities between preventive law and preventive medicine.

2. Explain why it is better to focus on a preventive law approach rather than a curative law approach.

3. Describe how therapeutic jurisprudence could be applied in the design and delivery of a workplace wellness program.

4. Discuss preventive law in terms of its relevance to a supportive organizational culture and a formal values statement.

5. Of the best practices described in this chapter, describe those that are in line with the principles of preventive law.

6. Explain why top-down initiatives can be perceived as adversarial by employees, and describe the potential negative effects this "us versus them" approach can have on workplace wellness programs.

7. Using the stop-sign analogy, explain how the law offers principled reasons and justifications for its existence.
8. Describe how your view of the law has changed after reading this chapter.

Key Terms

best practices
compliance program
curative law
preventive law

supportive organizational culture
therapeutic jurisprudence
values statement

3

To Plan or Not to Plan: A Historical Look at the Employer-Employee Relationship and the Birth of Employee Health Benefits

Learning Objectives

After reading this chapter, workplace wellness professionals will be able to:

1. Define "group health plan" and "medical care" as stated in the Employee Retirement and Income Security Act (ERISA).
2. Distinguish workplace wellness programs that qualify as group health plans (or part of one) from those that are non-group health plans (or outside the group health plan).
3. List and describe the federal laws applicable to wellness programs for group health plans and non-group health plans.
4. Summarize the historical issues that led Congress to enact the many different labor and employment laws.
5. Understand the terms "employee welfare benefit plan" and "exclusive benefit rule" as defined by ERISA.
6. Describe laws addressing employee benefit protections that were enacted after ERISA in 1974, and the rationale behind these protections.

Knowing yourself is the beginning of all wisdom.

—Aristotle

To be or not to be, that is the question.

—William Shakespeare

Introduction

Before embracing all the laws that impact workplace wellness programs, it is imperative that you first understand, or decide, your wellness program's "group health plan" status. Whether your workplace wellness program qualifies as a group health plan or a non-group health plan dictates which laws apply. See Table 3.1. The Employee Retirement and Income Security Act (ERISA) defines **group health plan** as "an employer-sponsored welfare benefit plan to the extent that the plan provides medical

Law	Group Health Plan Wellness Programs*	Non-Group Health Plan Wellness Programs
ACA—Affordable Care Act	X	
ERISA—Employment Retirement and Income Security Act	X	
HIPAA—Health Insurance Portability and Accountability Act	X	
COBRA—Consolidated Omnibus Budget Reconciliation Act	X	
ADA—Americans with Disabilities Act	X	X
GINA—Genetic Information Nondiscrimination Act	X	X
FLSA—Fair Labor Standards Act	X	X
IRC—Internal Revenue Code	X	X
NLRA—National Labor Relations Act	X	X
Title VII of the Civil Rights Act, which prohibits discrimination by employers on the basis of race, color, religion, sex, or national origin	X	X
State laws	Depends	X

Table 3.1   Federal Laws Applicable to Workplace Wellness Programs

*In addition to wellness programs that qualify as a group health plan on their own merit, workplace wellness programs that are part of an employer's group health plan (e.g., offered only to group health plan enrollees) also must comply with these laws.

care to employees or their dependents directly or through insurance or otherwise."[1] **Medical care** costs include amounts paid for:

- The diagnosis, cure, mitigation, treatment, or prevention of disease, or amounts paid for the purpose of affecting any structure or function of the body;
- Transportation primarily for and essential to this medical care; and
- Insurance covering this medical care.[2]

Medical care does not include anything that is merely beneficial to the general health of an individual, such as a vacation.[3] Thus, if an employer maintains a program that furthers general good health, but the program does not relate to the relief or alleviation of health or medical problems and is generally accessible to and used by employees without regard to their physical condition or state of health, that program is not considered a program that provides health care and so is not a group health plan. For example, if an employer maintains a spa, swimming pool, gymnasium, or other exercise/fitness program or facility that is normally accessible to and used by employees for reasons other than relief of health or medical problems, such a facility does not constitute a program that provides medical care and thus is not a group health plan. If, however, an employer offers a fitness program to those employees who have been diagnosed with a medical condition, and the employee's medical provider has prescribed exercise as treatment for that condition, the fitness activity would qualify as medical care. Similarly, if an employer maintains a drug or alcohol treatment program or a health clinic, or any other facility or program that is intended to relieve or alleviate a diagnosed physical condition or health problem, the facility or program is considered to be the provision of medical care and so the wellness program would qualify as a group health plan.[4]

---

1 ERISA §§ 607 and 733.
2 26 U.S.C. § 213(d); ERISA § 733(a)(2).
3 26 C.F.R. § 54.4980B-2(b). Although this regulatory reference defines *medical care* for COBRA purposes only, one could argue that the guidance is relevant to the group health plan definitions found in other parts of ERISA, such as HIPAA and the ACA. *Ratzlaff v. United States*, 510 U.S. 135, 143 (1994) (stating that a "term appearing in several places in a statutory text is generally read the same way each time it appears").
4 26 C.F.R. § 54-4980B-2(b).

If your wellness program either meets the definition of group health plan itself, or is tied to an employer's group health plan, such as by linking rewards to group health plan premiums or cost-sharing or offering the wellness program as a benefit to group health plan participants, the wellness program must also comply with a number of additional laws, as outlined in Table 3.1. This is because the Affordable Care Act (ACA) wellness program provisions, the Health Insurance Portability and Accountability Act (HIPAA) nondiscrimination provisions, and the Consolidated Omnibus Budget Reconciliation Act of 1985 (COBRA) apply only to group health plan wellness programs.[5]

If your wellness program does not qualify as a group health plan, then these laws would not apply, but the Americans with Disabilities Act (ADA), the Genetic Information Nondiscrimination Act (GINA), the Fair Labor Standards Act (FLSA), the Federal Trade Commission Act (FTCA), the Internal Revenue Code (IRC), the National Labor Relations Act (NLRA), Title VII, state privacy laws, and other state laws (such as workers' compensation, professional or institutional licensing, or state nondiscrimination laws) would still apply. Also, different parts of GINA apply to group health plans as compared to employer programs outside of group health plans. GINA Title I applies to group health plans and GINA Title II applies to employers. With Subchapters I–III of Chapter 126, the ADA also carves out from compliance the performance of benefit plan administration activities by group health plans and others.[6] This "safe harbor" within the ADA permits medical examinations by group health plans.[7] In Chapter 4, you will see how the group health plan distinction matters, and how the Equal Employment Opportunity Commission views the applicability of the ADA safe harbor to workplace wellness programs.

---

5 ERISA pt. 6 (COBRA applying to group health plans and defining *group health plan*, at § 607); ERISA pt. 7 (applying to group health plans HIPAA nondiscrimination rules, at § 7002, and defining "group health plan" at § 733); 42 U.S.C. § 300gg-41 (applying the ACA nondiscrimination rules to group health plans and health insurance issuers in the group or individual market).
6 42 U.S.C. § 12201(c).
7 42 U.S.C. § 12112(d).

Why Are There So Many Laws for Workplace Wellness, Particularly for Group Health Plans?

This is a fundamental question, the exploration of which may give you a greater appreciation for labor and employment laws generally. There is a long history of battle between worker interests and employer interests. One poignant poem puts the worker perspective in historical context:

A Worker Reads History

Who built the seven gates of Thebes?
The books are filled with names of kings.
Was it kings who hauled the craggy blocks of stone?
And Babylon, so many times destroyed,
Who built the city up each time? In which of Lima's houses,
That city glittering with gold, lived those who built it?
In the evening when the Chinese wall was finished
Where did the masons go? Imperial Rome
Is full of arcs of triumph. Who reared them up? Over whom
Did the Caesars triumph? Byzantium lives in song,
Were all her dwellings palaces? And even in Atlantis of the legend
The night the sea rushed in,
The drowning men still bellowed for their slaves.
Young Alexander conquered India.
He alone?
Caesar beat the Gauls.
Was there not even a cook in his army?
Philip of Spain wept as his fleet
Was sunk and destroyed. Were there no other tears?
Frederick the Great triumphed in the Seven Years War. Who
Triumphed with him?
Each page a victory,
At whose expense the victory ball?
Every ten years a great man,
Who paid the piper?
So many particulars.
So many questions.[8]

---

8 Bertolt Brecht, *Selected Poems*, trans. H. Hays (New York, NY: Harcourt, Brace Javanovich, 1947), 109.

At the risk of imposing on the reader an interpretation of this poem, we could all probably agree that at a minimum, this poem shines a light on the humanity behind many of the great leaders and moments in history. Not only does it remind the reader that behind great accomplishments are numerous, nameless laborers, but also that these laborers have feelings and lives beyond the work they did. Yet, we do not learn of the particulars of those laborers' lives, and therefore we as a society forget to appreciate the progress they helped create.

The lack of concern for workers permeates throughout history, and it was not until the 20th century that the United States started enacting laws to protect workers. In the early part of the 20th century, working men, women, and children had no legal protections with regard to working hours, minimum wages, compensation for accidents on the job, pensions, unemployment compensation, or occupational safety.[9] At the same time, industrial accidents in the United States were the highest in the world; about a half million workers were injured and 30,000 killed at work each year.[10] The lack of legislative protection of workers was primarily the result of "collusion of businesses and their representatives in state legislatures and the U.S. Senate to block laws that would bring the state into the workplace or mandate expensive safety measures."[11] The employer community preferred "freedom of contract" and "individual rights" workers. Contractual obligations may work when employers are very small, as they were in the earliest days of America. But, with the rise of factories and corporations, honoring promises made to individual workers became impractical. Thus, the only tools available to workers to protest terms and conditions of employment were the strike and the boycott. Early 20th-century courts, however, were not friendly to labor protests, and granted injunctions against labor on the ground that staging such protests violated antitrust laws.[12] It was not until labor became involved in politics that

---

9 Robert J. Rabin et al., *Labor and Employment Law* (West Casebook Series: The Labor Law Group, 1995), at 19 (citing Nell Painter, *Standing at Armageddon*, at 206–212).
10 *Id.*
11 *Id.*
12 *Id.*

some champions for labor causes were elected to office and could help enact pro-labor laws.[13]

These labor and employment laws, still in place today, include an exemption from prosecution under the federal antitrust laws (allowing worker organizations, strikes, and boycotts),[14] the National Labor Relations Act (NLRA; guaranteeing covered workers the right to organize and join labor movements, to choose representatives and bargain collectively, and to strike),[15] the Fair Labor Standards Act (FLSA; prescribing standards for wages and overtime pay as well as restricting the hours and types of jobs children can work),[16] the Worker Adjustment, Retraining and Notification Act (WARN; requiring advance notification to workers of employer shutdowns or layoffs),[17] the Occupational Health and Safety Act (OSHA; creates standards and protects health and safety of workers),[18] the Family and Medical Leave Act (FMLA; permits workers to take up to 12 weeks unpaid leave for family and medical reasons),[19] and Title VII (guards against discrimination based on a worker's race, color, religion, sex, or national origin),[20] among numerous others.

As alluded to earlier, labor and employment laws came into being to balance out an unequal bargaining relationship between employer and employee. Without these laws, employees would likely not have enough negotiating power to ensure that their employer looked out for their health and wellness. Employers and employees often have different, divergent interests, particularly when it comes to employee benefits. In general, employees want to maximize the value of the benefits employers obtain for them, whereas employers want to minimize the cost of obtaining the level and quality of benefits that the labor market

---

13 Painter, *Standing at Armageddon*, at 20–22.

14 "Federal Labor Laws," *Congressional Digest* (June-July 1993).

15 *Id.*

16 U.S. Department of Labor, "Summary of the Major Laws of the Department of Labor," http://www.dol.gov/opa/aboutdol/lawsprogr.htm.

17 *Id.*

18 *Id.*

19 *Id.* Applies only to employers of 50 or more employees. *Id.*

20 "Employment Discrimination: An Overview," Cornell Legal Information Institute, https://www.law.cornell.edu/wex/employment_discrimination.

demands.[21] Additional laws regulating employee benefits exist to ensure that the employer fulfills promises and expectations regarding benefits.

Employers entered the world of benefits in part because of tax incentives. The Revenue Acts of 1921 and 1926 allowed employers to deduct pension contributions from corporate income, and allowed income of the pension fund's portfolio to accumulate tax free.[22] World War II froze wages, but the War Labor Board permitted fringe benefits to continue to expand in lieu of wages.[23] The IRS considered health benefits to be "in-kind" compensation, deductible as a business expense and excluded from employees' taxable income.[24] In 1954, 70 percent of all workers were covered under employer-based health insurance contracts.[25]

Despite these tax incentives and the popularity of employee benefits, abuses occurred. For example, companies used pensions to shelter payments to their executives, but even when pension availability spread to rank-and-file employees, many companies failed to fund those pensions.[26] When companies dissolved, workers lost much of their promised benefit.[27]

One of the most publicized stories of an employee benefit disaster was the Studebaker plant closure in 1963. Like many manufacturers in the 1950s and 1960s, Studebaker-Packard had an employee pension plan that promised retirees and active employees around $2.50/month per year of service.[28] However, in December 1963, Studebaker-Packard announced that it would close its South Bend, Indiana, plant.[29] At that time, the Studebaker pension plan obligations exceeded its assets by

---

21 Dayna Bowen Matthew, "Controlling the Reverse Agency Costs of Employment-Based Health Insurance: Of Markets, Courts and a Regulatory Quagmire," in *Cases and Materials on Employee Benefits Law* (West, 1998), at 494–495.
22 U.S. Department of Labor, "History of EBSA and ERISA," http://www.dol.gov/ebsa/aboutebsa/history.html.
23 Matthew, "Controlling the Reverse Agency Costs of Employment-Based Health Insurance," 493.
24 *Id.* at 495.
25 *Id.*
26 Roger Lowenstein, "The End of Pensions," *N.Y. Times Magazine* (Oct. 30, 2005), http://www.nytimes.com/2005/10/30/magazine/the-end-of-pensions.html.
27 *Id.*
28 James A. Wooten, "The Most Glorious Story of Failure in the Business: The Studebaker-Packard Corporation and the Origins of ERISA," *Buffalo Law Review* 49 (2001), 683, 727.
29 *Id.*

$15 million.[30] This shortfall left 4,400 employees without any of their anticipated pension benefits.[31]

The Studebaker incident sparked earnest advocacy by unions to create a federal pension insurance program.[32] That effort culminated in the passage of ERISA in 1974; that law provides a legislative incentive to limit employer divergence from employees' interests. ERISA covers both retirement plans (including traditional pension plans as well as individual account plans like 401(k) plans) and welfare benefit plans (which include employment-based medical and hospitalization benefits).[33] Specifically, ERISA defines **employee welfare benefit plan** as:

> [A]ny plan, fund, or program which was heretofore or is hereafter established or maintained by an employer or by an employee organization, or by both, to the extent that such plan, fund, or program was established or is maintained for the purpose of providing for its participants or their beneficiaries, through the purchase of insurance or otherwise (A) medical, surgical, or hospital care or benefits, or benefits in the event of sickness, accident, disability, death or unemployment, or vacation benefits, apprenticeship or other training programs, or day care centers, scholarship funds, or prepaid legal services, or (B) any benefit described in section 302(c) of the Labor Management Relations Act, 1947 (other than pensions on retirement or death, and insurance to provide such pensions).[34]

As evidenced by this definition, ERISA welfare benefit plans cover most nonpension benefits that employees obtain through their workplace, including health, disability, childcare, and vacation benefits. ERISA does not, however, cover benefits an employee would obtain outside of work, such as an individually purchased health insurance plan.

---

30 *Id.*
31 *Id.*; *see also* Maria O'Brien Hylton and Lorraine A. Schmall, *Cases and Materials on Employee Benefits Law* (St. Paul, MN: West, 1998), at 9 (citing Ralph Nader and Kate Blackwell, *You and Your Pension* (1973)).
32 Lowenstein, "The End of Pensions."
33 U.S. Department of Labor, "History of EBSA and ERISA," http://www.dol.gov/ebsa/aboutebsa/history. html.
34 29 U.S.C. § 1002.

To address the concerns highlighted by the Studebaker plant shutdown, ERISA established an insurance program to protect private pensions from lack of funding.[35] ERISA also contains an **exclusive benefit rule** that requires employers to serve employee interests in terms of benefits offered.[36] ERISA imposes a fiduciary duty to manage employee benefit plans solely in the interest of the beneficiaries and for the exclusive purpose of providing benefits to participants and their beneficiaries.[37] ERISA also prohibits employers from discriminating against employees who exercise their rights under the plan.[38]

Within ERISA exist a number of other employee benefit protections that have appeared since 1974 when ERISA first came on the scene. These laws include COBRA, which added a new Part 6 to Title I of ERISA to provide for the continuation of healthcare coverage for employees and their beneficiaries for a limited period of time; HIPAA, which added a new Part 7 to Title I of ERISA to make healthcare coverage more portable and secure for employees; the Newborns' and Mothers' Health Protection Act of 1996, which requires plans that offer maternity coverage to pay for at least a 48-hour hospital stay following childbirth (96-hour stay in the case of a cesarean section); the Mental Health Parity Act of 1996, which required parity with respect to aggregate lifetime and annual dollar limits for mental health benefits; the Women's Health and Cancer Rights Act of 1998, which provides protections to patients who choose to have breast reconstruction in connection with a mastectomy; GINA, which protects individuals against discrimination based on their genetic information in health coverage and in employment; and the Mental Health Parity and Addiction Equity Act of 2008, which requires group health plans and health insurance issuers to ensure that financial requirements (such as co-pays, deductibles) and treatment limitations (such as visit limits) applicable to mental health or substance use disorder (MH/SUD) benefits are no more restrictive than the predominant requirements or limitations applied to substantially all medical/surgical

35 Lowenstein, "The End of Pensions."
36 Matthew, "Controlling the Reverse Agency Costs of Employment-Based Health Insurance," at 500.
37 Id.
38 Id.

benefits.[39] The ACA also amended ERISA to implement a number of the ACA's health insurance market reforms.[40] Some of these reforms include extending dependent coverage to age 26, eliminating lifetime and annual limits on most benefits, requiring coverage of preventive services, and prohibiting preexisting condition exclusions, to name a few.[41] The ACA also created statutory provisions permitting workplace wellness programs to discriminate based on health status if certain requirements are met.[42] (These requirements are covered in the next chapter.) Thus, in the wake of the ACA's restrictions on traditional insurance practices, workplace wellness programs offer employer health plans another way to manage employee healthcare costs.

The Impact of Group Health Plan Status on Workplace Wellness Programs

As shown in Table 3.1, group health plan wellness programs must comply with more laws than non-group health plan wellness programs. Incentives offered as part of a group health plan wellness program must comply with ACA, HIPAA, ERISA fiduciary and notice rules, and be offered as part of a COBRA continuation coverage package. Group health plan wellness programs must also comply with HIPAA privacy and security requirements as HIPAA "covered entities."[43] It also appears that group health plan wellness programs are included in the calculation of whether an employer owes the ACA "Cadillac tax" starting in 2020.[44]

---

39 U.S. Department of Labor, "History of EBSA and ERISA."
40 *Id.*
41 *Id.*
42 Karen Pollitz and Matthew Rae, "Workplace Wellness Programs Characteristics and Requirements" (Kaiser Family Foundation Issue Brief, May 19, 2016), http://kff.org/private-insurance/issue-brief/workplace-wellness-programs-characteristics-and-requirements/.
43 45 C.F.R. §§ 160.102, 160.103 (applicability to "health plans" and definition of "health plan" including a "group health plan").
44 26 U.S.C. § 4980I(d) (defining "applicable employer-sponsored coverage" as "coverage under any *group health plan* made available to the employee by an employer which is excludable from the employee's gross income under section 106 or would be so excludable if it were employer-provided coverage" [emphasis added].) The Consolidated Appropriations Act of 2016 delayed the effective date of the "Cadillac tax" by two years. See Pub. L. No. 114–113, Division P, Title I, § 101, https://www.gpo.gov/fdsys/pkg/BILLS-114hr2029enr/pdf/BILLS-114hr2029enr.pdf.

If a wellness program qualifies as a group health plan on its own, the program will also have to comply with ACA requirements regarding provision of free preventive care,[45] expanded claims and appeals procedures,[46] and requirements for summary of benefits and coverage.[47] However, it is possible that some of these ACA provisions may be repealed in the future. Nevertheless, these are just a sampling of additional compliance issues that group health plan wellness programs face.

RULE THE RULES

Key Points in Chapter 3

For this chapter, the key points are summarized in the answers to three true/false questions that test your knowledge and understanding of workplace wellness programs that qualify as a group health plan. This will be important before moving to Chapter 4.

> Q: *True or false:* A key factor in determining whether a wellness program qualifies as a group health plan is whether the program provides "medical care."
>
> A: *True.* Recall that a group health plan is an employer-sponsored welfare benefit plan to the extent that the plan provides *medical care* to employees or their dependents, directly or through insurance or otherwise. *Medical care* includes amounts paid for the diagnosis, cure, mitigation, treatment, or prevention of disease, or amounts paid for the purpose of affecting any structure or function of the body; transportation primarily for and essential to the medical care thus referred to; and insurance covering medical care. Not everything offered in workplace wellness programs qualifies as medical care. The Internal Revenue Service (IRS) regulations give examples of what does not constitute medical care. Specifically,

45 Public Health Service Act § 2713.
46 45 C.F.R. § 147.136; *see also* 76 *Fed. Reg.* 37208 (June 24, 2011).
47 45 C.F.R. § 147.200; *see also* 80 *Fed. Reg.* 34292 (June 16, 2015).

benefits that promote general well-being do not qualify as medical care. Hence, benefits such as vacation benefits, spas, swimming pools, and fitness center or gym memberships fit into that category. These benefits may improve employee health by being available, but they are generally accessible to and used by employees for reasons other than relief of health or medical problems. Also outside the category of medical care in workplace wellness programming would be educational materials and "Lunch-N-Learn" sessions about wellness topics that are open or available to all employees.

Q: *True or false:* A reward offered to employees enrolled in the employer's health plan that reduces the cost of employee health coverage (e.g., a reduced premium, co-pay, etc.) in exchange for attending a fitness class qualifies as a group health plan.

A: *Most likely true.* Based on the facts presented, it appears that the employer is offering the wellness activity to health plan participants only. As a result, the wellness activity is likely part of the employer's group health plan. Although the activity is a general well-being activity (a fitness class), the reward is tied to the group health plan. Because the activity is part of the group health plan, the requirements of ACA, HIPAA, ERISA, and COBRA would apply to the wellness program, with some caveats. Because the program is part of the group health plan, compliance with ERISA requirements should occur automatically, as the employer complies with those requirements for its major medical plan. A more interesting issue is whether the reward must be offered to COBRA beneficiaries. If the reward for attending this fitness class is a reduced premium, arguably COBRA beneficiaries would not have to be eligible for that reward, as the employer can require the beneficiary to pay 102 percent of the cost of coverage under 26 C.F.R. § 54.4980B-8. However, if the reward reduces the deductible in exchange for participation, there is an argument that the plan should offer the COBRA beneficiary the opportunity to earn that reward. This is because COBRA coverage must be identical to the coverage provided under the plan to similarly situated beneficiaries under the plan with respect to whom a qualifying event has not occurred. *See* ERISA § 602(1).

Q: *True or false*: An employer-sponsored health assessment (e.g., health risk assessment) would always qualify as medical care and therefore would always be considered part of a group health plan. A: *False in theory, but not in practice in light of the EEOC rules.* *Medical care* includes amounts paid for the diagnosis, cure, mitigation, treatment, or prevention of disease, or amounts paid for the purpose of affecting any structure or function of the body; transportation primarily for and essential to such medical care; and insurance covering medical care. A health risk assessment alone arguably does not diagnose, cure, mitigate, treat, or prevent disease. However, paired with health or wellness coaching after taking the health assessment looks more like medical care. So, if a wellness program includes a health assessment only, there is a strong argument that the program falls outside the ambit of group health plans (unless tied to the group health plan in another way) and therefore would not have to comply with the group health plan laws of ERISA, HIPAA, ACA, and COBRA. However, according to the EEOC's final rule regarding wellness program ADA compliance, tying a reward to health assessment completion would not be reasonably designed to promote health.[48] The final rule states that the mere collection of health information without any follow-up is not a program reasonably designed to promote health or prevent disease. Thus, a workplace wellness program that collects medical information should provide follow-up information or advice, such as providing feedback about risk factors or using aggregate information to design programs or treat any specific conditions.[49] A wellness program that tries to avoid group health plan status by limiting the program to a health assessment only would not be in compliance with the ADA health promotion requirement.[50]

---

48 81 *Fed. Reg.* 31126, 31139 (May 17, 2016).
49 *Id.*
50 *Id.*

Study Questions

1. Given the definitions of *group health plan* and *medical care* as stated in ERISA, prepare a list of wellness programs that would qualify as a group health plan or non-group health plan.
2. Identify the federal laws that all wellness programs must follow regardless of their status (i.e., group health plan or non-group health plan).
3. Explain why many of the labor and employment laws described in this chapter were passed by Congress.
4. Describe what happened in the Studebaker-Packard case and why ERISA was enacted in 1974 to address this employee benefit disaster.
5. Given ERISA's definition of *employee welfare benefit plan*, describe the types of benefit plans it covers.
6. After ERISA was enacted in 1974, many other laws involving employee benefits protections were passed. Make a list of these and include the major purpose of each.

Key Terms

employee welfare benefit plan

exclusive benefit rule

group health plan

medical care

4

The Law of Wellness Incentives and Screening

Learning Objectives

After reading this chapter, workplace wellness professionals will be able to:

1. Describe the history and purposes of the HIPAA/ACA, ADA, and GINA laws.
2. Identify the types of wellness programs for which incentives are allowable under the HIPAA/ACA law.
3. Identify the types of wellness programs in which incentives can be used when following the ADA and GINA laws.
4. Describe how the incentive (or penalty) limitations are calculated when applying the HIPAA/ACA, ADA, and GINA laws.
5. Apply the HIPAA/ACA regulations to the design of both participatory and health-contingent (activity-only and outcome-based) wellness programs.
6. Apply the ADA and GINA regulations to the design of wellness screening programs that incorporate health risk assessments and biometric screenings.
7. Explain why the EEOC decided, in the final ADA rules, that the insurance "safe harbor" does not apply to wellness programs.
8. Explain how the EEOC interprets a "voluntary" wellness program when applying the ADA regulations.
9. Understand that screening laws such as CLIA (federal law) and state laws, as well as pre-activity screening standards and guidelines, also must be considered in the design of wellness programs.
10. Understand the need to consult with legal counsel to help ensure compliance with all laws applicable to workplace wellness programs.

*If you look at history, innovation doesn't come just from giving
people incentives; it comes from creating environments where
their ideas can connect.*

—Steven Johnson

*Act in such a way that you treat humanity, never merely
as a means to an end, but always at the same time as an end.*

—Immanuel Kant, Grounding for the Metaphysics of
Morals (1785)

Introduction

The issue that seems to be igniting the most pushback from employees
and the government is financial incentives, the use of which by employers is gaining popularity. According to a Rand Corporation study, of
the 51 percent of employers that offer workplace wellness programs,
69 percent use financial incentives as a strategy to encourage employees to use those wellness programs.[1] Incentives are most common for
health risk assessment completion and lifestyle management programs,
with about 30 percent of employers that have a wellness program
offering such incentives.[2] Financial incentives may include cash, cash
equivalents (e.g., discounted gym memberships), and novelty items
(e.g., t-shirts or gift cards).[3] Employers also link incentives to the
employees' share of health plan premiums, health reimbursement or
savings account contributions, and plan cost-sharing, with incentives
affecting the employee share of health plan premiums being the most
popular.[4]

---

1 Soeren Mattke et al., *Workplace Wellness Programs Study* (Final Report), RAND Health (2013): 69,
http://www.rand.org/content/dam/rand/pubs/research_reports/RR200/RR254/RAND_RR254.pdf.
2 *Id.* at 69.
3 *Id.* at 71.
4 *Id.* (finding that 37 percent of employers that use incentives use them toward health plan premiums,
5 percent use them toward health reimbursement account contributions, and 3 percent use them to
adjust health plan cost-sharing).

Another Rand Corporation study found that employers that do not use incentives had a median employee participation rate of 20 percent, compared to a 40 percent median employee participation rate for employers that used monetary or nonmonetary incentives.[5] Employers that used penalties or surcharges for not participating boosted their median employee participation rates to 73 percent.[6] Other studies find that older men are most likely to respond to incentives, as are employees who were in generally poorer health, and that most employees want incentives to help motivate them to make lifestyle improvements.[7]

Three key federal laws permit wellness programs to adopt financial incentives. Those laws are the Health Insurance Portability and Accountability Act (HIPAA), the Americans with Disabilities Act (ADA), and the Genetic Information Nondiscrimination Act (GINA). Two of those laws, the ADA and GINA, apply to incentives used for screening purposes only. Screening can include health risk assessments or biometric screens. **Health risk assessments** or HRAs can have different meanings in different states and contexts. As one example, Wisconsin law defines an HRA as follows:

> "Health risk assessment" means a computer-based health-promotion tool consisting of a questionnaire; a biometric health screening to measure vital health statistics, including blood pressure, cholesterol, glucose, weight, and height; a formula for estimating health risks; an advice database; and a means to generate reports.[8]

The Centers for Disease Control and Prevention (CDC) defines **biometric screening** as the measurement of physical characteristics, such as height, weight, body mass index (BMI), blood pressure, blood cholesterol,

---

5 Soeren Mattke et al., *Workplace Wellness Programs: Services Offered, Participation and Incentives* (Rand Corp., 2014): xii–xiii.
6 *Id.*
7 John Wilcox, "Those Who Need Wellness Most Respond to Incentives," *Business Management Daily* (April 10, 2015), http://www.businessmanagementdaily.com/43247/those-who-need-wellness-most-respond-to-incentives; Andrea Davis, "Employees Want Wellness Incentives, Despite Regulatory Uncertainty," *Employee Benefits News* (January 30, 2015), http://ebn.benefitnews.com/news/health-care/employees-want-wellness-incentives-despite-regulatory-uncertainty-2745521-1.html.
8 Wis. Stat. § 250.21(1)(a).

blood glucose, and aerobic fitness that can be taken at the workplace and used as part of a workplace health assessment to benchmark and evaluate changes in employee health status over time.[9]

Before diving into the specific requirements of HIPAA, ADA, and GINA, it is important first to appreciate why those laws exist in the first place: to prevent discrimination. It is a fundamental principle of the American legal system that all people should be afforded equality of legal rights,[10] which is evident from the Fourteenth Amendment to the U.S. Constitution:

> All persons born or naturalized in the United States, and subject to the jurisdiction thereof, are citizens of the United States and of the State wherein they reside. No State shall make or enforce any law which shall abridge the privileges or immunities of citizens of the United States; nor shall any State deprive any person of life, liberty, or property, without due process of law; nor deny to any person within its jurisdiction the equal protection of the laws.

Congress enacted the Fourteenth Amendment in 1868 in direct response to the continued discriminatory treatment of the freed slaves by the reconstructed states of the South after the Civil War.[11] Although the U.S. Constitution applies to state action, other laws require equal treatment of "protected classes" by private organizations such as private employers. Indeed, the legislative history of HIPAA, ADA, and GINA demonstrate the need for added protection to ensure equal treatment of those with health disadvantages.

---

9 "Consensus Statement of the Health Enhancement Research Organization, American College of Occupational and Environmental Medicine, and Care Continuum Alliance, Biometric Health Screening for Employers," *J. Occupational & Envtl. Med.* 55, no. 10 (Oct. 2013): 1244, http://www.acoem.org/uploadedFiles/Public_Affairs/Policies_And_Position_Statements/Guidelines/Position_Statements/Biometric%20Hlth%20Screening%20Statement.pdf [hereinafter "Biometric Health Screening for Employers"].
10 Karen L. Loewy, "Lawyering for Social Change," *Fordham Urb. L.J.* 27, no. 6 (2000): 1891.
11 Richard Kluger, *Simple Justice* (New York, NY: Vintage Books, 1975), 45–48.

HIPAA/ACA

This section on the HIPAA/ACA first provides a historical perspective on the HIPAA and the purposes behind this law. The many provisions related to workplace wellness are then discussed based on the ACA's expansion of HIPAA.

HIPAA History

Congress passed HIPAA in 1996 to eliminate insurer practices that discriminated against employer groups and their members on the basis of health status, industry, or other characteristics.[12] Health insurers redlined (i.e., excluded) specific types of businesses from coverage, denied coverage to employees with poor health or to the entire group that included such employees, and excluded coverage for pre-existing conditions.[13] Indeed, "[d]iscrimination against unhealthy persons is deeply ingrained in the health insurance industry and traditionally has been generally accepted as a legitimate application of underwriting and risk-classification principles."[14] HIPAA put limits on that discrimination by prohibiting group health plans from excluding individuals from a group or varying benefits, cost-sharing, and premiums based on their health status.[15] Health status factors include medical conditions, claims experience, medical history, genetic information, receipt of health care, and evidence of insurability or disability.[16]

Legal scholars have pointed out that HIPAA's prohibitions of overt discrimination based on health status may have led to more subtle forms of discrimination against unhealthy persons, particularly through workplace

---

12 Stephen H. Long and M. Susan Marquis, *Potential Effects of HIPAA: A Review of the Literature* (Rand Corp., October 1998), http://aspe.hhs.gov/health/reports/hipabase/toc.htm.

13 *Id.*

14 Mary Crossley, "Discrimination Against the Unhealthy in Health Insurance," *Kansas L.R.* 54, at 74 (2005).

15 *Id.*; *see also* 29 C.F.R. § 2590.702(a)(1).

16 29 C.F.R. § 2590.702(a)(1). Thus, there is some overlap between HIPAA nondiscrimination goals and the nondiscrimination goals of the Americans with Disabilities Act (ADA) ("evidence of insurability or disability") and the Genetic Information Nondiscrimination Act (GINA) ("genetic information").

wellness programs.[17] This fear of more subtle forms of discrimination based on health status is due in part to a carve-out for workplace wellness programs under HIPAA and the ADA: HIPAA permits variation in benefits, cost-sharing, and premiums (i.e., **financial incentives**) based on health status if such variation is part of a wellness program.[18] As discussed further later in this chapter, the ADA and GINA also carve out an exception for employers to conduct voluntary medical exams, including voluntary medical histories (which might reveal information about a disability or genetic problem) if part of a workplace wellness program.[19]

HIPAA/ACA Provisions Related to Workplace Wellness

HIPAA nondiscrimination rules first created this carve-out for wellness programs, and the Affordable Care Act (ACA) expanded upon it.[20] Because the wellness program carve-out existed before the ACA, any repeal of ACA provisions will likely have minimal impact on the HIPAA wellness rules. The HIPAA/ACA law divides wellness program activities into two groups: (1) participatory and (2) health-contingent. Health-contingent programs are further divided between activity-only and outcomes-based programs.

In a **participatory wellness program**, a participant earns incentives merely by participating in the program. The participant is not expected to achieve a certain wellness goal, such as losing a certain amount of weight or having a certain blood pressure level. That is in contrast to participants in **health-contingent wellness programs**. In those programs, incentives are tied to achieving a health status goal, such as a certain weight or blood pressure (outcomes-based), or completing an activity that some individuals may be unable to do or have difficulty doing because of a health factor (activity-only) such as severe asthma,

17 *See, e.g.*, Anna Kirkland, "Critical Perspectives on Wellness," *J. of Health Politics, Pol'y & L.* 39, no. 5 (October 2014): 971; Jill Horowitz et al., "Wellness Incentives in the Workplace: Cost Savings Through Cost Shifting to Unhealthy Workers," *Health Affairs* 32, no. 3 (March 2013): 468; Carrie Griffin Basas, "What's Bad About Wellness? What the Disability Rights Perspective Offers About the Limitations of Wellness," *J. of Health Pol., Pol'y & L.* 39, no. 5 (October 2014): 1035; Crossley, "Discrimination against the Unhealthy in Health Insurance," 75.
18 29 C.F.R. § 2590.702(c)(3).
19 29 C.F.R. § 1630.14(d).
20 78 Fed. Reg. 3315833159 (June 3, 2013).

pregnancy, or a recent surgery. Some examples of activity-only programs are walking, diet, or exercise programs.[21]

The law limits incentives to no more than 30 percent of the cost of health coverage, but the incentive can climb as high as 50 percent of the total cost of coverage to the extent that the additional 20 percent is in connection with a program designed to prevent or reduce tobacco use.[22] The law calls these incentives "rewards," but the law's definition of *reward* is a bit misleading. The law defines *reward* as including both obtaining a reward and imposing a penalty.[23] So, the 30 percent (or 50 percent for tobacco cessation programs) limit can be applied to the amount of the reward or the amount of the penalty.

In addition to the maximum reward limit, the HIPAA/ACA rules require health-contingent programs to meet four other tests for compliance. Thus, in total there are five tests for compliance. These are:

1. **Frequency of opportunity to qualify.** The program must give individuals eligible for the program the opportunity to qualify for the reward at least once per year.[24]

2. **Size of reward.** The total reward for all wellness activities and/or goals must not exceed 30 percent (or 50 percent for tobacco cessation programs) of the total cost of employee-only coverage under the plan (or, if an employee's family can participate in the wellness program, the reward must not exceed 30 percent (or 50 percent if tobacco cessation programs are included) of the total cost of coverage in which an employee and any dependents are enrolled. The cost of coverage includes the total amount of employer and employee contributions toward the benefit package under which the employee is (or the employee and any dependents are) receiving coverage.[25]

3. **Reasonable design.** The wellness program must be reasonably designed to promote health or prevent disease. That is, it must

---

21 45 C.F.R. § 146.121(f).
22 *Id.*
23 *Id.*
24 45 C.F.R. § 146.121(f)(3)(i), (4)(i).
25 45 C.F.R. § 146.121(f)(3)(ii), (4)(ii).

have a reasonable chance of improving the health of, or preventing disease in, participating individuals, and it should not be overly burdensome or a subterfuge for discriminating based on a health factor.[26] Unlike the final ADA rules, discussed later, the HIPAA/ACA rules did not provide examples as to what would make a wellness program reasonably designed to promote health or prevent disease. The preamble to the HIPAA/ACA rules states that health-contingent wellness programs are not required to be accredited or based on particular evidence-based clinical standards, although if they are, such standards may increase the likelihood of wellness program success.[27] In contrast, as discussed in the following section on the ADA, the EEOC was much more explicit in asserting that wellness programs that collect health information must use that information to design a program that addresses at least a subset of conditions identified. This might be through providing follow-up information or advice designed to improve the health of participating employees.[28]

4. **Uniform Availability and Reasonable Alternative Standards.** The full reward under the program must be available to all similarly situated individuals. To achieve this, health-contingent wellness programs must allow a **reasonable alternative standard** (or waiver of the initial standard) for obtaining the reward for any individual for whom, for that period, it is unreasonably difficult due to a medical condition or medically inadvisable to satisfy the initial standard. For activity-only programs, plans may seek verification from an individual's personal physician that a health factor makes it unreasonably difficult for him or her to satisfy, or medically inadvisable for him or her to attempt to satisfy, the initial standard. Plans may not seek physician verification for health-contingent programs. If an individual's personal physician states that a plan standard (including, if applicable, the recommendations of the plan's medical professional) is not medically

---

26 45 C.F.R. § 146.121(f)(3)(iii), (4)(iii).
27 78 Fed. Reg. 33158, 33162 (June 3, 2013).
28 81 Fed. Reg. 31126, 31133 (May 17, 2016).

appropriate for that individual, the plan must prov
able alternative standard that accommodates the rᴄᴄᴏ......
tions of the individual's personal physician with regard to
medical appropriateness. Plans may impose standard cost-
sharing under the plan for medical items and services furnished
pursuant to the physician's recommendations.

The reasonable alternative standard cannot be a requirement
to meet a different level of the same standard without additional
time to comply that takes into account the individual's circumstances. For example, if the initial standard is to achieve a BMI
less than 30, the reasonable alternative standard cannot be to
achieve a BMI less than 31 on that same date. However, if the
initial standard is to achieve a BMI less than 30, a reasonable
alternative standard for the individual could be to reduce the
individual's BMI by a small amount or percentage over a realis-
tic period of time, such as within a year. Moreover, an individual must be given the opportunity to comply with the
recommendations of the individual's personal physician as a second reasonable alternative standard to meeting the reasonable
alternative standard defined by the plan, but only if the physician joins in the request. The individual can make a request to
involve a personal physician's recommendation at any time and
the personal physician can adjust the physician's recommendations at any time, consistent with medical appropriateness.

As for when the full reward to those who meet the reasonable
alternative standard must be available, the plan must provide the
full reward even for the months during which the individual did
not meet the reasonable alternative standard. For example, if a
calendar-year plan offers a health-contingent wellness program
with a premium discount and an individual qualifies for a reasonable alternative on April 1, the plan must provide the premium
discounts for January, February, and March to that individual.
Plans have flexibility to determine how to provide the portion of
the reward corresponding to the period before an alternative was
satisfied (e.g., payment for the retroactive period or pro rata over

the remainder of the year), as long as the method is reasonable and the individual receives the full amount of the reward. In some circumstances, an individual may not satisfy the reasonable alternative standard until the end of the year. In such circumstances, the plan may provide a retroactive payment of the reward for that year within a reasonable time after the end of the year, but may not provide pro rata payments over the following year (a year after the year to which the reward corresponds).

Individuals must request the reasonable alternative standard (and they must be notified of the opportunity to make such a request, as noted later). Plans are not required to determine a particular reasonable alternative standard in advance of an individual's request; they merely must make it available upon request. If the reasonable alternative standard is an educational program, the plan must make the educational program available or assist the employee in finding such a program, and may not require the individual to pay for the cost of the program. If the reasonable alternative standard is a diet program, the plan may require the individual to pay for the cost of food, but not any membership or participation fee. Moreover, the time commitment required for the reasonable alternative standard must be reasonable. For example, requiring attendance nightly at a one-hour class would be unreasonable.[29]

5. **Notice of Other Means to Qualifying for the Reward.** The plan must disclose in all plan materials describing the terms of a wellness program the availability of a reasonable alternative standard to qualify for the reward (and, if applicable, the possibility of waiver of the initial standard) including contact information for obtaining a reasonable alternative standard and a statement that recommendations of an individual's personal physician will be accommodated. These plan materials may include the summary plan description as well as any notice that an individual did not meet the initial standard to earn the incentive. If plan

29 45 C.F.R. § 146.121(f)(3)(iv), 4(iv).

materials merely mention that a wellness program is available, without describing its terms, this disclosure is not required.[30]

The final regulations provide the following sample notice language:

> Your health plan is committed to helping you achieve your best health. Rewards for participating in a wellness program are available to all employees. If you think you might be unable to meet a standard for a reward under this wellness program, you might qualify for an opportunity to earn the same reward by different means. Contact us at [insert contact information] and we will work with you (and, if you wish, with your doctor) to find a wellness program with the same reward that is right for you in light of your health status.[31]

There are two key points to remember about the HIPAA/ACA incentive law: First, it applies to group health plans only. As discussed in Chapter 3, if a wellness program is not a group health plan program, this incentive law does not apply. Second, the HIPAA/ACA five-factor test, including the incentive limit, applies to health-contingent wellness programs only. The five-factor test does not apply to participatory programs. See Figure 4.1 for a summary of the HIPAA/ACA nondiscrimination rules regarding incentives.

One other point to remember is that because HIPAA nondiscrimination rules apply to group health plans, those same plans are also subject to HIPAA privacy and security rules. Group health plans are "covered entities" subject to HIPAA privacy and security rules.[32] Those privacy rules include the requirement for an employer that administers all or part of its health plan and that wishes to receive from the plan individually identifiable health information to certify to the group health plan, as provided by 45 C.F.R. § 164.504(f)(2)(ii), that it will not use or disclose the information for purposes not permitted by its group health plan documents and the HIPAA privacy rule. Those employers that do not

---

30 45 C.F.R. § 146.121(f)(3)(v), (4)(v); *see also* 78 Fed. Reg. 33158, 33163 (June 3, 2013).
31 45 C.F.R. § 146.121(f)(6).
32 45 C.F.R. § 160.103 (definitions of *covered entity*, *health plan*, and *group health plan*).

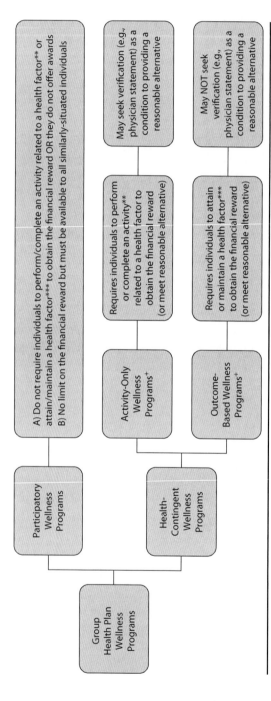

Figure 4.1 Summary of the HIPAA/ACA Nondiscrimination Rules Regarding Financial Incentives*

*Financial incentives can also be financial penalties, e.g., paying a higher monthly premium, monthly surcharge – but cannot exceed the limits specified in Test #2 (Size of Reward).

**An activity related to a health factor can be participation in program, e.g., walking, nutrition, smoking cessation, etc. but must be reasonably designed

***Health factor refers to a specific health outcome, e.g., BMI < 30, Cholesterol < 200 mg/dl

+ Activity-only and Outcome-based programs must meet the requirements specified in the five (5) tests, which are basically the same except for the requirements in Test #4 (reasonable alternative) which are different – see text for explanation. Five Tests for Health-Contingent Programs: (1) Frequency of Opportunity to Qualify; (2) Size of Reward; (3) Reasonable Design, (4) Uniform Availability and Reasonable Alternative Standard, and (5) Notice of Other Means of Qualifying for the Reward

administer any part of the health plan should only receive from the group health plan summary health information for purposes of obtaining premium bids or modifying, amending, or terminating the group health plan.[33]

ADA

This section on the ADA first provides a historical perspective of the ADA and the purposes behind this law. The general ADA provisions related to workplace wellness are then discussed, followed by a detailed description of the final ADA rule and its many applications to workplace wellness programs.

ADA History

President Bush signed the ADA into law on July 26, 1990, in front of 3,000 people on the White House lawn.[34] The president's directive that day: "Let the shameful walls of exclusion finally come tumbling down."[35] This statement and the enactment of the ADA recognize that Americans with disabilities are full-fledged citizens and are entitled to legal protections that ensure them equal opportunity and access to the mainstream of American life.[36] The ADA, like other civil rights laws, reflects the principle that the surest path to America's continued vitality, strength, and vibrancy is through the full realization of the contributions of all its citizens.[37] In essence, the ADA is an antidiscrimination statute designed to remove barriers that prevent qualified individuals with disabilities from enjoying the same employment opportunities that are available to persons without disabilities.[38] Specifically, Title I of the ADA prohibits employers from discriminating against individuals who have, had, or are perceived to have a

---

33 45 C.F.R. § 164.504(f)(2)(ii).
34 EEOC and U.S. Department of Justice (USDOJ), *Americans with Disabilities Act Handbook* (EEOC-BK-19) (October 1992): Preamble.
35 *Id.*
36 *Id.*
37 *Id.*
38 *Id.* at I-1.

disability as to the terms, conditions, or privileges of employment.[39] The law defines *disability* as a physical or mental impairment that substantially limits one or more major life activities.[40]

Through passage of the ADA and other efforts, disability rights advocates have sought to untangle a long history of assumptions that people with disabilities are dependent on the charitable acts of others, not suitable for work, and offer very little to the economy and society.[41] They have also challenged the subliminal message that moral or personal failings have led to an undesirable health state that employers and others can use to judge the character and worth of the disabled person.[42] The ADA challenges workplaces to be flexible and adaptive in their thinking, and to be disability-aware and difference-respectful in creating new programs and policies.[43]

This raised awareness is especially important in light of the amendments to the ADA, signed into law by the second Bush president, George W. Bush, on September 25, 2008. These amendments are known as the ADA Amendments Act (ADAAA). The ADAAA broadened the coverage of the ADA and aims to make it easier for an individual seeking protection under the ADA to establish that he or she has a disability within the meaning of the ADA.[44] In other words, under the ADAAA, the primary object of attention for employers is to determine whether they have complied with their obligations under the law and whether discrimination has occurred, not whether the individual meets the definition of disability.[45]

Specifically, the ADAAA expanded the definition of *disability* to include disabilities in their "unmitigated" state (i.e., untreated, such as

---

39 29 C.F.R. § 1630.4; 29 C.F.R. § 1630.2. Congress patterned the definition of *disability*—the "actual," "record of," and "regarded as" prongs—after the definition of *handicap* found in the Rehabilitation Act of 1973. Congress intended that the relevant case law developed under the Rehabilitation Act would be generally applicable to the term *disability* as used in the ADA. *See* 76 Fed. Reg. 17004 (March 25, 2011).
40 29 C.F.R. § 1630.2.
41 Basas, "What's Bad About Wellness?," 1048.
42 *Id.*
43 *Id.*
44 EEOC Notice Concerning the Americans with Disabilities Act (ADA) Amendments Act of 2008, http://www.eeoc.gov/laws/statutes/adaaa_notice.cfm.
45 Sheree Wright, *Protecting Your Employees from Harm While Accommodating Mental Illness—Are Employers in a Bind?* (Paper for the American Bar Association Annual Meeting, Section of Labor and Employment Law) (August 7, 2014), 4, http://www.americanbar.org/content/dam/aba/events/labor_law/am/2014/1d_mental_illness.authcheckdam.pdf.

through medication).[46] That is, employers may not consider the employee's use of a medication or device to mitigate the effects of a disability when determining whether that employee is in fact disabled. It also added to the list of "major life activities," to include "caring for oneself, performing manual tasks, seeing, hearing, eating, sleeping, walking, standing, lifting, bending, speaking, breathing, learning, reading, concentrating, thinking, communicating and working."[47]

ADA Provisions Relevant to Workplace Wellness

The ADA requires employers with 15 or more employees to provide **reasonable accommodations** to qualified individuals with a disability, unless the employer can demonstrate undue hardship.[48] *Qualified individuals* are those individuals who can perform the essential functions of their jobs with or without reasonable accommodation.[49] *Qualified* means that the individual satisfies the requisite skill, experience, education, and other job-related requirements of the position.[50] Thus, unless an employer can show undue hardship, that employer must provide reasonable accommodations to those employees who can otherwise perform the fundamental job duties of the position. Reasonable accommodations include modifications or adjustments to the work environment.[51] They also include modifications or adjustments that allow an employee with a disability to enjoy equal benefits and privileges of employment as are enjoyed by similarly situated employees without a disability.[52]

Title I of the ADA is enforced by the **Equal Employment Opportunity Commission (EEOC)** and prohibits discrimination by employers on the basis of disability in regard to terms, conditions, and privileges of

---

46 *Id.*
47 42 U.S.C. § 12102(a)(A).
48 42 U.S.C. §§ 12112(b)(5)(A), 12111(5)(A) (defining *employer* as "a person engaged in an industry affecting commerce who has fifteen or more employees for each working day in each of 20 or more calendar weeks in the current or preceding calendar year.").
49 42 U.S.C. §§ 12111(8), 12112(a).
50 29 C.F.R. § 1630.2(m).
51 *EEOC Enforcement Guidance: Reasonable Accommodation and Undue Hardship under the Americans with Disabilities Act*, http://www.eeoc.gov/policy/docs/accommodation.html#general; *see also* 29 C.F.R. § 1630.2(o)(1)(i)(iii).
52 *Id.*

employment.[53] Those terms, conditions, and privileges of employment can include participating in wellness programs. Thus, workplace wellness program designers must ensure that all employees, regardless of disability, have an equal opportunity to participate in the program and must offer reasonable accommodations so that such employees may participate and earn any financial incentives.

Discrimination under the ADA includes requiring medical examinations and making disability-related inquiries, including medical history inquiries, unless one of two exceptions applies: (1) such exam or inquiry is job-related and consistent with business necessity; or (2) the medical exam is *voluntary* and part of an employee health program available at the worksite.[54] The restriction on asking questions about an employee's medical status or conducting medical screenings applies regardless of whether the employee is disabled.[55] The EEOC has defined a **medical exam** as "a procedure or test that seeks information about an individual's physical or mental impairments or health."[56] These exams may include: (1) vision tests; (2) blood, urine, and breath analyses to check for alcohol use or to detect disease or genetic markers; (3) blood pressure screening and cholesterol testing; (4) range-of-motion tests that measure muscle strength and motor function; (5) pulmonary function tests; and (6) psychological tests that are designed to identify a mental disorder or impairment.[57] Medical exams do not include tests to determine the current illegal use of drugs; general well-being questions; physical agility tests or physical fitness tests to measure an employee's ability to perform job tasks; or psychological tests that measure personality traits such as honesty, preferences, and habits.[58]

For purposes of workplace wellness programs, a key term in the ADA prohibition against employee medical exams and medical history inquiries is the word *voluntary*; the ADA permits such exams and inquiries if

---

53 29 U.S.C. § 12112(a).
54 42 U.S.C. § 12112(d)(4) (emphasis added).
55 42 U.S.C. § 12112(d)(1).
56 *EEOC Enforcement Guidance* No. 915-002 (July 27, 2000).
57 *Id.*
58 *Id.*

they are part of a **voluntary workplace wellness program.** Until recently, the only guidance the EEOC provided with regard to the meaning of "voluntary" was that the employer could neither require participation nor penalize employees who do not participate.[59] However, recent final rules by the EEOC under the ADA shed additional light on what the EEOC means by "voluntary."

ADA Final Rule on Wellness Programs

The EEOC issued a final rule on the ADA's applicability to workplace wellness programs on May 17, 2016.[60] The final rule applies only to workplace wellness programs that conduct medical examinations or disability-related inquiries, such as through health risk assessments or biometric screens. To comply with the final ADA rule, wellness program designers must meet the following ADA requirements:[61]

1. **Incentives must be limited to 30 percent of the cost of self-only coverage.** The ADA permits incentives for wellness programs as long as the value of that incentive does not exceed 30 percent of the total cost of employee-only coverage.[62]

   a. *Incentive limit applies regardless of group health plan status.* The 30 percent incentive limit applies to all employer wellness programs, regardless of whether that program is part of a group health plan. To quote the EEOC, this means that "this rule applies to wellness programs that are: offered only to employees enrolled in an employer-sponsored group health plan; offered to all employees regardless of whether they are enrolled in such a plan; or offered as a benefit of employment by employers that do not sponsor a group health plan or group health insurance."[63]

---

59 *Id.*
60 81 Fed. Reg. 31126 (May 17, 2016).
61 81 Fed. Reg. 31126 (May 17, 2016); 29 C.F.R. § 1630.14(d).
62 81 Fed. Reg. 31126, 31141 (May 17, 2016).
63 81 Fed. Reg. 31132 (May 17, 2016).

b. *Calculating the incentive*[64]

  i. **Incentive limited to employees enrolled in employer's group health plan**

   1. Thirty percent of total cost of self-only coverage (including both employee's and employer's contribution).[65]

   2. Example calculation: The only group health plan offered costs $6,000/year for self-only coverage. The maximum allowable incentive is $1,800 (30 percent of $6,000).

  ii. **Incentive available to all employees regardless of their enrollment in the plan**

   1. Thirty percent of total cost of self-only coverage under the employer's group health plan.[66]

   2. Example calculation: The only group health plan offered costs $6,000/year for self-only coverage. The maximum allowable incentive is $1,800 (30 percent of $6,000), even for employees who are not enrolled in the group health plan but are still eligible to participate in the employer's wellness program.

  iii. **Incentive available to all employees when employer offers multiple plan options**

   1. Thirty percent of the total cost of the lowest-cost self-only coverage under a major medical group health plan.[67]

   2. Example calculation: Employer offers three different group health plans ranging in cost from $5,000 to $8,000 annually for self-only coverage. Employer wants to offer employees an incentive to participate in a wellness program that includes a health risk assessment and medical examination, regardless of whether the employee is enrolled in a particular health plan. In this case, the maximum allowable

---

64 81 Fed. Reg. 31141 (May 17, 2016).
65 29 C.F.R. § 1630.14(d)(3)(i).
66 29 C.F.R. § 1630.14(d)(3)(ii).
67 29 C.F.R. § 1630.14(d)(3)(iii).

incentive is $1,500 (30 percent of $5,000—the
lowest-cost plan).

iv. **Incentive available to all employees when employer does
not offer health coverage**

1. Thirty percent of the cost of self-only coverage under
the second lowest-cost Silver Plan for a 40-year-old
nonsmoker on the state or federal health care
exchange in the location that the employer identifies
as its principal place of business.[68]

2. Example calculation: Such a plan costs $4,000 in the
employer's state. If employer does not offer health
insurance but wants to offer an incentive for employees to participate in a wellness program that includes
disability-related inquiries or medical examinations,
the maximum allowable incentive is $1,200
(30 percent of $4,000).

c. *Applies to both participatory and health-contingent programs.* The 30 percent incentive limit applies to both participatory and health-contingent programs that involve
disability-related inquiries or medical examinations, such
as health risk assessments or biometric screens. As noted
later, the ADA incentive rules do not apply to wellness
programs that do not involve disability-related inquiries or
medical examinations in order to earn the incentive.
Examples include attending nutrition, weight loss, or
smoking cessation classes. However, to the extent the wellness program qualifies as a health-contingent program as
defined by the HIPAA/ACA rules, such program would
have to comply with the HIPAA/ACA incentive
requirements.

d. *All types of incentives (financial and in-kind) count.* The
EEOC specifies that the 30 percent financial incentive maximum applies to both financial and in-kind incentives, such as

---

68 29 C.F.R. § 1630.14(d)(3)(iv).

time-off awards, prizes, or other items of value.[69] A number
of commenters on the proposed ADA rule complained that it
will be hard to place a dollar value on in-kind incentives. The
EEOC stated in response that employers should be able to
find a dollar value as long as the method used is reasonable.[70]

   e. *Tobacco cessation programs have some special treatment.*[71]
   The EEOC does not consider tobacco cessation programs
   that merely ask employees whether they use tobacco and
   whether they ceased using tobacco upon completion of the
   program to be making "disability-related inquiries or medical examinations." Therefore, the HIPAA/ACA incentive
   maximum of 50 percent of the total cost of employee coverage applies to those programs. However, if the tobacco cessation program includes a biometric screen or other medical
   exam that tests for the presence of nicotine or tobacco, such
   program would qualify as a medical examination subject to
   the ADA 30 percent maximum financial incentive.

2. **Employers may not deny or limit coverage for, or retaliate
   against, nonparticipants in an employee wellness program.**[72] This
   is an important consideration for wellness program designers.
   The final ADA rule provides additional insight into the meaning
   of this requirement by discussing the employer trend of offering
   tiered health benefits or "gateway plans." Many employers are
   beginning to offer tiered health plan structures that base eligibility for more comprehensive or less expensive health coverage if
   the employee completes a health risk assessment or biometric
   screen. Employees who choose not to participate in the health
   risk assessment or biometric screen are offered less comprehensive or more expensive plans (higher premium or cost-sharing).

   The EEOC concludes that employers who deny employees the
   more comprehensive or less expensive coverage option because

---

69 81 Fed. Reg. 31126, 31141 (May 17, 2016).
70 81 Fed. Reg. at 31135.
71 81 Fed. Reg. 31136 (May 17, 2016).
72 29 C.F.R. § 1630.14(d)(2)(ii), (iii); 81 Fed. Reg. 31133 (May 17, 2016).

those employees refuse to participate in the health risk assessment or biometric screen violate the ADA.[73] The employer should allow employees who refuse to participate in those wellness screens to select the higher-tiered plan, even if that employee must pay more for the insurance because of their lack of participation. Of course, the amount of the higher payment should fall within the 30 percent incentive limits, discussed earlier.

Employers should also avoid retaliating against nonparticipants in wellness programs by not taking adverse employment actions against such employees. Employers should also avoid interfering with, coercing, intimidating, or threatening employees who do not participate.

> To increase participation in a health risk assessment, the employer asks the wellness professional to provide the names of nonparticipants to the nonparticipants' supervisors. The supervisors plan to personally entreat the nonparticipants to participate. Is this a good idea? Probably not, as even a friendly nudge from a supervisor could be interpreted as coercion or intimidation by the nonparticipating employee, which would violate the ADA rules on wellness programs.

3. **Wellness programs that collect medical information must provide employees with a notice.**[74] This notice requirement applies even if the employer does not offer incentives for providing the medical information. This notice must:
   a. Be written in a manner that is understandable to the employee.
   b. Describe the type of medical information that will be obtained.
   c. Describe the specific purposes for which the medical information will be used.
   d. Indicate who will receive the medical information.
   e. Describe the restrictions on the disclosure of the medical information.

---

73 81 Fed. Reg. at 31133.
74 29 C.F.R. § 1630.14(d)(iv).

f. Describe the methods the employer will use to prevent improper disclosure of the medical information

If an employer already provides a notice that contains all of these elements, the employer can continue using that notice. If the employer does not have such a notice, it must obtain such a notice. A sample notice is available on the EEOC website at https://www.eeoc.gov/laws/regulations/ada-wellness-notice.cfm.[75]

4. **Employers and vendors must protect the confidentiality of the health information collected through the wellness program.**[76] The EEOC expects both employers and wellness program vendors to ensure compliance with confidentiality rules, such as set forth in the HIPAA privacy, security, and breach notification rules for group health plans, as well as the ADA rules. Data privacy and security requirements for wellness programs are covered more thoroughly in Chapter 9. Briefly, however, the ADA requires employers to collect and maintain employee medical information on separate forms and in separate medical files and to treat such information as a confidential medical record. Unless an employer administers part or all of its health plan, both vendors and employers must ensure that an employer does not receive individually identifiable health information collected through a wellness program. In those instances, employers should only receive medical information in aggregate terms.[77]

Employee wellness programs that are part of a group health plan must abide by HIPAA privacy rules, as discussed earlier as well as more fully in Chapter 9. To the extent that an employer receives individually identifiable medical information for purposes of administering the wellness program, it is a good practice to provide that information to individuals who are not responsible for making employment-related decisions. Use of a third-party vendor may reduce the risk of disclosure of medical information for improper purposes. Small

---

75 81 Fed. Reg. 31134 (May 17, 2016).
76 81 Fed. Reg. 31136, 31142 (May 17, 2016); *see also* 80 Fed. Reg. 21659, 21669 (April 20, 2015).
77 29 C.F.R. § 1630.14(d)(4)(iii).

employers that administer their own wellness programs should not use the information to discriminate on the basis of disability.

5. **Employers may not require an employee to agree to the sale, exchange, sharing, transfer, or other disclosure of medical information.**[78] In response to the proposed ADA rule issued in April 2015, advocacy groups raised concerns that employees may unwittingly "waive" their privacy rights when completing online health risk assessments.[79] To address this concern, the final ADA rule prohibits employers from requiring employees to agree to the use or disclosure of their medical information in exchange for wellness program participation or an incentive. Of course, employers may share employee medical information in order to carry out specific activities related to the wellness program.[80] Beyond that, however, wellness program designers should ensure that employees are not required to waive ADA confidentiality protections or agree to the sale, exchange, sharing, or transfer of their medical information. Wellness professionals and organizations should evaluate their program's privacy and security policies and procedures, as well as those of downstream vendors, to determine whether this new requirement is met. If the wellness program is part of a group health plan or is offered or administered through a business associate of a group health plan, those programs are also prohibited under the HIPAA privacy rules from selling protected health information.[81]

6. **Like the HIPAA/ACA rules, the ADA requires wellness programs to be reasonably designed to promote health or prevent disease.**[82] Recall that the HIPAA/ACA rules require only health contingent wellness programs to be reasonably designed to

---

78 29 C.F.R. § 1630.14(d)(3)(iv).
79 81 Fed. Reg. 31126, 31137 (May 17, 2016).
80 *Id.*
81 45 C.F.R. § 164.502(5)(ii).
82 29 C.F.R. § 1630.14(d)(1).

promote health and prevent disease.[83] However, the ADA rules require both participatory and health-contingent programs that collect health information to be reasonably designed to promote health or prevent disease. A key point the EEOC makes about this provision is that collecting medical information on a health questionnaire without providing follow-up information or advice to employees, such as providing feedback about an employee's risk factors, would *not* be reasonably designed to promote health.[84]

There is an exception to this prohibition on merely collecting health information: The final ADA rule states that a wellness professional or organization can collect information without any follow-up if the information is used to design a program that addresses at least some of the conditions identified. Thus, a wellness professional or organization could conduct a preliminary employee survey to help determine the types of programming activities that would help that employee population.

However, wellness programs that collect medical information mainly to shift costs from the employer to targeted employees based on their health, or to give an employer information to estimate future healthcare costs, are not reasonably designed to promote health or prevent disease. Such wellness programs are prohibited under the final rule.[85]

7. **Employers must provide reasonable accommodations.**[86] Regardless of whether a wellness program includes disability-related inquiries or medical examinations, the employer must provide reasonable accommodations, absent undue hardship, to enable employees with disabilities to earn whatever financial incentive an employer offers. These reasonable accommodations apply to *both* participatory and health-contingent wellness programs.

---

83 45 C.F.R. § 146.121(f)(2).
84 81 Fed. Reg. 31126, 31139 (May 17, 2016); 29 C.F.R. § 1630.14(d)(1).
85 81 Fed. Reg. 31140 (May 17, 2016).
86 81 Fed. Reg. 31141 (May 17, 2016).

The EEOC provides some helpful examples in the interpretive guidance to the final rule:

a. Employers that offer a financial incentive to attend a nutrition class would have to provide a sign language interpreter so an employee who is deaf and who needs an interpreter to understand the information communicated in the class could earn the incentive.

b. Programs that require employees to read written materials should provide those materials in large print or on a computer disk for someone with a vision impairment.

c. Employers that offer rewards for completing a biometric screen that includes a blood draw should provide an alternative test (or certification requirement) so that an employee with a disability that makes drawing blood dangerous can participate and earn the incentive.[87]

8. **Compliance with the ADA rules does not guarantee compliance with other laws.**[88] The final rule mentions specifically that ADA compliance does not translate to compliance with Title VII, the Equal Pay Act, the Age Discrimination in Employment Act (ADEA), Title II of the Genetic Information and Nondiscrimination Act (GINA), or other sections of Title I of the ADA.

   For a summary of the ADA final rules regarding financial incentives, as well as additional ADA rules related to workplace wellness programs, see Figure 4.2.

   Two other points worth emphasizing about the final rule are that:

   1. Other than the equal opportunity requirements, the ADA incentive rules do not apply to wellness programs that do not collect health information as part of the program.

   2. The EEOC has determined that the ADA insurance safe harbor does not apply to wellness programs. A number of employers have challenged this determination in court cases brought by the EEOC involving those employers' wellness programs. These cases are discussed later in this chapter.

---

87 *Id.*
88 29 C.F.R. § 1630.14(d)(5).

All Wokplace Wellness "Screening" Programs (HRAs, Biometric Screening)
*Non-Group Health Plans
*Group Health Plans (GHPs) – Participatory and Health-Contingent

The financial incentive or penalty (whether monetary or in-kind) is limited to 30% of the total employee-only coverage regardless of GHP enrollment status (applies only to wellness programs that collect health information)

A) Enrolled in the employer-sponsored GHP
B) Not enrolled in the employer-sponsored GHP
C) Enrolled in a GHP outside the employer-sponsored GHP
D) No GHP offered by the employer

Tobacco Cessation Programs

A) The HIPAA/ACA limit of 50% is applicable to programs that only inquire about smoking status (50% of the total cost of employee-only coverage).

B) Programs that include biometric screening or other medical exams that test for the presense of nicotine or tobacco must follow the 30% limit.

Additional ADA Final Rules for Employee Wellness Programs

➤ Employers cannot require employees to complete medical exams (including disability-related or medical history inquiries) unless they are (a) job-related, or (b) "voluntary" as part of a wellness program.
➤ Employers may not deny (or limit) health coverage for, or retaliate against nonparticipants in employee wellness programs.
➤ Wellness programs that collect medical information must provide employees with a notice regardless if incentive offered.
➤ Employers and vendors must protect the confidentiality of the medical information collected through a wellness program.
  o Employees cannot be required to waive ADA confidentiality protections or agree to sale, exchange, sharing, or transfer of their medical information.
➤ Like the HIPAA/ACA rules for health-contingent programs only, wellness programs must be reasonably designed to promote health or prevent disease but for both health-contingent and participatory programs.
  o After collecting medical information (e.g. health assessments, biometric screenings), wellness programs must provide follow-up in order to meet "promote health or prevent disease" requirements.
➤ Must provide reasonable accommodation (reasonable alternative).
➤ Compliance with the ADA rules does not mean compliance with other laws.
➤ The incentive rules do not apply to wellness programs that do not collect medical information.
➤ According to the EEOC, "safe harbor" does not apply to workplace wellness programs.

Figure 4.2 Summary of the ADA Final Rules Regarding Financial Incentives

According to the EEOC, the final ADA rule applies to all workplace wellness programs that ask employees to respond to disability-related inquiries and/or undergo medical examinations.[89] Wellness programs that do not include such inquiries or examinations (such as those that provide general health and educational information) are not subject to the final ADA rule.[90] Thus, wellness programs that consist of nutrition or fitness classes only (i.e., no health information is collected), for example, would not be limited to the 30 percent incentive limit under the final ADA rules.[91] Those programs would still have to meet the ADA requirement of being available to all employees and providing reasonable accommodations to employees with disabilities.[92]

As for the applicability of the ADA insurance safe harbor, the EEOC explained its position in the preamble to the final ADA rule, and included a provision in the regulation carving out its applicability to workplace wellness programs. Before diving into the EEOC's position on the ADA safe harbor, it is important first to understand what the safe harbor provides.

The ADA Safe Harbor and Its Application to Workplace Wellness Programs

The ADA **safe harbor** provision reads as follows:

> (c) INSURANCE. Subchapters I through III of this chapter and title IV of this Act shall not be construed to prohibit or restrict—
> (1) an insurer, hospital or medical service company, health maintenance organization, or any agent, or entity that administers benefit plans, or similar organizations from underwriting risks, classifying risks, or administering such risks that are based on or not inconsistent with State law; or
> (2) a person or organization covered by this chapter from establishing, sponsoring, observing or administering the terms of a

---

89 81 Fed. Reg. 31126 (May 17, 2016).
90 *Id.*
91 81 Fed. Reg. 31141 (May 17, 2016).
92 81 Fed. Reg. 31126 (May 17, 2016).

bona fide benefit plan that are based on underwriting risks, classifying risks, or administering such risks that are based on or not inconsistent with State law; or

(3) a person or organization covered by this chapter from establishing, sponsoring, observing or administering the terms of a bona fide benefit plan that is not subject to State laws that regulate insurance.

Paragraphs (1), (2), and (3) shall not be used as a subterfuge to evade the purposes of subchapter[s] I and III.[93]

Thus, according to Sections (c)(2) and (3) of the safe harbor, an organization covered by the ADA, such as an employer with 15 or more employees, is allowed to sponsor, observe, or administer the terms of a bona fide benefit plan, as well as administer the plan based on underwriting risks, classifying risks, or administering risks.

At least two federal courts have concluded that the safe harbor applies to workplace wellness programs; when the safe harbor applies, an employer arguably can administer a disability-related inquiry or medical examination without considering the voluntary nature of that inquiry or examination. In other words, the employer could require the employee to participate in the disability-related inquiry or medical examination by forcing the employee to pay 100 percent of the cost of health coverage.

The first federal court to apply the ADA safe harbor to workplace wellness programs was *Seff v. Broward County*.[94] The employer's wellness program included a biometric screening and online health risk assessment.[95] The employer used the results to identify employees who had one of five disease states: asthma, hypertension, diabetes, congestive heart failure, or kidney disease.[96] Employees suffering from any of these five disease states received an opportunity to participate in a disease management coaching program, after which they were eligible to receive co-pay waivers for certain medications.[97] Employees who were enrolled

---

93 42 U.S.C. § 12201(c).
94 *Seff v. Broward Cty.*, 691 F.3d 1221 (11th Cir. 2012).
95 *Id.* at 1222.
96 *Id.*
97 *Id.*

in the employer's group health plan but who refused to participate in the wellness program incurred a $20 charge on each biweekly paycheck.[98]

The *Seff* court found the wellness program to be a "term" of the employer's group health plan because: (1) it was part of the employer's group health plan; (2) the employer offered the program to group health plan enrollees; and (3) the employer presented the program as part of its group health plan in at least two employee handouts.[99] Because the program was a term of the group health plan, the court could find that the program fit within the safe harbor.[100]

Specifically, the district court found, and the appeals court affirmed, that the wellness program functioned as underwriting and classifying risks on a macroscopic level so that the plan could form economically sound benefits plans for the future.[101] In addition, the court viewed the wellness program as an initiative designed to mitigate risks; the program encouraged employees to get involved in their own health care, which leads to a healthier employee population that costs less to insure.[102] The EEOC has disagreed with the *Seff* court's reasoning, stating that reading the ADA insurance safe harbor as exempting workplace wellness programs from ADA restrictions would render the ADA's "voluntary" provision for wellness programs "superfluous."[103]

The safe harbor also won the day in the district court opinion in *EEOC v. Flambeau, Inc.*[104] Flambeau's wellness program was available to health plan enrollees and consisted of a health risk assessment and a biometric test.[105] The health risk assessment required each participant to complete a questionnaire about his or her medical history, diet, mental and social health, and job satisfaction.[106] The biometric test was similar to a routine physical examination: Among other things, it involved height and weight measurements, a blood pressure test, and a blood draw.[107] Flambeau used

---

98 *Id.*
99 *Seff v. Broward Cty.*, at 1224.
100 *Id.*
101 *Id.*; *Seff v. Broward Cty.*, 778 F. Supp. 2d 1370, 1374 (S.D. Fla. 2011).
102 *Id.*
103 80 Fed. Reg. 21659, 21662, n. 24 (April 20, 2015).
104 *EEOC v. Flambeau, Inc.*, 14-CV-638, Opinion and Order, Dkt. #38 (W.D. Wis. 2014).
105 *Id.* at 34.
106 *Id.*
107 *Id.*

this information to identify the health risks and medical conditions common among the plan's enrollees.[108] In particular, it used the information to estimate the cost of providing insurance, set participants' premiums, evaluate the need for stop-loss insurance, adjust the co-pays for preventive exams, and adjust the co-pays for certain prescription drugs.[109] Except for information regarding tobacco use, the health risks and medical conditions identified were reported to Flambeau in the aggregate, so that it did not know any participant's individual results.[110]

The incentives for Flambeau's wellness program changed from 2011 to 2012. In 2011, the financial incentive offered for participating in the health risk assessment and biometric test was a $600 credit.[111] In 2012 and 2013, however, Flambeau adopted a policy of offering health insurance only to those employees who completed the health risk assessment and biometric test.[112] The *Flambeau* court noted that participating in the wellness program was not a condition of continued employment; it was only a condition for enrolling in Flambeau's self-insured health plan, the cost of which was heavily subsidized by Flambeau.[113] The court also noted that Flambeau also sponsored weight loss competitions, modified vending machine options, and made other "organization-wide changes" aimed at promoting health in light of the fact that a high percentage of Flambeau's employees appeared to suffer from nutritional deficiencies and weight management problems.[114]

The district judge concluded that Flambeau's wellness program requirement was a "term" of its benefit plan and therefore the plan could collect and use the health information to administer the terms of the plan.[115] The court did not need to analyze Flambeau's wellness program under the ADA's "voluntary" medical exam exception because Flambeau tied the health risk assessment and biometric screen to its health plan.[116]

---

108 *Id.*
109 *Id.*
110 *Id.*
111 *EEOC v. Flambeau, Inc.*, at 4.
112 *Id.*
113 *Id.*
114 *Id.*
115 *EEOC v. Flambeau, Inc.*, at 10.
116 *Id.* at 8–9.

The *Flambeau* court noted that consultants who worked for Flambeau used the information gathered from the health risk assessment and biometric screen to classify plan participants' health risks and calculate Flambeau's projected insurance costs for the benefit year.[117] The information also helped the consultants decide whether the employer should charge the plan participants for maintenance medications and preventive care.[118] The information further helped the consultants make recommendations regarding plan premiums, which included a recommendation that Flambeau charge tobacco users higher premiums.[119] Finally, the information helped Flambeau decide to purchase stop-loss insurance.[120] The court viewed these types of decisions as a fundamental part of developing and administering an insurance plan, which falls squarely within the ADA insurance safe harbor.[121] Because Flambeau's wellness program fell within the insurance safe harbor, Flambeau did not violate the ADA and the court dismissed the case, entering judgment in Flambeau's favor.[122]

EEOC's Reaction to the Flambeau and Seff "Safe Harbor" Rulings

In the preamble to the final ADA rules, the EEOC chastised these court conclusions, as well as reacting to criticisms by members of Congress who have accused the EEOC of inappropriately seeking to rewrite the ADA and vacate court decisions through regulation.[123] The EEOC concluded that it does indeed have authority to determine the applicability of the safe harbor provision to workplace wellness program incentives that involve health information collection.[124] It also rejected the *Flambeau* court's position that the ADA wellness program rules apply only to programs that are not part of a group health plan.[125]

The EEOC points out that when the ADA was enacted in the early 1990s, health plans were allowed to engage in practices that are no

---

117 *Id.* at 12–13.
118 *Id.*
119 *Id.*
120 *Id.*
121 *Id.*
122 *EEOC v. Flambeau, Inc.*, at 15.
123 81 Fed. Reg. 31130-31131 (May 17, 2016).
124 *Id.*
125 *Id.*

longer permitted. For example, before HIPAA made the practice illegal in 1996, group health plans could charge individuals in the plan higher rates based on increased risks associated with their medical conditions.[126] The safe harbor protected individuals from this practice by ensuring that their differential treatment was based on real risks and costs associated with those medical conditions.[127]

The EEOC notes that wellness programs are not referred to anywhere in the ADA legislative history regarding the safe harbor provisions.[128] In fact, according to the EEOC, the only reference to wellness programs is in connection with the voluntary health program provision of the ADA.[129] The EEOC interprets this legislative history as supporting its conclusion that the ADA safe harbor does not apply to a workplace wellness program, regardless of whether that program is part of a group health plan.[130] Even if an employer uses a wellness program to make its employees healthier and thus ultimately reduce its healthcare costs, the EEOC does not believe that such use constitutes underwriting or risk classification protected by the ADA safe harbor.[131]

With regard to the court decisions in *Seff v. Broward County* and *EEOC v. Flambeau* specifically, the EEOC observes that neither court ruled that the language of the ADA safe harbor was unambiguous.[132] Under the U.S. Supreme Court decision in *Chevron U.S.A. Inc. v. National Resources Defense Council*,[133] courts must give deference to interpretation of ambiguous statutes made by federal agencies like the EEOC. This legal principle is called "*Chevron* deference." Because neither the *Seff* nor *Flambeau* court concluded that the ADA safe harbor language was unambiguous, the EEOC's interpretation should trump that of any federal court.[134] Also, to be clear on how it interprets the safe harbor, the EEOC inserts into the final rule language stating that the

---

126 81 Fed. Reg. 31130 (May 17, 2016).
127 *Id.* at 31131.
128 *Id.*
129 81 Fed. Reg. 31131.
130 *Id.*; *see also* 29 C.F.R. § 1630.14(d)(6).
131 81 Fed. Reg. 31131.
132 *Id.*
133 467 U.S. 837 (1984).
134 81 Fed. Reg. 31131.

ADA safe harbor provisions "do not apply to wellness programs, even if such plans are part of an [employer's] health plan."[135]

The EEOC also contends that even if the safe harbor could apply to workplace wellness programs, the employers in *Seff* and *Flambeau* did not use the safe harbor provisions for their intended purpose. The EEOC states that in neither case did the employer nor its health plan use wellness program data to determine insurability or to calculate insurance rates based on risks associated with certain conditions—the practices the safe harbor provisions were intended to permit.[136]

One court recently found the EEOC's final rule to be reasonable. The relevant facts in *EEOC v. Orion Energy Systems* are very similar to the facts in the *Flambeau* case: Orion Energy Systems offered employees who elected to enroll in its health plan a wellness program that included an HRA and a biometric screen.[137] Orion required employees who refused to complete the HRA to pay 100 percent of their health insurance premium.[138] Just as in the *Flambeau* case, the company in the *Orion* case argued that the ADA safe harbor applied to its wellness program, and therefore the 100 percent of premium incentive did not violate the ADA's voluntary medical exam exception.[139]

In a surprising twist after the *Flambeau* case, the *Orion* court refused to apply the ADA safe harbor to Orion's wellness program.[140] The court agreed with the EEOC and its interpretation of the ADA safe harbor.[141] It applied *Chevron* deference to the EEOC's final rule, stating that Congress was not clear as to if and how the ADA safe harbor should apply to workplace wellness programs.[142] The *Orion* court also found the EEOC's interpretation of the ADA safe harbor to be reasonable.[143] It agreed that applying the safe harbor to workplace wellness programs, even those programs that are part of a group health plan, is at odds with

---

135 29 C.F.R. § 1630(d)(6).
136 81 Fed. Reg. 31131.
137 *EEOC v. Orion Energy Sys.*, 14-cv-1019, Dkt. #51 (E.D. Wis. Sept. 19, 2016), at 3.
138 *Id.* at 3.
139 *Id.* at 7–8.
140 *Id.* at 17.
141 *Id.* at 15.
142 *Id.* at 11.
143 *Id.* at 12.

the intent of the safe harbor.[144] According to the *Orion* court, the purpose of the safe harbor is to protect the basic business operations of insurance companies.[145] Workplace wellness programs do not fit within that purpose, as companies usually implement them after they set premiums and wellness programs are usually unrelated to basic underwriting and risk classification.[146]

Even though the *Orion* court rejected the application of the ADA safe harbor to Orion's wellness program, it still found the program to be voluntary and therefore not in violation of the ADA voluntary medical exam exception.[147] It reasoned that even a strong incentive, such as an employee having to pay 100 percent of his or her health insurance premium, is not compulsion.[148] In the *Orion* case, an employee who refused to participate in the HRA could still enroll in Orion's health plan, albeit at a much higher cost.[149] As noted by the court, a "hard choice is not the same as no choice."[150] The court was able to reach this conclusion because the EEOC's final ADA rule that now limits incentives to 30 percent of the cost of self-only coverage does not apply retroactively; the wellness program at issue in the *Orion* case existed in 2009, seven years before the EEOC issued its final ADA rule.[151]

As of the publication date of this book, it is uncertain and doubtful that either party in the *Orion* case will appeal the district court's decision to the Seventh Circuit Court of Appeals. However, the EEOC did appeal the *Flambeau* decision to the Seventh Circuit Court of Appeals.[152] In early 2017, the Seventh Circuit found the issues raised in the *Flambeau* case to be moot and therefore did not rule on the merits of EEOC's interpretation of the ADA.[153]

As noted earlier, certain members of Congress believe the EEOC has exceeded its authority in issuing the final rules. Senator Lamar Alexander

---

144 *Id.* at 15.
145 *Id.*
146 *Id.*
147 *EEOC v. Orion Energy Sys.*, at 18.
148 *Id.*
149 *Id.*
150 *Id.*
151 *Id.*
152 *EEOC v. Flambeau, Inc.*, 16-cv-1402 (7th Cir. 2016).
153 *EEOC v. Flambeau*, No. 16-1402 (7th Cir. Jan. 25, 2017).

said he might seek to revive the Preserving Employee Wellness Programs Act, which would allow, for example, participatory wellness programs (as defined by HIPAA/ACA) to offer rewards of any amount.[154] Despite this congressional criticism, the federal District Court of the District of Columbia in *AARP v. EEOC* recently determined that, based on the record before it at the time, the EEOC was within its authority to impose a 30 percent maximum incentive on wellness program activities.[155] Thus, until there is change imposed by Congress, wellness professionals and organizations would be wise to comply with the final ADA rules and avoid using the ADA insurance safe harbor as guidance for incentive limits.

GINA

This section on the Genetic Information Nondiscrimination Act (GINA) first provides a historical perspective of GINA and the purposes behind the law. This chapter then addresses the GINA provisions related to workplace wellness, followed by a discussion of financial inducements under GINA and a detailed description of the final GINA rules for workplace wellness programs.

GINA History

President George W. Bush signed the Genetic Information Nondiscrimination Act in 2008.[156] The law recognizes advancements in the field of genetics and the potential for using genetic information to identify the risks of disease and health conditions before they develop. However, the law also recognizes the risk that **genetic information** could be used to discriminate.

The law took root in the 1990s, when the Human Genome Project built on decades of genetic research and ultimately announced in 2003

---

154 "Alexander: EEOC Workplace 'Wellness' Rules Will Make It Harder for Employees to Choose Healthy Lifestyles and Save Money," *The Chattanoogan.com* (Tuesday, May 17, 2016), http://www.chattanoogan.com/2016/5/17/324342/Alexander-EEOC-Workplace-Wellness.aspx; H.R. 1189, 114th Congress (March 2, 2015), https://www.congress.gov/114/bills/hr1189/BILLS-114hr1189ih.pdf.
155 *AARP v. EEOC*, 16-cv-2113 (D. D.C. filed December 29, 2016).
156 Pub. L. No. 110-223, 122 Stat. 881 (May 21, 2008), https://www.congress.gov/110/plaws/publ233/PLAW-110publ233.pdf.

that scientists had sequenced the human genome.[157] By 2006, genetic testing could identify hereditary risks for more than 1,000 diseases.[158] As of February 2016, more than 33,000 different genetic tests are used to identify more than 6,000 health conditions.[159] These numbers will only increase as genetic science advances.

GINA was enacted amidst a rapidly advancing period for genetics. Bills to ban genetic discrimination had surfaced as early as the 1990s,[160] but after such huge breakthroughs in genetic science in the early 2000s, Congress recognized the growing need and public pressure to protect individuals who wanted to pursue genetic testing as a way to minimize health risks.[161]

For instance, members of Congress heard about a railroad company that in 2000 performed genetic tests on employees, without their knowledge, to undermine their workers' compensation claims.[162] They also heard about other individuals who were denied jobs or insurance because of health conditions that were identified through family histories or involuntary genetic testing.[163] Surveys revealed the public's fear that genetic testing could lead to adverse insurance decisions, or adverse employment decisions if employers had access to their genetic information.[164] Because of those fears, people were less likely to seek such tests.

"GINA provides the protections from genetic discrimination that Americans want and would allow genetic research to move forward in this country so we can all live healthier lives," Rep. Louise McIntosh Slaughter (New York), a microbiologist with a master's degree in public health, told members of the U.S. House of Representatives in 2007.[165] When the U.S. Senate considered GINA days later, former U.S. Sen. Olympia Snowe

---

157 National Human Genome Research Institute, "An Overview of the Human Genome Project," https://www.genome.gov/12011238.
158 Louise McIntosh Slaughter, "Genetic Testing and Discrimination: How Private Is Your Information?," 17 *Stan. L. & Pol'y Rev.* 67 (2006).
159 National Center for Biotechnology Information, Genetic Testing Registry, "Transparency in Genetic Testing: Data, Trends, and Uses," http://epostersonline.com/acmg2016/node/775?view=true.
160 *Id.*
161 *Id.*
162 *Id.*
163 *Id.*
164 *Id.*
165 Speech of Hon. Louise M. Slaughter of New York in the House of Representatives (Jan. 16, 2007), http://thomas.loc.gov/cgi-bin/query/R?r110:FLD001:E00121.

(Maine) suggested that it was the "first civil rights act of the 21st century," repeating the words of a colleague.[166] She said that "[d]iscrimination based on genetics is just as wrong as discrimination based on race or gender."[167] GINA, which was enacted with bipartisan support, prohibits discrimination based on genetic information, and placed restrictions on the collection and disclosure of genetic information.

Enacting GINA, Congress found that "[d]eciphering the sequence of the human genome and other advances in genetics open major new opportunities for medical progress," including early detection of illness and the development of better therapies.[168] However, it also found that "[t]hese advances give rise to the potential misuse of genetic information to discriminate in health insurance and employment."[169] Congress noted that genetics formed the basis for state laws requiring sterilization for presumed genetic defects, such as mental disease or blindness, starting in 1907,[170] and by 1981, a majority of states had sterilization laws to "correct" flawed genetic traits.[171] Although those state laws have since been repealed, a bipartisan Congress noted, in 2008, that "the current explosion in the science of genetics, and the history of sterilization laws by States based on early genetic science, compels Congressional action in this area."[172]

Congress also noted that many genetic conditions are associated more closely with certain racial or ethnic groups.[173] GINA prohibits the type of genetic discrimination that can occur based on genotype misconceptions about an otherwise healthy person's predisposition for health conditions that may never actually develop.[174] Finally, Congress concluded that a

---

166 Introductory remarks of Sen. Olympia J. Snowe, Senate Bill 358, in Cong. Rec.-Senate (Jan. 22, 2007): S846, https://www.gpo.gov/fdsys/pkg/CREC-2007-01-22/pdf/CREC-2007-01-22-pt1-PgS828-3.pdf#page=19.
167 *Id.* at S847.
168 122 Stat. 882.
169 *Id.*
170 *Id.*
171 *Id.*
172 *Id.*
173 *Id.*
174 *Id.; see also* H. Rep. 110-28, pt. 1, 28 (Mar. 5, 2007), https://www.gpo.gov/fdsys/pkg/CRPT-110hrpt28/pdf/CRPT-110hrpt28-pt1.pdf ("Enabling employers, health insurers, and others to base decisions about individuals on the characteristics that are assumed to be their genetic destiny would be an undesirable outcome of our national investment in genetic research, and may significantly diminish the benefits that this research offers").

federal nondiscrimination law would better protect American citizens than the patchwork of state nondiscrimination laws then in existence.[175]

GINA Provisions Related to Workplace Wellness

GINA has two titles of relevance to workplace wellness program design. Title I applies to "group health plans" and Title II applies to employers. The EEOC enforces GINA Title II, while the Departments of Labor, Health and Human Services, and Treasury enforce GINA Title I. GINA Title I prohibits group health plans from collecting genetic information, either for underwriting purposes or prior to or in connection with enrollment.[176] "Underwriting purposes" include changing deductibles or other cost-sharing mechanisms, or providing discounts, rebates, or other premium differential mechanisms in return for activities such as completing a health risk assessment or other wellness activity.[177] Thus, group health plans that offer premium discounts, for example, in exchange for completing a health risk assessment or biometric screen that collects genetic information (defined later) likely implicate GINA.

Other key terms and definitions that apply to workplace wellness programs include "genetic information," "family medical history," "manifestation," and "family." *Genetic information* means information about (1) the individual's genetic tests; (2) the genetic tests of an individual's family members; and (3) the manifestation of a disease or disorder in the individual's family member (i.e., family medical history).[178] **Family medical history** means information about the **manifestation of disease or disorder** in family members of the individual.[179] *Manifestation of disease* means a person has been or could reasonably be diagnosed by a healthcare professional with appropriate training and expertise in the field of medicine involved.[180] **Family** includes individuals related to the employee

---

175 Snowe, Senate Bill 358, Cong. Rec.-Senate (Jan. 22, 2007): S846.
176 45 C.F.R. § 146.122(d).
177 45 C.F.R. § 146.122(d)(1)(ii).
178 29 C.F.R. § 1635.3(c).
179 29 C.F.R. § 1635.3(b).
180 29 C.F.R. § 1635.3(g).

by blood, marriage, or adoption.[181] Therefore, GINA considers an employee's spouse or adopted child a family member subject to the rule.

GINA Title II prohibits employers from requesting, requiring, or purchasing genetic information with respect to an employee or an employee's family member, with certain limited exceptions.[182] One of those exceptions applies to voluntary wellness programs.[183] The EEOC issued final Title II regulations in 2010,[184] clarifying the requirements that must be met when employers offer to collect genetic information as part of a voluntary wellness program. The regulations are codified at 29 C.F.R. Part 1635.

First, the employer must not require individuals to provide genetic information nor penalize those who choose not to provide it.[185] Second, the individual must provide knowing, voluntary, and written authorization (including authorizations in electronic format).[186] The authorization form must be "written so that the individual from whom the genetic information is being obtained is reasonably likely to understand it."[187] It must also describe "the type of genetic information that will be obtained and the general purposes for which it will be used," as well as the safeguards in place to assure confidentiality.[188]

Third, employers must ensure that individually identifiable genetic information "is provided only to the individual (or family member if the family member is receiving genetic services) and the licensed healthcare professionals or board certified genetic counselors involved in providing such services, and is not accessible to managers, supervisors, or others who make employment decisions, or to anyone else in the workplace."[189]

In addition, the EEOC says that the regulations specifically allow employers to contract with third parties "to operate a wellness program or to provide other health or genetic services, or may provide such programs and services through an in-house health services office, as long as

---

181 29 C.F.R. § 1645.3(a).
182 42 U.S.C. § 2000ff-1.
183 29 C.F.R. 1635.8(b)(2).
184 75 Fed. Reg. 68912 (Nov. 9, 2010).
185 29 C.F.R. § 1635.8(b)(2)(A).
186 29 C.F.R. § 1635.8(b)(2)(i)(B).
187 29 C.F.R. § 1635.8(b)(2)(i)(B)(1).
188 29 C.F.R. § 1635.8(b)(2)(i)(B)(2)(3).
189 29 C.F.R. § 1635.8(b)(2)(i)(C).

individually identifiable genetic information is accessible only to the individual and the healthcare provider in providing such services."[190]

Finally, individually identifiable information can only be used for the purposes described through the authorization form and cannot be disclosed to the employer.[191] The employer can only receive identifiable genetic information "in aggregate terms that do not disclose the identity of specific individuals."[192] If the employer learns the source of individually identifiable information for reasons outside of its control, the employer does not violate GINA.[193] This could happen, for instance, if a small number of individuals participated in voluntary genetic testing.[194]

Financial Inducements and GINA

Under the EEOC regulations, an employer "may not offer a financial inducement (or incentive) for individuals to provide genetic information, but may offer financial inducements for completion of health risk assessments that include questions about family medical history or other genetic information, provided the [employer] makes clear, in language reasonably likely to be understood by those completing the health risk assessment, that the inducement will be made available whether or not the participant answers questions regarding genetic information."[195]

Under this requirement, the regulations provide two examples, one that would violate GINA and one that would not. In the first example, an employer offers employees cash rewards to complete an HSA, even if they do not answer the last 20 questions, which concern family medical history and genetic information.[196] In the second example, which would violate GINA, the employer does not make clear which questions relate to genetic information and does not make clear which questions must be answered to obtain the cash reward.[197]

---

190 75 Fed. Reg. 68924 (November 9, 2010).
191 29 C.F.R. § 1635.8(b)(2)(i)(D).
192 Id.
193 Id.
194 Id.
195 29 C.F.R. § 1635.8(b)(2)(ii).
196 29 C.F.R. § 1635.8(b)(2)(ii)(A).
197 29 C.F.R. § 1635.8(b)(2)(ii)(B).

The regulations also determine that employers may offer financial inducements to employees who voluntarily provided genetic information "that indicates that they are at increased risk of acquiring a health condition in the future to participate in disease management programs or other programs that promote healthy lifestyles, and/or to meet particular health goals as part of a health or genetic service."[198] However, the employer must also offer these programs to "individuals with current health conditions and/or to individuals whose lifestyle choices put them at increased risk of developing a condition."[199] Again, the regulations provide examples.

For instance, employees who voluntarily disclose a family medical history of heart disease or diabetes on a health risk assessment (HRA) and those who currently have those conditions are offered money to participate in a wellness program. This financial inducement does not violate GINA.[200] It also would not violate GINA to offer additional financial inducements for achieving certain health outcomes, such as losing weight or lowering blood pressure.[201]

When offering financial inducements to encourage participation in wellness programs, employers must also remember that other federal laws may apply, including the ADA and HIPAA/ACA. For instance, as discussed in the previous section, employers that offer financial inducements to participate in a wellness program that collects health information may have to limit the amount of the incentive to comply with the ADA rules.[202]

Similarly, if the wellness program provides direct medical care, such as genetic counseling, or reimbursement for medical care, the program may be considered a "group health plan" and "must comply with the special requirements for wellness programs that condition rewards on an individual satisfying a standard related to a health factor, including the requirement to provide an individual with a 'reasonable alternative

198 29 C.F.R. § 1635.8(b)(2)(iii).
199 *Id.*
200 29 C.F.R. § 1635.8(b)(2)(iii)(A).
201 29 C.F.R. § 1635.8(b)(2)(iii)(B).
202 29 C.F.R. § 1635.8(b)(2)(iv).

(or waiver of the otherwise applicable standard)' under HIPAA, when 'it is unreasonably difficult due to a medical condition to satisfy' or 'medically inadvisable to attempt to satisfy' the otherwise applicable standard."[203]

Final GINA Wellness Regulation

Putting together the preceding GINA requirements, one can surmise that GINA concerns arise when a workplace wellness program conducts health risk assessments that ask family medical history questions of the employee and family members or conducts biometric screens of an employee's family members whose results can show "manifestation" of a disease or disorder. An employee wellness program, whether sponsored by a group health plan or not, that asks employees and family members questions about whether anyone in their family has or had a disease or disorder may violate GINA if it ties financial incentives to answering those questions. Specifically, health risk assessments or biometric screens of family members may reveal the manifestation of a disease or disorder in those family members.

The EEOC issued final rules under GINA on May 16, 2016, the same day it issued the final rules under ADA.[204] The final rule clarifies when workplace wellness programs may financially induce family members to provide genetic information.

Here are the key provisions of the final GINA rule:

1. **Limited to spousal information.** The final GINA rule serves a very limited purpose. That purpose is to allow an employer to offer inducements to an employee for the employee's spouse to provide information about the spouse's manifestation of disease or disorder.[205] The spouse may provide that information as part of a health risk assessment (which includes biometric screens) administered in connection with a workplace wellness

---

203 29 C.F.R. § 1635.8(b)(2)(iv).
204 81 Fed. Reg. 31126, 31143 (May 17, 2016).
205 *Id.* at 31146.

program.[206] Recall that spousal health information qualifies as "genetic information" for an employee because GINA includes in the definition of *family member* a spouse (as well as adopted children). GINA allows employers to request an employee's genetic information, on a voluntary basis, for the purpose of providing wellness programs. However, current regulations prohibit a wellness program from requiring employees to provide their genetic information as a condition of receiving incentives.

The final rule makes a limited exception to this prohibition by allowing wellness programs to offer employees incentives (which may take the form of a reward or penalty and may be financial or in-kind) for an employee's spouse to provide information about the spouse's own manifestation of disease or disorder as part of a health risk assessment or medical examination (e.g., to detect high blood pressure or high cholesterol or both).

The incentive is for obtaining the spouse's manifestation of disease or disorder *only*; no reward is allowed to obtain other genetic information about the spouse, such as results of genetic tests.[207] Also, no incentives are allowed for obtaining manifestation of disease or disorder information for an employee's children or for other genetic information of an employee's child, regardless of the child's age.[208]

2. **Applies to all wellness programs.** Just like the final ADA rule, the final GINA rule allowing incentives to obtain spousal manifestation of disease or disorder information applies regardless of whether the spouse or employee are enrolled in an employer's health plan.[209]

3. **Incentive limit calculation.** The amount of the incentive for obtaining manifestation of disease or disorder information from the employee's spouse is 30 percent of the total cost of self-only coverage.[210] A separate 30 percent incentive limit applies to the employee for his or her participation in a workplace wellness

---

206 29 C.F.R. § 1635.8(b)(2)(iii).
207 81 Fed. Reg. 31153 (May 17, 2016).
208 *Id.* at 31147–31148.
209 *Id.* at 31151.
210 29 C.F.R. § 1635.8(b)(2)(iii).

program.[211] Consequently, when an employee and the employee's spouse are given the opportunity to enroll in an employer-sponsored wellness program, the inducement to each may not exceed 30 percent of the total cost of:

a. Self-only coverage under the group health plan in which the employee is enrolled (including both employee and employer cost), if enrollment in the plan is a condition for participation in the wellness program.

> i. Example Calculation: If the employee is enrolled in employer health plan and total cost of family coverage is $14,000 and the self-only option is $6,000, the employer may not offer more than $1,800 to the employee (30 percent of $6,000) and $1,800 to the spouse (30 percent of $6,000) for participating in a wellness program that collects information about the spouse's manifestation of disease or disorder as part of a health risk assessment or biometric screen.[212]

b. Self-only coverage under the group health plan offered by the employer (including both employee and employer cost) where the employer offers a single group health plan, but participation in a wellness program does not depend on the employee's or spouse's enrollment in that plan.

> i. Example Calculation: Employer offers a single health plan that costs $7,000 for self-only coverage, but enrollment in that plan is not necessary to participate in the wellness program that collects information about a spouse's manifestation of disease or disorder. The maximum inducement the employer can offer the employee and spouse is $2,100 each (which equals 30 percent of $7,000).[213]

c. Lowest-cost self-only coverage under a major medical group health plan offered by the employer (including both employee

---

211 Id.
212 29 C.F.R. § 1635.8(b)(2)(iii)(A).
213 29 C.F.R. § 1635.8(b)(2)(iii)(B).

and employer cost), where the employer has more than one group health plan, but enrollment in a particular plan is not a condition for participating in the wellness program. *like (b)*

  i. Example Calculation: Employer offers multiple group health plan options that range in cost from $5,000 to $8,000. Employees do not have to be enrolled in any of the options to participate in the wellness program that collects information about a spouse's manifestation of disease or disorder. The maximum incentive that the employer may offer the employee and spouse is $1,500 each (30 percent of $5,000).[214]

limited

ER offers NO health plan

(d) The second-lowest cost Silver Plan available on the exchange in the location that the employer identifies as its principal place of business if the employer offers no group health plan. The maximum inducement should be equal to 30 percent of the cost of covering an individual who is a 40-year-old nonsmoker.

  i. Example Calculation. The cost of second-lowest cost Silver Plan available to a 40-year-old nonsmoker on the exchange in the location of the employer is $4,000 annually. Therefore, an employer that does not offer employee health coverage but does offer a wellness program that collects information about a spouse's manifestation of disease or disorder can offer an inducement of $1,200 (30 percent of $4,000) each to the employee and spouse.[215]

These incentive limits align with the ADA incentive limits that employers can offer employees to participate in a wellness program that includes disability-related questions or medical examinations.

It is important to note that the final rule does not require the employer to pay the spouse's inducement directly to the spouse.

---

214 29 C.F.R. § 1635.8(b)(2)(iii)(C).
215 29 C.F.R. § 1635.8(b)(2)(iii)(D).

Rather, the employer may pay the spouse's portion of the inducement in whatever way the remaining portion of the inducement is made, such as, for example, part of a reduction in premium.[216]

4. **No agreement to sale or waiver of confidentiality of genetic information.** Like the final ADA rule, the final GINA rule prohibits employers from conditioning participation in a wellness program or providing any reward to an employee, spouse, or other covered dependent in exchange for their agreement permitting the sale, exchange, sharing, transfer, or other disclosure of genetic information, including information about the manifestation of disease or disorder of an employee's family member.[217] It is very important for wellness professionals and organizations to determine where the information they collect goes and whether any vendor agreements permit the downstream sale, exchange, sharing, or transfer of genetic information, unless that exchange is permitted by GINA (such as disclosing the information to licensed or certified professionals for the provision of genetic services[218]).

Also similar to the ADA rules, GINA requires employers that possess genetic information to maintain it in medical files (including where the information exists in electronic forms or files) that are separate from personnel files and to treat such information as a confidential medical record.[219] Moreover, GINA prohibits disclosure of genetic information except in six very limited circumstances, such as to the employee, by order of a court, or to government officials to ensure GINA compliance or for public health purposes.[220]

Although the final rule did not include additional protections for the confidentiality of genetic information, the EEOC urged

216 81 Fed. Reg. 31154 (May 17, 2016).
217 29 C.F.R. § 1635.8(b)(2)(iv).
218 29 C.F.R. § 1635.8(b)(2)(i)(D).
219 81 Fed. Reg. 31148 (May 17, 2016) (citing 29 C.F.R. § 1635.9).
220 29 C.F.R. § 1635.9.

employers to consider adopting best practices such as adopting strong privacy policies, training individuals who handle confidential medical information, encrypting electronic files, and notifying employees whose information is compromised because of a data breach.[221] The EEOC encourages these best practices for purposes of ADA confidentiality as well.[222]

5. **Authorizations are required for both employee and spouse.** Before an employee or spouse provides genetic information as part of a health risk assessment or biometric screen, the final rules state that the spouse must provide prior, knowing, voluntary, and written authorization.[223] GINA already requires such authorization for employees who provide genetic information.[224] The final rule ensures that spouses who agree to provide information about their manifestation of disease or disorder through a health risk assessment or biometric screen also provide such authorization.

The **authorization form** that employees and spouses sign should meet the following requirements:

a. Be easy to understand

b. Describe the type of genetic information that will be obtained and the general purpose for which it will be used

c. Describe the restrictions on the disclosure of genetic information.[225]

The employee does not have to sign a separate authorization for the collection of the spouse's manifestation of disease or disorder information.[226] Furthermore, GINA requires that individually identifiable genetic information be provided only to the individual (or family member if the family member is receiving genetic services) and the licensed healthcare professionals or board-certified genetic counselors involved in providing

---

221 81 Fed. Reg. at 31150–31151.
222 *Id.*
223 29 C.F.R. § 1635.8(b)(2)(iii).
224 42 U.S.C. § 2000ff-1(b)(2)(B); 29 C.F.R. § 1635.8(b)(2)(i).
225 81 Fed. Reg. 31155, n. 47 (May 17, 2016) (citing 29 C.F.R. § 1635.8(b)(2)(i)).
226 *Id.*

such services, and not be accessible to managers, supervisors, or others who make employment decisions, or to anyone else in the workplace.[227] The authorization form should include language to that effect as well. Moreover, it is a good idea for the authorization to state that the genetic information is only available for purposes of providing health or genetic services and is not disclosed to the employer except in aggregate terms that do not disclose the identity of specific individuals.[228]

6. **Information disclosure must be part of a larger effort to promote health or prevent disease.** Similar to the final ADA rules, the EEOC added language that would allow employers to obtain genetic information (whether through incentives or otherwise) only if acquiring that information is part of offering a wellness program that is "reasonably designed to promote health or prevent disease."[229] In other words, the program must have a reasonable chance of improving the health of, or preventing disease in, participating individuals, and must not be overly burdensome, a subterfuge for violating GINA or other laws prohibiting employment discrimination, or highly suspect in the method chosen to promote health or prevent disease.

   The final rule states that a program is not reasonably designed to promote health or prevent disease if it imposes a penalty or disadvantage on an individual because a spouse's manifestation of disease or disorder prevents or inhibits the spouse from participating or from achieving a certain health outcome.[230] For example, an employer may not deny an employee an inducement for participation of either the employee or spouse in an employer-sponsored wellness program because the employee's spouse has a blood pressure, a cholesterol level, or a blood glucose level that the employer considers too high.[231]

---

227 *Id.*
228 *Id.*
229 29 C.F.R. § 1635.8(b)(2)(i)(A).
230 *Id.*
231 *Id.*

In addition, for a wellness program to be reasonably designed to promote health or prevent disease, the collection of information on a health questionnaire must include follow-up information or advice, or the information must be used to design a program that addresses at least some of the conditions the information collection identified.[232] Thus, it is a good idea for companies that ask their plan participants to provide health information via health risk assessments or biometric screens to use the services of health coaches or health educators to help those employees benefit from the health information collection activity.

7. **Employers may not deny access to health coverage based on spouse's refusal to provide information.** Employers will violate GINA if they deny access to health benefits to an employee and/ or his or her family members based on a spouse's refusal to provide genetic information as part of a workplace wellness program.[233] Employers may also not retaliate against an employee based on a spouse's refusal to provide information about his or her manifestation of disease or disorder as part of a workplace wellness program.[234]

For a summary of the GINA regulations (2008 provisions and 2016 final rules) related to workplace wellness programs, see Figure 4.3.

When Complying with HIPAA, ADA, and GINA Is Not Enough

Despite the conditions wellness programs must meet to comply with HIPAA, ADA, and GINA, those conditions do not allay the fear expressed by some scholars that disparate impact discrimination may still occur under the guise of a corporate wellness program. Specifically, their argument is that unhealthy or disabled employees will bear more of

---

232 *Id.*
233 29 C.F.R. § 1635.8(b)(2)(v).
234 *Id.*

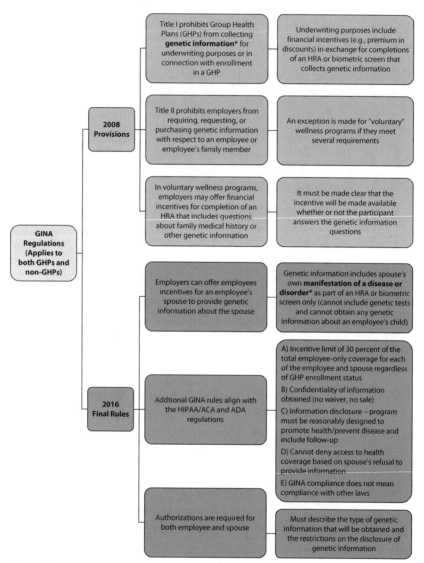

*Genetic information means (a) genetic tests of an individual, (b) genetic tests of an individual's family member, and (c) the manifestation of a disease or disorder in the individual's family member.

*Manifestation of disease or disorder means a person has been or could reasonably be diagnosed with a condition by a health-care professional.

Figure 4.3   Summary of GINA Regulations and Financial Incentives in Workplace Wellness "Screening" Programs

the financial burden of health coverage because they will be unable to earn the financial incentives. Studies point out that powerful personal, social, and financial incentives to be healthy, nonsmoking, and thin already exist and that obese workers, on average, earn lower wages than others; yet, people often fail at efforts to lose weight and stop smoking over the long term.[235] Moreover, the studies find that health-contingent programs that impose financial risk on unhealthy employees are likely to be regressive because the prevalence of unhealthy conditions typically targeted by wellness programs is highest among people with low socio-economic status, as well as racial minorities and women.[236]

As one example, a female healthcare system employee was unable to meet the body mass index (BMI) standard set by her employer wellness program. Those unable to meet the standard or who refused to participate in the program had to pay higher health insurance premiums. This employee's premiums increased from $175 per month to $320 per month, even though she also suffered from Type 1 diabetes and was breastfeeding. Moreover, the employee's doctor advised her not to lose weight. As an alternative standard, the employer required that she work out with a trainer at the company gym for 130 minutes per week at her own cost.[237] Had the employer practiced preventive law in this situation, it might have considered the fact that the employee was a new mother and likely facing new stress at home and that going to the gym for two hours each week on her own time was not reasonable given her personal situation. It would likely also have considered the advice of the employee's doctor to not lose weight at this time. As alternatives, the employer could have proposed to waive meeting the standard for the employee to earn the incentive, or ask that she work with her doctor to find a standard that was a better fit for her unique situation. Perhaps she could have attended a nutrition class on controlling diabetes or obtained counseling from a wellness coach to earn the reward.

---

235 Jill Horowitz et al., "Wellness Incentives in the Workplace: Cost Savings Through Cost Shifting to Unhealthy Workers," *Health Affairs* 32, no. 3 (March 2013): 469–471.

236 *Id.*

237 Jane Norman, "Workplace Wellness Programs May Punish Workers, Researchers Warn," *Washington Health Policy Week in Review* (March 5, 2012), http://www.commonwealthfund.org/publications/newsletters/washington-health-policy-in-review/2012/mar/march-5-2012/workplace-wellness-programs-may-punish-workers.

Instead, the employer in this example used a top-down, paternalistic, and insensitive approach in dictating the reasonable alternative standard. One could argue that the reasonable alternative standard in this case did not meet HIPAA/ACA requirements because it was overly burdensome: It required the employee to pay for the cost of the training program and it required a commitment of more than two hours each week. In addition, even if the reasonable alternative standard complied with the HIPAA/ACA requirements, the employer's approach may have caused discontent for the employee. It may also have adversely impacted female employees who were pregnant or had added stress at home, and the approach certainly was not the least risky strategy that the wellness program could have adopted.

Nudges versus Coercion

In fact, attending a class instead of dictating a certain amount of exercise would have fallen under the category of a "nudge," which feels less like coercion. The fields of psychology, sociology, and organizational development have studied the effectiveness of *nudges*, or supportive environments, as compared to coercion, on human behavior.[238] *Nudges*, as defined by Richard Thaler and Cass Sunstein in their seminal book, *Nudge: Improving Decisions About Health, Wealth, and Happiness*, provide people easy and cheap choices that alter their behavior in a predictable way without telling them what to do.[239] Individuals value the ability to control their lives, paths, and choices.[240] Research suggests that if human beings lose their ability to control things at any point in their lives, they become unhappy, helpless, hopeless, and depressed.[241] Thus, nudges create greater liberty than mandates.[242] As an example in the wellness world, the authors highlight the program implemented by Destiny Health Plan, offered in Illinois, Wisconsin, Michigan, and Colo-

---

238 *See, e.g.*, Salveo Partners, "Resources," http://salveopartners.com/free-resources/.
239 Richard H. Thaler and Cass R. Sunstein, *Nudge: Improving Decisions About Health, Wealth, and Happiness* (New York, NY: Penguin Books, 2008, 2009), at 6.
240 On Amir and Orly Lobel, "Stumble, Predict, Nudge: How Behavioral Economics Informs Law and Policy," *Colum. L. Rev.* 108, no. 2098 (2008): 2126.
241 Thaler and Sunstein, *Nudge*, at 6.
242 *Id.* at 188.

rado. The Health Vitality Program gives people incentives to make healthy choices. In particular, participants are able to earn "Vitality Bucks" if they work out at a health club in a particular week, have a child join a soccer league, or complete a blood-pressure check with normal results. Vitality Bucks can be used to obtain airline tickets, hotel rooms, magazine subscriptions, and electronics.[243]

In addition to the social sciences, the law offers guidance and insight into the shortcomings of coercion. Coercion by authorities, be it by government or an employer, antagonizes principles of individual freedom that are ingrained in the American spirit. The Declaration of Independence, a founding document of the United States, speaks of a right to "life, liberty, and ... happiness," not because the government granted it, but because all people naturally have it simply because they are people.[244] The Constitution's Bill of Rights guarantees freedoms of free speech, free press, freedom of worship and assembly, and other fundamental rights such as the right to privacy.[245] The U.S. Supreme Court notes that these rights cultivate a diverse culture with exceptional minds.[246] It also states that the nation should not fear disintegration of the social organization because of occasional eccentricity or abnormal attitudes that individual freedoms may foster; that is a small price to pay in exchange for freedom to be intellectually and spiritually diverse.[247] Moreover, it says that the right to exercise such individual freedoms should not be put to a vote or depend on the outcome of elections.[248] Only when the freedom to differ risks the safety or welfare of the common good should authority intervene.[249]

Coercive financial inducements imposed by the federal government against the states were the subject of a 2012 Supreme Court case

---

243 *Id.* at 235.
244 Daniel Farber et al., *Constitutional Law* (St. Paul, MN: West Group, 1998): 398.
245 *West Va. State Bd. of Educ. v. Barneete*, 319 U.S. 624, 638–641 (1943).
246 *Id.*
247 *Id.*
248 *Id.*
249 *Id.*; *see also Jacobson v. Massachusetts*, 197 U.S. 11, 27 (1905) (noting that "the liberty secured by the Constitution of the United States to every person within its jurisdiction does not import an absolute right in each person to be, at all times and in all circumstances, wholly freed from restraint. There are manifold restraints to which every person is necessarily subject for the common good. On any other basis organized society could not exist with safety to its members.").

involving the ACA's Medicaid expansion provision.[250] That provision threatened to withhold all of a state's Medicaid grants unless the state accepted the new expanded funding to cover more people under Medicaid.[251] Many states did not want to expand Medicaid, but felt forced to do so for fear of losing all of their Medicaid funding, which amounts to more than 20 percent of the average state's total budget.[252] The Supreme Court found the ACA's financial inducement so coercive as to pass the point at which pressure turns into compulsion, which, as Chief Justice Roberts stated, was like a "gun to the head."[253] This ruling gave states a choice to expand Medicaid funding versus requiring them to do so.

EEOC Cases Against Workplace Wellness Programs

Closer to the workplace wellness arena, one finds valuable lessons from three lawsuits filed by the EEOC regarding employer wellness program financial incentives. In 2014, the EEOC brought a series of cases challenging the legality of workplace wellness programs under the ADA and GINA: *EEOC v. Orion Energy Systems, EEOC v. Flambeau, Inc.,* and *EEOC v. Honeywell International, Inc.* Some of these cases were discussed earlier in the context of the ADA safe harbor, but the cases are worthy of further exploration in terms of applying the principles of nudges, coercion, and preventive law.

In the *Orion Energy* case, the EEOC alleged that Orion implemented a wellness program that included a health risk assessment and fitness test for its employees.[254] The health risk assessment asked the employees medical history questions and also had a blood work component.[255] According to the EEOC complaint, Orion required nonparticipants in the program to pay the entire premium cost of their health insurance coverage, while Orion paid much of the cost of coverage for employees who did participate in the program.[256]

---

250 *Nat'l Fed'n of Indep. Bus. v. Sebelius*, 132 S. Ct. 2566, 2604 (2012).
251 *Id.*
252 *Id.*
253 *Id.*
254 *EEOC v. Orion Energy Sys.*, Case No. 2:14-cv-1019 (E.D. Wis. 2014), Complaint, ¶ 10.
255 *Id.* at ¶ 11.
256 *Id.* at ¶ 16.

Similarly, the EEOC alleged that Flambeau implemented a wellness program that required employees to undergo biometric testing and a health risk assessment.[257] According to the EEOC, employees who failed to complete the biometric test and health risk assessment were responsible for paying 100 percent of their health insurance premium, while employees who did complete the test and health risk assessment paid a much lower cost.[258]

Finally, in the *Honeywell* case, the EEOC alleged that Honeywell required its high-deductible health plan participants (including spouses) to submit to a biometric test.[259] Failure to do so resulted in denial of a $250–$1,500 health savings account contribution, a $500 surcharge, and a $1,000 tobacco surcharge.[260] With regard to the tobacco surcharge, Honeywell offered three alternatives to the biometric test to avoid the surcharge: (1) enroll in a tobacco cessation program (actual cessation not required); (2) submit a physician report indicating that neither the employee nor spouse uses tobacco; or (3) work with a health advocate to establish that the employee or spouse is not a tobacco user.[261]

In all three of these EEOC cases, the EEOC alleged that the companies' wellness programs violated the ADA. The EEOC contended that the health risk assessment or biometric test constituted an involuntary medical examination that was not job-related.[262] As noted earlier, the ADA prohibits employee medical examinations, such as health risk assessments or biometric tests, unless those inquiries are job-related and consistent with business necessity.[263] The ADA provides an exception for medical inquiries that are part of a "voluntary" wellness program.[264]

---

257 *EEOC v. Flambeau, Inc.*, 3:14-cv-638 (W.D. Wis. 2014), Complaint, ¶¶ 10–11.

258 *Id.* at ¶ 16.

259 *EEOC v. Honeywell, Inc.*, 2014 WL 5795481, * 1 (D. Minn. 2014).

260 *Id.* at * 1–2. It should be noted that the $500 surcharge was not levied against employees whose spouses refused to undergo the biometric test.

261 *Id; see also EEOC v. Honeywell, Inc.*, Case No. 14-CV-04517, Memorandum of Law in Opposition to Plaintiff's Motion for Temporary Restraining Order and Expedited Preliminary Injunction, Dkt. #20, at 11 (D. Minn. Oct. 30, 2014).

262 *See, e.g., EEOC v. Honeywell*, 2014 WL 5795481, at * 4.

263 *Id.*, citing 42 U.S.C. § 12112(d)(4)(A) ("A covered entity shall not require a medical examination and shall not make inquiries of an employee as to whether such employee is an individual with a disability or as to the nature or severity of the disability, unless such examination or inquiry is shown to be job-related and consistent with business necessity.").

264 42 U.S.C. § 12112(d)(4)(B); *see also EEOC Enforcement Guidance: Disability-Related Inquiries and Medical Examinations of Employers under the Americans with Disabilities Act* (2000), Q. 22 ("A wellness program is 'voluntary' as long as an employer neither requires participation nor penalizes employees who do not participate.").

The EEOC did not view having to pay 100 percent of one's health insurance premium for failing to participate in the wellness program, as was the case in *Orion* and *Flambeau*, to be voluntary. It also did not view the large penalties imposed by Honeywell as promoting a voluntary program. Furthermore, in the *Honeywell* case, the EEOC alleged a violation of GINA because the biometric screen offered a financial inducement in exchange for information about the manifestation of disease in employees' spouses, who are considered "family" under GINA.[265]

Despite the alleged ADA and GINA violations, the wellness programs at each of these employers complied with the HIPAA/ACA incentive rules.[266] Specifically, these programs were "participatory" wellness programs under HIPAA/ACA, meaning that to obtain the reward, the participant did not have to satisfy a health status factor.[267] Unlike health-contingent programs, which do have a limit on the amount of a "reward," participatory programs have no limit on the financial reward that is used to encourage participation.[268] Indeed, the employers in all three cases pointed out that their wellness programs complied with the HIPAA/ACA nondiscrimination standards.[269] As a result, under the employers' reasoning, the wellness programs were legal and should not be facing EEOC criticism.

The preventive law lesson to be learned from the EEOC cases is that just because a program can arguably fit within legal parameters does not mean the program will be accepted by those it is intended to help. Some employees from those HIPAA-/ACA-compliant programs likely felt coerced: The financial incentive in each of those cases put at stake their ability to enroll in the group health plan. The EEOC did not view the

---

265 *EEOC v. Honeywell*, 2014 WL 5795481, * 5; *see also EEOC v. Honeywell, Inc.*, Case No. 14-CV-04517, Memorandum in Support of EEOC's Application for Temporary Restraining Order and an Expedited Preliminary Injunction, Dkt. #4 (D. Minn. Oct. 30, 2014), at 19–26.
266 Public Health Service Act § 2705.
267 42 U.S.C. § 300gg-4(j)(1)(B).
268 42 U.S.C. § 300gg-4(j)(1)(B); 42 U.S.C. § 300gg-j(3) (limiting the "reward" to no more than 30 percent of the cost of health coverage under the plan and defining "reward" to include a discount, rebate, waiver of cost-sharing, absence of surcharge, or value of a benefit that would otherwise not be provided under the plan); *see also* 42 C.F.R. § 146.121(f)(5) (allowing reward of up to 50 percent of cost of coverage for tobacco prevention programs).
269 *See, e.g., EEOC v. Honeywell*, 2014 WL 5795481, * 5 (noting Honeywell's argument that "Congress would not expressly endorse in one federal statute what is illegal under another pre-existing federal statute").

financial incentive at issue in those cases as a mere "nudge," but as closer to a mandate because of the size of the financial penalty. The employees pushed back by filing complaints with the EEOC in the hope that the EEOC would rule in their favor and not require them to reveal private information to their employer.[270]

Current Status of the EEOC Cases

According to the Public Access to Court Electronic Records (PACER) system, it appears that the parties in the *Honeywell* case have settled, as PACER indicates that the case is now closed. As a result, the public will not benefit from a court analysis of the legality of the Honeywell wellness program under the ADA or GINA. Moreover, as mentioned earlier, the appellate court dismissed the Flambeau case as moot, prohibiting a ruling on the merits of using the ADA safe harbor in workplace wellness programs or the EEOCs final ADA rules. Neverthless, the *Orion* court rejected the application of the ADA safe harbor to workplace wellness programs and found the EEOC's final ADA rule to be reasonable. It is uncertain whether the parties will appeal the court's decision regarding the ADA safe harbor.

Other Laws Affecting Screening

As noted at the very beginning of this chapter, two of the incentive-based laws, ADA and GINA, are tied to wellness programs that have screening components. However, those are not the only laws that are implicated when wellness programs contain a screening component. Other laws about which wellness professionals and organizations should be aware include the Clinical Laboratory Improvement Amendments of 1988 (CLIA) and state laws that govern drawing of blood and laboratory testing. Although not laws, pre-activity screening standards and guidelines published by professional organizations should be followed in

---

270 *See, e.g., EEOC v. Honeywell, Inc.*, Case No. 14-CV-04517, Memorandum in Support of EEOC's Application for Temporary Restraining Order and an Expedited Preliminary Injunction, Dkt. #4 (D. Minn. Oct. 30, 2014), at 3, 23.

all fitness facilities to help avoid negligence lawsuits that can result for failing to conduct pre-activity screening.

CLIA

The federal Centers for Medicare and Medicaid Services (CMS) regulates all laboratory testing (except research) performed on humans in the United States through CLIA.[271] CLIA was established to strengthen federal oversight of clinical laboratories to ensure the accuracy and reliability of patient test results.[272] Federal law defines a **laboratory** to be a facility that performs certain testing on human specimens in order to obtain information that can be used for the diagnosis, prevention, or treatment of any disease or impairment of a human being; or the assessment of the health of a human being; or procedures to determine, measure, or otherwise describe the presence or absence of various substances or organisms in a human body.[273] Given this broad definition, many workplace wellness biometric screening activities involve a CLIA "laboratory" at some point during the testing process. All facilities that meet the definition of "laboratory" under CLIA must obtain an appropriate CLIA certificate prior to conducting patient testing.[274] However, facilities that only collect or prepare specimens (or both), or only serve as a mailing service and do not perform testing, are not considered laboratories under CLIA.[275]

CLIA's regulatory requirements vary according to the kind of tests each laboratory conducts.[276] Tests are categorized as:

- Waived
- Moderate complexity
- High complexity[277]

---

271 "Biometric Health Screening for Employers," *supra* note 179, at 1246.
272 CMS, "Direct Access Testing (DAT) and the Clinical Laboratory Improvement Amendments (CLIA) Regulations, Fact Sheet," https://www.cms.gov/Regulations-and-Guidance/Legislation/CLIA/Downloads/directaccesstesting.pdf.
273 *Id.* (citing 42 C.F.R. § 493.2).
274 *Id.*
275 42 C.F.R. § 493.2 (definition of *laboratory*).
276 CMS, "Direct Access Testing (DAT) and the Clinical Laboratory Improvement Amendments (CLIA) Regulations, Fact Sheet."
277 *Id.*

Most onsite, point-of-care biometric screens in workplace wellness programs fall within the CLIA waived test category.[278] Laboratories that perform waived tests must obtain a certificate of waiver under CLIA.[279] Waived tests must meet the following criteria:

- Are cleared by the FDA for home use;
- Employ methodologies that are so simple and accurate as to render the likelihood of erroneous results negligible; or
- Pose no reasonable risk of harm to the patient if the test is performed incorrectly.[280]

One can see a full list of the tests that are waived under CLIA, and the manufacturers of those tests, at https://www.cms.gov/Regulations-and-Guidance/Legislation/CLIA/downloads/waivetbl.pdf.

The significance of being categorized as a waived test is that there are fewer regulatory requirements for the laboratory conducting those tests. Laboratories eligible for a certificate of waiver must (1) follow the manufacturers' instructions for performing the test; and (2) meet the certificate of waiver requirements found at 42 C.F.R. §§ 493.35–493.39.[281] The certificate of waiver requirements includes:

- Filing an application with the Department of Health and Human Services (HHS)
- Making records available and submitting reports to HHS to ensure compliance with 42 C.F.R. § 493.15(e)
- Agreeing to permit announced and unannounced inspections by HHS
- Remitting a certificate of waiver fee[282]

---

278 "Biometric Health Screening for Employers," *supra* note 179, at 1246.
279 42 C.F.R. § 493.15.
280 42 C.F.R. § 493.15(b).
281 42 C.F.R. § 439.15(e).
282 42 C.F.R. §§ 493.35–493.37. Current CLIA certificate of waiver fee is $150 for two years. *See* https://www.cms.gov/Regulations-and-Guidance/Legislation/CLIA/downloads/clia_certificate_fee_schedule.pdf.

The certification is good for two years.[283] After that, the laboratory must renew the certificate.[284]

It is important for wellness professionals and organizations that include screening activities as part of a workplace wellness program to assess whether the appropriate CLIA certificates have been issued.

State Screening Laws

State laws can sometimes override or go beyond CLIA requirements, including for waived tests.[285] State regulations may limit the tests that can be run, dictate who can run certain tests, require certain practitioner oversight, or regulate the way results can be provided or reported to employees.[286] There are also state laws that address transport, storage, and disposal of biometric specimens.[287]

Some states also prohibit direct access testing (DAT), which refers to laboratory tests that are allowed without a physician's order.[288] In those states that prohibit DAT, physicians must order the test and the results must be reported to the ordering physician.[289]

An examination of each state's laws that govern biometric screening is beyond the scope of this book. Nevertheless, wellness professionals and organizations should be aware that such state laws exist, and should consult with legal counsel when assessing a wellness program's compliance with those laws.

Pre-Activity Screening Standards and Guidelines

Several professional organizations have published standards and guidelines either requiring or recommending that fitness facilities conduct pre-activity screening; they include such bodies as the American College of Sports Medicine (ACSM), the Medical Fitness Association (MFA), and the National Strength and Conditioning Association (NSCA). The major

---

283 42 C.F.R. § 493.37(e).
284 42 C.F.R. § 493.37(f).
285 "Biometric Health Screening for Employers," *supra* note 179, at 1246.
286 *Id.*
287 *See, e.g.*, Wis. Admin. Code §§ NR 526.07-08 and 526.10 (addressing transport, containment, and handling of infectious waste).
288 "Biometric Health Screening for Employers," *supra* note 179, at 1246.
289 *Id.*

purpose of pre-activity screening is to identify individuals who may be "at risk" for an untoward event during exercise, such as a cardiac arrest. As a precaution, the professional standards and guidelines recommend that "at risk" individuals seek medical clearance or consultation prior to starting an exercise program.

Generally, there are two approaches to pre-activity screening: (a) self-guided (e.g., participants complete a simple questionnaire such as the PAR-Q & You[290] and are informed to follow the recommendations on the questionnaire regarding whether or not to consult with a medical provider before beginning an exercise program), and (b) professionally guided (e.g., participants complete a pre-activity screening questionnaire which is then interpreted by an exercise professional to determine whether or not the participant needs to obtain medical clearance prior to participation in physical activity.

It is important for workplace wellness professionals to develop and implement pre-activity screening procedures that reflect these standards and guidelines, not only from a fitness safety perspective, but also from a legal perspective. As discussed in Chapter 1, expert witnesses in negligence cases often refer to these types of published statements in their testimony to help educate the court as to the duty the defendant owed to the plaintiff and if the defendant breached its duty. There have been many negligence claims/lawsuits against fitness professionals and facilities that failed to conduct pre-activity screening.[291] However, workplace fitness facilities appear to be doing a good job of conducting pre-activity screening procedures. In a 2015 national study[292] that investigated adherence to ACSM's pre-activity screening procedures among fitness facilities, 78 percent of workplace fitness facilities required new participants to complete a pre-activity screening device compared to other settings: (a) clinical—93 percent, (b) government—67 percent, (c) university—56 percent, (d) community—54 percent, and (e) commercial—40 percent.

290 Canadian Society for Exercise Physiology, "PAR-Q & You, Physical Activity Readiness Questionnaire," http://www.csep.ca/CMFiles/publications/parq/par-q.pdf.

291 JoAnn M. Eickhoff-Shemek, David L. Herbert, and Daniel P. Connaughton, *Risk Management for Health/Fitness Professionals: Legal Issues and Strategies* (Baltimore, MD: Lippincott Williams & Wilkins, 2009).

292 Aaron C. Craig and JoAnn Eickhoff-Shemek, "Adherence to ACSM's Pre-Activity Screening Procedures in Fitness Facilities: A National Investigation," *J. Physical Educ. & Sports Mgmt.* 2, no. 2 (2015): 120–137.

Often there is inconsistency among professional standards and guidelines published by professional organizations.[293] When this occurs, it is recommended professionals follow "the most authoritative or safety-oriented in their approach."[294] The pre-activity screening procedures published in *ACSM's Guidelines for Exercise Testing and Prescription (ACSM's GETP)* are considered some of the most authoritative and safety oriented. For the past 30 years (third edition through the current ninth edition), these procedures have involved asking participants if they have (a) known cardiovascular, pulmonary, and/or metabolic disease; (b) any signs and symptoms suggestive of known disease; and (c) risk factors associated with cardiovascular disease (CVD). After collecting this information, the exercise professional then classifies the individual into a low, moderate, or high risk category following the criteria specified in the *ACSM's GETP*.[295] All individuals classified as high risk and some individuals classified as moderate risk (e.g., those who want to participate in a "vigorous"[296] exercise program) should obtain medical clearance and/or a medical exam prior to participation in an exercise program.

In the current edition of the *ACSM's GETP*,[297] one of the nine CVD risk factors includes family history and states: "myocardial infarction, coronary revascularization or sudden death before 55 yr in father or other male first-degree relative or before 65 yr in mother or other female first-degree relative."[298] If a workplace fitness program requires an employee to complete a screening device that includes family history information, there may be GINA implications. So, to reduce the risk of a GINA violation, it might be best to (a) have the completion of the screening questionnaire voluntary, to avoid a potential violation of GINA (although this would go against the standards/guidelines that require fitness facilities to conduct pre-activity screening); or (b) leave out the risk factor involving family history on the screening device. Using

293 Eickhoff-Shemek, Herbert, and Connaughton, *Risk Management for Health/Fitness Professionals.*
294 *Id.* at 53.
295 Linda S. Pescatello, Ross Arena, Deborah Riebe, and Paul D. Thompson, *ACSM's Guidelines for Exercise Testing and Prescription,* 9th ed. (Baltimore, MD: Lippincott Williams & Wilkins, 2014).
296 *Id.* at 28. This publication identifies exercise intensity levels as (a) very light, (b) light, (c) moderate, (d) vigorous (hard), (e) vigorous (very hard), and (f) maximal. *Id.* at 5.
297 Pescatello, Arena, Riebe, and Thompson, *ACSM's Guidelines for Exercise Testing and Prescription.*
298 *Id.* at 27.

the *ACSM's GETP* criteria, anyone who has two or more CVD risk factors would be classified as moderate risk, even if that person has no known diseases and/or no signs/symptoms of disease.

The next edition (10th) of the *ACSM's GETP* will be available in early 2017. There are significant changes regarding the pre-activity screening criteria in this new edition.[299] No longer will participants need to answer any questions regarding CVD risk factors including family history. Therefore, applying these new criteria in the creation of a pre-activity screening device will no longer have GINA implications. The main reason for the deletion of CVD risk factors (as well as other changes) was that the screening guidelines were resulting in excessive physician referrals. It is believed that removing this barrier will help more individuals adopt and maintain a regular exercise program. It also will make the pre-activity screening procedures easier and more efficient for fitness facilities to carry out.

RULE THE RULES

Key Points in Chapter 4

As in Chapter 3, the "key points" in this chapter are summarized in the answers to three case-study questions that test your understanding and application of the HIPAA/ACA, ADA, and GINA laws with regard to financial incentives.

> Q: My employer wants to create a wellness program that financially rewards participants in a daily noon-time walking program. The walking program is open to all employees and is not part of our health plan. The incentive amount being tossed around is

---

299 Deborah Riebe, Barry A. Franklin, Paul D. Thompson et al., "Updating ACSM's Recommendations for Exercise Preparticipation Health Screening," *Med. & Sci. in Sports & Exercise* 47, no. 11 (2015): 2473–2479.

$150 for those who walk daily for at least one month. Is this incentive okay?

A: In this case, because the walking program is not part of a group health plan, HIPAA/ACA does not apply. Also, according to the EEOC ADA incentive rules, $150 is likely within the 30 percent maximum incentive range. Regardless of the amount of the incentive, the ADA reasonable accommodation requirement would apply. Remember, the premise behind the ADA is to provide an equal opportunity to those who have or are perceived to have disabilities to enjoy the same terms and conditions of employment, which includes wellness program incentives. So, for those employees who are unable to participate in the wellness program due to a disability, the program should offer a reasonable alternative method to earn the reward. This might be a different type of exercise, or attending a nutrition class, as examples. It is important to recognize that employees, like people in greater society, have different abilities. We can't all be triathletes.

How You Rule the Rules: The ADA in particular serves as a reminder to consider the needs of those who might have trouble walking during their lunch break. Perhaps they have a medical condition that requires a certain diet and therefore can't use their lunch break to walk because they need the time to prepare certain food. Or perhaps they are on crutches, wheelchair bound, or use other mobility assisters that would make walking at lunch every day impossible or at least cumbersome. Perhaps they have a skin condition that would make walking outdoors medically inadvisable. There could be a myriad of reasons, and the ADA's equal opportunity requirements should serve as a trigger to remember the varying abilities of your workforce, even if some of those inabilities do not technically qualify as disabilities under the law. The ADA can help sensitize you to the unique needs of your workforce and stand ready to offer alternatives to earn the $150 incentive. Moreover, even though HIPAA/ACA do not apply in this case, using the reasonable alternative standard and notice requirements in that law may be good practice. In other words, when announcing the walking program to employees, you could mention the availability of a reasonable alternative standard for those who are unable to participate in the walking program. You do not have to devise the alternative standard up front, but could offer to work with individuals to find an alternative that suits them and that puts them on the path to becoming their best self. Isn't that the whole point of a wellness program?

Let's look at another example:

> **Q:** An employer wants its group health plan participants, including spouses and children, to complete a health risk assessment. The plan notified the plan participants that they will be responsible for paying 100 percent of the plan premium if they do not complete the questionnaire. The employer is just asking them to complete the assessment. What the participants do with the results is their business. Is this okay?
>
> **A:** Under the HIPAA/ACA rules, yes, because the program is participatory only. However, under the new ADA rules, no, because the incentive exceeds 30 percent of the cost of coverage and the ADA rules apply to both participatory and health-contingent programs that involve disability-related inquiries or medical exams. Moreover, the ADA rules expect employer plans that collect medical information to provide employees with follow-up information or advice, such as providing feedback about risk factors or using aggregate information to design programs or treat any specific conditions. Employee follow-up is necessary, according to the EEOC, to promote health. Without follow-up, the collection of employee health information is not permissible. In addition, follow-up of health assessments is considered a "best practice" and one of the key components of a comprehensive wellness program. Moreover, this employer is violating the GINA rules by including children in the incentive program and exceeding the 30 percent maximum incentive for collecting information on spousal manifestation of disease or disorder.

How You Rule the Rules: The EEOC's ADA and GINA rules try to fill a gap left by the HIPAA/ACA rules, which do not cap incentive amounts for participatory programs. As seen from the *Flambeau, Orion Energy,* and *Honeywell* cases, some employees at those companies rebelled against divulging their personal health information through a participatory wellness program or face having to pay 100 percent (in the case of Flambeau and Orion Energy) of their health insurance premium, by filing a complaint with the EEOC. Even though a mere few employees filed a complaint, it is very possible that many more felt the same way. The EEOC claimed that the 100 percent incentive made the program involuntary; it did not give the employees a real choice. Employer-sponsored health insurance is a valuable benefit for many employees. Tying the disclosure of sensitive information to such a benefit, with no apparent purpose articulated by the employer plan, undermines employee trust in the employer. It also violates the ADA and GINA requirements that wellness programs be reasonably designed to promote health and prevent disease.

Proper wellness program planning that incorporates the program into the employer's value statement can help employees understand the purpose of the program and create trust in the program. Moreover, following up with employees after they divulge their health information, such as through health coaching or using the results to improve wellness opportunities in the workplace (and communicating those results), solidifies the health promotion purpose of the program.

Another question:

> **Q:** Our group health plan wellness program sponsors a walking program. Participants earn a $100 gift card for completing the eight-week program. An employee approached me stating that he is unable to participate because of a medical condition. Can we ask him to provide a verification of his condition from his physician before agreeing to offer him an alternative way of earning the incentive?
>
> **A:** Yes. HIPAA/ACA rules permit activity-only wellness programs to require verification by the individual's physician that a health factor makes it unreasonably difficult or medically inadvisable for

the individual to satisfy the activity. However, asking for physician verification is prohibited for outcomes-based programs. Thus, a weight loss program that requires participants to lose a certain number of pounds could not ask an individual's physician to verify that losing that amount of weight would be unreasonably difficult or medically inadvisable before offering the individual an alternative standard (or waiving the standard altogether).

How You Rule the Rules: It is important to remember that health measures such as BMI, cholesterol, blood pressure, and the like are very personal, which is why there are a number of laws that protect the privacy of health information. Whether one wants or is able to achieve certain health measures is also a personal decision or circumstance that may reflect a person's values, beliefs, culture, and social, economic, and physical environment. Asking or requiring a person to meet a certain health measure can be perceived as invasive and possibly coercive. Moreover, seeking information from an employee's physician about whether an employee is able to meet a measure will likely infringe upon the physician-patient relationship. The reasons why an employee may not be able to meet a measure can be many and varied. Asking the physician to verify whether an employee can achieve a certain outcome places the physician in an uncomfortable position about whether to disclose the employee's health information, and how much information to disclose, to justify the need for a reasonable alternative standard. So, rather than placing the employer, physician, or employee in that uncomfortable position, the ACA prohibits seeking physician verification for outcomes-based programs.

One final scenario:

Q: ABC Wellness Company conducts biometric screens in the workplace. ABC sends the collected blood samples to a laboratory for analysis. Does ABC need a CLIA waiver?
A: No. ABC is merely collecting the blood samples. The laboratories to which ABC sends the specimens should have the CLIA certificates, however. ABC should verify that the laboratories with which it works have the appropriate certifications in place before doing business with them.

How You Rule the Rules: The CLIA law aims to protect public health and safety to ensure that entities that handle and interpret biological materials do so safely and accurately. As you will read in Chapter 10, the healthcare industry has many regulations for the protection of the public. Because laboratories are part of the healthcare landscape, wellness professionals must be aware of these healthcare laws when relying on healthcare entities such as laboratories, drug manufacturers, hospitals, physicians, nurses, and others for assistance with workplace wellness programs.

Study Questions

1. Briefly describe the legislative history of the HIPAA, ADA, and GINA laws and how these laws reflect a need for added protection to ensure equal treatment for all Americans.
2. Explain the distinctions under the HIPAA/ACA law between "participatory" and "health-contingent" wellness programs.
3. List and describe the five tests under the HIPAA/ACA law that health-contingent programs must meet and then describe (a) the differences for test #4 (reasonable alternative standard) between activity-only and outcome-based programs, and (b) the financial incentive limitations for health-contingent programs.
4. Describe how the ADA Amendments Act expanded the coverage of the ADA and potential implications that the ADAAA may have for workplace wellness programs.
5. Using the preamble to the final ADA rule described in this chapter, explain how the EEOC concluded that "safe harbor" provisions do not apply to wellness programs under the ADA.
6. Using case law examples (*Orion, Honeywell,* and *Flambeau*) described in this chapter, explain the EEOC's position with regard to voluntary wellness programs under the ADA regulations.
7. For both the ADA and GINA final rules, describe the financial incentive limitations for wellness screening programs (health risk assessments and biometric screenings), as well as other key regulations applicable to wellness programs.

8. Prepare a written policy for a workplace wellness program that reflects compliance with additional screening laws (e.g., CLIA and state laws) and pre-activity standards and guidelines published by professional organizations.

Key Terms

authorization form

biometric screening

Equal Employment Opportunity Commission (EEOC)

family

family medical history

financial incentives

genetic information

health-contingent wellness program

health risk assessment (HRA)

laboratory

manifestation of disease or disorder

medical exam

participatory wellness program

reasonable accommodations

reasonable alternative standard

safe harbor

voluntary workplace wellness program

APPENDIX

Making the Argument to Avoid Large Financial Incentive and Disincentive Programs

Before making decisions to spend a lot of money on financial rewards and penalizing employees with financial disincentives, wellness professionals should read an excellent white paper published by Health Enhancement Systems entitled "How Financial Incentives/Disincentives Undermine Wellness: Making Wellness Rewarding without Rewards."[1] The following are discussed in this paper to shed some light about financial incentives and disincentives:

1. Financial rewards undermine autonomy
2. Excessive controls lead to defiance
3. Employees who aren't ready or willing to change...won't
4. Monetary incentives aren't sustainable
5. Bribery fosters a "What have you done for me lately?" mentality
6. Financial incentives aren't enough to change complex behaviors
7. Extrinsic controls sabotage skills needed for well-being[2]

Financial incentives (or other tangible awards) and disincentives may entice employees to participate in a wellness program, especially initially. These incentives focus on "extrinsic" motivation, meaning individuals participate in order to earn a reward or avoid a penalty. In order for workplace wellness programs to gain and sustain positive health outcomes for both individuals and organizations, it will be important to focus on programs that lead to "intrinsic" motivation, meaning individuals realize the many nontangible benefits from participating in wellness programs. For example, individuals who have exercised regularly all

---

1 How Financial Incentives/Disincentives Undermine Wellness: Making Wellness Rewarding Without Rewards. Health Enhancement Systems (2012). Available at: https://www.hesonline.com/free-stuff/white-papers/rewards (last visited July 8, 2016).
2 *Id.* at 2.

their life do not do it to receive some kind of tangible reward, but for the many personal (intrinsic) physical and psychological benefits that result from exercise. This white paper describes 20 ways to boost intrinsic motivation in wellness programs. Helping employees to change and sustain their behavior and achieve intrinsic motivation is quite complex. Wellness professionals not only need to understand behavior theories (e.g., theory of planned behavior, health belief model, transtheoretical model, social cognitive theory) but must also understand how to apply the constructs (e.g., self-efficacy) within these theories in the design and delivery of wellness programs.

Fidelity and the National Business Group on Health (NBGH) conducted a couple of studies in 2013[3] and 2014.[4] The 2013 study found that (a) 90 percent of employers offered financial incentives in 2013 whereas 57 percent did so in 2009, and (b) spending on wellness-based incentives doubled between 2009 ($260/employee) and 2013 ($521/ employee). This study also found that financial incentives included (a) decrease in premiums (61 percent), (b) cash or gift cards (55 percent), and (c) contribution to employer-sponsored health savings accounts or similar accounts (27 percent). The 2014 study reported that four out of ten companies planned to offer financial incentives to spouses/domestic partners with an average cost of $530. Of the companies surveyed, 93 percent indicated they planned to expand or maintain funding for their wellness programs over the next three to five years. Also, 41 percent of employers currently included or planned to include outcome-based programs where employees need to meet a specific goal (e.g., lowering cholesterol 30 percent, lowering blood pressure 29 percent, or reducing waist circumference 11 percent) to earn the financial reward. However, in their 2015 study, Fidelity and NBGH found that the number of

---

3 New Health Care Survey Finds Spending on Wellness Incentives Has Doubled in the Last Four Years. National Business Group on Health (February 27, 2013). Available at: http://www.businessgrouphealth. org/pressroom/pressRelease.cfm?ID=207 (last visited July 8, 2016).
4 Health Care Survey Finds Spending on Corporate Wellness Incentives to Increase 15 Percent in 2014. National Business Group on Health (February 20, 2014). Available at: http://www.businessgrouphealth. org/pressroom/pressRelease.cfm?ID=225 (last visited July 8, 2016).

employers utilizing outcome-based incentives was expected to drop in 2016 to help encourage employee participation.[5]

The expansion of offering financial incentives and the increases in the amounts of the incentives pose an important question that all wellness professionals need to ask: Are large financial incentives the most cost-effective way to spend the dollars allocated for the wellness program? Cost-effective in this context means achieving the most "bang for the buck"—the most effective way to achieve positive health outcomes for individuals and organizations given the dollars spent. The results of one study[6] involving a wellness coaching intervention actually showed that the employers who offered higher financial incentives tended to have lower rates of risk reduction than those who offered lower financial incentives. The authors of this study concluded that offering financial incentives may be slightly effective for increasing participation and completion rates but may not be effective to improve health outcomes (reducing risk factors). A systematic review[7] of smoking cessation interventions at the workplace showed that financial incentives may entice enrollment, participation, and initial quit rates, but generally did not achieve long-term behavior change.

The American Heart Association's (AHA's) position statement on worksite wellness financial incentives[8] is also recommended for wellness professionals to read prior to offering large financial rewards/penalties. The AHA states the premise of the part of the ACA that allows financial incentives/disincentives is that it will motivate employees to take responsibility to change their behavior. But, this premise is not well supported

---

5 Companies Expand Wellness Programs to Focus on Improving Employee's Emotional and Financial Well-Being. National Business Group on Health (April 1, 2016). Available at: http://www.businesswire.com/news/home/20160401005372/en/Companies-Expand-Wellness-Programs-Focus-Improving-Employees%E2%80%99 (last visited July 9, 2016).

6 Research Brief. Impact of Financial Incentives on Behavior Change Program Participation and Risk Reduction. StayWell Health Management. (2012). Available at: http://staywell.com/wp-content/uploads/2012/11/ResearchBrief_Impact-of-financial-incentives.pdf (last visited July 9, 2016).

7 Kate Cahill and Rafael Perera, Competitions and Incentives for Smoking Cessation. Cochrane Database of Systematic Reviews (April 13, 2011). Available at: http://onlinelibrary.wiley.com/doi/10.1002/14651858.CD004307.pub4/abstract (last visited July 9, 2016).

8 Position Statement on Financial Incentives within Worksite Wellness Programs. American Heart Association, American Stroke Association. (n.d.). Available at: https://www.heart.org/idc/groups/heart-public/@wcm/@adv/documents/downloadable/ucm_428966.pdf (last visited July 10, 2016).

by evidenced-based research. The AHA calls for more research to determine (a) both short-term and long-term impact of financial incentives, (b) whether financial incentives or disincentives have the greatest impact, and (c) any unintended consequences, e.g., those paying a higher premium (disincentive) may delay medical care because they cannot afford to participate in their health plan. The AHA claims that penalizing individuals for their health status violates a major purpose of the ACA, which is to preserve and expand "access to affordable, adequate, high quality insurance coverage for all Americans"[9] and may negatively affect the most vulnerable employees by denying them access to the medical care they need.

Potential problems with large financial penalties go beyond whether they are effective in achieving and sustaining behavior change. They can lead to litigation, as demonstrated in the EEOC cases described above (*Orion*, *Flambeau*, and *Honeywell*). Obviously, the employees in these companies who filed their complaints with the EEOC were angry with management's decision to impose hefty financial penalties (e.g., paying the entire premium, surcharges in the hundreds of dollars) and felt discriminated against. How does this "us-them" approach lead to positive feelings toward an employer? How does this approach lead to an environment or culture to promote positive health behaviors? It doesn't. To be effective, workplace wellness programs need to use a "we" approach, meaning we (management and employees) are all in this effort together. Some of the WELCOA benchmarks (e.g., creating cohesive diverse wellness teams, creating a supportive culture) and the best practices defined by Pronk (e.g, integrating partnerships with stakeholders, engaging co-ownership of the programs) described in Chapter 2 reflect a "we" approach. Also, one of the key components of a comprehensive program is to provide "supportive physical and social environments for health improvement," which also reflects a "we" approach. Unfortunately, the employees in the EEOC cases likely felt "coerced" into participation in the health activities. Coercion approaches do not reflect the definition of health education, i.e., learning experiences designed to predispose,

---

9 *Id.* at 2.

enable, and reinforce "voluntary" behavior. Programs that are truly voluntary enhance autonomy and lead to intrinsic motivation.

Financial incentives (or other tangible incentives) should be included in behavior change programs. Positive reinforcement can be helpful especially to encourage initial participation. However, just because the ACA allows for large financial incentives/disincentives, does not mean they should be implemented. Dean Witherspoon recommends spending no more than $19 on recognition, e.g., use small prizes such as t-shirts, gym bags, water bottles to reward participation because they are long-lasting reminders of personal achievement.[10] He states that "giving people money to coerce them to do something we want them to *want* to do for themselves is at best ineffective and at worst degrading."[11] Also, as described in Chapter 5, employees will need to pay income tax on large financial incentives whereas they will not for small incentives (de minimis fringe benefits) such as t-shirts and gym bags.

The large amounts of money that companies are budgeting for financial incentives may be better spent on hiring additional wellness staff members to improve the wellness staff/employee ratios. Having more staff resources will increase opportunities for staff members to engage with employees. The first step to help an employee change his/her behavior may be for a wellness staff member to establish a relationship with the employee. It takes time and effort to develop a trusting, respectful relationship. We all know that businesses that have positive relationships with their customers or clients are often more successful than those that do not. In the case of workplace wellness, the employees of the company are the customers of the wellness staff. The wellness staff members "serve" the employees. Personal approaches that foster positive relationships can be effective in improving individual and organizational health outcomes.

As described in this chapter, there are many complex regulations with each of the laws related to workplace wellness programs, more so

---

10 How Financial Incentives/Disincentives Undermine Wellness: Making Wellness Rewarding Without Rewards. Health Enhancement Systems (2012). Available at: https://www.hesonline.com/free-stuff/white-papers/rewards (last visited July 8, 2016).
11 *Id.* at 9.

for programs that offer incentives than for those that do not. Failure to follow the regulations can result in the company having to pay the federal government large fines (see Chapter 1 for examples of companies that had to pay large fines due to violations of the HIPAA privacy rule). From an administrative perspective, it may be easier and will take less time for wellness professionals to comply with the regulations that apply to incentive-free programs. For example, wellness professionals will need time to consult with legal counsel to develop procedures that will help ensure compliance with all of the incentive-based regulations, such as HIPAA/ACA, ADA and GINA. Once the regulatory procedures are developed, it will take additional staff time to administer them (e.g., effective communication with employees, calculating and tracking of incentives, etc.). Of course, wellness professionals need to consult with legal counsel to be sure they are compliant with all laws applicable to their programs. However, by not offering incentive-based programs, wellness programs avoid the time and effort of both wellness staff members and legal counsel to develop/implement the many legal requirements of these types of programs.

A specific example of the additional time and effort associated with incentive-based programs is calculating the cost or value of all the incentives, financial and in-kind, to ensure that the amount does not exceed the 30 percent maximum incentive limit (or 50 percent if there is a tobacco cessation component). Another example of additional time one may need to spend on incentive-based programs is keeping records of employees that have been given a reasonable alternative (i.e., maintaining documentation/progress toward the alternative, time frame, etc.). Given about 50 percent of adults in the United States have at least one chronic condition and 25 percent have two or more chronic conditions,[12] there may be a high number of employees requesting a reasonable alternative. Seeking verification from a physician in an activity-only program as a condition to providing a reasonable alternative may be time consuming and difficult. Physicians do not give out their email addresses, direct

---

12 Brian W. Ward, Jeannine S. Schiller, and Richard A Goodman, Multiple Chronic Conditions Among U.S. Adults: A 2012 Update, *Preventing Chronic Disease,* 11: E62 (April 17, 2014). Available at: http://www.ncbi.nlm.nih.gov/pmc/articles/PMC3992293/ (last visited July 10, 2016).

phone numbers, and the like. So wellness staff members will have a difficult time in communicating with an employee's physician in an effective, timely manner. It may be best for the employee to obtain this verification statement from his/her physician, but the employee may feel this is an added burden. For example, obtaining physician clearance for participation in exercise programs for moderate-high risk individuals has been shown to be a burden (or barrier) for participants and fitness facility staff members.[13]

The information in this appendix has attempted to make some good arguments for small financial incentives and incentive-free wellness programs. However, Michael O'Donnell perhaps makes the best argument in a few short words. Although workplace wellness programs are well positioned for continued growth, there are certain factors that could derail this growth.[14] He states that "the biggest risk to workplace health promotion programs is the possible loss of its soul. If the field becomes dominated by financial incentives that create winners among the healthy and losers among the unhealthy, or if the predominate programs are impersonal web-based approaches, or if business people with a profit motive and no knowledge of the art and science of health behavior change become the driving force of the field, the workplace health promotion field has the potential to wither away."[15]

---

13 Deborah Reibe, Barry Franklin, Paul D. Thompson, P.D. et al., Updating the American College of Sports Medicine's Recommendations for the Exercsie Pre-Participation Health Screening Process. *Medicine & Science in Sports & Exercise,* 47(11), 2473–2479, (Novembr 2015).
14 Michael P. O'Donnell (Ed.), *Health Promotion at the Workplace* (4th ed.), Troy, MI: American Journal of Health Promotion, (2014).
15 *Id.* at xxv–xxvi.

5

The Taxing Truth

Learning Objectives

After reading this chapter, workplace wellness professionals will be able to:

1. Understand the origins of the U.S. income tax.
2. Describe the social purposes behind income taxes.
3. Distinguish tax policy from conservative and progressive perspectives.
4. Describe the purpose behind medical care expense deductions and how these deductions qualify as both involuntary expenses and intermediate expenses.
5. Understand *medical care* as defined in Internal Revenue Code (IRC) § 213.
6. Explain the potential benefits of the Personal Health Investment Today (PHIT) Act from a tax perspective.
7. Apply taxation laws in the design and delivery of workplace wellness incentive programs (e.g., incentives that are exempt from income tax and those that are not exempt).
8. Define *de minimis fringe benefits* and explain their application to workplace wellness incentive programs.
9. Understand why legal counsel is needed when designing wellness incentives that affect contributions to FSAs, HRAs, or HSAs.
10. Understand that wellness cash (or cash equivalent) incentives are always taxable as income even if the employer uses a third-party vendor to issue the incentives.

The hardest thing in the world to understand is the income tax.

—Albert Einstein

*No government can exist without taxation. This money must nec-
essarily be levied on the people; and the grand art consists of
levying so as not to oppress.*

— Frederick the Great, 18th-century Prussian king

Introduction

Workplace wellness incentives implicate the U.S. tax code in a number
of ways. Many workplace wellness program designers are surprised to
learn that certain incentives are taxable as wages, while others are not.
Workplace wellness incentives may also affect an employee's ability to
change cafeteria plan elections, such as pretax salary reductions that are
used to pay health coverage premiums. There are also nondiscrimination
and reporting issues to consider under the tax code.

Before we jump into these tax compliance issues, learning the background of the U.S. income tax can help shed light on why certain wellness incentives are excludable from tax (and must adhere to certain tax
code requirements to stay that way) while other incentives are subject to
tax in all cases.

Origins of the U.S. Income Tax

The origin of the individual income tax is generally cited as the passage
of the Sixteenth Amendment to the U.S. Constitution, passed by Congress on July 2, 1909, and ratified February 3, 1913. However, the individual income tax history actually goes back even further. In 1862,
President Lincoln signed into law a revenue-raising measure to help pay
for Civil War expenses. The measure created a Commissioner of Internal
Revenue and the nation's first income tax. It levied a 3 percent tax on
incomes between $600 and $10,000 and a 5 percent tax on incomes of
more than $10,000. This tax was repealed 10 years later. So, from 1868
until 1913, 90 percent of all revenue came from taxes on liquor, beer,
wine, and tobacco, not from income. However, in 1894 Congress tried

again to impose an income tax, enacting a flat-rate federal income tax. This tax was ruled unconstitutional the following year by the U.S. Supreme Court because it was a direct tax not apportioned according to the population of each state. The Sixteenth Amendment, ratified in 1913, removed this objection by allowing the federal government to tax the income of individuals without regard to the population of each state.[1]

Today, **income taxes** are the largest source of revenue for the United States government. In 2014, the federal government collected nearly $1.4 trillion from individual income taxes. Federal individual income taxes fund 46.2 percent of the U.S. government, compared to 33.9 percent from payroll taxes (taxes that pay for Social Security and Medicare), 10.6 percent from corporate income taxes, 3.1 percent from excise taxes, and 6.3 percent from other sources. These "other sources" include gasoline and cigarette taxes, estate taxes, customs duties, and payments from the Federal Reserve. The individual income tax contribution percentage of just less than half of all federal revenue sources has been roughly constant since World War II.[2]

The Social Purpose Behind Income Taxes

"Taxation has always been intimately related to democracy," said Sidney Ratner, author of the 1942 book *American Taxation*.[3] Especially in the United States, taxation has always been a major source of conflict among different economic groups and sections. Some seek to create and use a tax system as an important instrument for concentrating wealth and income in the hands of a certain class and section. Others strive for a society free of glaring inequalities and try to develop and control a revenue system that counteracts the centralization of economic power.[4]

---

1 Library of Congress, *IRS History*, https://www.loc.gov/rr/business/hottopic/irs_history.html; Internal Revenue Service, *Historical Highlights of the IRS*, https://www.irs.gov/uac/Historical-Highlights-of-the-IRS.
2 Drew Desliver, "High-Income Americans Pay the Most Income Taxes, But Enough to Be 'Fair?'," Pew Research Center (March 24, 2015), http://www.pewresearch.org/fact-tank/2015/03/24/high-income-americans-pay-most-income-taxes-but-enough-to-be-fair/.
3 S. Ratner, *American Taxation: Its History as a Social Force in Democracy* (New York, NY: W.W. Norton, 1942): 13.
4 *Id.* at 13.

132

According to one tax expert, **tax policy** is a "group contest in which powerful interests vigorously endeavor to rid themselves of present or proposed tax burdens .... Class politics is the essence of taxation."[5]

Among the taxes which are regarded as well suited for achieving and preserving the economic objectives of democracy are income, gift, inheritance, and excess-profit taxes. These levies place the weight of taxation on those best able to bear it or on those receiving "unearned" or "undeserved" gains.[6] Those who desire such taxes support them to minimize existing economic inequalities and prevent their further growth. These champions of taxation regard increasing social welfare as a legitimate objective of revenue policy. They reject the doctrine of laissez-faire economists and conservatives that taxation can and should only be used for the production of revenue and not for the social control of business or the redistribution of wealth and income.[7]

On the flip side, conservative tax policy relies on taxation for revenue and prefers tariff duties and sales taxes over income, gift, and inheritance taxes. Sales taxes burden those with lower incomes more than those with higher incomes, which allows those with higher incomes to more easily build up their capital. The premise defending this tax policy is that a high concentration of wealth and income promotes capital investment and business prosperity.[8] Those in the conservative tax policy camp believe that high, progressive income tax rates equate to confiscation of property and offer an opening wedge for socialism.[9]

The historic struggle for control of the state by the middle classes in England, France, and America during the 17th and 18th centuries was inspired to some degree by their desire to secure a more equitable tax system, in which they would not bear the major tax burden without receiving commensurate benefits.[10] The democracy that Americans cherish today is the product of the evolution of the American people toward the achievement of the satisfactions which the natural and social resources

---

5 *Id.* at 14.
6 *Id.*
7 *Id.*
8 *Id.*
9 *Id.*
10 Ratner, *American Taxation*, at 15.

of the United States make possible. Mere aspiration by the common people for a fuller and richer life would be ineffectual without a national government endowed with powers to counteract the concentration of economic and political power in the hands of an oligarchy. The economic basis for the creation and preservation of democracy is the distribution of wealth and income among the majority of the people in such a fashion that no elite can permanently dominate the community.[11]

Because of this history and these varied social goals, the government of the United States is authorized to—and does—tax income and other monies received by individuals and organizations. Yet, there are some items and services that the government has decided should be excluded from tax. One of those exclusions is medical care.

The Purpose Behind the Medical Care Expense Deduction

As just discussed, taxation is a means of improving social welfare. Generally speaking, **tax deductions** function as indirect subsidies which are alternatives to budget outlays, credit assistance, or other instruments of public policy.[12] Some contend that tax deductions are not the most equitable means of achieving direct government support because the amount of a deduction depends on the individual taxpayer's marginal tax rate.[13] Thus, tax deductions are most beneficial to the relatively wealthier taxpayers in higher tax brackets.[14]

Nevertheless, tax scholars explain that tax deductions for goods and services that are involuntary or intermediate (i.e., they are a step toward

---

11 *Id.* at 22.
12 David W. Ichel, "Note: Defining 'Medical Care': The Key to Proper Application of the Medical Expense Deduction," *Duke L.J.* 1977 (1977): 909, 910, http://scholarship.law.duke.edu/dlj/vol26/iss4/4 [hereinafter Ichel, "Defining Medical Care"].
13 *Id.*
14 *Id.* "Since the deduction will reduce an individual's tax bill by a percentage of the deducted amount equal to his tax rate, the wealthier taxpayer in a higher income bracket will receive a greater benefit from an amount deducted." The percentage floor to section 213 medical expense deductions, however, mitigates this upside-down effect by disallowing deductions for medical expenses unless the total exceeds a certain percentage of the taxpayer's gross income. *Id.* For 2015, the percentage floor was 10 percent of a person's adjusted gross income or 7.5 percent if the taxpayer or taxpayer's spouse is age 65 or older. *See* https://www.irs.gov/taxtopics/tc502.html.

producing income or maintaining the status quo) are justifiable. In the case of **involuntary expenses**, such expenses take away from the taxpayer's ability to build his or her material wealth.[15] In the case of **intermediate expenses**, such expenses provide no benefit to the taxpayer other than to aid in the production of money.[16] Hence, tax deductions for business expenses exist because they are intermediate in nature.

Tax deductions for medical care expenses exist because they are involuntary as well as intermediate. Specifically, medical expenses are involuntary because individuals do not usually choose to fall ill, and when an individual does, he or she is unable to build his or her material wealth; the illness often prevents the individual from earning money at his or her full potential, and the ill individual must spend the money he or she does have on medical expenses.[17] Thus, a tax deduction on medical expenses can help relieve the financial burden of those expenses. Medical expenses can also be intermediate because they do not increase a taxpayer's material well-being, except to improve a person's poor health.[18] Usually, the taxpayer with extraordinary medical expenditures is at most made whole by the expenditure, not made better off.[19]

The Revenue Bill of 1942, introduced by the Senate Finance Committee, included a medical care tax deduction.[20] In its report, the Senate Finance Committee stated:

> The term "medical care" is broadly defined to include amounts paid for the diagnosis, cure, mitigation, treatment, or prevention of disease, or for the purpose of affecting any structure or function of the body. It is not intended, however, that a deduction should be allowed for any expense that is not incurred primarily for the prevention or alleviation of a physical or mental defect or illness.[21]

---

15 Ichel, "Defining Medical Care," at 912–913.
16 *Id.* at 913.
17 *Id.*
18 *Id.*
19 *Id.*
20 Ichel, "Defining Medical Care," at 917.
21 *Id.*

The bulk of this Senate Finance Committee language defining *medical care* made its way into **Internal Revenue Code (IRC) § 213**.[22] Section 213 is an exception carved out of the general rule of IRC § 262, which prohibits deductions for personal, living, or family expenses.[23] According to one researcher, underlying the overall purpose of § 213 is the premise that **medical care expenses** are something other than personal expenses—that to constitute a medical care expense, an expenditure must be intermediate in nature, at most returning the taxpayer to a status quo, a whole position of good health.[24] "Thus, expenditures which are not for the diagnosis, prevention or treatment of a specific defect—even if they be for the general improvement of one's health—should not constitute medical care expenses."[25]

Most expenses associated with medical treatment have been held by the courts and the Internal Revenue Service (IRS) to constitute medical care expenditures deductible under § 213.[26] Expenses for services performed by medical professionals, including laboratory work, x-rays, and hospital care, are deductible medical care expenses. So are legally procured medicines and drugs.[27] However, expenses for cosmetics, toiletries, weight-loss programs that are not to treat a specific disease diagnosed by a physician, vitamins, health club dues, and other general well-being activities or items are not deductible.[28]

Taxation Issues of Wellness Incentives

As noted earlier, wellness activities and products are often taxable. In the eyes of the Department of Treasury, wellness activities and products often fall within the voluntary choice category of expenditures, and therefore would be subject to tax. As a result, employer reimbursements of health

22 IRC § 213(d).
23 Ichel, "Defining Medical Care," at 914.
24 *Id.* at 914–915.
25 *Id.* at 915.
26 *Id.* at 923.
27 *Id.*
28 Ichel, "Defining Medical Care," at 923–924; *see also* IRS Publication 502, https://www.irs.gov/publications/p502/index.html.

club dues or costs of weight loss or nutrition programs, are generally subject to tax.[29] In that case, an employer must treat the reimbursement, or the fair market value of the program, as income and wages reportable in Box 1, 3, and 5 on Form W-2.[30] However, such expenses may be excludable from income and wages if the taxpayer can show that the expenses were to treat a specific disease and would not have been incurred but for the disease.[31] According to the IRS, objective factors indicating that an otherwise personal expense is for medical care include:

- The taxpayer's motive or purpose for making the expenditure
- A physician's diagnosis of a medical condition and recommendation of the item as treatment or mitigation
- The relationship between the treatment and the illness
- The effectiveness of the treatment
- The proximity in time of the expenditure to the onset or recurrence of a disease[32]

The IRS will not permit a taxpayer to deduct a personal expense as medical care if the taxpayer would have paid the expense in the absence of a medical condition.[33] Also, health club or weight loss program fees may be deductible as medical expenses only when a physician prescribes the treatments and provides a statement that the treatments are necessary for the alleviation of a physical or mental defect or illness of the individual receiving the treatments.[34] Finally, access to an employer's onsite fitness facility, such as the company gym or pool, may be excludable from employees' income and wages if the facility is operated by the employer and substantially all use is by employees and family members only.[35]

---

29 IRS Information Letter 2010-0175 (June 25, 2010); Brandon Lafving, "Why Your Employer's Gym Membership Perk May Cost You at Tax Time," U.S. Tax Center article (June 17, 2013), http://www.irs.com/articles/why-your-employers-gym-membership-perk-may-cost-you [hereinafter Lafving article]; IRS Publication 502, https://www.irs.gov/taxtopics/tc502.html.
30 Lafving article.
31 IRS Information Letter 2010-0175 (June 25, 2010).
32 *Id.* at 2.
33 *Id.*
34 *Id.*
35 26 U.S.C. § 132(j)(4); *see also* Lafving article.

Of course, it is appealing to argue that wellness expenditures such as (offsite) health club memberships or weight loss programs should be deductible as a medical care expense because such expenses may be for the prevention of hypertension, obesity, cardiovascular disease, or other ailments. Recall that the definition of *medical care* under § 213 includes expenditures related to the prevention of disease. Thus, it would not be too much of a stretch to exclude many wellness expenditures from income taxation for the very reason that those expenses help prevent disease. Yet, the IRS has stated that an "expense qualifies as medical care as preventing disease only if a *present existence or an imminent probability* of developing a disease, physical or mental defect, or illness exists."[36] For example, prediabetes or metabolic syndrome may reflect an imminent probability of a medical condition. But, for those who want to adopt healthy lifestyles to stave off illness or disease that may occur in the far distant future, the IRS prohibits deducting such expenses from income.

To change the income deduction and exclusion rules, Congress must change the law. Indeed, congressional leaders introduced H.R. 1218, the **Personal Health Investment Today (PHIT) Act,** in March 2015. Although the PHIT Act is not law, it shows what legal changes Congress could make to advance wellness initiatives. The PHIT Act proposes to amend the IRC to allow a medical care tax deduction for up to $1,000 ($2,000 for a joint return or head-of-household return) of qualified sports and fitness expenses, such as amounts paid for fitness facility memberships, physical exercise programs, and exercise equipment.[37] Of course, expanding what constitutes medical care under the tax deduction rules may have the unintended consequence of expanding the types of employer-sponsored wellness programs that may constitute "group health plans" which, as discussed in Chapter 3, creates more legal obligations for the program.

Nevertheless, allowing tax deductions or exclusions for wellness activities and products may induce people to adopt healthier lifestyles. As noted in Chapter 4, incentives can increase participation and may lead to behavior change/risk reduction, at least in the short term. Some

---

36 Lafving article (citing *Daniels v. Commissioner*, 41 T.C. 324 (1963) and *Stringham v. Commissioner*, 12 T.C. 580 (1949); emphasis added).
37 H.R. 1218, 114th Cong. (2015–2016), https://www.congress.gov/bill/114th-congress/house-bill/1218.

incentives associated with certain wellness programs already are exclud-able from income tax. For example, reimbursement for smoking cessa-tion classes, high blood pressure screenings, or vaccinations would be excludable because such activities qualify as medical care.[38]

In addition, **de minimis fringe benefits** are nontaxable.[39] These bene-fits include awards such as t-shirts, tickets, healthy snacks, water bottles, and the like. According to the IRS, a "de minimis benefit is one for which, considering its value and the frequency with which it is provided, is so small as to make accounting for it unreasonable or impractical."[40] How much is beyond de minimis? It depends on all the facts and circum-stances, but if a benefit is too large to be considered de minimis, the entire value of the benefit is taxable to the employee, not just the excess over a designated de minimis amount.[41] The IRS has previously ruled that items with a value exceeding $100 cannot be considered de mini-mis, even under unusual circumstances.[42] This may be another reason for avoiding large financial incentives, which are not excludable from income, in workplace wellness programs.

Another category of **tax-deductible wellness benefits** that are exclud-able from income and wages consist of certain employer subsidies for health coverage, such as premium contributions or other health plan cost-sharing reductions. These incentives are generally exempt from income tax under IRC §§ 105 and 106.[43] Wellness rewards consisting of employer contributions to health flexible spending accounts (FSAs), health reimbursement accounts (HRAs), or health savings accounts (HSAs) can also be excluded from an employee's income and would not be subject to wage withholding or employment taxes, provided that

---

38 IRS Publication 502, https://www.irs.gov/taxtopics/tc502.html (specifying that smoking cessation costs are deductible medical expenses). Arguably, screenings for a particular medical condition, such as high blood pressure, or vaccines, constitute medical care as defined by IRC § 213(d), and are therefore tax-deductible expenses, because such activities are for the diagnosis, treatment, or prevention of disease.
39 26 U.S.C. § 132(a)(4).
40 IRS Fact Sheet, "De Minimis Fringe Benefits," https://www.irs.gov/Government-Entities/Federal,-State-&-Local-Governments/De-Minimis-Fringe-Benefits.
41 *Id.*
42 *Id.*
43 26 U.S.C. § 105 (exclusion from federal gross income for reimbursements paid from an accident or health plan); 26 U.S.C. § 106(a) (exclusion for employer-provided coverage under accident or health plan).

applicable nondiscrimination requirements (and dollar limits, in the case of HSAs) are satisfied.[44] Simply put, employer contributions to employee FSAs, HRAs, or HSAs cannot discriminate in terms of eligibility or contributions in favor of highly compensated or key employees.[45]

There are various nondiscrimination rules that apply to these accounts. Some rules apply to contributions through cafeteria plans, and others apply to contributions made outside of cafeteria plans. HRA contributions cannot be made through an employer's cafeteria plan, and are subject to nondiscrimination requirements under IRC § 105(h).[46] Contributions to accounts through cafeteria plans, such as to FSAs, must comply with cafeteria plan nondiscrimination rules. With regard to FSA contributions, those contributions would also need to analyze compliance under IRC § 105(h) as well.[47]

Which set of nondiscrimination rules apply to HSA contributions depends on whether the employer contribution is made through or outside a cafeteria plan. An employer that chooses to make contributions to its employees' HSAs outside a cafeteria plan, which typically is not advisable in the context of wellness program incentives, must comply with separate "comparable contribution" requirements in lieu of the cafeteria plan nondiscrimination rules.[48] Thus, an employer FSA, HRA, or

---

44 Thomson Reuters Checkpoint, EBIA Benefits Library, *Consumer-Driven Health Care* (2015): 205 (citing IRC § 105(h)) [hereinafter *Consumer-Driven Health Care*].

45 *Id.* at 208B.

46 *Id.* at 209 and 1058I.

47 *Id.* at 208B.

48 *Id* at 209; *see also* IRC §§ 105(h), 125(b)(1), 4980G, 4980E; 26 CFR § 1.105-11(e); 26 C.F.R. § 1.125-7 (proposed); IRS Notice 2004-2, Q&A 32; IRS Notice 2004-50, Q&A 49. An excise tax equal to 35 percent of the total amount of employer HSA contributions applies to any employer that contributes to its employees' HSAs outside of a cafeteria plan and fails to satisfy the comparability rules. Those rules require all HSA-eligible employees in the same non-collectively bargained category (i.e., current full-time, current part-time, or former employees), who have the same High Deductible Health Plan (HDHP) coverage tier (i.e., self-only, self-plus-one, self-plus-two, or self-plus-three-or-more), to receive HSA contributions in the same dollar amount or the same percentage of the deductible under their HSA-compatible high deductible health plan. Because wellness rewards are earned on the basis of whether a particular employee participates in or satisfies the wellness program activity, the resulting HSA contributions likely would not be comparable unless each employee in the same category happened to earn the same HSA incentive amount. 26 CFR §§ 54.4980G-4, Q/A – 9 and 54.4980G-5. Stated another way, if an employer wanted to offer wellness program awards in the form of HSA contributions outside a cafeteria plan, the employer would need to make the same contribution amount on behalf of all "comparable" employees, regardless of whether they participated in the wellness program (thus effectively negating the "incentive" aspect of the wellness program). Therefore, it is recommended that employers make any such wellness program incentive HSA contributions through a cafeteria plan established under IRC § 125.

HSA contribution that is set as a percentage of compensation may discriminate in favor of highly compensated individuals, because such individuals would earn a proportionately larger dollar reward.[49] If wellness rewards offered under an HRA fail the nondiscrimination rules under IRC § 105(h), certain highly compensated or key employees will be subject to income tax on at least a portion of the "discriminatory" HRA amounts.[50] Employers that contract with an insurance company to provide health coverage (i.e., insured plans) could face an excise tax of up to $100 per day per individual for each day of noncompliance with the nondiscrimination rules similar to IRC § 105(h).[51]

The cafeteria plan and other nondiscrimination requirements are complex and discussing those complexities is beyond the scope of this book. Nevertheless, wellness professionals should be aware that these nondiscrimination laws exist and should work with legal counsel when designing wellness incentives that impact FSA, HSA, or HRA contributions. Working with legal counsel is especially important if the contributions are different among employees, particularly in terms of the award amount and who can earn the reward.

Although employer contributions to FSAs, HRAs, and HSAs can be excluded from income tax, premium reimbursements by an employer are subject to tax. According to an IRS memorandum released in 2016, if an employer reimburses an employee for a premium amount paid through a § 125 "cafeteria plan," as a reward for participating in a wellness program, for example, the employer's reimbursement amount is taxable income to the employee.[52] Under § 125 of the Internal Revenue Code, an employer may establish a cafeteria plan that permits an employee to choose among two or more benefits, consisting of cash (generally, salary)

---

49 *Consumer-Driven Health Care* at 209.
50 *Id.* at 208B; *see* § 2716 of the Public Health Service Act (PHSA), IRC §§ 4890D, 9815.
51 As of the publication of this book, these nondiscrimination rules as applied to insured group health plans were not yet being enforced by the IRS, pursuant to a temporary grace period. See IRS Notice 2011-1, Affordable Care Act Nondiscrimination Provisions Applicable to Insured Group Health Plans, https://www.irs.gov/pub/irs-drop/n-11-01.pdf. However, a failure to comply with these nondiscrimination rules could still subject the employer/plan sponsor to a private right of action in federal court under § 502(a) of the Employee Retirement Income Security Act of 1974 (ERISA). *See* ERISA § 715, PHSA § 2716.
52 IRS Memorandum 201622031 (May 27, 2016), https://www.irs.gov/pub/irs-wd/201622031.pdf.

and qualified benefits, including accident or health coverage.[53] Pursuant to § 125, the amount of an employee's salary reduction applied to purchase such coverage is not included in the employee's gross income, even though it was available to the employee and the employee could have chosen to receive cash instead.[54] If an employee elects health coverage through the cafeteria plan, the coverage is excludable from gross income under § 106 as employer-provided health coverage.[55] But, if an employer reimburses any part of that salary reduction (which was used to pay the premium for health coverage or perhaps to participate in the wellness program), the IRS considers that reimbursement amount as taxable wages to the employee.[56]

It is important to note that cash and cash equivalent rewards for wellness programs (like gift cards) are always taxable, regardless of the amount (i.e., cash can never qualify as a de minimis fringe benefit).[57] The IRS considers payment or reimbursement of gym fees as a cash benefit that is taxable as income.[58] Thus, employers must report these cash incentives on the recipient's Form W-2 and withhold applicable income and employment taxes.[59] Even if an employer uses a third-party wellness vendor to issue the cash incentives, the employer typically is still responsible for withholding applicable income and employment taxes, and reporting the taxable wellness rewards on an employee's Form W-2.[60] However, there may be scenarios where a third party (such as a health insurer for an insured group health plan) administers a wellness program that provides a taxable incentive (e.g., cash or a gift card), and the third party is actually deemed the "statutory employer" for purposes of complying with related income and employment tax withholding and

---

53 Id.
54 Id.
55 Id.
56 Id.
57 26 U.S.C. § 61; IRS Fact Sheet, "De Minimis Fringe Benefits," supra note 40.
58 IRS Memorandum 201622031, supra note 52.
59 IRS Form W-2 (Wage and Tax Statement).
60 ABA Joint Committee on Employee Benefits, meeting with IRS officials, Q/A-2 (May 8–10, 2008), http://www.americanbar.org/content/dam/aba/migrated/2011_build/employee_benefits/irs_treas_2008.authcheckdam.pdf.

Form W-2 reporting responsibilities (in contrast to the general rule that imposes these obligations upon the common law, or "true," employer).[61]

Whether an insurer or other third party constitutes the statutory employer for this purpose is very fact-specific, and generally turns on which entity has "control of the payment" of the taxable reward or incentive (i.e., which party determines when an employee is eligible for the incentive, provides funding for the incentives, etc.).[62] If the third party's role with regard to the incentive is more ministerial and the real decision-maker with regard to who qualifies for the incentive as well as who funds the incentive lies with the employer, then the third party generally would not have any related withholding or reporting obligations. In those cases, the common law employer would have the obligation to comply with the relevant requirements.[63]

Finally, some wellness activities and products, particularly those offered outside the group health plan context, will likely be subject to tax even if the taxpayer uses such services and products to mitigate a specific ailment such as stress or depression. For example, the United States Tax Court ruled, in *Huff v. Commissioner of Internal Revenue*, that the massages, yoga classes, and vitamin supplements that Nancy Huff paid for to alleviate her depressive state did not constitute medical care and were therefore taxable.[64] At the time of these expenditures, Ms. Huff was going through a difficult financial crisis and rather than seeing a psychiatrist, sought to relieve her stress through other means such as massage, yoga, acupuncture, chiropractic treatments, and a change in diet.[65] The Tax Court permitted Ms. Huff to deduct the acupuncture and chiropractic care (as well as traditional medical and dental expenses), but not the massages, yoga, or vitamins and food supplements. The Tax Court found that the massages and yoga were for Ms. Huff's general well-being and were personal within the meaning of IRC § 262 and therefore not deductible under IRC § 213.[66] The

61 IRC § 3401(d).
62 See IRC § 3401(d); 26 CFR § 31.3401(d)-1(f).
63 See IRS Chief Counsel Advice 200415008 (Apr. 9, 2004); PLR 200128018 (July 13, 2001).
64 *Huff v. Comm'r of Internal Revenue*, T.C. Memo 1995-200 (1995).
65 Id.
66 Id.

Tax Court also concluded that Ms. Huff failed to show how her special diet and food supplements were for her medical care and not just random purchases.[67]

Thus, although wellness services and products may serve as alternative methods of addressing specific diseases or ailments, such services and products will be subject to close scrutiny by the IRS. Until there is a widespread paradigm shift toward recognizing the value and validity of alternative wellness therapies, employers and wellness vendors who encourage employee wellness may want to educate employees about the taxable nature of many wellness services and products.

RULE THE RULES

Key Points in Chapter 5

1. Federal individual income taxes fund 46.2 percent of the U.S. government.
2. Tax policy can vary depending on conservative or progressive perspectives.
3. There is a general consensus that tax deductions involving involuntary expenses and intermediate expenses are justifiable.
4. Taxpayers with extraordinary "medical care" expenses, as defined by IRC § 213, in excess of a specified threshold, can deduct these expenses because they are involuntary and intermediate.
5. Only items and services that qualify as medical care (under the IRC definition) are generally deductible from income tax. Hence, employer reimbursement for gym memberships or weight loss programs not tied to treatment of any specific disease would be subject to tax. Reimbursement for smoking cessation classes, high blood pressure screenings, or vaccinations would be excludable because such activities qualify as medical care.

---

67 *Id.*

6. Employers who have onsite fitness facilities generally can exclude the value of employees' access to those facilities from the employees' income and wages if the facility is largely utilized by employees and family members only.

7. Wellness rewards that constitute group health plan premium or cost-sharing reductions, or employer contributions to FSAs, HRAs, or HSAs, may be excluded from an employee's income and wages (and thus exempt from tax) as long as specified non-discrimination rules are followed. It is a good idea to work with your employee benefits attorney to ensure that the requirements of those rules are met.

8. Cash and cash equivalents (such as gift cards) are always taxable income, no matter the amount. Also, in most cases, the employer, not the vendor or other third party, is responsible for reporting the cash reward on the employee's Form W-2.

9. The Personal Health Investment Today (PHIT) Act, if passed by Congress, would amend the IRC to allow a medical care tax deduction up to $1,000 ($2,000 for a joint return) of qualified fitness expenses, including facility memberships.

10. De minimis fringe benefits such as t-shirts, water bottles, inexpensive event tickets, and snack items are excluded from taxable income.

Study Questions

1. Briefly describe the origins of the U.S. income tax.
2. Although taxpayers often have a negative view of federal income taxes, what are some of the social and economic benefits of governmental expenditures?
3. Distinguish involuntary expenses and intermediate expenses with regard to medical care tax deductions.
4. Describe what constitutes "medical care" as defined by IRC § 213.
5. List the workplace wellness incentives that are considered taxable and nontaxable income, and describe why each item is so classified.

6. If passed by Congress, do you believe the Personal Health Investment Today (PHIT) Act would increase physical activity among Americans? Why or why not?
7. Explain why workplace wellness professionals need to seek legal counsel for wellness incentives associated with contributions to FSAs, HRAs, or HSAs.
8. Describe the types of medical care expenses incurred by Nancy Huff in the *Huff v. Commissioner of Internal Revenue* case that the court ruled as taxable and nontaxable deductions. On what basis did the Tax Court make these distinctions?

Key Terms

de minimis fringe benefits

income taxes

intermediate expenses

Internal Revenue Code (IRC) § 213

involuntary expenses

medical care expenses

Personal Health Investment Today (PHIT) Act

tax-deductible wellness benefits

tax deductions

tax policy

6

Are They Qualified to Do That?

Learning Objectives

After reading this chapter, workplace wellness professionals will be able to:

1. Explain the difference between a "qualified" and a "competent" professional.
2. Describe four levels of credentialing: accreditation, licensure, certification, and statutory certification.
3. Distinguish government-regulated and self-regulated professions.
4. Explain the job task analysis (JTA) process and its potential limitations in the development of an accredited certification exam.
5. Describe the steps to obtain licensure for registered dietitians and athletic trainers.
6. List common certifications in the fitness/wellness field and their eligibility requirements.
7. Describe scope of practice from a legal perspective (e.g., how practicing outside one's scope can lead to criminal charges and civil lawsuits).
8. Establish policies and procedures regarding scope of practice for employees to follow.
9. Define *respondeat superior* and explain why employers have a vested interest in hiring only qualified and competent employees.
10. Describe the professional standard of care with regard to three factors: (a) nature of the activity, (b) type of participants, and (c) environmental conditions.
11. Develop risk management strategies to properly hire, train, and supervise employees.
12. Understand various legal issues related to hiring independent contractors and selecting wellness vendors.

You cannot have qualifications without experience; and you cannot have experience without personal interest and bias. That may not be an ideal arrangement; but it is the way the world is built and we must make the best of it.

—George Bernard Shaw, *Dramatic Opinions and Essays* (vol. 1, p. 242)

No letters after your name are ever going to be a total guarantee of competence any more than they are a guarantee against fraud. Improving competence involves continuing professional development .... That is the really crucial thing, not just passing an examination.

—Colette Bowe

Introduction

The healthcare industry, for the most part, is government-regulated, meaning that healthcare professionals must possess a state license in order to practice in a certain profession (e.g., medicine, nursing, physical therapy, etc.). However, the fitness and wellness field is self-regulated through voluntary accreditation and certification programs, meaning that virtually anyone can practice in the field. This creates several challenges for employers that want to hire both qualified and competent staff members to lead their workplace fitness/wellness programs.

There can be a difference between qualified and competent staff members. *Qualified* staff members possess certain educational credentials and *competent* staff members know how to properly carry out their responsibilities: namely, to safely and effectively design/deliver fitness and wellness programs. Therefore, a qualified professional is not necessarily a competent professional. This chapter first covers four types of credentialing and points out the many limitations of voluntary self-regulation. Then scope of practice, which is difficult to define for unlicensed professions, is discussed from a legal context applicable to fitness and wellness professionals. Next, risk management strategies are described to help minimize legal liability related to the hiring, training, and supervision of fitness and wellness employees. The chapter ends by describing important issues related to independent contractors and criteria to consider when selecting wellness vendors.

Types of Credentialing

There are various types of credentialing, as shown in Table 6.1. Credentialing can be government-regulated through licensure or statutory certification, or self-regulated through accreditation or certification. Fitness and wellness professionals do not have to possess any government-regulated credentials, in contrast to professionals in many other allied health areas such as athletic training and dietetics/nutrition, who must possess a state license to practice in most states. The many issues surrounding the credentialing of fitness/wellness professionals have been hot topics for many years—and the issues have still not been resolved. This first section describes the four types of credentialing.

Self-Regulated	Government-Regulated
Accreditation Examples Organizations (e.g., hospitals, universities) Educational programs (e.g., provided by academic institutions or professional organizations) Certification examinations	**Licensure Examples** Individuals: license required to practice (e.g., dietitians, athletic trainers, physical therapists) Organizations: healthcare facilities may need state licensure to operate (e.g., nursing homes, hospitals)
Certification Examples Individuals: certification not required to practice, but employers may demand it Individuals: may be required first in order to obtain a license to practice	**Statutory Certification Examples** Individuals: specific credentials are required to use a certain title (e.g., certified dietitian, certified nutritionist) Organizations: healthcare facilities may have to have state certification to operate (e.g., adult family homes)

Table 6.1   Types of Credentialing

Accreditation

Accreditation can be awarded to (a) organizations and programs, and (b) certification exams. Organizations such as hospitals can receive accreditation through the Joint Commission on Accreditation of Healthcare Organizations (JCAHO, now The Joint Commission), and universities can become accredited through one of six regional accrediting agencies recognized by the United States Department of Education (USDE) and the Council for Higher Education Accreditation (CHEA); for instance, the University of South Florida is accredited through the Southern Association of Colleges and Schools (SACS). Academic programs also can become accredited: for example, athletic training programs through the Commission on Accreditation of Athletic Training Education (CAATE), nutrition/dietetics programs through the Accreditation Council for Education in Nutrition and Dietetics (ACEND), exercise science programs through the Commission on the Accreditation of Allied Health Education Programs (CAAHEP), community health education and public health programs through the Council on Education for Public Health (CEPH), and health promotion/wellness programs through the National Wellness Institute (NWI) Council on Wellness Accreditation and Education (CWAE). To earn accreditation, organizations/programs must meet certain standards established by the accrediting agency. This process is lengthy, complex, and often costly. It usually includes preparation of numerous documents to show that the standards have been met, as well as a site visit by members of the accrediting agency. Once accreditation is awarded, it is often used for marketing and public image purposes to help demonstrate the commitment to quality of the organization/program. Maintaining accreditation or accredited status is an ongoing process; for example, an academic program may have to submit an annual report and pay an annual fee and complete a comprehensive review every 10 years.

Accreditation of certification exams involves a somewhat different process. For example, several fitness and wellness organizations have opted to have their exams accredited by the National Commission for Certifying Agencies (NCCA), including the American College of Sports Medicine (ACSM), the American Council on Exercise (ACE), and the

Cooper Institute. Other organizations, such as the Aerobics and Fitness Association of America (AFAA), have obtained accreditation for their personal trainer and group exercise instructor educational programs through the Distance Education and Training Council (DETC) and accreditation for both their written and practical certification exams through Vital Research.[1] The National Commission on Health Education Credentialing (NCHEC) provides two levels of certification: Certified Health Education Specialist (CHES) and Master Certified Health Education Specialist (MCHES). Both exams are accredited by the NCCA.

Each accrediting agency has certain standards that must be met for the exam to earn accreditation. For example, the NCCA recently adopted 24 standards.[2] Most of the standards deal with "administrative" procedures that the certifying organization must follow to help ensure the integrity and quality of the exam. One important procedure is to conduct a **job task analysis (JTA)**. According to the NCCA,[3] "job/practice analysis must be conducted leading to clearly delineated performance domains and tasks, associated knowledge and/or skills, and ... be used as the basis for developing each type of assessment instrument."[4] The NCCA also states that the "validation of performance domains, tasks, and associated knowledge and/or skills is typically accomplished by conducting a survey of current certificants and/or individuals providing services or performing a job consistent with the purpose of the credential."[5] For example, health and wellness coaches recently completed a JTA that led to 21 tasks listed under 4 performance domains, along with a listing of knowledge and skills necessary for competent and effective performance of health and wellness coaches.[6]

1 David L. Herbert and Marcia M. Ditmyer, "Isn't It Time for Education & Evaluation of Hands-On Competence in Personal Training?," *American Fitness* 32, no. 4 (July/August 2014): 38–41.
2 Institute for Credentialing Excellence, "NCCA Accreditation" (2016), http://www.credentialingexcellence .org/p/cm/ld/fid=66.
3 National Commission for Certifying Agencies and National Organization for Competency Assurance, *Standards for the Accreditation of Certification Programs* (2004).
4 *Id*. at 10.
5 *Id*.
6 Meg Jordan, Ruth Q. Wolever, Karen Lawson, and Margaret Moore, "National Training and Education Standards for Health and Wellness Coaching: The Path to National Certification," *Global Advances in Health and Medicine* 4, no. 3 (May 2015): 46–56.

The next step is to use this information to develop a national certification exam that is accredited. Therefore, the quality of the JTA is essential, because the information that is gathered and summarized is used to develop certain outcomes such as the certification exam. See Figure 6.1 for a typical model and Figure 6.2 for a professional model.

Figure 6.1   Outcomes of a Job Task Analysis: Typical Model

*No formal education and practical skills training required prior to taking certification exams.

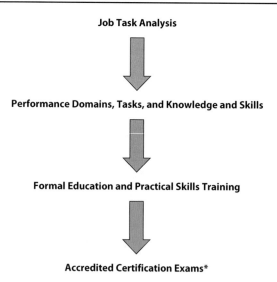

Figure 6.2   Outcomes of a Job Task Analysis: Professional Model

*Formal education and practical skills training are required prior to taking certification exams, as in almost all other professions.

If the JTA process is invalid, the resulting exam may not really adequately measure important competencies needed to safely and effectively perform a job. As individuals complete a JTA survey that includes a listing of job tasks, they give a rating as to how important that task is and how frequently they perform that task. A couple of concerns can arise that can affect the validity of the process as these tasks are rated: (a) Are the persons doing the rating qualified to perform the task (what credentials do they have to perform such a task)?, and (b) do they fully understand what is meant by each task? For example, if personal fitness trainers are asked to rate a task such as "the personal fitness trainer conducts fitness assessments," a concern may be that they are not qualified to perform that task in the first place. Perhaps they should first be asked if they have the credentials (e.g., formal education/training) to perform such a task before rating its importance and frequency, and if so, what those credentials are. If not, they may be rating a task they really should not be performing (or may not know much about), which could lead to a validation problem with the JTA process and its outcomes. In addition, the JTA survey may include task statements that are not fully understood by the respondent. For example, a JTA recently completed by health and wellness coaches led to the following tasks being listed under Domain IV: "Health and wellness coaches practice in accordance with (a) applicable laws and regulations" and (b) "accepted professional standards and within the limits of their scope of practice."[7] Just by virtue of these tasks being listed in the JTA survey, it is likely that they would be rated high regarding importance and frequency. However, it also is likely that most health and wellness professionals are not aware of all the applicable laws and regulations (not to mention how to integrate compliance with those laws and regulations into their practice), and that they do not fully understand the scope of practice from a standard of care and legal perspective (as described later). If the respondents do not fully understand each task and all it entails prior to giving it a rating, those inadequacies could compromise the JTA process and the outcomes that build upon it, such as the certification exam.

---

7 *Id.* at 52.

To help address these concerns, validation of the JTA survey is often done. For the JTA completed by health and wellness coaches,[8] 38 coaches and 15 subject matter experts were involved in the development and validation of the survey items (tasks) before it was sent out to 4,026 health and wellness coaches. It could be that those involved in this validation process (and similar validation processes for other JTA surveys) have credentials (e.g., formal education and training) and thus understand the task statements they developed for a JTA survey. However, that might not be the case for the individuals who complete a JTA survey, because no educational requirements are necessary for those practicing in the fitness and wellness field. Therefore, it is easy to understand how this could taint the JTA process and its outcomes, and produce such things as a certification exam that does not adequately measure important knowledge and skills. To the credit of the National Consortium for Credentialing Health and Wellness Coaches (NCCHWC), the purpose of its JTA was not merely to lead to an accredited certification exam (scheduled to begin in 2017[9]), as is the case with most fitness/wellness accredited certification exams. Rather, the NCCHWC's major purpose was to produce accredited educational programs that must be completed by an individual before he or she can be eligible to sit for the national certification exam. The accredited educational programs will have to meet certain standards (e.g., cover the domains and tasks resulting from the JTA) and include formal education and practical skills training. This credentialing model is similar to licensing models used in the allied health field, as described later.

Understanding the Limitations of Accredited Certification Exams

If the JTA process (or other subsequent steps in the preparation of the exam) is invalid, fitness/wellness professionals may be led into falsely believing that they are qualified and competent to perform a job when they pass an accredited written exam. Many employers require that their fitness/wellness staff members have accredited certifications (e.g., NCCA,

---

8 *Id.*
9 National Consortium for Credentialing Health & Wellness Coaches, "News Release: Historic Agreement in Place to Nationally Certify Health & Wellness Coaches," http://www.ncchwc.org/wp-content/uploads/2015/03/5-25-2016-NCCHWC-NBME-Press-Release-May-25.pdf.

or those recognized by the USDE and/or the CHEA). If this is the only qualification needed, employers may also believe, in error, that these staff members are qualified and competent upon hiring. This limitation is best expressed by a well-known expert witness, Dr. Anthony Abbott, who has taken more than 30 certification exams in the fitness field, with most of them being accredited exams.[10] He states that "the concept of accreditation has lost most of its value" because, "although accredited exams are testing appropriate content areas, they are posing poorly written and simplistic questions"; "without using well-constructed and challenging application and analysis questions, exams are unable to probe the depth of a trainer's knowledge base."[11]

Another major limitation of accredited certification exams is that in most instances, no formal education or practical experience is needed to be eligible to sit for (take) the exam, as shown in Figure 6.1. For example, none of the 24 NCCA standards require an individual to have any formal coursework or practical work experience prior to sitting for the exam. Although an academic degree may be required by the certifying organization to be eligible to sit for its accredited exam, the majority of certifications in the fitness/wellness field do not require a college degree, only a high school diploma (see the subsection on "Certification").

To prepare for an accredited certification exam, candidates often take an online self-study course, attend a one- to two-day workshop, or read recommended resources. This failure to require any formal education (e.g., academic coursework) or practical experience before entering the field has been a concern for some time, and many are questioning if the field is regressing when it comes to preparing qualified and competent professionals and if the self-regulated approach is working. When certifications first became available back in the late 1970s and 1980s, a candidate first had to pass a written exam and then pass a practical exam; all of the ACSM certifications at that time required both a written and practical exam, but now none of them do. As the number of professional fitness organizations increased tremendously in the 1980s and 1990s, so did the number of

---

10 Anthony A. Abbott, "Fitness Professionals: Certified, Qualified and Justified," *The Exercise Standards and Malpractice Rep.* 23, no. 2 (March 2009): 17, 20–22.
11 *Id.* at 21.

certifications. Many of these organizations realized that they can make a lot more money with written-only certification exams than with having both written and practical exams. Some of these organizations have stated that adding a practical exam would be too costly, create a burden for candidates, and could not be designed to be fair and unbiased.[12]

A written-only exam cannot adequately measure important practical skills necessary to safely perform the job of a fitness professional (e.g., taking blood pressures, doing fitness testing, giving proper instruction, and designing/delivering a program that incorporates basic principles of safe exercise). As described in Chapter 1, if a fitness or wellness professional's conduct (actions/behaviors) causes harm, he or she can be found liable for negligence. Thus, teaching and evaluation of practical skills are essential to include in a formal education program to help minimize injuries and subsequent litigation. This concern regarding the lack of practical training is described by Herbert and Ditmeyer.[13] They discuss the rise in fitness-related injuries (see the data in Table 6.2) to help demonstrate that accredited written-only exams are not leading to fewer injuries, explain why practical testing should be a requirement for certification from a consumer safety perspective, and argue that virtually all other healthcare professionals are required to complete formal education (including practical skills training)

Year	Number of Exercise and Exercise Equipment Injuries*
2009	349,543
2010	382,970
2011	410,024
2012	459,978
2013	472,212 (35 percent increase since 2009)

Table 6.2   Exercise and Exercise Equipment Injuries, 2009–2013

* The total number of injuries presented in the table reflects estimates based on data obtained from U.S. hospital emergency departments across the country through the National Electronic Surveillance System (NEISS); https://www.cpsc.gov/research--statistics/neiss-injury-data.

---

12 Herbert and Ditmyer, "Isn't It Time for Education & Evaluation of Hands-On Competence in Personal Training?," at 38–41.
13 *Id.*

prior to sitting for a national certification exam. They call for dual accreditation, meaning that individuals should pass accredited practical and written exams to earn certification, but first should complete an accredited educational program that includes practical skills training in order to be eligible to sit for the exam; in short, they should follow the professional model as shown in Figure 6.2.

Licensure

Almost all allied health professionals must have a license to practice in their field. **Licensure** is decided by state governments, not by the federal government. Therefore, licensure requirements can vary from state to state. If a person moves from one state to another that requires licensure, he or she will need to obtain a license in the new state before practicing in the field. This might involve obtaining a license in the first place. For example, some states, such as Arizona, Colorado, Michigan, and New Jersey, do not require a license to practice as a dietitian/nutritionist.[14] In these states anyone, including individuals with no educational credentials, can practice as a dietician/nutritionist. A dietitian/nutritionist who has practiced in one of these states and then moves to another state that requires licensure will first need to meet the state licensure requirements before being allowed to practice (e.g., obtaining educational credentials, passing a qualifying exam). Thirty-six states require licensure to practice dietetics/nutrition.[15] The licensure requirements for registered dietitians (RDs), or registered dietitian nutritionists (RDNs), are provided in Table 6.3. The licensure requirements for athletic trainers follow a similar model. First, individuals must complete an academic program that is accredited by the Commission on Accreditation of Athletic Training Education that then qualifies them to sit for the Board of Certification (BOC) examination for athletic trainers. Upon successful completion of this national certification examination, the professional earns the title of *certified athletic trainer.* This certification is the qualification needed for

1. Complete the minimum of a baccalaureate degree from a U.S. regionally accredited college or university or foreign equivalent.
2. Complete an accredited didactic program in dietetics (accredited by the Accreditation Council for Education in Nutrition and Dietetics).
3. Complete an ACEND-accredited dietetic internship (DI) program that includes at least 1,200 hours of supervised practice experience.
4. Successfully complete the Registration Examination for Dietitians (eligible to take exam after successful completion of academic and supervised practice requirements).

Table 6.3   Requirements for Registered Dietitian Nutritionists (RDNs)

Source: Commission on Dietetic Registration of the Academy of Nutrition and Dietetics; https://www .cdrnet.org.

licensure in most states.[16] Once they obtain a license to practice in a given state, licensed professionals need to keep their licenses current by meeting certain requirements (e.g., continuing education) for renewal as specified in that state's statutes.

As demonstrated in these models, licensure prevents unqualified individuals from practicing in a certain profession. It helps ensure that the public is receiving quality (safe and effective) services from individuals who meet minimum educational requirements. Because certain educational requirements are needed to qualify for licensure, it raises the bar from certifications, which may not require any educational requirements, which is the case for most certifications in the fitness field (as described later).

When preparing a proposed licensure bill, several factors are considered, such as (a) qualifications for licensure and renewal, (b) definition of the scope of practice distinguishing this profession from other similar professions, (c) qualifications of the members of the licensing board and their powers/duties, and (d) criminal penalties for violations of the licensing statutes. In addition, other issues must be taken into consideration when licensure legislation is proposed for any profession. For example, is there a need for government regulation? In July 2015, the White House released a publication entitled *Occupational Licensing: A Framework*

---

16 Board of Certification for the Athletic Trainer, "State Regulation," http://www.bocatc.org/index.php/ state-regulation.

Ensure That Licensing Restrictions Are Closely Targeted to Protecting Public Health and Safety, and Are Not Overly Broad or Burdensome

1. In cases where public health and safety concerns are mild, consider using alternative systems that are less restrictive than licensing, such as voluntary state certification ("right-to-title") or registration (filing basic information with a state registry).
2. Make sure that substantive requirements of licensing (e.g., education and experience requirements) are closely tied to public health and safety concerns.
3. Minimize procedural burdens of acquiring a license, in terms of fees, complexity of requirements, processing time, and paperwork.

Facilitate a Careful Consideration of the Costs and Benefits of Licensure

1. Carry out comprehensive cost-benefit assessments of licensing laws through both sunrise and regular sunset reviews.

Work to Reduce Licensing's Barriers to Mobility

1. Harmonize licensing requirements to the maximum extent possible across states.
2. Form interstate compacts that make it easier for licensed workers to practice and relocate across state lines, while also enabling state regulators to share practitioners' performance histories.

Table 6.4   Licensing Best Practices (partial)*

*Adapted from *Occupational Licensing: A Framework for Policy Makers* (2015): 42–43, https://www .whitehouse.gov/sites/default/files/docs/licensing_report_final_nonembargo.pdf.

for Policy Makers. See Table 6.4 for a partial listing of licensing best practices, provided in this publication, to consider when establishing state licensure. Many professionals in the field would agree that item #2 in Table 6.4 related to health and safety under the first category would apply to the fitness field, especially given the continued increase of injuries and subsequent litigation in the fitness field, which are often due to the improper design and delivery of exercise programs by unqualified and incompetent fitness practitioners.[17] Well-known legal experts in the fitness field have stated that improper instruction is one of the most common allegations of negligence.[18] Many believe that licensure for fitness professionals is the only remedy to truly protect the public, because the certification-only credential has proven to be inadequate.

17 JoAnn Eickhoff-Shemek, David L. Herbert, and Daniel P. Connaughton, *Risk Management for Health/Fitness Professionals: Legal Issues and Strategies* (Baltimore MD: Lippincott Williams & Wilkins, 2009).
18 Betty van der Smissen, *Legal Liability and Risk Management for Public and Private Entities,* vol. 2 (Cincinnati, OH: Anderson, 1990); Harvey C. Voris and Marc Rabinoff, "When Is a Standard of Care Not a Standard of Care?," *The Exercise Standards and Malpractice Rep.* 25, no. 2 (March 2011): 20–21.

The Licensure Debate

Licensure does not appear to be a hot issue in the health education, health promotion, or wellness fields, although it is in the fitness field. The risk of personal injury to participants in health education programs such as stress management or smoking cessation, or to those who participate in health assessments and biometric screenings, is low. Therefore, there have been no efforts to license health and wellness professionals. However, legislative bills to license personal fitness trainers and group exercise leaders have been proposed in several states. Those proposing these licensing bills believe that the number of injuries (and subsequent litigation) could be reduced by raising the bar for those who want to practice in the field, as licensure would require certain educational credentials. However, none of these proposed state licensing bills have passed into law. Washington, D.C., did pass a law to regulate personal trainers in 2014, but then repealed it before it went into effect.[19]

Licensure for exercise professionals is required in only one state, Louisiana, but only for clinical exercise physiologists who work in a clinical setting under a physician.[20] This law went into effect on January 1, 1996. It was believed that other states would follow suit to license clinical exercise physiologists who work in clinical settings alongside other licensed professionals, but this has not been the case. For example, Massachusetts proposed a similar bill, but it was met with strong opposition from both outside the field (American Physical Therapy Association of Massachusetts) and inside the field (American Society of Exercise Physiologists), albeit for different reasons.[21]

Proposed licensure bills for personal trainers and group exercise leaders start out with good intentions. For example, the initial New Jersey proposed bill required an associate's degree in the health and fitness field or 200 classroom hours, at least 50 hours of an internship, and passage of an examination administered and approved by the state licensing board.[22]

19 Emily Hull, "D.C. Delays Personal Trainer Legislation," *Washington, D.C. News*, September 28, 2015, http://dc.suntimes.com/dc-news/7/82/243111/d-c-delays-personal-trainer-legislation.
20 La. Stat. Ann. 37:3422 (1996).
21 JoAnn M. Eickhoff-Shemek and David L. Herbert, "Is Licensure in Your Future? Issues to Consider—Part 2," *ACSM's Health & Fitness Journal* 12, no. 1 (January/February, 2008): 36–38.
22 David L. Herbert, "New Jersey Reintroduces Personal Trainer Legislation," *The Exercise Standards and Malpractice Rep.* 24, no. 3 (May 2010): 37–41.

Later, when the bill was reintroduced, a new section was added that would allow someone to qualify for a license that did not meet the initial educational requirements, but only possessed an NCCA-accredited certification. Again, the NCCA does not require any educational credentials to be eligible to sit for a certification examination. If proposed licensure bills water down the credentials to obtain a license (e.g., do not require any formal education, only NCCA-accredited certification), it will not raise the bar for entry into the field. There will be virtually no distinction between self-regulation through certification and government regulation through licensure.

There is often a strong and effective lobbying effort to oppose licensure bills that require formal education and practical experience, often mounted by organizations that make a lot of money from certifications (and their continuing education programs that are required for individuals to keep the certifications current) or by the health club industry, which believes that licensure will drive up operating costs and negatively affect their bottom line. For example, one nonprofit certifying organization that provides many different fitness certifications reported its revenue (certification and continuing education income) to be more than $15 million in 2014, with several of its top executives making more than $300,000 in annual salaries.[23] Some individuals argue that the organizations that oppose licensure are more concerned with their profits than with the safety of the public. These same individuals also argue that many occupations, that pose much less risk of personal injury to the consumer than those leading exercise programs, require formal education and practical experience to be eligible to obtain a license to practice (e.g., hair stylists/barbers and massage therapists). It is predicted that licensure will continue to be a hot topic in the fitness field, especially as injuries and litigation continue to increase. For more information on licensure issues in the fitness field, see the three-part article entitled "Is Licensure in Your Future? Issues to Consider."[24]

---

23 For salary ranges, *see* GuideStar, http://www.guidestar.org.
24 Eickhoff-Shemek and Herbert, "Is Licensure in Your Future? Issues to Consider—Part 1," *ACSM's Health & Fitness Journal* 11(5): 35–37 (September/October 2007); Eickhoff-Shemek and Herbert, "Is Licensure in Your Future? Issues to Consider—Part 2," *ACSM's Health & Fitness Journal* 12, no. 1 (January/February, 2008): 36–38; JoAnn Eickhoff-Shemek and David L. Herbert, "Is Licensure in Your Future? Issues to Consider—Part 3," *ACSM's Health & Fitness Journal* 12, no. 3 (May/June 2008): 36–38.

Certification

In the early days, earning a **certification** that required passing both written and practical exams enhanced the credibility and marketability of fitness/wellness professionals. Employers could be somewhat confident that these certified candidates possessed certain knowledge and skills that would enable them to safely and effectively perform the job. However, that is no longer the case, given the tremendous growth of certifications over the past several years that require only passage of a written examination. Back in 2004, it was reported that there were as many as 250 fitness certifications offered by 75 organizations.[25] Since then, the number of organizations and certifications has continued to grow, especially in the area of specialty certifications such as senior fitness, mind/body, nutrition/weight management, functional training, health/wellness coaching, and the like. Given that there is no government regulation, anyone can form an organization and start offering certifications, which can reap large profits for the organization. As stated earlier, many believe that much of the fitness/wellness certification business is profit-driven rather than quality-driven, especially when the certifying organizations make it easy for someone to earn a certification, even an accredited one. Additional profits are made when certified individuals need to submit continuing education credits or units to the certifying organization to keep their certifications current.

Until leading organizations in the field work together toward licensure that requires certain educational credentials, or begin requiring formal education and practical experience as qualifications to sit for a certification examination, the hiring dilemma for employers will continue. Self-regulation could still be considered a viable option to advance the profession and protect the public if all certifying organizations would implement a model like the one being adopted by NCCHWC (described earlier) for health and wellness coaches. Because this is unlikely, though, employers need to understand that just because someone possesses a fitness or wellness certification—even an accredited one—the employers cannot assume that the individual is qualified (possesses certain educational credentials) and competent (knows how to safely and effectively perform the job). Employers must fully understand the

25 Andrew Cohen, "It's Getting Personal," *Athletic Business* (July, 2004): 52–54, 56, 58, 60.

qualifications (or lack of) that are required to sit for various certification exams; see Table 6.5 for the prerequisites needed for certain certifications in the field. This table does not include requirements for any of the numerous specialty certifications. Employers need to investigate the certifications that candidates indicate they possess on their résumés to determine the quality of those certifications. It is also recommended that they follow the strategies described in the section on "Risk Management Strategies" when hiring, training, and supervising fitness/wellness staff members.

Most full-time jobs in workplace wellness (e.g., managers and program coordinators) require at least an undergraduate degree and maybe a graduate degree in the field (e.g., exercise science, health education, public health) or outside the field (e.g., nursing, business administration, human resources). They also may require professional certifications in which an academic degree is needed such as Exercise Physiologist-Certified (EP-C) or the Certified Health Education Specialist (CHES) as shown in Table 6.5. It is best for the workplace wellness leadership team

Professional Certifications in Exercise and Health Education: Require an Academic Degree
ACSM—Exercise Physiologist (EP-C), formerly called Health Fitness Specialist Bachelor's degree in exercise science, exercise physiology, or kinesiology from a regionally accredited university or college; must include coursework that covers certain content Adult CPR/AED certification
NCHEC—Certified Health Education Specialist (CHES) Bachelor's degree with a major in health education (e.g., Health Education, Community Health Education, Public Health Education, School Health Education) OR Bachelor's degree with 25 semester hours or 37 quarter hours of coursework (with a grade "C" or better) with specific preparation addressing the Seven Areas of Responsibility and Competency for Health Educators

ACSM—Clinical Exercise Physiologist (CEP)
Bachelor's degree in exercise science, exercise physiology, or kinesiology from a regionally accredited university or college
BLS/ACLS or CPR for the "Professional Rescuer" certification
Practical experience in a clinical exercise program
    400 hours in a CAAHEP-accredited program
    500 hours in a non-CAAHEP-accredited program

Table 6.5   Examples of Fitness and Wellness Certifications and Their Prerequisites*

Practitioner Certifications: Do Not Require an Academic Degree or Coursework
ACSM—Personal Trainer and Group Exercise Instructor 18 years of age High school diploma or equivalent Adult CPR/AED certification
American Council on Exercise (ACE)—Personal Trainer and Group Fitness Instructor 18 years of age High school diploma or equivalent Adult CPR/AED certification
Certifications in Workplace Wellness
National Wellness Institute (NWI)—Certified Workplace Wellness Specialist (CWWS) Participation in a two-day, in-person course and passage of an online exam within two weeks of the training (no degree requirements specified on website)
Wellness Councils of America (WELCOA)—WELCOA Certified Completion of online training of approximately six hours (no degree requirements specified on website)
Chapman Institute WellCert Program—Certified Wellness Program Coordinator (CWPC) Completion of approximately two days of training, delivered online or onsite (no degree requirements specified on website)

Table 6.5 *(continued)*

*For more information about these certifications, as well as other certifications offered by these organizations, see their websites:
- ACE: http://www.acefitness.org/fitness-certifications
- ACSM: http://www.acsm.org/certification
- Chapman Institute: https://chapmaninstitute.com/courses/certification
- NCHEC: http://www.nchec.org/overview
- NWI: http://www.nationalwellness.org/?page=WorksiteWellnessCert
- WELCOA: https://www.welcoa.org/training/certification-schedule

to have varied backgrounds and expertise, given that wellness programs offered to employees are comprehensive in nature. For example, the exercise professional should have a great deal of knowledge regarding the many professional standards, guidelines, and position papers that need to be addressed in the design and delivery of safe/effective exercise programs and the health education professional should have a great deal of knowledge regarding the professional standards and methods for designing and delivering all types of quality health education programs.

As noted, individuals who need to obtain a license to practice as dietitians and athletic trainers must first complete an academic program that is accredited by ACEND and CAATE, respectively, before they are eligible to sit for the national certification/registration examinations. Accreditation of academic programs helps ensure that some level of consistency exists with regard to the knowledge and skills taught across all programs. Graduating from an accredited academic program is not required for fitness/health education/wellness professionals to obtain their certifications or to begin practicing in the field. Therefore, employers should recognize that these academic programs can vary in terms of the quality of education provided and the knowledge/skills taught and evaluated. Currently, accreditation is voluntary through CAAHEP (exercise science), CEPH (community health education/public health), and NWI CWAE (health promotion/wellness). As the profession evolves, these academic programs may be required to become accredited. Right now, it is something that academic programs should seriously consider in order to be competitive and nationally recognized as quality programs.

Statutory Certification

In lieu of licensure, some states have opted for **statutory certification,** which allows only professionals with specific credentials to use certain titles as stated in the statute. For example, 10 states have opted for statutory certification (or title protection) rather than licensure for nutrition and dietetics professionals.[26] Only those professionals who possess the credentialing requirements specified in the statute (e.g., the RDN credential) can use certain titles such as "certified dietitian" or "certified nutritionist." All other individuals, no matter what credentials they have or do not have, can practice as dietitians or nutritionists in these states, but they must use some other title. Therefore, fitness/wellness professionals can practice as dietitians/nutritionists in these states, but need to be sure they are not using any protected titles. There are only four states that have no government regulation for the practice of dietetics/

---

26 State Licensure. Commission on Dietetic Registration—the credentialing agency of the Academy of Nutrition and Dietetics. Available at: https://www.cdrnet.org/vault/2459/web/files/Licensurelawsregulations.pdf.

nutrition—Arizona, Colorado, Michigan, and New Jersey—and in these states anyone can practice dietetics/nutrition and call themselves whatever they want. However, it will be important to understand the potential legal consequences for practicing in this area without adequate education and training, such as civil claims (discussed later) that can be brought if anyone is harmed by following the nutritional advice that is provided. Statutory certification could be an option for the fitness profession to consider, perhaps as a starting point that might gain more support than licensure and help address some of the credentialing issues that exist.

Scope of Practice: The Legal Context

The following definition of **scope of practice** is provided by the Federation of State Medical Boards:

> Scope of practice is defined as the activities that an individual health care practitioner is permitted to perform within a specific profession. Those activities should be based on appropriate education, training, and experience. Scope of practice is established by the practice act of the specific practitioner's board, and the rules adopted pursuant that act.[27]

This description is applicable to "licensed" healthcare occupations: The scope of practice is specified in the licensing statutes. But how is "scope of practice" defined for professionals who are not licensed, such as the fitness and wellness professionals? Some certifying organizations provide a "scope of practice" description of sorts for their various levels of certification. It is likely that these are derived from the job task analyses (JTAs) discussed earlier. However, these can vary among organizations even for the same type of job (see the example for personal trainers

---

27 Federation of State Medical Boards, *Assessing Scope of Practice in Health Care Delivery: Critical Questions in Assuring Public Access and Safety* (2005), https://www.fsmb.org/Media/Default/PDF/FSMB/Advocacy/2005_grpol_scope_of_practice.pdf.

in the sidebar). Notice that the NSCA description includes "assess ... health and fitness needs" and the ACSM description does not.

Scope of Practice Descriptions for the Certified Personal Trainer

1. National Strength and Conditioning Association (NSCA)

NSCA-Certified Personal Trainers (NSCA-CPT®) are health/fitness professionals who, using an individualized approach, assess, motivate, educate, and train clients regarding their personal health and fitness needs.

A personal training certification will help to design safe and effective exercise programs, provide the guidance to help clients achieve their personal health/fitness goals, and respond appropriately in emergency situations.

Recognizing their own area of expertise, a personal trainer will refer clients to other healthcare professionals when appropriate.[28]

2. American College of Sports Medicine (ACSM)

ACSM Certified Personal Trainers® are fitness professionals who develop and implement personalized exercise programs for individuals across a diverse set of health and fitness backgrounds, from professional athletes to individuals only recently cleared to exercise.

Becoming an ACSM CPT means that you'll have the practical and scientific knowledge to work in a variety of facilities, including health clubs, gyms, university, corporate, and community or public fitness centers, and positions ranging from freelance to full-time and beyond. ACSM Certified Personal Trainers® are respected across the industry as high-achieving, knowledgeable professionals who represent the gold standard of health fitness certifications, no matter where their career takes them.

ACSM Certified Personal Trainers® are motivated fitness leaders, backed by knowledge and abilities that set the standard for the industry.[29]

---

28 National Strength and Conditioning Association, "NSCA-Certified Personal Trainer® (NSCA-CPT®)," https://www.nsca.com/Certification/CPT.
29 American College of Sports Medicine, "ACSM Certified Personal Trainer®," http://certification.acsm .org/acsm-certified-personal-trainer.

To fully understand scope of practice, the concept must be explained from a legal context, not just descriptions professional organizations might provide on their websites. In fact, it is highly unlikely that courts will consider scope of practice descriptions provided by professional organizations when analyzing scope of practice violations. Courts will determine scope of practice violations in two ways: (a) criminal charges due to crossing over the line into a licensed practice, and (b) civil claims such as negligent conduct (resulting in harm to someone) due to practicing outside one's credentials (e.g., education, training, and experience). Each of these is described using legal cases.

Criminal Charges

In their practice, fitness and wellness professionals could cross over into licensed professions such as medicine (e.g., diagnosing and treating a medical condition), physical therapy, athletic training, and others. However, the biggest concern is in the areas of nutrition/dietetics. Fitness and wellness professionals often have (a) received some nutrition education in their academic programs, (b) one or more of the many available nutrition certifications, or (c) even a degree in nutrition. But none of these qualifications allows one to practice dietetics/nutrition in any of the 36 states that require a license to practice.

Another concern, especially for personal trainers and health/wellness coaches, is crossing over into the licensed practice of counseling. Sometimes clients will share their personal problems (e.g., financial, drugs/alcohol, relationships, etc.) with their trainers/coaches and it will be important for these trainers/coaches to refer such clients to a licensed professional counselor when appropriate. In a worksite setting, this referral can be done through the company's employee assistance program (EAP). If the company does not have an EAP, clients can be referred to a licensed professional counselor in the community. Licensed professional counselors first complete a qualifying master's degree and then need to obtain a passing score on the National

Counselor Examination for Licensure and Certification (NCE), which is the credential needed for licensure.[30] The National Board of Certified Counselors (NBCC) administers the licensure examinations in all 50 U.S. states.

Regarding referrals, it is important for all professionals who make referrals to another professional to be sure that they are referring their clients/patients only to properly credentialed (i.e., qualified and competent) professionals. If the referral is made to someone who does not have the proper credentials and then that individual gives instructions or advice that harms the client/patient, the referring professional can potentially be held liable for the harm and named as a co-defendant in a negligence lawsuit. The plaintiff can claim that he or she relied on the referral and thus the one making the referral was, in part, the cause of the plaintiff's harm.

Penalties for violating state licensing statutes are specified in the statute. See the sidebar for the types of penalties that someone can face who has crossed over the line into a licensed practice. To prevent these types of penalties, fitness and wellness professionals need to be aware of how *scope of practice* is defined in applicable state statutes. For example, if fitness and wellness professionals provide "individualized" nutrition advice and services (e.g., nutrition assessments, nutrition counseling), they would likely be considered to be practicing dietetics without a license. However, if they stick to providing "general" nutrition education, their actions likely will not constitute the practice of dietetics. Ohio statutes provide guidance to help understand the distinction between what licensed dietitians do in their practice and what nonlicensed (unlicensed) individuals can do to prevent being exposed to any criminal penalties. See the sidebar.

---

30 National Board of Certified Counselors, "Apply for Certification," http://nbcc.org/Certification/ApplyForCertification.

Sample Penalties for Violating State Licensing Statutes

These examples are based on Florida's law, "Unlicensed practice of a health care profession," Fla. Stat. § 456.065.

- **A cease–and–desist notice**: Issued to any person violating this statute. The violation can result in a fine between $500 and $5,000. Each day the unlicensed practice continues after the notice, a separate violation can be charged.
- **3rd-degree felony**: Minimum penalty—Fine of $1,000 and mandatory period of incarceration of 1 year.
- **2nd-degree felony**: Practice results in serious bodily injury; minimum penalty same as 3rd-degree felony.
- **1st-degree misdemeanor**: Minimum penalty is a fine of $500 and imprisonment for 30 days.

Practice of Dietetics and General Non-Medical Nutrition Information
Practice of Dietetics*—restricted to those with a license

- Nutritional assessment to determine nutritional needs and to recommend appropriate nutritional intake, including enteral and parenteral nutrition
- Nutritional counseling or education as components of preventive, curative, and restorative health care
- Development, administration, evaluation, and consultation regarding nutritional care standards
* Dietetics. Ohio Rev. Code Ann. § 4759-01 (2013); http://codes.ohio. gov/orc/4759.

General Non-Medical Nutrition Information**—not restricted

Providing information on the following:
- Principles of good nutrition and food preparation;
- Food to be included in the normal daily diet;
- The essential nutrients needed by the body;
- Recommended amounts of the essential nutrients;
- The actions of nutrients on the body;
- The effects of deficiencies or excesses of nutrients; or
- Food and supplements that are good sources of essential nutrients
** Dietetics. Ohio Rev. Code Ann. § 4759-2-01(M) 2009; http://www.dietetics.ohio.gov/bulletins/bulletin8.pdf.

The practice-of-dietetics statute featured in the sidebar became relevant in *Ohio Board of Dietetics v. Brown*.[31] In that case, the defendant, who represented himself as a nutritionist, was charged with practicing

31 *Ohio Bd. of Dietetics v. Brown*, 83 Ohio App. 3d 242 (Ohio Ct. App. 1993).

dietetics as defined by the Ohio statute (Ohio Rev. Code § 4759.01). In his practice, he performed nutritional assessments, recommended nutritional supplements, and engaged in nutritional counseling specifically for the purpose of treating certain complaints and ailments of his clients. After determining that the defendant was practicing dietetics as defined in the scope of practice in the Ohio statute, the appellate court granted the request from the Ohio Board of Dietetics for an injunction. (An *injunction* is similar to a cease-and-desist notice, referred to in the Florida statute sidebar.) Even though the defendant in this case called himself a nutritionist (not a registered dietitian), it made no difference to the court's ruling. Courts may analyze the conduct (i.e., the behavior and/or actions) of the defendant as it did in this case to determine if there was a violation of state licensing statutes.

Given that fitness and wellness professionals often have some level of nutrition education, they may believe that they can provide individualized nutrition assessments, counseling, and the like—which they could, but only in the four states that have no licensure or in the 10 states that have statutory certification. Of course, in those 10 states, they would need to be sure to avoid using any protected titles as specified in the statute. An excellent case to demonstrate this is the *Liz Lipski* case.[32] At the time this case was brought, Dr. Lipski possessed several nutrition certifications (e.g., Certified Clinical Nutrition and Certified Nutrition Specialist), as well as a doctoral degree in clinical nutrition. She was practicing nutrition in the state of North Carolina until the North Carolina Board of Dietetics/Nutrition denied her the right to continue her practice and recommended that she return to college to complete the requirements to become a Registered Dietitian. Instead, she moved to Maryland to serve as the "Academic Director of Nutrition and Integrative Health Programs" at Maryland University of Integrative Health.[33] Maryland also requires a license to practice dietetics/nutrition, but she could practice in neighboring Virginia as long as she did not use a title that is protected by Virginia's statutory certification statute.

---

32 Liz Lipski, "Stories from the Field," Center for Nutrition Advocacy, http://nutritionadvocacy.org/stories/liz-lipski.
33 "Dr. Liz Lipski," http://lizlipski.com.

The *Cooksey v. Futrell*[34] case, which was also brought in North Carolina, is relevant for fitness and wellness professionals who provide nutrition education on a website or by email. An administrative code in North Carolina[35] states: "Any person, whether residing in this state or not, who by use of electronic or other medium performs any of the acts described as the practice of dietetics/nutrition, but is not licensed ... shall be deemed by the [state] Board as being engaged in the practice of dietetics/nutrition and subject to the enforcement provisions available to the Board."[36] Cooksey started a website, called "Diabetes Warrior," that provided various types of nutrition information, including a fee-based "Diabetes Support Life-Coaching" service in which Cooksey charged a fee for providing individualized dietary advice. Once informed of this website, the executive director of the North Carolina Board of Dietetics/Nutrition informed him that his website—the part regarding the Diabetes Support Life-Coaching services—had to be taken down because these services constituted practicing dietetics without a license. The director stated: "You should not be addressing diabetic's [sic] specific questions. You are no longer just providing information when you do this, you are assessing and counseling, both of which require a license."[37] An important lesson from this case is that fitness and wellness professionals who intend to give nutrition information to clients via a website or email should first seek legal counsel before providing these types of services. If they do not, they run the risk of violating state licensing laws and/or administrative codes.

Civil Claims—Negligence

In the criminal cases just described, the issues dealt with conduct that violated state licensing statutes, not any conduct that caused harm. If individuals are harmed (physically or emotionally) by following the instructions/advice given to them by a fitness/wellness professional, they can bring various civil claims, including for negligence and gross negligence, against the professional and his or her employer. As described in

---

34 *Cooksey v. Futrell*, 721 F.3d 226 (4th Cir. 2013).
35 N.C. Admin. Code § 17.0403 (2006), "Electronic Practice."
36 *Id*. at 231.
37 *Id*. at 232.

Chapter 1, there is a legal principle called ***respondeat superior*** under which employers can be held liable for the negligent acts of their employees; this is a form of strict liability. Therefore, employers have a vested interest in properly hiring, training, and supervising their employees. Because of the many unresolved credentialing issues (addressed earlier in this chapter), this becomes quite challenging for employers who hire staff members to lead fitness/wellness programs for their employees. To help address this challenge, some companies opt to have the employee wellness program managed by a third party: a management company that handles the hiring, training, and supervision of staff members as well as the overall operations of the wellness program. Nevertheless, careful consideration in selecting a management company is needed to help ensure that the company has qualified, competent, and experienced leadership and has a good track record in providing excellent customer service.

Additional issues that must be addressed include: (a) what action(s) an employee can take if he or she is injured while participating in the company's fitness/wellness programs (e.g., a negligence claim or workers' compensation claim), and (b) whether employees should sign a waiver prior to participation. Both types of claims can be costly for the employer, so focusing on the prevention of injuries is essential. Generally, if an injury is compensable under workers' compensation, the employee cannot sue the employer for negligence. For more on workers' compensation, see Chapter 7. The following discussion addresses prevention of injuries and subsequent negligence claims/lawsuits.

Scope of Practice and the Professional Standard of Care

This section describes a few negligence cases in which fitness professionals were practicing outside their scope of practice. First, though, it is important to understand the standard of care (duty) or the professional standard of care to which fitness/wellness professionals will likely be held in a negligence case. A **professional standard of care** is defined as an "ethical or legal duty of a professional to exercise the level of care, diligence, and skill prescribed in the code of practice of his or her profession, or as other professionals in the same discipline would in the same or similar circumstances."[38] To meet the professional standard of care, fitness/wellness professionals need to possess a certain level of knowledge and skills to safely and effectively perform the job that is well above and distinct from the skills possessed by the general public. Individuals who practice in the field without adequate education and training will likely not fully understand and appreciate the professional standard of care, or legal duties, that they will be held to in a court of law. They also might not understand that expert witnesses will most likely be judging their conduct to determine whether or not it met the professional standard of care: That is, did they breach their duty or not (as described in Chapter 1)?[39]

Legal scholar Betty van der Smissen states that "if one accepts responsibility for giving leadership to an activity or providing a service, one's performance is measured against the standard of care of a qualified professional **for that situation.**"[40] *Qualified professional*, in this context, means not only someone who possesses the necessary credentials (education, certification, experiences), but who is also competent (e.g., knows how to design and deliver a safe and effective exercise program). As van der Smissen explains, "'for that situation'" means that the professional standard of care is situationally determined using any of three factors: (a) nature of the activity, (b) type of participants, and (c) environmental conditions.[41] Each of these is explained here as it applies to exercise programs.[42] The second factor (type of participants) would also be applicable to any nutrition/diet instruction or other health advice given to participants.

---

38 Business Dictionary.com, s.v. Professional Standard of Care. Definition, http://www.businessdictionary.com/definition/professional-standard-of-care.html.

39 See the *Mimms* case described in Chapter 1 to help understand how the professional standard of care is established in negligence cases (e.g., expert witnesses introduce standards, guidelines, and position papers published by professional organizations to help demonstrate the duty or professional standard of care).

40 Betty van der Smissen, "Elements of Negligence," in *Law for Sport and Recreation Managers*, 4th ed., ed. Doyice J. Cotten and John T. Wolohan (Dubuque, IA: Kendall Hunt, 2007), at 41 [emphasis in original quote].

41 *Id.* at 41–42.

42 JoAnn Eickhoff-Shemek, "Legal Considerations," in *Fitness Professional's Handbook*, 7th ed., Edward T. Howley and Dixie L. Thompson, eds. (Champaign, IL: Human Kinetics, 2016).

A. Nature of the activity. The professional must be aware of the skills and abilities a participant needs to participate "safely" in the activity (e.g., the exercise professional must possess adequate knowledge and skills to lead "safe" exercise programs). To meet the requirements implied by this factor, exercise professionals must fully understand and apply numerous safety principles (e.g., warm-up, progression, overload, cool-down) when leading even a basic or beginning exercise program. If the exercise program is complex or poses additional risks (e.g., Olympic lifting, high-intensity exercise), the professional needs to possess the advanced knowledge and skills necessary to safely teach and lead these types of programs.

B. Type of participants. The professional must be aware of individual factors of the participant (e.g., medical conditions that can impose increased risks) and know how to minimize those risks. To meet this factor, exercise professionals who train individuals with medical conditions (e.g., diabetes, back problems, pregnancy, hypertension, etc.) need to possess advanced credentials in the exercise sciences, such as academic coursework/certification in clinical exercise, and be familiar with the numerous position papers published by professional organizations that address exercise guidelines for individuals with all types of medical conditions. See the published systematic review by Warburton and colleagues for more on this topic.[43]

C. Environmental conditions. The professional must be aware of any conditions that may increase risks (e.g., weather conditions such as heat/humidity, floor surface conditions, exercise equipment condition) and know how to minimize those risks. To meet the requirements inherent in this factor, exercise professionals need to have the knowledge and skills to minimize injuries related to weather conditions, slips and falls, exercise equipment maintenance, and development/enforcement of fitness facility safety policies.

---

43 Darren E. R. Warburton, Shannon S. D. Bredin, Sarah A. Charlesworth et al., "Evidence-Based Risk Recommendations for Best Practices in the Training of Qualified Exercise Professionals Working with Clinical Populations," *Applied Physiology Nutrition and Metabolism* 36 (July 2011): S232–S265.

Scope of Practice—Negligence Cases

In *Capati v. Crunch Fitness*,[44] Mrs. Capati, a young mother of two children, was taking medication for hypertension. While she was on this medication, her personal fitness trainer at Crunch Fitness Club advised her to take a variety of nutritional and dietary supplements, including some that contained ephedra. One day, while performing squats at the Club, Mrs. Capati became very ill, and later died of a stroke at the hospital. Her husband filed a $320 million wrongful death claim against the defendants (the trainer, the Club, and a variety of other defendants, including Vitamin Shoppe Industries) seeking both compensatory and punitive damages. The trainer testified that he did give Mrs. Capati advice as to certain foods and supplements, but he did not inform her that there might be negative health consequences to consuming those foods or supplements while on hypertension medication and while working out. The trainer probably did not realize that the combination of hypertension medication and ephedra can be lethal; that is, he did not understand the precautions he needed to take for someone on hypertension medication. The case was settled out of court for more than $4 million, with the trainer and Club being liable for $1.75 million and the other defendants being liable for the remaining amount.

In addition to risks associated with recommending supplements (see the sidebar), fitness/wellness professionals need to realize that any nutritional/dietary advice they provide to someone who is later harmed by that advice can lead to a negligence claim/lawsuit against them. Fitness/wellness professionals cannot claim, as a legally effective defense, that they were unaware of any harmful consequences that occurred due to the nutritional advice they provided. As described in Chapter 1, legal defenses to refute negligence lawsuits do exist—but ignorance or lack of knowledge is not one of them. Fitness/wellness professionals can be

---

44 David L. Herbert, "1999. $320 Million Lawsuit Filed Against Health Club," *The Exercise Standards and Malpractice Rep.* 13, no. 3 (June 1999): 33, 36; "Wrongful Death Case of Anne Marie Capati Settled for Excess of $4 Million," *The Exercise Standards and Malpractice Rep.* 20, no. 3 (May 2006): 36.

found negligent for any harm they caused by their improper instruction or advice. It is best to provide only general, nonmedical nutritional information (as described earlier) and refer participants/clients to a qualified dietitian/nutritionist or their primary care doctors for individualized or specific advice. It also is important to realize that RDNs conduct different health screenings than do fitness/wellness professionals. For example, they screen for all types of medical conditions, and they also know the specific nutritional needs for individuals with various medical conditions.

The Truth About Nutritional/Dietary Supplements

Facts from: *Dietary Supplements: Promising Panaceas or Pandora's Potion?*[45]
- 1994: 4,000 supplements; Now: 85,000 supplements (2,100 percent increase)
- $25 billion per year industry
- Supplements not tested prior to going to market
- No FDA regulation (but most consumers believe the FDA imposes premarket regulation)

Facts from: *Risky Business: Dietary Supplements Use by Athletes*[46]
- Benefit claims are not to be trusted
- Products are sometimes contaminated with banned substances
- Dietary supplements for muscle building and weight loss pose the highest risk of containing prohibited substances
- There are four third-party agencies that certify supplements for prohibited substances (there is, however, no 100 percent guarantee)

Government Websites/Resources

- Office of Dietary Supplements—https://ods.od.nih.gov
- National Center for Alternative and Complementary Medicine—http://nccam.nih.gov/health/supplements/wiseuse.htm

---

45 Benjamin T. Gordon, "Dietary Supplements: Promising Panaceas or Pandora's Potion?," *ACSM's Certified News* 24, no. 3 (Third Quarter, 2014): 12–13.
46 Christine Rosenbloom and Bob Murray, "Risky Business: Dietary Supplements Use by Athletes," *Nutrition Today* 50, no. 5 (September/October 2015): 240–246.

The four additional negligence cases summarized in Table 6.6 demonstrate that the personal trainers and group exercise leaders did not have the basic knowledge and skills to safely lead exercise programs. Individuals who practice in this manner and do not have the necessary knowledge and skills to do so are practicing outside their scope. As described in Table 6.6, this was evident in the personal trainer cases of *Rostai*[47] and *Proffitt*,[48] and the group exercise leader cases, *Stelluti*[49] and *Santana*.[50] It appears that neither of the latter two trainers knew how to design an exercise program for these clients (or any client, for that matter) because they did not:

- Conduct pre-activity health screenings to determine if medical clearance was needed
- Perform a fitness assessment to ascertain initial fitness levels and abilities
- Understand how to design and implement a proper workout for deconditioned, novice exercisers (such as knowing how to properly apply a basic safety principle of exercise called *progression*)
- Realize that signs and symptoms of overexertion can lead to serious consequences such as rhabdomyolysis or a heart attack, especially if strenuous exercise continues
- Grant the repeated requests for a break made by their clients during the workout, instead pushing them further and further above their limits

The negligent conduct, which included actions and inactions of the personal trainers, led to the injuries suffered by the plaintiffs. Negligent conduct was also evident in *Stelluti*, in which the indoor cycling instructor failed to give very important safety instructions. In *Santana*, the step aerobics instructor gave improper instruction. These cases underscore the basic requirement:

---

47 *Rostai v. Neste Enters.*, 41 Cal. Rptr. 3d 411 (Cal. Ct. App., 4th Dist. 2006).
48 *Proffitt v. Global Fitness Holdings, LLC et al.* as discussed in David L. Herbert, "New Lawsuit Against Personal Trainer and Facility in Kentucky—Rhabdomyolysis Alleged," *The Exercise, Sports and Medicine Standards & Malpractice Rep.* 2, no. 1 (January 2013): 1, 3–10; "Rhabdomyolysis Lawsuit in Kentucky Settled," *The Exercise, Sports and Medicine Standards & Malpractice Rep.* 2, no. 4 (July 2013): 58.
49 *Stelluti v. Casapenn Enters., LLC*, 203 N.J. 286, N.J. LEXIS 750 (2010).
50 *Santana v. Women's Workout & Weight Loss Ctrs., Inc.*, 2001 WL 1521959 (Cal. Ct. App., 2001).

Case	Facts—What Happened	Harm/Injury to Plaintiff	Negligence Claims Against the Defendant(s)	Court's Ruling—For or Against Plaintiff and Court's Reasoning
Rostai v. Neste Enterprises	During his first personal training session, the plaintiff (Rostai, who was 46 years old, overweight, and inactive) suffered a heart attack toward the end of his 60-minute session.	Heart attack	Rostai claimed that the defendants (the trainer and facility) were negligent because the trainer (1) failed to assess his health and physical condition, in particular, his cardiac risk factors prior to exercise, and (2) aggressively challenged him to perform beyond his level of physical ability and fitness even after observing him exhibiting certain signs/symptoms and (3) denied his several requests for a break throughout the session.	AGAINST—The court ruled that the Rostai "assumed the risks" even though the court acknowledged that the trainer was negligent, *i.e.*, did not access plaintiff's level of fitness and may have interpreted plaintiff's complaints (tiredness, shortness of breath, profuse sweating) as usual signs of physical exertion vs. signs/symptoms of a heart attack. The court also indicated that there was no evidence of *intentional* or *reckless* conduct on the part of the trainer, and therefore the plaintiff assumed the risks. NOTE: The assumption of risk defense is usually effective in protecting defendants for injuries due to inherent risks but not negligent conduct.

Table 6.6 Scope of Practice Negligence Cases

Case	Facts—What Happened	Harm/Injury to Plaintiff	Negligence Claims Against the Defendant(s)	Court's Ruling—For or Against Plaintiff and Court's Reasoning
Proffitt v. Global Fitness Holdings, LLC et al.	The personal fitness trainer, in the first session with the plaintiff (Proffitt), had him perform numerous bouts of strenuous exercises and directed him to continue the exercises even after signs/symptoms of overexertion and requests by Proffitt to stop. For many hours after the session, Proffitt experienced extreme pain and fatigue and after 38 hours he noticed his urine was dark brown. He went to the emergency room where he was diagnosed with Rhabdomyolysis and hospitalized for 8 days.	Rhabdomyolysis resulting in permanent injuries including 30 percent loss of muscle tissue in both quadriceps muscles	The plaintiff filed a negligence lawsuit against the trainer and the facility claiming the personal trainer failed to (1) assess the health/fitness status of the client, (2) provide an exercise program within client's safe fitness capacity, and (3) respond to client's complaints of fatigue during training session.	SETTLED—for $75,000 that included medical expenses of $20,000 and lost wages of $6,000.

Table 6.6 *(continued)*

Case	Facts—What Happened	Harm/Injury to Plaintiff	Negligence Claims Against the Defendant(s)	Court's Ruling—For or Against Plaintiff and Court's Reasoning
Stelluti v. Casapenn Enterprises, LLC	The plaintiff (Stelluti), prior to her first indoor cycling class, was not given any instruction on safe use of the bike. When she stood, the handlebars dislodged from the bike and she fell forward while her feet remained strapped to the bike.	Serious back and neck injuries	The plaintiff claimed the cycling instructor failed to properly instruct Stelluti on safe use of the bike. The instructor did not inform her to check that the "pop pin" was fully engaged to make sure the handlebars were secure. An expert witness stated that "users should be aware of... functions and proper operation of the cycle."	AGAINST—New Jersey Supreme Court upholds the waiver. The waiver protected the defendants from their negligent instruction. However, two dissenting judges disagree with the majority opinion regarding the enforceability of waiver
Santana v. Women's Workout and Weight Loss Centers, Inc.	During a steps aerobics class, the plaintiff (Santana) fell while performing simultaneous exercises (stepping and arm exercises with a Dynaband) as directed by the instructor. While performing the simultaneous exercises, the participants were instructed to look straight ahead at their reflection in a mirror versus looking at their feet.	Fractured ankle requiring surgery	The plaintiff claimed that the step aerobics instructor failed to provide a safe exercise class when she created an inherently dangerous situation, as described in the testimony of an expert witness. The expert witness stated that the instructor "increased the risks over and above those inherent in the activity" when participants performed the simultaneous exercises.	FOR—Appellate court ruled that the assumption of risk and waiver defenses did not protect the defendants. Assumption of risk would be effective for injuries due to inherent risks only and the waiver (exculpatory language) was on the back side of the membership agreement making it inconspicuous and, therefore, unenforceable.

Table 6.6 *(continued)*

All fitness trainers and instructors must know how to design and deliver safe and effective programs. Formal education, including coursework and practical training, is needed to acquire the necessary knowledge and skills to do so. *Note:* When reviewing the cases in Table 6.6, take note of the courts' rulings. The defenses of assumption of risk and waiver, as described in Chapter 1, were used by the defendants in three of these negligence cases. Courts examine a variety of factors bearing on each of these defenses to determine if the defenses can be effective in protecting the defendants.

Practice outside one's scope of practice can also occur when an exercise professional does not have the advanced knowledge and skills needed for a particular client (e.g., training someone with medical conditions). To meet the professional standard of care, as described earlier, exercise, nutrition, and other professionals must be aware of individual medical conditions of the participant that can impose increased risks and know how to minimize those risks. If they do not know how to minimize the risks, the professionals should refer the individual to a qualified professional who does, such as a professional with education/training/certification in clinical exercise or nutrition. This is evident in *Baldi-Perry v. Kaifas & 360 Fitness Center, Inc.*[51]

Baldi-Perry, a female with known back/neck injuries, informed her personal trainer (Kaifas) of her health history prior to training. He told her that he had extensive experience training individuals with such injuries and that he could design a safe program for her. One day prior to starting the training session, Kaifas informed Baldi-Perry that he had established a new routine for her (circuit training with no/little rest periods) that was being performed by many at 360 Fitness Center. She reminded him of her past injuries and he responded by stating that she needed to trust him; he was the professional and did this for a living. So she performed the routine, but it resulted in many injuries and serious outcomes such as herniated cervical discs, required surgery to decompress and fuse cervical discs, ongoing pain/medical care, and future surgery. In her negligence lawsuit, Baldi-Perry filed 27 claims against the trainer and 14 claims against the facility.

51 *Baldi-Perry v. Kaifas & 360 Fitness Ctr., Inc.*, as reported in David L. Herbert, "New York Case Against Personal Trainer Results in $1.4 Million Verdict," *The Exercise, Sports and Sports Medicine Standards & Malpractice Rep.* 4, no. 4 (July 2015): 49, 51–55.

Against the trainer:
- Failed to perform proper health appraisal and fitness evaluation
- Failed to meet the representations made to the plaintiff
- Failed to distinguish exercises that were safe from those that were dangerous

Against the facility:
- Failed to hire properly trained personal trainers
- Failed to ensure that trainers conduct proper health appraisals and fitness evaluations
- Negligently hired trainers who were not qualified to design exercise programs for individuals with injuries

Baldi-Perri won her case, receiving a jury verdict of $1.4 million. She was awarded $980,000 (instead of the $1.4 million) due to her being 30 percent at fault. This case was brought in New York, which has a comparative negligence rule; this means that damages are proportionally awarded based on the amount of fault. In this case, the court determined that the defendants were 70 percent at fault and the plaintiff was 30 percent at fault.

Important lessons can be learned from this case. First, clients will trust their wellness professionals, such as personal trainers, and follow their instructions, as demonstrated in this case and in the cases described in Table 6.6. The general public often believes that if a fitness trainer or instructor is "certified," he or she is automatically qualified and competent. However, a certification does not carry much merit or credibility, as discussed earlier in this chapter. Much more credentialing information is needed to help determine if a particular exercise professional is qualified and competent.

Second, it is essential that only exercise professionals with advanced knowledge and skills train individuals who have medical conditions. About 50 percent of adults in the United States have at least one chronic condition, and 25 percent have two or more chronic conditions.[52] Many U.S. adults also have major risk factors for chronic illnesses. For example,

---

52 Brian W. Ward, Jeannine S. Schiller, and Richard A. Goodman, "Multiple Chronic Conditions among U.S. Adults: A 2012 Update," *Preventing Chronic Disease* 11 (April 17, 2014): E62, http://www.ncbi. nlm.nih.gov/pmc/articles/PMC3992293/.

less than 50 percent meet the minimum cardiovascular (aerobic) physical activity guidelines, and less than 25 percent meet the minimum muscle-strengthening activity guidelines.[53] Given these statistics, it is essential to have qualified and competent fitness staff members to lead exercise programs. In their systematic review, Warburton and colleagues[54] make seven recommendations regarding the qualifications of exercise professionals working with clinical populations. Two of these are:

- Professionals should possess a series of discipline-specific core competencies for work with prominent higher-risk conditions. Core competencies ($n = 15$) are listed and include:
  - An in-depth knowledge of acute and chronic responses and adaptations to exercise in healthy and clinical populations
  - A clear understanding of the influence of commonly used medications on the response to exercise
  - A comprehensive knowledge regarding the design and implementation of safe and effective exercise prescriptions for patients with chronic disease, functional limitations, and disabilities
- The qualifications for an exercise professional should include completion of an undergraduate degree in the exercise sciences and the passing of rigorous, independent, national written and practical exams demonstrating competency to work with at-risk populations.[55]

The third lesson from *Baldi-Perri* (and many other negligence lawsuits in the fitness field) is that employers can be held liable for the negligent conduct of their employees through the legal principle of *respondeat superior*. In addition, if employers do not properly hire, train, and supervise their employees, they may have many negligence claims brought against them, as demonstrated in *Baldi-Perri*. Therefore, workplace

---

53 Healthy People 2020, "Physical Activity Objectives," http://www.healthypeople.gov/2020/topics-objectives/topic/physical-activity/objectives.
54 Warburton, Bredin, Charlesworth et al., "Evidence-Based Risk Recommendations for Best Practices in the Training of Qualified Exercise Professionals Working with Clinical Populations," *supra* note 43.
55 *Id.* at S252.

wellness managers have a vested interest, as well as an important legal duty, in developing and implementing risk management strategies when hiring, training, and supervising fitness/wellness staff members.

Risk Management Strategies

Because the fitness/wellness field is not regulated by the government through licensure, there are many hiring challenges for managers of workplace wellness programs. It is very different from hiring in a licensed field. For example, when a manager of an athletic training program is hiring professional staff members, the minimum qualification for all candidates will be that they possess a state license to practice. The manager already knows that they have graduated from an accredited academic program (that meets national standards regarding important knowledge and skills) and are certified (passed the national BOC examination). Thus, the manager can be somewhat confident that candidates have the necessary credentials to perform the job and can focus on other characteristics to find the best employees.

Workplace wellness professionals in management or leadership roles who have responsibility for the company's fitness/wellness programs need to be aware of the many credentialing concerns in the field, as discussed in this chapter. Many of these credentialing issues can be addressed by establishing risk management strategies related to hiring, training, and supervision of fitness/wellness staff members. In addition to a general legal duty to properly hire, train, and supervise employees, employers need to be aware of the many employment laws affecting this area (e.g., smoker protection laws at the state level, as well as federal laws such as the Age Discrimination in Employment Act and Title VII of the Civil Rights Act). These two federal laws are addressed briefly in Chapter 8 from training and supervision perspectives.

Hiring of Employees
When hiring workplace wellness managers and other professional staff members who will serve in supervisory roles, it will be best to hire

individuals with academic degrees in exercise science or health education (or related areas) and who have professional certifications that require a degree, such as the ACSM EP-C and the NCHEC CHES. Graduation from an accredited program might provide some assurance as to their knowledge and skills. Again, it is important to realize that accreditation of academic programs in these disciplines is voluntary, and that more effort will be required to determine the qualifications for candidates who have not graduated from an accredited program. Given the risks of injuries that can occur in fitness programs compared to health education programs, it will be essential to have a well-qualified and competent exercise professional on staff who will have oversight of the fitness programs and staff members.

Hiring other fitness staff members (e.g., personal trainers, group exercise leaders) becomes much more challenging because "certification" is the main credential that employers often require. As discussed in length in this chapter, many fitness certifications (even accredited certifications) are not all that credible or worthwhile, because no formal education or practical training is required by the certifying organizations before a person sits for the certification examination. The fitness/wellness professionals who hire these individuals should take careful steps in the hiring process to help ensure they select qualified and competent individuals. For example, in the interview process, (a) ask questions that will assess candidates' knowledge and skills; (b) ask situational-type questions (common situations that occur in training sessions/group exercise classes) to determine if they know how to properly handle the situation; and (c) have them teach a mock group exercise class or mock personal training session.

Similar hiring procedures should take place for health educators, such as selecting degreed individuals (e.g., RDN) to develop or teach nutrition/weight management and stress management programs. When hiring health and wellness coaches, it would be best to consider individuals who have completed an accredited educational program that meets the NCCHWC standards.

Another important consideration relevant to the hiring process is the performance of criminal background checks, especially for those employees and independent contractors (discussed later) who will be performing personal fitness training, massage therapy, or working with vulnerable populations (children, older adults, and those with disabilities). In addition, prior to hiring, employers should purchase professional liability insurance for their fitness and wellness staff members and require independent contractors to provide proof of general and professional liability insurance.

Training of Employees

Training of employees is always an important function of those serving in management or supervisory roles. Because of the risk of injuries in exercise programs, training is absolutely essential for fitness staff members. Given the tremendous variation in the types of education/training (or lack of) that new fitness employees may bring to the job, it will be up to management to provide the initial training. However, it will be important for management to first establish some policies and procedures (to be discussed in the training) with regard to the scope of practice for all fitness/wellness employees. Examples of policies might be:

a. Exercise staff members who work as personal trainers and group exercise leaders must first complete a formal education course (e.g., classroom instruction and practical training) if they have no previous formal education and practical training.

b. Exercise staff members (and health educators, health/wellness coaches) do not provide "individualized nutritional advice" but only "general, non-medical nutrition education" to participants.

c. Health education staff members (nutrition educators, RDNs, health/wellness coaches) do not provide "individualized" exercise programs, but may provide "general" education covering topics such as the U.S. physical activity guidelines and health benefits of physical activity.

d. Only exercise professionals with advanced knowledge and skills will work with clinical populations.

e. Fitness/wellness staff members do not conduct professional counseling with participants.

Once the policies are formed, specific procedures that accompany each policy must also be developed. For example, for general nonmedical nutrition education, the nutrition education that can be provided by nonlicensed individuals should be clearly specified in the procedures. Once policies and procedures are developed and approved (e.g., by upper management, human resources, and/or legal counsel) they can be placed into a *Risk Management Policies and Procedures Manual* that can be given to staff members, either in hard copy or electronically via the company's intranet.

The next step is to conduct in-service-trainings for all fitness/wellness employees to go over the policies and procedures. The workplace wellness managers and supervisors who lead the trainings need to have good teaching skills (e.g., know how to put a lesson plan together and conduct training activities that engage the staff members). For example, an in-service training regarding the policy related to "general, non-medical nutrition information" might start by explaining the policy and procedures and why they were developed from both a safety and a legal perspective. The next activity could be role-playing. Prior to the training, the staff members could submit a list of nutrition/weight management questions often asked by participants. Then, pair up staff members, with one playing the role of the exercise leader (or health educator such as a wellness coach) and the other playing the role of the participant. Each pair role-plays (the "participant" asks one of the nutrition questions on the list and the "leader" answers) in front of the entire group. The entire group then critiques the responses of the exercise leader/health educator to evaluate if his or her response was consistent with the policy/procedures. If it was not, explain why it was not and then have members of the group share answers that properly reflect the policy/procedures. An outcome of this initial training should be that staff members know how to provide "general non-medical nutrition education" when communicating with participants and can recognize situations that warrant a referral to an RDN.

For training related to the professional counseling policy and procedures, it might be wise to bring in a professional counselor from the company's employee assistance program to give a presentation. This counselor could help reinforce the importance of the policy/procedures using several examples. He or she could also inform the fitness/wellness staff members about the EAP program, how to refer an employee to the program, and how it benefits employees.

Although initial in-service trainings are important for new employees, it is important to realize that staff training does not only occur upon hiring. Regular in-service trainings are needed to refresh staff members' memories of the policies/procedures and when any changes or revisions occur.

Another important risk management strategy related to in-service training is documentation. Be sure to store, in a safe place, items such as the lesson plans, dates of the trainings, staff members attending, and the instructor(s) who led the training. This evidence may be helpful in refuting claims such as those brought against the facility in the *Baldi-Perri* case. Documentation of hiring procedures (discussed earlier) and supervision procedures (discussed next) should also be created and retained.

Supervision of Employees

Supervising new employees during a probationary period requires observing them as they are performing their jobs and providing feedback on their performance. The feedback can be both informal (given privately at the time of observation) or formal (e.g., use of a performance appraisal tool to evaluate all important job tasks/responsibilities). Supervision during the probationary period is essential so that employees get off to a good start and learn how to properly carry out their job responsibilities. This also helps them feel confident that they are performing their jobs according to the program's policies and procedures.

An example of informal feedback would be informing a personal trainer that she was teaching an exercise incorrectly soon after an informal observation by the personal trainer supervisor (again, privately). Unsafe exercise teaching must be corrected right away. In contrast, formal job performance appraisals should be done a couple of times during a probationary period for new employees and on at least an annual basis for all employees. Such an appraisal involves direct observation by the program supervisor of an entire personal training session, group exercise class, or wellness coaching session. A written and comprehensive performance appraisal tool should be used to evaluate the staff member's job performance. A tool for group exercise leaders has been developed and validated.[56] This tool can also be adapted to evaluate the job performance of personal trainers. After the direct observation/evaluation, the supervisor and employee discuss the performance appraisal, highlighting both strengths and areas where improvement is needed. For areas needing improvement, an action plan should be developed. The performance appraisal process is described in detail elsewhere.[57]

Independent Contractors and Wellness Vendors

The preceding information focused on fitness and wellness staff members (employees); however, many workplace wellness programs also utilize independent contractors (e.g., health and wellness coaches, personal fitness trainers, group exercise leaders) and wellness vendors (e.g., companies that provide various services such as biometric screenings and management of the entire workplace wellness program). *Black's Law Dictionary*[58] defines an **independent contractor,** in part, as "one who renders service in course of self-employment or occupation, and who follows employer's desires only as to the results of the work"[59]; it defines a **vendor** as a "seller of goods or services."[60] When hiring either, a well-written contract that explicitly describes the responsibilities of each party (and meets all four elements of a contract, as described in Chapter 1) should be prepared by a competent lawyer.

Independent Contractor versus Employee

From a legal perspective, there is a distinction between an independent contractor and an employee. IRS Publication 1779—a two-page form available at https://www.irs.gov/pub/irs-pdf/p1779.pdf—describes these

---

56 Eickhoff-Shemek, Herbert, and Connaughton, *Risk Management for Health/Fitness Professionals.*
57 JoAnn Eickhoff-Shemek and Susan Selde, "Evaluating Group Exercise Leader Performance: An Easy and Helpful Tool," *ACSM's Health & Fitness J.* 10, no. 1 (January/February 2006): 20–23.
58 Henry C. Black, Joseph R. Nolan, Jacqueline M. Nolan-Haley et al., *Black's Law Dictionary,* 6th ed. (St. Paul, MN: West, 1991).
59 *Id.* at 530.
60 *Id.* at 1079.

differences, which are related to *behavioral control, financial control,* and *relationship between the parties.* For example, an employer has *behavioral control* over an employee, but does not over an independent contractor. If an individual receives extensive instructions and training to perform the job, he or she would likely be classified as an employee. Therefore, when considering the use of independent contractors, more scrutiny is needed in the hiring process than what was described for employees. Once someone is hired as an independent contractor, the employer cannot control the job performance of that individual via training/supervision; it can only accept or reject the "results" of the work.

In addition to applying these IRS guidelines, it is important that independent contractors do not hold themselves out as or appear to be employees (e.g., wearing a shirt with the company logo on it); perhaps they could wear badges indicating they are independent contractors. If they appear to be ostensible agents of the employer, the employer could be held liable for their negligent acts, as it could be with employees under the legal doctrine of *respondeat superior.* Generally, employers are not liable for the negligent acts of independent contractors. Employers could also be held liable for paying or withholding taxes on the independent contractor's compensation if a state or federal agency, such as the IRS, deems the independent contractor an employee.[61] Thus, many factors should be considered when developing an independent contractor contract, including liability insurance, indemnification, and scope of practice. A competent lawyer should be involved in the writing of such a contract.

Selecting Wellness Vendors
As stated in the introduction, there are more than 8,000 wellness vendors.[62] When selecting a vendor, there are a variety of criteria to consider. General criteria include (a) pricing, (b) quality of programs/services (e.g., do the programs/services reflect best practices?), (c) integrity and

---

61 IRS, "Independent Contractor or Employee?" Publication 1779 (2012): 2, https://www.irs.gov/pub/irs-pdf/p1779.pdf.
62 Steven Ross Johnson, "Firms Revamping Employee Wellness Programs," *Modern Healthcare* (May 24, 2014), http://www.modernhealthcare.com/article/20140524/MAGAZINE/305249980.

professionalism of the managers/employees, (d) quality of customer service, (e) recommendations/feedback from current or previous clients, and (f) quality of data collected (e.g., how are reliability and validity determined?). Companies must also consider important legal criteria when selecting a vendor. (See the sidebar; also see the Compliance Checklist in Chapter 9. Many of the items on that checklist regarding data privacy and security pertain to wellness vendors. By no means do the criteria in the sidebar constitute an inclusive list.)

Legal Criteria to Consider When Selecting Wellness Vendors

1. Litigation history (e.g., describe current or previous legal claims or lawsuits against the vendor).
2. Audit history (e.g., describe current or previous audits by a federal, state, or county regulatory agency).
3. Written policies and procedures that demonstrate compliance with applicable federal laws, such as those discussed in this book.
4. Written policies and procedures that demonstrate compliance with applicable state or local laws (e.g., state privacy laws, state licensing laws for employees).
5. Description of the medical advisory board and/or medical director if providing health screenings or other medical services.
6. Willingness to indemnify.
7. Description of qualifications of all staff members, including degrees, certifications, licenses, and years of professional experience, as well as criminal background checks conducted prior to hiring.
8. Description of all staff trainings that are designed to help staff members comply with applicable laws (e.g., provide written procedures discussed in staff trainings that address privacy, confidentiality, and security of employee data, as well as written agreements signed by staff members regarding compliance with laws).
9. Verification of insurance (e.g., general and professional liability, workers' compensation, ratings of insurance providers).
10. Description of quality control procedures related to the safety and effectiveness of any equipment used or provided.

Companies that decide to hire a vendor to manage an in-house fitness facility should also consider the criteria listed in the sidebar. For companies that opt not to have an in-house fitness facility and encourage their employees to use a local fitness facility instead, the same criteria can be used when establishing a contract with a facility such as a YMCA or health club. Many of these facilities offer corporate discounts to local businesses, but it will be essential to check upfront that the facility provides safe and effective programs and services. Making a concerted effort to help ensure that a management company and/or local facility meet certain criteria will help minimize the liability risk of the company when establishing such contracts. It is also important that legal counsel be directly involved in the development of vendor contracts.

Once a company establishes all the criteria that it will want to consider when hiring a wellness vendor, the criteria can then be used to develop a document that lists and describes the proposal guidelines for vendors to follow. Providing proposal guidelines will also help to objectify the evaluation process when making a vendor selection.

Criteria to Consider When Selecting a Vendor for Fitness Facility Management or Contracting with a Local Fitness Facility

1. Qualifications, competence, and experience of the facility manager and all staff members (e.g., in addition to degrees/certifications, what formal practical training have the staff members had? Are there exercise staff members with formal educational background in clinical exercise?)

2. Quality and effectiveness of programs and services (e.g., do they reflect best practices, and are they based on sound principles of safe/effective exercise? Do staff members have the freedom to develop programs, or can they only offer those programs developed by the management company or fitness facility?)

3. Risk management policy and procedures manual (e.g., does the manual have a section reflecting each of the major liability exposures associated with fitness programs/facilities, as well as applicable laws such as the ADA and OSHA's bloodborne pathogens standard?)

4. National safety standards, guidelines, and position papers (e.g., does the program follow standards/guidelines published by professional and independent organizations?)

5. Risk management advisory committee (e.g., who are the members of this committee, such as medical, legal, and insurance experts? What are their backgrounds? How does the vendor or facility utilize the advisory committee?)

6. Initial and ongoing training of all staff members (e.g., who provides the training, and what content is covered?)

RULE THE RULES

Key Points in Chapter 6

1. In the fitness/wellness profession, there can be a difference between a "qualified" employee who possesses certain credentials (e.g., degrees, certifications) and a "competent" professional who not only possesses credentials but also knows how to design and deliver safe/effective programs.

2. There are four types of credentialing: (a) accreditation and (b) certification are self-regulated/voluntary, and (c) licensure and (d) statutory certification are government-regulated/required.

3. Given that the fitness/wellness profession is self-regulated through voluntary accreditation and certification, certain challenges are created for employers in hiring qualified and competent employees.

4. Other than certain certification exams that require a degree in the field (e.g., ACSM EP-C and CHES), most fitness/wellness certifications exams do not require any formal education or assessment of practical skills prior to sitting for the exam. Therefore, there can be many limitations with certification credentials.

5. Given the risk of injuries that can occur in exercise programs, employers need to take special precautions to hire only qualified and competent fitness staff members who know how to safely design and deliver exercise programs for both healthy and clinical populations.

6. Conduct outside one's scope of practice can lead to both criminal charges (e.g., practicing dietetics without a license) and civil claims (e.g., negligence such as negligent instruction), as demonstrated by the case law examples in this chapter.

7. It is likely that fitness/wellness professionals will be held to a professional standard of care if they are ever named as defendants in a negligence lawsuit.

8. Employers can be liable for the negligent conduct of their employees based on a legal principle called *respondeat superior;*

therefore, they should develop and implement risk management strategies for hiring, training, and supervision of their employees.

9. When hiring independent contractors, employers need to realize their limits with regard to behavioral and financial controls as established by the IRS.

10. When selecting a vendor to provide wellness programs/services or to manage an in-house fitness facility, several criteria should be considered, including those described in this chapter.

Study Questions

1. List and describe the four levels of credentialing and indicate which ones are government-regulated and which are self-regulated.

2. Explain why employers should be cautious of accredited certifications, especially if these are the only credentials that a candidate possesses.

3. Should fitness and wellness professionals be licensed? Using information presented in this chapter, make a good argument for or against licensure.

4. Using case law examples described in this chapter, describe how practicing outside one's scope can lead to both criminal charges and civil lawsuits such as negligence.

5. Develop an outline (topics/activities to be covered) for an in-service training on scope of practice.

6. Describe policies and procedures that should be developed to address each of the three factors related to the professional standard of care: (a) nature of the activity, (b) type of participants, and (c) environmental conditions.

7. Employers have a legal duty to properly (a) hire, (b) train, and (c) supervise employees. List and describe risk management strategies that can help minimize legal liability for each of these duties.

8. List the legal issues associated with independent contractors and wellness vendors.

9. Describe the legal criteria that should be used to select a wellness vendor.
10. Describe the criteria that should be considered before contracting with a company to manage an in-house fitness facility.

Key Terms

accreditation

certification

independent contractor

job task analysis (JTA)

licensure

professional standard of care

respondeat superior

scope of practice

statutory certification

vendor

7

Is That Part of Their Workday?

Learning Objectives

After reading this chapter, workplace wellness professionals will be able to:

1. Understand the purpose of the Federal Labor Standards Act (FLSA) and its application to workplace wellness programs.
2. Based on the FLSA, describe situations in which an employer needs to pay (or not pay) employees for their participation in workplace wellness programs.
3. List the benefits of workers' compensation statutes for both employers and employees.
4. Identify factors that courts consider to determine whether or not an injury is compensable under workers' compensation, and explain how these can vary from state to state.
5. Analyze legal cases involving employee injuries occurring in company-sponsored fitness and recreation programs that resulted in workers' compensation claims.
6. Develop risk management strategies, in consultation with a competent lawyer, to address the many factors related to workers' compensation statutes and company-sponsored fitness and recreation programs.

The only pride of her workday was not that it had been lived, but that it had been survived. It was wrong, she thought, it was viciously wrong that one should ever be forced to say that about any hour of one's life.

—Ayn Rand, Atlas Shrugged

Better a thousand times careful than once dead.

—Proverb

Introduction

This chapter addresses the Fair Labor Standards Act (FLSA) and work-ers' compensation laws. The FLSA is a federal law, and workers' compen-sation is based on individual state statutes. The FLSA may be applicable to workplace wellness programs if participation in such a program is per-ceived as mandatory and the employer does not pay employees for their participation. Whether a wellness activity is perceived as mandatory could arguably be influenced by the presence and amount of any incen-tives to participate. Workers' compensation is applicable to workplace wellness programs in a couple of ways: (a) healthy employees experience fewer and less severe injuries (physically and psychologically) on the job, which can lead to decreased workers' compensation claims; and (b) if injuries do occur in a company-sponsored fitness or recreational pro-gram, workers' compensation *may* be applicable and available.

The Federal Labor Standards Act

The major provisions of the Fair Labor Standards Act of 1938 (FLSA)[1] guarantee minimum wage and overtime pay. The FLSA was intended to establish a minimum standard of living for American workers.[2] It also sets recordkeeping and child labor standards.[3] The FLSA, along with other labor laws strengthening workers' rights, such as the National Labor Relations Act of 1935, was one piece of President Franklin Roosevelt's New Deal during the Great Depression.[4]

Employees are covered under the FLSA if they work for covered "enter-prises" with at least two employees engaged in commerce or in the produc-tion of goods for commerce and have annual revenues of at least $500,000.[5] Private and public hospitals, and certain medical care facilities, schools,

---

1 52 Stat. 1060, as amended, 29 U.S.C. §§ 201 *et seq.*
2 Pamela Williams, "Historical Overview of the Fair Labor Standards Act," 10 *Fla. Coastal L. Rev.* (Sum-mer 2009): 657, 669.
3 *Id.*
4 Williams, "Historical Overview," at 666–667.
5 80 Fed. Reg. 38516, 38545.

and public agencies are also covered "enterprises" under the FLSA, regardless of their annual revenues.[6] Even if an employer is not considered a covered enterprise, the FLSA covers domestic service workers (e.g., housekeepers) and individuals "engaged in interstate commerce or in the production of goods for commerce."[7] For instance, workers in small businesses that ship goods out of state would be covered under FLSA even if the employer is not considered an enterprise.[8]

The minimum wage under the FLSA is currently $7.25 per hour.[9] The FLSA also requires that covered employees who work more than 40 hours per week receive compensation "at a rate not less than one and one-half times the regular rate at which he is employed."[10] Alternatively, covered employees may receive "compensatory time off at a rate not less than one and one-half hours for each hour of employment for which overtime compensation is required."[11]

Under FLSA's so-called "white collar" exemption, executive, administrative, professional, computer, and outside sales employees are exempt from minimum wage and overtime pay regulations.[12] In general, white-collar workers are exempted if their salaries exceed a certain amount, set at $23,660 per year since 2004.[13] Just recently, the U.S. Department of Labor (DOL) increased the salary threshold to $47,476 ($913 per week).[14] That means a much larger number of U.S. workers will be required to receive overtime pay (or compensatory time off) if they work more than 40 hours per week.

---

6 *Id.*; 29 U.S.C. §§ 203(d), (e), (s)(1), 206(a), 207(a), 778.0; DOL, Wages and Hours Worked: Minimum Wage and Overtime Pay, available at www.dol.gov/compliance/guide/minwage.htm; Technical Release 2013-02, Section III.A (May 8, 2013), available at http://www.dol.gov/ebsa/pdf/tr13-02.pdf.
7 *Id.*
8 *See* U.S. Department of Labor, Wage and Hour Division, "Fact Sheet #14: Coverage Under the Fair Labor Standards Act (FLSA)" (July 2009), https://www.dol.gov/whd/regs/compliance/whdfs14.pdf.
9 29 U.S.C. § 206.
10 29 U.S.C. § 207(a).
11 29 U.S.C. § 207(o).
12 29 C.F.R. §§ 541.100-541.504; *see also* U.S. Department of Labor, "Fact Sheet #17a, Exemption for Executive, Administrative, Professional, Computer and Outside Sales Employees Under the Fair Labor Standards Act (FLSA)," https://www.dol.gov/whd/overtime/fs17a_overview.pdf.
13 29 C.F.R. § 541.600 ($455 per week).
14 The final rule was published on May 23, 2016; *see* https://www.federalregister.gov/articles/2016/05/23/2016-11754/defining-and-delimiting-the-exemptions-for-executive-administrative-professional-outside-sales-and.

A relevant provision of the FLSA for workplace wellness programs concerns payment for attendance at lectures, meetings, training programs, and similar activities. The FLSA considers such attendance "working time," and therefore subject to FLSA minimum wage and overtime provisions, unless the following four criteria are met:

1. Attendance is outside of the employee's regular working hours;
2. Attendance is in fact voluntary;
3. The course, lecture, or meeting is not directly related to the employee's job; and
4. The employee does not perform any productive work during such attendance.[15]

All four of these criteria must be met.[16] Thus, if the wellness program takes place during the employee's regular working hours or attendance is mandatory, the employer should consider such participation compensable work time.

A court evaluates whether a wellness program activity is mandatory from the employee's reasonable perspective.[17] "Attendance is not voluntary, of course, if it is required by the employer. It is not voluntary in fact if the employee is given to understand or led to believe that his present working conditions or the continuance of his employment would be adversely affected by nonattendance."[18]

Although the authors of this book could not find any cases involving wellness programs, employees have sued their employers for FLSA violations for failing to pay them for time spent in "mandatory" trainings.[19] In one case, the employees viewed the trainings as mandatory because their attendance was tied to wage increases, and the company president would call employees who missed the training.[20] Similar arguments could be made in the workplace wellness context if employee participation in wellness

---

15 29 C.F.R. § 785.27.
16 *Id.*
17 *See, e.g., Wicke v. L&C Insulation, Inc.*, 12-CV-638, at 17 (W.D. Wis. 2014).
18 29 C.F.R. § 785.28.
19 *See, e.g., Wicke v. L&C Insulation, Inc.*, 12-CV-638, at 17 (W.D. Wis. 2014).
20 *Id.*

programs affects an employee's working conditions or employment at a company. For example, if an employer tied wellness program participation to a large incentive or had supervisors "encourage" employee participation, an employee may view participation as mandatory. In such a case, if an employer did not pay an employee for his or her time spent participating in the wellness activity, an employee could presumably raise an FLSA claim.

Employers can reduce their FLSA risk by paying employees for the time spent participating in the workplace wellness program. If employers do not pay for that time, then the employer must make sure that participation meets all four of the criteria previously listed. Moreover, it is not clear at this time whether scenarios could arise in which the Department of Labor or a court might deem monetary incentives or other rewards for attending a course offered as part of a wellness program (e.g., a nutritional counseling or health education seminar) to cause the course not to be "voluntary." This determination likely would require a case-by-case analysis of the particular facts and circumstances at issue.[21] Employers thus need to analyze whether an employee's participation in a wellness program could give rise to compensable work hours under the minimum wage and overtime provisions described above. A failure to comply with these requirements could subject the employer to a civil action brought by the affected employee(s) (or the Department of Labor) to recover any unpaid minimum wages and/or overtime compensation, additional liquidated damages, and possibly attorneys' fees and costs.[22] In addition, although seemingly very unlikely to arise in connection with a wellness program, any person who repeatedly or willfully violates the FLSA's minimum wage and overtime provisions could be subject to civil penalties and, perhaps in the most extreme cases, imprisonment.[23]

---

21 *See Wetzel v. Town of Orangetown*, No. 06-15190, 2013 U.S. Dist. LEXIS 37352 (S.D.N.Y. 2013), aff'd, No. 06-15190, 2014 U.S. App. LEXIS 3879 (2d Cir. 2014) (whether or not attendance is voluntary requires case-by-case analysis); DOL, Employment Standards Administration (Wage & Hour Division), FLSA 2006-5 (Mar. 3, 2006) (time spent by non-English-speaking restaurant employees voluntarily studying employer-provided English lesson materials was not compensable work time); FLSA 2006-2NA (time that police recruits spent outside class typing notes from academic training was not voluntary, and thus was compensable, because recruits were "penalized" (but not terminated) for failing to submit typed notes, and program "directly related" to recruits' jobs).
22 29 U.S.C. §§ 211(a), 216(b)-(c), 217.
23 29 U.S.C. § 216(a), (e)(2); 29 C.F.R. § 578.3.

Workers' Compensation Statutes

As briefly discussed in Chapter 1, workers' compensation is a form of **strict liability** imposed upon the employer without fault—meaning that the injured employee is compensated (e.g., medical expenses, portion of lost wages) regardless of who is at fault for the injury. According to *American Jurisprudence 2d*,[24] the purposes of workers' compensation statutes include: (a) to protect and compensate workers, providing financial protection by compensating for medical costs due to work-related injuries (including disability benefits); (b) to replace wages for workers by providing compensation for loss or reduction of wages; (c) to promote efficiency by offering an efficient system to provide prompt relief to injured employees; (d) to protect employers by precluding the employee from bringing a tort lawsuit for negligence against the employer, and through subrogation preventing double recovery and allowing employers to shift liability onto third parties whenever possible; and (e) to promote safety by motivating employers to make workplaces safer.

Making the workplace safer for employees should be a major motivation for employers who want to minimize the frequency and severity of job-related injuries and costs associated with workers' compensation claims. Workplace wellness programs have been shown to reduce workers' compensation costs. In a meta-evaluation of workplace wellness economic return studies conducted by Chapman, 7 of the 62 studies selected (62 studies that met the inclusion criteria) found an average of a 32 percent decrease in workers' compensation costs and disability management claims cost.[25] Although these data reflect positive findings, additional studies are needed to investigate injury prevention programs and their economic outcomes. As demonstrated in this meta-evaluation, economic return studies have focused mainly on healthcare costs and sick leave absenteeism (e.g., 32 and 26 of these studies investigated return on

---

24 82 AM. JUR. 2d *Workers' Compensation* §§ 10, 11, 12, 13, 14 (2016) (Workers' Compensation, I. In General, B. Purposes of Workers' Compensation Acts).

25 Larry Chapman, "Meta Evaluation of Worksite Health Promotion Economic Return Studies: 2012 Update," *The Art of Health Promotion—American Journal of Health Promotion* (March/April 2012): TAHP 1-TAHP 12.

investment (ROI) for healthcare costs and sick leave absenteeism, respectively).[26] As stated by Chapman, few wellness programs have included injury prevention or initiatives to address injury-related costs.[27] O'Donnell[28] agrees, identifying a need to focus more on the health risks that are most costly, such as injury and musculoskeletal problems, instead of the health risks associated with chronic illnesses.

The Affordable Care Act (ACA) may have an impact on workers' compensation. A 2015 law review article on this topic[29] discussed several opportunities and considerations, including the expansion of health, wellness, and safety programs. Because the ACA encourages employers to offer wellness programs to their employees, the institution of such programs could lead to more employees becoming healthier and fitter, and thus less susceptible to injury. For example, more than 50 percent of workers' compensation claims are due to back injuries.[30] Low back exercise programs, such as a daily "prework" stretching and strengthening program, have been effective in preventing low back injuries.[31] Workplace wellness programs can keep healthy employees healthy, but can also help reduce risk factors and chronic illnesses. Studies have shown that employees with risk factors and chronic illnesses (comorbidities) are more likely to be injured on the job, and also that their injuries are more severe and costly when compared to employees facing the same type of injury without the medical conditions.[32] In addition to physical injuries, there are many stress-related injuries that have led to subsequent workers' compensation claims. Examples of these types of claims are discussed in Chapter 8. It is important to realize that comprehensive workplace

---

26 *Id.*

27 *Id.*

28 Michael P. O'Donnell, ed., *Health Promotion at the Workplace*, 4th ed. (Troy, MI: American Journal of Health Promotion, 2014).

29 David A. North, "The Impact of the Affordable Care Act on Workers' Compensation: Opportunities and Considerations," 41 *Wm. Mitchell L. Rev.* (2015): 1445.

30 David H. Chenoweth, *Worksite Health Promotion*, 3rd ed. (Champaign, IL: Human Kinetics, 2011).

31 *Id.*

32 Harry Shuford and Tanya Restrepo, *How Obesity Increases the Risk of Disabling Workplace Injuries* (NCCI Research Report), https://www.ncci.com/Articles/Documents//II_obesity_research_brief.pdf; *see also* Eric Finkelstein, Ian Fiebelkorn, and Guijing Wang, "The Costs of Obesity Among Full-Time Employees," *American J. Health Promotion* 20, no. 1 (September/October 2005): 45–51.

wellness programs can have a positive impact on workers' compensation claims by decreasing injuries, both physical and psychological.

Injuries Occurring in Workplace Fitness and Recreation Programs: Are They Compensable Under Workers' Compensation?

As discussed in Chapter 1, injuries in physical activity programs can be due to **inherent risks, negligent conduct,** defects in exercise equipment, and—in rare cases—even **intentional acts** (e.g., sexual assault committed by a personal fitness trainer). Injuries suffered while participating in workplace fitness or recreation programs, which are associated with inherent risks and negligent conduct, may be compensable under workers' compensation. Injuries caused by defects in exercise equipment could give rise to a products liability claim against the equipment manufacturer. If a wellness staff member commits an intentional act (e.g., sexual assault) that harmed a fellow employee or a client of the employer, that employee/client could bring criminal charges against the wellness staff member and, depending on the circumstances, could also bring a legal action against the employer. For example, if an employee commits a sexual assault while on the job, the general rule is that the employer would not be held liable for that employee's conduct, because that type of conduct is not within the scope of employment. However, if the employer had constructive (prior) knowledge of this type of conduct and chose to do nothing about it, then the employer could be liable. An employer's intentional or egregious conduct will not be compensable under workers' compensation, but the employee/client who is harmed by such conduct may pursue other legal actions against the employer.

The following cases describe injuries that have occurred to employees while participating in company-sponsored fitness and recreation programs, and detail the factors that courts consider to determine whether or not the injury is compensable under workers' compensation. Obviously, the goal is to prevent injuries in the first place. Fitness/wellness managers need to implement risk management strategies to address the many legal liability exposures that exist with physical activity programs, as described in Chapter 1.

Before discussing these cases, we present a necessarily basic review of the procedures involved in workers' compensation claims when disputes occur, such as when an employee is denied benefits by the workers' compensation insurance carrier. These procedures are set forth in the workers' compensation acts in each state, and thus can vary. However, in general most states suggest **arbitration** as the first means of resolving such disputes; in arbitration, usually the parties voluntarily agree to use an independent arbitrator.[33] Decisions made by an arbitrator are rarely binding,[34] and an employee can appeal to an administrative body such as the state's Workers' Compensation Board, an industrial commission, or a state court.[35] For example, in the *Stanner* case analyzed in the next subsection, the petitioner, a widow of an employee who died, was denied workers' compensation death benefits by the arbitrator. Upon her appeal, the Pennsylvania Workers' Compensation Board affirmed the arbitrator's decision. She then appealed that decision to a state intermediate court of appeals, the Commonwealth Court of Pennsylvania, which reversed the decision of the Workers' Compensation Board and awarded her the benefits.

Stanner v. Compensation Appeal Board[36]

Anthony Stanner (Stanner) was a manager at Westinghouse Electric Company. Stanner, who had a history of coronary heart disease, worked out in the company's fitness center two or three times per week. One day, shortly after a workout in the company's in-house fitness center, he died due to sudden death syndrome. His widow, Molly Stanner, filed a fatal claim petition to seek workers' compensation death benefits, alleging that her husband died as a result of a work-related myocardial infarction. The referee, or arbitrator, dismissed the claim. Mrs. Stanner appealed this decision to the Pennsylvania Workers' Compensation Board, but the board affirmed the referee's dismissal of the claim. The referee claimed that Molly Stanner was unable to establish a work-related injury resulting in

33 Lindsey Shafar, "What Happens if You Lose a Worker's Comp Case at Arbitration?," *Nolo* (2016), http://www.disabilitysecrets.com/workmans-comp-question-7.html.
34 *Id.*
35 Beth Laurence, "How Do You Start the Workers' Comp Process?" *Nolo* (2016), http://www.disabilitysecrets.com/workmans-comp-question-18.html.
36 *Stanner v. Compensation Appeal Bd. (Westinghouse Elec. Co.)*, 604 A.2d 1167 (Pa. Commw. 1992).

her husband's death. This decision was primarily based on the testimony of the medical expert, who stated that Stanner was a "walking time bomb" given his severe coronary artery disease, and that his sudden death could have happened anywhere. However, this expert also stated that the high level of physical exercise just prior to his death was the immediate and significant precipitating cause of Mr. Stanner's sudden death.

Molly Stanner further appealed this decision to an intermediate court of appeals in Pennsylvania, claiming that her husband sustained the injury leading to his death while he was actually engaged in activities in further-ance of his employer's business or affairs. The employer counter-argued that even if he was engaged in such activities, the state workers' compensa-tion act requires heart-related injuries to be compensable under the Act if they (a) arise out of the course of employment and (b) are causally related thereto. The court referred to a section within the Act which states:

> The terms "injury" and "personal injury," as used in this act, shall be construed to mean an injury to an employee, regardless of his previous physical condition, arising in the course of his employment and related thereto ... . The term "injury arising in the course of his employment," as used in this article, ... shall include all other injuries sustained while the employee is actually engaged in the furtherance of the business or affairs of the employer, whether upon the employer's premises or elsewhere, and shall include all injuries caused by the condition of the premises or by the operation of the employer's business or affairs thereon, sustained by the employee, who, though not so engaged, is injured upon the premises occupied by or under the control of the employer, or upon which the employer's business or affairs are being carried on, the employee's presence thereon being required by the nature of his employment.[37]

To assist in analysis of this case, the court relied upon previous cases which have liberally interpreted "engaged in the furtherance of the

---

37 *Id.* at 1169.

business or affairs of the employer." One of these cases was *Hemmler v. Workmen's Compensation Appeal Board.*[38] That court stated:

> In *Hemmler*, the claimant suffered sprain to his ankle and torn ligaments while playing basketball during his lunch break with other employees in the gymnasium on the employer's premises. The sole issue in *Hemmler* was whether the claimant was in the course of his employment at the time of his injury. This Court reversed the Board and reinstated the referee's award of benefits concluding that the claimant was engaged in an activity in furtherance of the employer's business or affairs, and, therefore, was in the course of his employment. In *Hemmler*, the following factors were crucial to the Court's conclusion: *the employer encouraged its employees to participate in activities to improve their health, relieve the stress of their work and promote better mental attitude in the performance of their work; the employer posted information on the bulletin board encouraging employees to engage in sports activities; and the employer's gymnasium was used for the employees during breaks to play basketball"*[39]

The *Stanner* court used similar reasoning based on the testimony of the director of the employer's health/fitness center. "The fitness center was owned, operated and staffed by Employer's employees for exclusive use of its employees; the employees were encouraged to participate in its fitness program; flexible working hours were available to the employees to enable them to use the facility; Employer distributed brochures to its employees describing the program and stating, *inter alia*, that the employees' participation in the program benefits both Employer and the employees; Employer's manager of healthcare costs felt that the employees' participation in the program could reduce healthcare costs to Employer; and Stanner's exercise program was specifically developed by

---

38 *Hemmler v. Workmen's Compensation Appeal Bd. (Clarks Summit State Hosp.)*, 131 Pa. Commw. 24, 569 A.2d 395 (1990).
39 *Stanner v. Compensation Appeal Bd. (Westinghouse Elec. Co.)*, 604 A.2d at 1170 (emphasis added).

the staff of the fitness center."[40] Given its interpretation of the state's Workers' Compensation Act and the testimony of the medical expert who concluded that Stanner's death was caused by the decedent's strenuous exercise, the court ruled that there was substantial evidence to support a finding that the death was work-related. Therefore, it reversed the Board's decision and awarded benefits to Molly Stanner.

Estate of Gregory Sullwold v. Salvation Army[41]

This 2015 case deals with an employee's death that occurred at home. Given that many employees are working at home in recent years, many are also exercising at home rather than using the company's fitness center. Sullwold, who lived in Maine, was employed as a portfolio specialist and comptroller for the Salvation Army and was allowed to work from home. On the day he died, he began working at 8:30 a.m. in his office at home until about 3:30 when he took a break to walk on his treadmill. His wife found him about 30 minutes later, unconscious on the floor. Emergency personnel were called but were unable to save his life. Sullwold had known coronary artery disease (previous heart attack) and was being treated for it. He was encouraged by his doctors to make lifestyle changes with his diet and exercise. Prior to the incident, he suffered a panic attack, which he attributed to job stress from working long hours and traveling frequently.

His widow filed a petition for workers' compensation death benefits, claiming that her husband's workload, or work-related stress, caused the myocardial infarction that led to his death. (*Note:* The cause of death could also have been due to the exercise, as in the *Stanner* case, especially given the decedent's health history, but that was not addressed as a cause.) The Workers' Compensation Board granted the petition. However, the Salvation Army appealed the Board's decision and after further proceedings, the case was finally decided by Maine's Supreme Court. That court determined:

---

40 *Id.* at 1170–1171.
41 David L. Herbert, "Maine Supreme Court Determines Employee's Treadmill Related Death Is Compensable," *The Exercise, Sports and Sports Medicine Standards and Malpractice Rep.* 4, no. 2 (March 2015): 25.

Whether injury arose in the course of employment depends on "the time, place, and circumstances under which an injury occurs, the place where the employee reasonably may be in performance of the employee's duties, and whether it occurred while fulfilling those duties or engaged in something incidental to those duties.[42]

The hearing officer found that Sullwold "was walking on the treadmill at the time of his death, his injury occurred during work hours, in a place that the Salvation Army sanctioned for his work."[43] The Maine Supreme Court upheld the hearing officer's findings and therefore Sullwold's death was compensable.

Price v. Industrial Claim Appeals Office[44]

In this case, the Colorado Supreme Court analyzed two cases, Price[45] and Eltrich,[46] to determine if the injuries incurred were compensable under workers' compensation. Max Price, a prison guard for the Colorado Department of Corrections (DOC), was hanging upside down on a chin-up bar at home when he fell and landed on his neck, causing an injury. In his workers' compensation claim, he testified that his supervisor told him that in order to retain his job, he would need to lose weight. He also stated that his supervisor provided him with the DOC regulations that required him to maintain the physical condition to perform the job, and that was why he was exercising on the chin-up bar. Jeannine Eltrich was a police officer for the City of Northglenn. The Northglenn police department required all police officers to maintain certain fitness levels. They were required to complete a fitness examination every three months to demonstrate that they continued to meet the fitness standards. During one of these tests, Eltrich failed the running portion of the examination. To improve her performance, she began riding her bicycle during off-duty hours in the vicinity of her home. After she was injured when she fell from her bicycle, she filed a workers' compensation

---

42 *Id.* at 26.
43 *Id.*
44 *Price v. Industrial Claim Appeals Office*, 919 P.2d 207 (Colo. 1996).
45 *Price v. Industrial Claim Appeals Office*, 908 P.2d 136 (Colo. Ct. App. 1995).
46 *City of Northglenn v. Eltrich*, 908 P.2d 139 (Colo. Ct. App. 1995).

claim. In *Price*, the Industrial Claims Appeals Office (ICAO) decided that the injury was not compensable, and this decision was affirmed by the Colorado Court of Appeals. In *Eltrich*, the ICAO found that the injury was compensable. The Colorado Court of Appeals initially affirmed the ICAO's decision but, after further analysis and proceedings, reversed the ICAO's decision and indicated that Eltrich's injuries were not compensable.

Both Price and Eltrich petitioned the Colorado Supreme Court for **certiorari.** The state Supreme Court granted certiorari in both cases and decided to consolidate the cases given their similarity. To determine whether an employee's injury from participation in an exercise program is compensable under workers' compensation, the court provided a five-factor test:

> (1) Whether the injury occurred during working hours;
> (2) whether the injury occurred on the employer's premises;
> (3) whether the employer initiated the employee's exercise program; (4) whether the employer exerted any control or direction over the employee's exercise program; and (5) whether the employer stood to benefit from the employee's exercise program.[47]

The Colorado Supreme Court upheld the decisions of the courts of appeals in both cases, primarily because it gave greater weight to the first two factors than to the other three factors. The court stated that both Price and Eltrich failed to meet the first two factors and failed to make an extremely strong showing on the other factors. For example, in *Price*, the court concluded that the DOC exerted no control over the exercise program: It did not direct Price as to the type of exercise and certainly did not instruct him to hang upside down on a chin-up bar. In *Eltrich*, the court noted that she made a stronger showing than Price on employer initiative, given that there were direct orders from her supervisor that she pass the required fitness examination. However, her employer exerted no control over her exercise program: It did not furnish any of

---

47 *Price v. Industrial Claim Appeals Office*, 919 P.2d 207, 210–211 (Colo. 1996).

the equipment and did not direct her to as the type of exercise she should perform.

Workers' Compensation and Public Safety Officers

Many workplace fitness/wellness professionals design and deliver exercise programs for public safety workers such as police officers and firefighters. Major goals of these programs are to help prepare these workers for the physical demands of the job[48] and to help reduce injuries while performing the job (and thus subsequent workers' compensation claims).[49] Again, because workers' compensation is based on individual state laws, court opinions as to whether these workers are entitled to workers' compensation for injuries incurred while engaging in fitness and recreational programs vary from state to state. For example, the five-factor test set out by the Colorado Supreme Court may or may not be used in other states. Some courts have relied upon a three-prong test to determine if an injury was compensable: (1) Was the activity on the premises? (2) Was the activity required by the employer?, or (3) Did the employer derive a substantial benefit from it?[50]

The weight that courts accord to each factor can also vary. For example, one court awarded compensation to a police officer injured while participating in a benefit basketball game, and another court rejected the claim after applying the same test.[51] Regarding the requirement factor, some courts have ruled that injuries are not compensable unless the employer required the employees to participate in a specific activity as a condition of employment; other courts have awarded compensation when an employer encouraged employees to participate in the activity or derived substantial benefit from the activity.[52]

---

48 Patricia G. Barnes, *Workers' Compensation: Law Enforcement Officer's Recovery for Injury Sustained During Exercise or Physical Recreation Activities*, 44 A.L.R. 5th 569 (1996).

49 Kerry S. Kuehl, Yasemin Kisbu-Sakarya, Diane L. Elliot et al., "Body Mass Is a Predictor of Fire Fighter Injury and Workers' Compensation Claims," *J. Occupational & Envtl. Med.* 54, no. 5 (2013): 579–582; *see also* Stephanie C. Griffin, Tracy L. Regan, Phillip Harber et al., "Evaluation of a Fitness Intervention for New Firefighters: Injury Reduction and Economic Benefits," *Injury Prevention* (published online, November 11, 2015), http://injuryprevention.bmj.com/content/early/2015/11/11/injury-prev-2015-041785.full.

50 Patricia G. Barnes, *Workers' Compensation: Law Enforcement Officer's Recovery for Injury Sustained During Exercise or Physical Recreation Activities*, 44 A.L.R. 5th 569 (1996).

51 *Id.*

52 *Id.*

City of Kenosha v. Labor & Industry Review Commission[53]

In this case, the City of Kenosha appealed a decision of the Labor and Industry Review Commission (LIRC) that a firefighter suffered a compensable injury while playing basketball with fellow firefighters and while on active duty at the time. The city claimed that the "well-being activity exclusion" found in Wis. Stat. § 102.03(1)(c) prevented the firefighter from receiving workers' compensation benefits. This exclusion, in part, stated:

> An employee is not performing service growing out of and incidental to employment while engaging in a program, event, or activity designed to improve the physical well-being of the employee, whether or not the program, event, or activity is located on the employer's premises, if participation in the program, event, or activity is voluntary and the employee receives no compensation for participation.[54]

The city contended that at the time of the injury, all three prongs of this exclusion clause were satisfied: (a) the employee was engaged in an activity designed to improve his physical well-being, (b) his participation was voluntary, and (c) he received no compensation for participation. The court stated that the city would have to show that all three criteria were met to win its case. The court did not discuss the first two prongs, but did indicate that the city failed on the third prong because the firefighter was being compensated by the city to stand ready at the fire station at the time of his injury.

In his testimony, the city's fire chief explained that "it was common for on-duty firefighters to play basketball during their shifts .... He did not consider playing basketball while on active duty to be an abandonment of the job duties of a firefighter" and he "made clear that it is important for firefighters to be physically fit, due to the stress and demands of firefighting. He testified the City's fire department had no

---

53 *City of Kenosha v. Labor & Indus. Rev. Comm'n*, 332 Wis. 2d 448 (Wis. Ct. App. 2011).
54 *Id.* at 453.

formal fitness policy, but rather an informal fitness program under which the fire department encourages personnel to engage in physical fitness activities while on duty."[55] He also stated that the city provided a weight room, treadmills, and elliptical trainers for the firefighters to use. In its ruling to award compensation to the firefighter, the court said: "If the employer was compensating the employee when the injury occurred, it is the employer's acknowledgement that the employee was engaged in the employer's business and the well-being exception does not apply."[56] The court also indicated that the city would have to have paid the firefighter additional compensation for playing basketball in order to satisfy the third prong. Although not an issue in this case, this holding does pose an interesting question: If the firefighter would have received some type of financial incentive for participating in physical activity such as basketball, would this be considered additional compensation?

A couple of other firefighter workers' compensation cases are interesting in that they have different outcomes: In one, a firefighter was awarded compensation, and in the other a firefighter was not awarded compensation. In the first case,[57] a firefighter was injured while performing push-ups in his home basement to help prepare for one of his employer's required fitness tests. The Labor and Industry Review Commission awarded compensation to this firefighter because the upper body strength portion of the employer's test consisted of performing push-ups, even though the employer had no direct control of the off-premise exercise program. The LIRC indicated that there was a direct link between the type of exercise the employee performed when injured and the type the employer required in the fitness test.

In the other case,[58] a firefighter experienced a serious injury—a torn quadriceps tendon requiring surgery—while performing a "clean and jerk." On the day of the injury, the firefighter, along with other firefighters, was being pushed by the trainers to hit a new personal record (PR): lifting

---

55 *Id.* at 451–452.

56 *Id.* at 456.

57 *Nofzinger v. City of Appleton*, WC Claim No. 2009-009564 (LIRC, 1/27/2011), http://lirc.wisconsin.gov/wcdecsns/1365.htm.

58 Call the Cops, "Firefighter Injured On-Duty Denied Workers Comp Over a Technicality," February 10, 2014, http://www.callthecops.net/firefighter-injured-duty-denied-workers-comp-technicality.

weights heavier than they ever lifted before. The insurance company denied the workers' compensation claim filed by the firefighter. It did not provide a reason for the denial, stating that to do so would be a violation of HIPAA. However, it appeared that the city supported the insurer's decision and took the position that pushing people for a PR while on duty showed that the trainers were not responsible. The fire chief stated that the city was making it look like the firefighters were irresponsible, and he claimed that the trainers were well qualified. For example, one trainer had a degree in kinesiology and was also certified by CrossFit; another trainer was certified by the Cooper Institute and Russian Kettlebells.

Generally, workers' compensation benefits would be available if the trainers in this case were negligent, such as giving negligent instruction. It may be, though, that the insurance company viewed their conduct as intentional; if so, the injury would not be compensable under workers' compensation. This case is interesting for a couple of reasons: (a) just because someone has a degree and/or certifications does not mean he or she is qualified and competent to design and deliver safe and effective programs (see Chapter 6); and (b) given the trend toward and tremendous growth in extreme conditioning programs (ECPs), some military units and fire/police departments are including these ECPs in their physical training programs. Trainers of these programs not only need advanced knowledge and skills, but also need to take many precautions, given the increased risk of injuries with these programs. In fact, a consensus statement on the topic of ECPs was published in 2011 by the American College of Sports Medicine.[59] ECPs (e.g., CrossFit, Insanity) were defined in this statement as high-volume training workouts that use a variety of high-intensity exercises with short rest periods between sets. The authors discuss the emerging problem of injury risks associated with these programs and how they violate recognized accepted standards that should be used in the design of safe exercise programs. Exercise programs should not be designed to increase risks of injury above and beyond those risks that would be considered inherent.

---

59 Michael F. Bergeron, Bradley C. Nindl, Patricia A. Deuster et al., "Consortium for Health and Military Performance and American College of Sports Medicine Consensus Paper on Extreme Conditioning Programs in Military Personnel," *Current Sports Med. Reps.* 10, no. 6 (2011): 383–389.

Voluntary Recreational Activities

In the cases just discussed, the courts had to consider whether the employee's fitness/recreation injury arose out of and in the course of employment, to determine if the injury was compensable. But what about "voluntary" recreational activities, such as participating in a team sport league that the employer sponsors and encourages employees to participate in during non-work hours? Generally, "employment" does not include participation in a voluntary recreational activity. However, there is ample case law dealing with these types of activities, and the rulings vary among the states. The following summaries highlight a couple of state statutes and how they have defined voluntary recreational activity with regard to workers' compensation.

Pennsylvania—§ 4:84. Employer-sponsored teams and exertional activities encouraged by employer: 6 West's Pa. Prac., Workers' Compensation § 4:84 (3d ed., 2015).

- An injury suffered while participating in an employer-sponsored sports team is compensable because it benefits the employer by enhancing morale and fostering teamwork among employees as well as providing a favorable public image.
- An injury suffered while participating in an informal get together of employees playing sports is not compensable because it does not create a tangible employer interest.

According to this state's law, an injury suffered while participating in exertional activities (including exercising, playing basketball, or swimming) at the behest of the employer is compensable because it furthers the interests of the employer by enhancing the health of its employees.

New York—§ 437. Off-duty athletic activity: 110 N.Y. Jur. 2d Workers' Compensation § 437 (2016).

- A benefit to the employer is a factor but is not the only test for an injury to be compensable that occurred during voluntary participation in an off-duty athletic activity.

- An injury occurring during voluntary participation in an off-duty athletic activity is only compensable if it constitutes a part of the employee's work-related duties.
- If the employer (a) requires the employee to participate, (b) compensates the employee for participating, or (c) sponsors the activity (e.g., there is evidence that the employer encouraged employees to participate), the injury would be compensable.

Can Employees Waive Their Workers' Compensation Benefits by Signing a Waiver?

As briefly described in Chapter 1, waivers (or prospective releases) are signed by participants prior to participation in fitness/recreation programs to protect the defendants (e.g., exercise professionals and employers) from ordinary negligence. However, can employees validly sign a **waiver** of workers' compensation benefits before participating in employer-sponsored fitness and/or recreational activities? *Jones v. Multi-Color Corp.*[60] is an interesting case that addresses this issue. Before participating in a foot race (one of the activities employees could participate in during an employer-sponsored fitness day), Jones signed a waiver entitled "Waiver of Workers' Compensation Benefits for a Voluntary Participant in an Employer-Sponsored Recreation or Fitness Program/Activity" (the waiver), which stated:

> The undersigned declares that he or she is a voluntary participant in the employer's sponsored recreation fitness activity(s) listed above and hereby waives and relinquishes all rights to Workers' Compensation benefits under Chapter 4123 of the Revised Code for any injury or disability incurred while participating on an annual basis in the listed activity(s).[61]

Jones's family filed a workers' compensation claim seeking death benefits. The defendants (administrator of the Bureau of Workers' Compensation, the Industrial Commission, and Multi-Color Corporation) denied

---

60 *Jones v. Multi-Color Corp.*, 108 Ohio App. 3d 388 (Ohio Ct. App. 1995).
61 *Id.* at 391–392.

the benefits because Jones had signed the waiver and therefore his injury did not occur in the course of or arising out of employment. The trial court agreed and the family then appealed this decision.

According to Ohio law, the general rule was that it is invalid to have an employee waive his or her rights to workers' compensation. However, in 1986 the state legislature enacted new statutes creating exceptions to the general rule, due to the large number of employer challenges to compensation for recreational activities. These statutes allowed employers to have their employees sign a waiver of their workers' compensation benefits for an injury or disability incurred in voluntary participation in recreation or fitness activities sponsored by the employer.

The appellate court found that Jones's injury occurred during the course of or arising out of employment. The court stated that if Jones's injury was outside his employment:

> to allow this interpretation, which would remove such injuries from the workers' compensation system, employees injured in recreational activities could sue their employers for common-law negligence, and in the event of a fatal injury, dependents could bring wrongful death claims. Such an interpretation is completely at odds with the entire workers' compensation scheme ... . The Act [Rev. Code ch. 4123] operates as a balance of mutual compromise between the interests of the employer and the employee whereby employees relinquish their common law remedy and accept lower benefit levels coupled with the greater assurance of recovery and employers give up their common law defenses and are protected from unlimited liability.[62]

Regarding the language in the waiver, the court stated:

> Looking first at the release itself, even if a worker could waive benefits other than his own, we hold that the release in this case is wholly insufficient in law to accomplish such a waiver. It simply does not inform Jones that he is or might be waiving the right of

---

62 *Id.* at 394.

his dependents to any death benefits. The form does not even mention death benefits.[63]

The release in this case absolutely fails to inform Jones about the effect of his waiver on his dependents' benefits, and on this basis alone it would not operate as a waiver even if such a waiver were permissible. However, we also hold that even if the form Jones signed adequately advised him of what he was waiving, Jones could not, in law, waive his dependents' death benefits.[64]

The court concluded that its interpretation and ruling did not automatically entitle death benefits to the family, but it allowed them to prove the necessary compensable injury as if there had been no waiver at all.

Risk Management Strategies: Preventive Law

Given the many variations in state workers' compensation laws, workplace wellness professionals will need to seek legal advice to help develop risk management strategies involving injuries that occur when employees are participating in fitness and/or recreational activities. If companies have locations in multiple states, these strategies could vary from site to site. It is best to address the issue of workers' compensation prior to offering fitness and recreation programs. Knowing the state laws and understanding how courts have applied them is the first step. Legal counsel will be able to review the applicable workers' compensation statutes and any state court cases dealing with fitness and recreational activities. Wellness professionals should ask the following questions when developing risk management strategies:

1. What factors are specified in the law to determine if injuries that occur while participating in fitness and/or recreational activities are compensable? (As described earlier, there are many such factors:

---

63 *Id.* at 395.
64 *Id.* at 395–396.

e.g., was the activity required, encouraged, or voluntary; did the activity occur during work or outside of work; did the activity occur on the premises or off the premises; did the employer benefit from the activity and if so, how was "benefit" defined; etc.)

2. If workers' compensation does *not* apply to certain fitness and recreational activities, should employees sign a waiver prior to participating in such activities to help protect the employer from negligence?

3. If workers' compensation does apply to certain fitness and recreational activities, does state law allow employers to have their employees sign a waiver to forgo their workers' compensation benefits? If so, could this lead to the possibility of the employee suing the employer for negligence?

4. What about dependents who are not employees but are often involved in company-sponsored fitness and recreational activities: should they sign a waiver (for negligence)? Should dependents sign a waiver of workers' compensation death benefits, and does the state's law allow this in the event of an employee's death?

5. If a waiver is used for negligence, what is it required to contain (e.g., certain language, proper administration) to help ensure that it will be upheld by the court? (Waiver law varies from state to state, as do workers' compensation laws. See *Waivers & Releases of Liability*[65] for an analysis of each state's waiver law.)

RULE THE RULES

Key Points in Chapter 7

1. Based on the FLSA, if wellness programs take place during the employee's regular work time, or if attendance is required, the employer should consider such participation to be compensable work time.

---

65 Doyice J. Cotton and Mary B. Cotten, *Waivers & Releases of Liability,* 9th ed. (Statesboro, GA: Sport Risk Consulting, 2016).

2. If employers do not want to compensate employees for their participation in wellness programs, the FLSA requires certain criteria to be met.

3. Workers' compensation statutes benefit both the employer and the employee.

4. Workplace wellness programs have been shown to reduce workplace injuries and workers' compensation costs.

5. Employees cannot sue their employer for negligence if workers' compensation applies.

6. The procedures set forth in workers' compensation acts vary from state to state, as do the factors that courts use to determine if an injury is compensable under workers' compensation.

7. Most states use arbitration to solve disputes, but an employee can appeal a decision made by an arbitrator to the state's Workers' Compensation Board, an industrial commission, or a state court.

8. Generally, injuries occurring in employer-sponsored fitness and/ or recreation programs are compensable under workers' compensation, but not in all instances. State laws can vary; for example, compensability may depend on whether the program was required, encouraged, or voluntary.

9. Individual state statutes will determine whether employees can waive their workers' compensation benefits prior to participating in company-sponsored fitness and/or recreation programs.

10. Workplace wellness professionals need to address a variety of factors, in consultation with a competent lawyer, related to application of workers' compensation statutes.

Study Questions

1. Describe the purposes of the Fair Labor Standards Act and its application to workplace wellness programs.

2. List the four criteria that must be met if employers do not want to compensate their employees for participation in wellness programs.

3. Explain why workers' compensation is a form of strict liability and how it benefits both employees and employers.
4. Describe how workplace fitness and wellness programs can lead to fewer injuries and subsequent workers' compensation claims.
5. First, describe the facts (what happened) in the *Stanner* and *Estate of Gregory Sullwold* cases. Second, describe the procedural facts (appeal process) that led to awards of workers' compensation benefits to the widows in these cases.
6. Compare and contrast the factors that the courts in the *Price* and *City of Kenosha* cases used to determine if the injuries were compensable under workers' compensation.
7. Describe variations in state laws with regard to voluntary recreational activities and workers' compensation.
8. Given the issues involving a waiver of workers' compensation benefits in the *Jones* case, describe risk management issues that workplace wellness professionals (along with their legal counsel) should address.

Key Terms

arbitration

certiorari

inherent risks

intentional torts (acts)

negligent conduct

strict liability

waiver

8

What About Stress?

Learning Objectives

After reading this chapter, workplace wellness professionals will be able to:

1. Understand the prevalence and adverse consequences of occupational stress.
2. Describe how comprehensive workplace wellness programs can address workplace stress through two approaches: individual (e.g., EAPs, stress management workshops, exercise programs) and organizational (e.g., company efforts that lead to a healthy work culture).
3. Identify stress-related hazards that can be addressed through a comprehensive workplace wellness program.
4. Understand how federal laws such as OSHA, ADA, Title VII of the Civil Rights Act, ADEA, MHPAEA, and the ACA can help provide guidance and incentives for creating a healthy work environment.
5. Describe the purposes of state workers' compensation laws, as well as legal cases involving stress-related or psychological injuries.
6. Develop and implement preventive law strategies that not only comply with federal and state laws, but also, when properly designed into workplace wellness programs, can have a positive effect on workplace stress.

Workplace trauma has its roots in the culture of the organization. Recent court decisions have supported this notion by affirming that the creation of an environment that may be perceived as offensive, threatening or hostile is sufficient basis for liability on

the part of the employer, regardless of the direct experience of an individual member.

—T. R. Tyler[1]

When we downshift, we revert to the tried and true .... Our
responses become more automatic and limited. We are less able
to access all that we know or see what is really there. Our ability
to consider subtle environmental and internal cues is reduced.
We also seem less able to engage in complex intellectual tasks,
those requiring creativity and the ability to engage in open-ended
thinking and questioning.

—R. Caine and G. Caine[2]

Introduction

Occupational stress is a growing public health concern. Some have even
labeled it a "global epidemic."[3] The International Labor Office has recognized work stress as a major challenge to worker and organization
health.[4] According to the World Health Organization (WHO), workers
who are stressed are more likely to be unhealthy, poorly motivated, less
productive, and less safe at work.[5] Moreover, their organizations are less
likely to be successful in a competitive market.[6]

Work-related stress increases the risk for depression and anxiety disorders.[7] WHO estimates that depression will be the most prominent

---

1 "Do Employees Really Care About Due Process?" *In Proceedings of the 1989 Employee Responsibili-*
ties and Rights Conference, American Bar Association, Northwestern University, 1989.
2 *Making Connections: Teaching and the Human Brain* (New York, NY: Addison Wesley, 1994): 72.
3 *See, e.g.,* Lori Kozlowski, "Getting America to Check in with Itself," *Forbes* (January 28, 2013), http://
www.forbes.com/sites/lorikozlowski/2013/01/28/getting-america-to-check-in-with-itself/ (stating that the
World Health Organization has called stress the health epidemic of the 21st century).
4 Stavroula Leka et al., "Work Organization and Stress," *World Health Organization* (2004): 1.
5 *Id.*
6 *Id.*
7 Jong-Min Woo and Teodor T. Postolache, "The Impact of Work Environment on Mood Disorders and
Suicide: Evidence and Implications," *Int'l J. Disabil. Hum. Dev.* 7, no. 2 (2008): 185–200, http://www.
ncbi.nlm.nih.gov/pmc/articles/PMC2559945/pdf/nihms52245.pdf.

disability at work in the next decade.[8] Self-reported data from more than 1.3 million employees indicate that 30 percent experienced some depression or were in treatment.[9] Studies have shown a relationship between depression and chronic disease. Depression is found to co-occur in 17 percent of cardiovascular cases, 23 percent of cerebrovascular cases, and with 27 percent of diabetes patients and more than 40 percent of individuals with cancer.[10] Tobacco use is also about twice as high for those with mental illness compared to the general population.[11] Stress and mental illness contribute to occupational injury and illness. Specifically, injury rates are two to six times higher among individuals with a mental illness than in the overall population.[12]

The costs of workplace stress are also monumental. One study estimates that **mental health disorders** cost U.S. employers $317.5 billion annually, compared to the $310 billion employers spend each year on occupational injury and illness generally.[13] Most of the financial burden of mental health disorders is not from the cost to treat the illness, but from indirect costs,[14] such as workers' compensation, short- and long-term disability, **presenteeism** (the measurable extent to which health symptoms, conditions, and diseases adversely affect the work productivity of individuals who choose to remain at work), and absenteeism.[15]

The prevalence and adverse consequences of stress and mental illness are not lost on American employers. In a 2013 survey of employers, stress ranked as the number one workforce risk issue, ranking above

---

8 Laura Anderko et al., "Promoting Prevention Through the Affordable Care Act: Workplace Wellness," *Centers for Disease Control Preventing Chronic Disease*, 9 (December 13, 2012), http://www.cdc.gov/pcd/issues/2012/12_0092.htm.
9 *Id.*
10 Centers for Disease Control (CDC), *Mental Health and Chronic Diseases* (Issue Brief No. 2, October 2012), http://www.cdc.gov/nationalhealthyworksite/docs/Issue-Brief-No-2-Mental-Health-and-Chronic-Disease.pdf.
11 *Id.*
12 Jonathan C. Dopkeen and Renee Dubois, *Stress in the Workplace: A Policy Synthesis on Its Dimensions and Prevalence* (University of Illinois at Chicago Center for Employee Health Studies, March 2014): 3, http://indigo.uic.edu/bitstream/handle/10027/18751/Stress%20in%20the%20Workplace%20A%20Policy%20Synthesis%20on%20Its%20Dimensions%20and%20Prevalence.pdf?sequence=3.
13 *Id.*
14 CDC, *Mental Health and Chronic Diseases.*
15 *Id.*

physical inactivity and obesity.[16] Yet, despite the recognized importance, only 15 percent of employers identify improving the emotional/mental health of employees (i.e., lessening their stress and anxiety) as a top priority of their health and productivity programs.[17] This lack of interest in addressing mental health exacerbates the staggering statistic that 71 percent of workers with mental illnesses have never sought help from a medical or mental health specialist for their symptoms.[18] Stigma and discrimination associated with mental illness remain a significant barrier to seeking help.[19]

Most of the causes of work stress arise from the way work is designed and the way in which organizations are managed.[20] Stress results from a mismatch between the demands and pressures on the person, on the one hand, and the person's knowledge and abilities, on the other.[21] The more excessive or unmanageable the demands placed on workers in relation to their knowledge and abilities, coupled with little opportunity to exercise any choice or control and lack of support from others, the more likely it is that their jobs will be stressful.[22]

Stress is different from pressure. Pressure at work can be healthy, by keeping workers alert, motivated, and able to learn.[23] However, when pressure becomes excessive or otherwise unmanageable, it can lead to stress.[24] Other causes of stress include scheduling issues, such as shift-work or long hours; physical demands, such as positions that are mostly sedentary or involve heavy physical exertion; exposure to hazardous chemicals; and broader work environment conditions such as noise, heat, cold, and little access to healthy food.[25]

---

16 Towers Watson, "U.S. Employers Rank Stress as Top Workforce Risk Issue" (November 13, 2013) (describing survey conducted by Towers Watson and the National Business Group on Health), https://www.towerswatson.com/en-US/Press/2013/11/us-employers-rank-stress-as-top-workforce-risk-issue.
17 *Id.*; *see also* Jill Horowitz et al., "Wellness Incentives in the Workplace: Cost Savings Through Cost Shifting to Unhealthy Workers," *Health Affairs* 32, no. 3 (March 2013): 471 (noting that wellness programs infrequently target stress).
18 CDC, *Mental Health and Chronic Diseases.*
19 *Id.*
20 Leka et al., "Work Organization and Stress," at 1.
21 *Id.* at 4–5.
22 *Id.*
23 *Id.*
24 *Id.*
25 CDC, *Mental Health and Chronic Diseases.*

Comprehensive Workplace Wellness Programs Can Help

There are two general approaches to addressing workplace stress and mental illness: (1) individual and (2) organizational.[26] Individual approaches can include counseling through an **employee assistance program (EAP)** and participation in stress reduction programs, such as physical activity, meditation, or yoga.[27] Indeed, policies that enhance worksite lifestyle programs such as physical activity are good adjunct therapies in preventing and treating depression.[28] Individual approaches may also include screening for stress or substance misuse (an activity correlated with depression); creating standards-of-conduct policies; and training efforts to improve manager and employee understanding of and skills in problem solving, effective communication, and conflict resolution.[29]

Although in 2013, 85 percent of surveyed employers reported that they promote EAPs to help employees manage stress, only 39 percent offered overt stress management interventions to employees (such as stress management workshops, yoga, or tai chi).[30] Given these results, it should be obvious that those designing workplace wellness programs can do more to boost stress management program availability. For example, some workplace wellness programs have special relaxation areas/rooms and have incorporated mindfulness programs as part of their overall offerings.

Organizational approaches are equally important, but are much more difficult to implement. Organizational approaches focus on assessing hazardous work conditions and mobilizing organizational resources to support workers' mental health.[31] Organizational approaches aim to create a healthy work environment and culture. Employees in companies with a strong culture of health are three times as likely to report taking

---

26 Woo and Postolache, "The Impact of Work Environment on Mood Disorders and Suicide."
27 Id.; see also Centers for Disease Control, "Depression Fact Sheet" (October 23, 2013), http://www.cdc.gov/workplacehealthpromotion/implementation/topics/depression.html.
28 CDC, "Depression Fact Sheet."
29 Id.; see also Dopkeen and Dubois, "Stress in the Workplace," at 4.
30 Towers Watson, "U.S. Employers Rank Stress as Top Workforce Risk Issue."
31 Woo and Postolache, "The Impact of Work Environment on Mood Disorders and Suicide."

action to improve their health, and have better performance and higher job satisfaction.[32] In addition, such a company may experience better financial outcomes and lower employee turnover.[33] Another bonus of addressing organizational factors that lead to job stress, such as long working hours and job control, is an overall reduction in community health inequality. A 2015 study suggests that policies to encourage healthier psychosocial work environments, especially for jobs likely to be held by the most disadvantaged demographic groups, can help improve life expectancy across different socioeconomic groups.[34]

Despite these benefits, fewer than 26 percent of employees believe their company has a strong culture of health.[35] According to one researcher, employers have been fairly accepting of adopting workplace mental health promotion programs that focus on "fixing the worker," but are not taking steps to ensure that the workplace itself is optimal.[36] For example, as noted earlier, many employers promote EAPs—yet EAPs are often not able to address issues that relate to the work environment or organizational practice.[37] However, EAP benefits may include referral services and short-term substance use disorder or mental health counseling, as well as financial counseling and legal services.[38]

To sufficiently address job stress, an effective workplace wellness program will develop managers who support their employees, maximize employee autonomy, promote engagement in the value of employees' work in alignment with the organization's mission, and improve the work environment.[39] Improving the work environment may include instituting shorter or more flexible working hours, monitoring the

---

32 Anderko et al., "Promoting Prevention through the Affordable Care Act."

33 *Id.*

34 Joel Goh, Jeffrey Pfeffer, and Stefanos Zenios, "Exposure to Harmful Workplace Practices Could Account for Inequality in Life Spans Across Different Demographic Groups," *Health Affairs* 34, no. 10 (October 2015): 1761–1768.

35 Anderko et al., "Promoting Prevention through the Affordable Care Act."

36 Kirsten Weir, "Work, Stress and Health: Research from the 10th International Conference on Occupational Stress and Health," *American Psychological Association* 44, no. 8 (September 2013): 40, http://www.apa.org/monitor/2013/09/stress-health.aspx.

37 CDC, "Depression Fact Sheet."

38 79 Fed. Reg. 59130, 59132 (October 1, 2014). EAP benefits are typically available free of charge to employees and are often provided through third-party vendors. *Id.*

39 Dopkeen and Dubois, "Stress in the Workplace."

environmental risks to mood status, using noise-canceling headphones, allowing outdoor walks or rest time during the workday, or having access to a window.[40] According to WHO, workplace wellness program designers should assess risk of the following **stress-related hazards**:

- Job content (monotonous, understimulating, meaningless, or unpleasant tasks)
- Workload and work pace (having too much or too little to do and working under time pressures)
- Work hours (strict and inflexible working schedules, long and unsocial hours, unpredictable hours, badly designed shift systems)
- Participation and control (lack of participation in decision making; lack of control over work methods, pace, hours, and environment)
- Career development, status, and pay (job insecurity, lack of promotion prospects, overpromotion, piece-rate payment schemes, unclear or unfair performance evaluation systems, being over-skilled or underskilled for the job)
- Role in the organization (unclear role, conflicting roles within the same job, responsibility for people, continuously dealing with other people and their problems)
- Interpersonal relationships (inadequate, inconsiderate, or unsupportive supervision; poor relationships with coworkers; bullying, harassment, and violence; isolated or solitary work; no standard or agreed procedures for dealing with problems or complaints)
- Organizational culture (poor communication, poor leadership, lack of clarity about organizational objectives and structure)
- Home-work interface (conflicting demands of work and home, lack of support for domestic problems at work, lack of support for work problems at home)[41]

---

40 Woo and Postolache, "The Impact of Work Environment on Mood Disorders and Suicide."
41 Leka et al., "Work Organization and Stress," at 6–7.

Organizational assessment and change are a tall order for many organizations. Nevertheless, the law can help provide guidance and incentives to create a healthy work environment.

Preventive Law to the Rescue

Recall that in Chapter 2 we discussed the concept of preventive law and using the law as a tool to effectuate the law's purpose and therefore mitigate risk of employee discontent. Nowhere does it make more sense to adopt a preventive law approach than when addressing potential workplace stress. There are a number of laws that can help guide workplace wellness program designers in creating a positive organizational culture, thereby reducing the risk of workplace stress. These laws include workers' compensation, the Occupational Safety and Health Act (OSHA), the Americans with Disabilities Act (ADA), other civil rights laws like Title VII and the Age Discrimination in Employment Act (ADEA), the Mental Health Parity and Addiction Equity Act (MHPAEA), the Affordable Care Act (ACA), and recent rules regarding EAPs and excepted benefit status. Data privacy laws are also important in this context; they are addressed in the next chapter.

Each of these laws should remind the workplace wellness program designer that wellness programs must be about more than just diet and exercise. Although physical fitness and a healthy diet can help employees feel better about themselves, adequately addressing stress in the workplace requires broader programming. Ideally, this programming would encompass both individual and organizational approaches to minimizing occupational stress.

Workers' Compensation Laws

One of the more surprising, but significant, areas of law that protects workers from overburdening workplace stress is state workers' compensation laws. Wellness program designers should understand the legal risks that state workers' compensation laws may impose when a wellness program fails to account for the existence and alleviation of occupational stress. Before delving into some interesting workers' compensation cases addressing workplace stress, though, it is important to review the purpose of workers' compensation laws.

Workers' compensation laws are state-based laws.[42] As discussed more fully in Chapter 7, the basic aim of workers' compensation laws is to provide employers with "no-fault" insurance based on the premise that occupational accidents are not completely avoidable.[43] The no-fault aspect of workers' compensation laws means that employees are unable to sue the employer for their injuries.[44] Instead, most states have a workers' compensation board that initially handles any claims.[45] In return for forfeiting the right to sue, workers' compensation law imposes strict liability on the employer, regardless of who is actually at fault for the injury, and compensates the injured employee. A successful workers' compensation claim pays for the injured employee's lost wages (usually at about two-thirds salary) for the period of total disability and in the form of lump-sum payments for any residual permanent partial disability, as well as for the employee's medical and rehabilitation costs.[46]

Even though the purpose of workers' compensation laws is to avoid costly litigation for the employer, some claims do wind up in court.[47] Usually, courts are asked to resolve disputes relating to whether an injury was caused by the employee's work.[48] Employees have the burden of proving that their disability or injury was caused by or suffered in the course of their work.[49] Stress-related claims are particularly ripe for court involvement, as it can be difficult to prove that work caused a

---

42 John M. Ivancevich et al., "Who's Liable for Stress on the Job?," *Harvard Bus. Rev.* (1985), https://hbr.org/1985/03/whos-liable-for-stress-on-the-job.

43 Gregory P. Guyton, "A Brief History of Workers' Compensation," *Iowa Orthopaedic J.* 19 (1999): 106–110, at 108, http://www.ncbi.nlm.nih.gov/pmc/articles/PMC1888620/.

44 *Id.*; *see also* Ivancevich et al., "Who's Liable for Stress on the Job?"

45 Guyton, "A Brief History of Workers' Compensation," at 108–109. Apparently, in Wyoming, Tennessee, New Mexico, Alabama, and Louisiana, employees can take workers' compensation claims directly to court, but special state agencies exist to assist the processing of claims. *Id.*

46 *Id.* at 109.

47 Ivancevich et al., "Who's Liable for Stress on the Job?"

48 *Id.*

49 Rolf C. Schuetz, Jr., "Stress at Work? You Might Have a Workers' Compensation Claim," *American Bar Association GP Solo eReport* 2, no. 12 (July 2013), http://www.americanbar.org/publications/gpsolo_ereport/2013/july_2013/stressed_at_work_might_have_workers_compensation_claim.html.

psychological injury.[50] Courts divide claims of psychological injury into those arising from a discrete, identifiable accident and those arising from the effects of repetitive events, no one of which can be identified as causing the injury.[51] Courts more readily compensate for psychological injury that arises from an accident involving physical injury.[52] Cases involving psychological trauma resulting in physical illness or producing psychological injury are more difficult.[53] In either case, an employee will need to prove causation of the psychological injury with facts and medical testimony.[54] Although there are cases in which the employee is unsuccessful in proving that work caused a psychological injury,[55] this chapter focuses on cases in which the employee was successful. The following cases illustrate occupational stress claims in which the employee (or the employee's family) successfully showed a link between work conditions and psychological injury.

Harper v. Banks, Finley, White & Co. of Mississippi

Milton Harper was the managing partner and president of accounting firm Banks, Finley, White & Co. (Banks) who suffered a severe stroke on August 3, 2000, and died after suffering another stroke on July 10, 2001. His family sued Banks for workers' compensation benefits, alleging that Mr. Harper's death arose out of the scope and course of his employment at Banks. In 1995, Dr. Marvin Jeter diagnosed Mr. Harper with high blood pressure and prescribed him blood pressure medication, which Mr. Harper took intermittently for three years. On August 3, 2000, Mr. Harper suffered a stroke, and Dr. Jeter noted that Mr. Harper had not been taking his blood pressure medication. Mr. Harper rested for two weeks and then returned to work, initially part-time and then to his usual full-time schedule of 8:00 a.m. until 5:30 or 7:30 p.m.

---

50 *Id.*
51 Ivancevich et al., "Who's Liable for Stress on the Job?"
52 *Id.*
53 *Id.*
54 Schuetz, Jr., "Stress at Work? You Might Have a Workers' Compensation Claim."
55 Ivancevich et al., "Who's Liable for Stress on the Job?" (citing *Transportation Ins. Co. v. Maksyn*, 580 S.W. 2d 334 (Tex. 1979); *Peroti v. Atkinson*, 213 Cal. App. 2d 472 (Cal. Ct. App. 1963); *LaBuda v. Chrysler Corp.*, 232 N.W. 2d 686 (Mich. 1975); *Lockwood v. Indep. Sch. Dist. et al.*, Workers' Comp. L. Rep. 1054 (Minnesota Supreme Court Nos. 51976 and 51931, Dec. 4, 1981).

Almost a year later, on July 8, 2001, Mr. Harper suffered another stroke at home and died a few days later. Mr. Harper's wife and daughter sought workers' compensation benefits for his two strokes. Mr. Harper's wife described her husband as a "workaholic" and said that he was "constantly working." She stated that Mr. Harper kept saying that he was getting behind at work and having problems balancing being out of town for audits and trying to manage the office at the same time. She said that her husband was the type of person who liked to perform well and who pushed himself at work to receive bonuses. Mrs. Harper testified that over the years, Mr. Harper's work stress began to take a toll on him. She would advise him to cut back, but he would respond that he had to "go make a dollar." Mr. Harper told his wife that his stress had nothing to do with her or with their family life.

The Mississippi Workers' Compensation Commission found that Mr. Harper's family proved that his hypertension was caused by the stresses of work and that such hypertension caused his stroke on August 3, 2000, and his death on July 10, 2001. The commission found that Mr. Harper was under a considerable amount of stress from work which was more than the usual and everyday work stress, including but not limited to: (1) working long hours and working seven days a week; (2) having partners feuding over profit sharing; (3) having problems with new computer software shortly after his August 3, 2000, stroke; and (4) managing the office while simultaneously performing out-of-town audits and other accounting work. The commission concluded that Mr. Harper's stress was such that it caused an increase in his blood pressure, which in turn caused his strokes and death. The Supreme Court of Mississippi affirmed the commission's decision that Mr. Harper's stroke was a compensable injury under workers' compensation.[56]

Cox v. Saks Fifth Avenue

Jeremy Cox worked as a sales associate at Saks Fifth Avenue in its handbag department starting in November 2011. During a promotional event for a manufacturer of high-priced luxury goods, Mr. Cox's supervisor directed him to fabricate reserve orders by falsely indicating that

---

56 *Harper ex rel. Harper v. Banks, Finley, White & Co. of Miss., P.C.*, 167 So. 3d 1155 (Miss. 2015).

individual customers intended to purchase the manufacturer's handbags, for the purpose of increasing store inventory. Mr. Cox submitted two fabricated orders during the event, which required the inclusion of customers' personal information, including credit card numbers. The store's supervisors admitted that the submission of fabricated reserve orders on the day of a promotional event had occurred at the store in the past. Mr. Cox became upset during the promotional event and a supervisor heard Mr. Cox say that he did not want to submit false orders. The workers' compensation law judge concluded that Mr. Cox sustained a mental injury as a result of the stress from being directed to engage in a deceptive business practice. The judge found that this stress was greater than that experienced in the normal work environment, because pressure to engage in unethical and illegal practices cannot be considered a normal work environment. The New York Supreme Court, Appellate Division, agreed with the workers' compensation law judge's findings.[57]

Lucke v. Ellis Hospital

Caterina Lucke worked as a cardiothoracic physician's assistant. Her physician supervisor, a cardiothoracic surgeon, had a "difficult" personality. During an hours-long procedure in the operating room, the surgeon threatened Ms. Lucke with physical violence. The surgeon's supervisor removed Ms. Lucke from work for her safety until the surgeon began attending an intensive psychiatric counseling program. Ms. Lucke also sought psychiatric treatment and filed a workers' compensation claim for posttraumatic stress and adjustment disorder. The workers' compensation law judge found that Ms. Lucke's psychiatric diagnoses were caused by the surgeon's threat, and that threats of physical violence made by a supervisor constituted greater stress than that which normally occurs in similar work environments. As a result, Ms. Lucke sustained a compensable injury due to work-related stress.[58]

Dietz v. Workers' Compensation Appeal Board

Robert Dietz worked for the Lower Bucks County Joint Municipal Authority as a field maintenance worker for 20 years. His job involved heavy

---

57 *Cox v. Saks Fifth Ave.*, 130 A.D. 3d 1236 (N.Y. App. Div. 2015).
58 *Lucke v. Ellis Hosp.*, 119 A.D. 3d 1050 (N.Y. App. Div. 2014).

labor such as jackhammering to dig up roads, repairing water main breaks, and cutting tree roots out of the sewer system. Mr. Dietz frequently worked more than 40 hours per week and was always on call. On November 7, 2007, Mr. Dietz left the house at 6:00 a.m., as usual, and began work at 7:00 a.m. At 9:35 p.m., Mr. Dietz called his wife to tell her that he and the other crew members were still working but that the job would likely soon be finished. Mr. Dietz told his wife that he had been doing roadwork and jackhammering for hours and that he and his coworkers were tired because they had been "out there" at the job site for a long time. Mr. Dietz made no other complaints and everything seemed normal during the conversation with his wife. About an hour later, Mrs. Dietz learned her husband died of a heart attack, at age 48, after collapsing on the job.

Mrs. Dietz sought workers' compensation for her husband's death. She testified that Mr. Dietz smoked a pack of cigarettes a day during their marriage. He had been taking medication to treat high cholesterol, but he had not been diagnosed with heart disease. A physician testified that Mr. Dietz would not have had a fatal heart attack on November 7, 2007, if he had not worked such a long, strenuous day. The workers' compensation judge found that Mr. Dietz did not alternate between days of heavy duties and days of performing light office duties. Rather, his daily job involved strenuous physical activity. As a result, the workers' compensation judge found that exertion from Mr. Dietz's regular work activities over the course of a 14-hour workday caused his heart attack and that Mrs. Dietz was eligible for workers' compensation benefits.[59]

Hynes v. Good Samaritan Hospital

Kimberly Hynes worked as a registered nurse in the mental health unit of Good Samaritan Hospital in Kearney, Nebraska. On April 16, 2008, a patient "whipped" Ms. Hynes several times with a large vacuum cleaner cord and punched her jaw. Ms. Hynes suffered bruising and substantial pain as a result of the assault. Ms. Hynes sought medical treatment for her physical injuries. Following the incident, Ms. Hynes tearfully discussed the assault with an EAP counselor. Ms. Hynes reported having difficulty

---

59 *Dietz v. Workers' Comp. Appeal Bd.*, 2015 WL 7771080 (Pa. Cir. Ct. 2015).

eating and sleeping after the assault and stated that she did not feel safe returning to the adolescent unit. A few days later, Ms. Hynes told the EAP counselor that she had sensitivity to noises and movement, as well as nightmares and disturbing dreams. Follow-up appointments with the EAP counselor revealed increasing feelings of hopelessness and helplessness, flashbacks, dreams of the assault, strained communication problems, and difficulty functioning in her professional, social, and personal life.

Ms. Hynes experienced two more assaults at work: one where a patient kicked and bit her and another where a male adolescent patient grabbed Ms. Hynes and made "extremely aggressive" sexual comments to her. Ms. Hynes did not seek medical treatment for these other two assaults. Ultimately, Ms. Hynes was admitted to an inpatient psychiatric facility for major depressive disorder and posttraumatic stress disorder. Ms. Hynes sought workers' compensation for her mental injuries. The workers' compensation court found that Ms. Hynes's injuries were the result of the initial assault on April 16, 2008, and that the two subsequent incidents aggravated or cumulatively added to the injury. Therefore, the workers' compensation court awarded her benefits.[60]

What Workplace Wellness Lessons Can We Learn from These Cases?

Each of these cases teaches a key lesson for workplace wellness program designers: Job design and work environment play a crucial role in whether an employee experiences excessive stress. As noted by WHO, workload and working hours, as well as participation and control, are stress-related hazards. The employees in the cases just discussed were found to have suffered occupational stress because of being overworked, as was the case for Mr. Harper and Mr. Dietz; or put in uncomfortable positions, as was the case for Mr. Cox, Ms. Lucke, and Ms. Hynes. In the case of Mr. Harper, even though he was a workaholic, and as managing partner likely had more control over his work than most, the organizational design of the work (such as compensation structure) likely added undue pressure. Can and should workplace wellness program designers address such workplace features such as compensation structure? Ideally, yes,

---

60 *Hynes v. Good Samaritan Hosp.*, 291 Neb. 757 (2015).

because such features and systems create barriers to increased well-being and end up costing the organization in terms of loss of valuable employees, an unfavorable community reputation, and workers' compensation payments.

In the case of Mr. Dietz, the court hinted at how his job could have been designed differently to create greater well-being. Specifically, the court pointed out that the employer could have alternated heavy workload days with lighter office duty days. Of course, shorter workdays would have helped, too.

From the facts of the case, it appears that Ms. Hynes did not have much control over her work. After the initial assault, she had expressed to the EAP counselor that she did not feel safe returning to the adolescent unit, yet that is where she was when the subsequent incidents occurred. Even though Ms. Hynes's employer had an EAP (which she used), it was not enough to prevent further assaults and eventual need for inpatient psychiatric treatment. Giving Ms. Hynes an ability to choose where to work in the hospital might have prevented the subsequent attacks and reduced the need for inpatient treatment.

Finally, in the cases of Ms. Lucke and Mr. Cox, strong leadership and a corporate compliance program could have deterred the illegal or harassing behavior that caused their stress-related injuries. Workplace wellness program designers can use these workers' compensation cases to build a business case for implementing a more comprehensive wellness program that captures both individual and organizational approaches to managing and preventing occupational stress.

Occupational Safety and Health Act (OSHA)

OSHA became law in 1970.[61] Its purpose is to "assure safe and healthful working conditions for working men and women."[62] Congress enacted the law because it found that personal injuries and illnesses arising out

---

61 Pub. L. No. 91–596, https://www.osha.gov/pls/oshaweb/owadisp.show_document?p_table=OSHACT &p_id=2743.
62 *Id.*

of work situations impose a substantial burden upon, and are a hindrance to, interstate commerce in terms of lost production, wage loss, medical expenses, and disability compensation payments.[63] OSHA applies to private employers in the United States.[64]

The general duty clause, in § 5(a)(1), requires employers to provide their employees with a place of employment that is free from recognizable hazards that are causing or are likely to cause death or serious harm to employees.[65] The courts have interpreted the general duty clause to mean that an employer has a legal obligation to provide a workplace free of conditions or activities that either the employer or industry recognizes as hazardous and that cause, or are likely to cause, death or serious physical harm to employees when there is a feasible method to abate the hazard.[66]

The U.S. Department of Labor's Occupational Safety and Health Administration (the "Administration") considers workplace violence to be a preventable hazard.[67] Indeed, it has issued several guidebooks addressing workplace violence in particular situations, such as health care and social services, retail, and taxi or for-hire drivers. For healthcare and social service workers in particular, the Administration notes that between 2011 and 2013, 70 to 74 percent of the approximately 25,000 annual workplace assaults occurred in healthcare and social service settings.[68] For healthcare workers, assaults comprise 10 to 11 percent of workplace injuries involving days away from work, as compared to 3 percent of injuries of all private-sector employees.[69] These statistics show an increased risk of workplace violence facing healthcare and social service workers. Assaults result primarily from violent behavior of

---

63 *Id.*

64 29 U.S.C. § 652 (defining "employer" as a person engaged in a business affecting commerce who has employees—but this does not include the United States (not including the United States Postal Service) or any state or political subdivision of a state).

65 29 U.S.C. § 654.

66 U.S. Dep't of Labor, OSHA, "Enforcement Fact Sheet," https://www.osha.gov/SLTC/workplaceviolence/standards.html.

67 U.S. Dep't of Labor, OSHA, "Workplace Violence" website, https://www.osha.gov/SLTC/workplaceviolence/index.html.

68 *OSHA Guidelines for Preventing Workplace Violence for Healthcare and Social Service Workers* (OSHA Publication No. 2148-04R 2015), at 2, https://www.osha.gov/Publications/osha3148.pdf.

69 *Id.* at 2.

their patients, clients, and/or residents.[70] Certainly that was the case in Ms. Hynes's workers' compensation case (discussed previously).

Although the Administration's guidelines do not have the same status as law, they provide insight into how the Administration views the risks in certain industries and how the OSHA law relates to those risks. Thus, if workplace wellness program designers work in the healthcare, social services, retail, or transportation industries, it may be a good idea to review the OSHA and the Administration's guidelines to determine how those guidelines may be incorporated into an employer's wellness program. In fact, it is best for workplace wellness professionals and employees in the company's safety and health department to be continually working together on various efforts to prevent workplace injuries.

For example, under the healthcare and social service guidelines, the Administration recommends incorporating a written program for workplace violence prevention into an organization's overall safety and health program.[71] The Administration advises that an effective workplace violence prevention program will include management commitment and employee participation, a worksite analysis, safety and health training, recordkeeping, and program evaluation.[72] These steps overlap with the recommended steps for developing an effective workplace wellness program, as discussed in Chapter 2.

OSHA's general duty clause, which requires employers to provide a place of employment free from recognizable hazards that could cause injury or death, supports the implementation of comprehensive workplace wellness programs. Indeed, smaller employers in high-hazard industries such as health care, social services, retail, or transportation, may want to take advantage of the Administration's free onsite safety

---

70 *Id.* at 3.

71 *OSHA Guidelines for Preventing Workplace Violence for Healthcare and Social Service Workers*, at 5.

72 *Id.* OSHA notes, however, that employee participation should not infringe upon worker rights under the National Labor Relations Act (NLRA), 29 U.S.C. §§ 151–169. The NLRA gives employees the right to self-organize; to form, join, or assist labor organizations; to bargain collectively through representatives of their own choosing; and to engage in other concerted activities for the purpose of collective bargaining or other mutual aid or protection. 29 U.S.C. § 157. The NLRA prohibits employers from interfering with, restraining, or coercing employees in the exercise of these rights. 29 U.S.C. § 158.

and health consultation services.[73] These services are separate from enforcement and do not result in penalties or citations.[74] Consultants from state agencies or universities work with employers to identify workplace hazards, provide advice on compliance with OSHA standards, and assist in establishing safety and health management programs.[75] Workplace wellness program designers could leverage the expertise available through the free OSHA program to help design a more comprehensive wellness program that incorporates environmental and ergonomic improvements into the workplace. As noted in Chapter 2, environmental and policy supports are a critical component of successful workplace wellness programs.

Americans with Disabilities Act (ADA)

Conditions affecting a person's mental abilities and function can be dealt with through the ADA. Many courts have held that depression, anxiety, posttraumatic stress disorder, and panic attacks constitute mental impairments under the ADA.[76] Workplace wellness program designers should look to the requirements under the ADA to support wellness programming that reduces stress in the workplace. Being proactive about reducing stress hazards may help employers prevent ADA claims, which can be costly regardless of who wins.

As outlined in Chapter 4, Congress enacted the ADA in 1990 to establish rights and obligations with regard to persons with disabilities. Under the ADA, a *disability* is defined as: (1) a physical or mental impairment that substantially limits one or more major life activities of

---

73 *OSHA Guidelines for Preventing Workplace Violence for Healthcare and Social Service Workers,* at 47–48; *see also OSHA Factsheet on Consultations,* https://www.osha.gov/OshDoc/data_General_Facts/factsheet-consultations.pdf.
74 *OSHA Guidelines for Preventing Workplace Violence for Healthcare and Social Service Workers,* at 48.
75 *Id.*
76 Sheree Wright, *Protecting Your Employees from Harm While Accommodating Mental Illness—Are Employers in a Bind?* Paper for the American Bar Association Annual Meeting, Section of Labor and Employment Law (August 7, 2014), at 4, http://www.americanbar.org/content/dam/aba/events/labor_law/am/2014/1d_mental_illness.authcheckdam.pdf.

the individual; (2) a record of such an impairment; or (3) being regarded as having such an impairment.[77] Recall that Congress amended the ADA in 2008 with the ADA Amendments Act (ADAAA), which broadened the coverage of the ADA and aimed to make it easier for an individual seeking protection under the ADA to establish that he or she has a disability within the meaning of the ADA.[78] Specifically, the ADAAA expands the definition of *disability* to include disabilities in their "unmitigated" state (i.e., employers may not take into account medication or devices when considering whether an individual has a disability).[79] It also amended the list of "major life activities" to add "caring for oneself, performing manual tasks, seeing, hearing, eating, sleeping, walking, standing, lifting, bending, speaking, breathing, learning, reading, concentrating, thinking, communicating and working."[80] Based on this expanded list of major life activities, it is easy to see how someone feeling stressed or depressed at work could fall within the protection of the ADAAA. Working in an environment with stress-inducing hazards, such as those outlined by WHO, can exacerbate mental impairments. As a result, designing a workplace wellness program that reduces those stressors not only will create greater workplace well-being, but may automatically address employer obligations under the ADAAA.

When it comes to mental impairments, however, employees may be more reluctant to disclose (and an employer may not be aware of) such impairments until after inappropriate conduct occurs.[81] Unlike physical disabilities, employees experiencing anxiety or depression, for example, may not exhibit any outward manifestation of their impairment.[82] In addition, an employee may hesitate to report the condition and request accommodations because of fear of stigma or invasion of privacy.[83]

---

77 42 U.S.C. § 12101(1).
78 *EEOC Notice Concerning the Americans with Disabilities Act (ADA) Amendments Act of 2008*, http://www.eeoc.gov/laws/statutes/adaaa_notice.cfm.
79 *Id.* at 2.
80 42 U.S.C. § 12102(a)(A).
81 Wright, *Protecting Your Employees from Harm While Accommodating Mental Illness*, at 5–6.
82 *Id.*
83 *Id.*

Finally, the employee may not be aware, or be in denial, that he or she has a mental impairment.[84]

When an employee finally does speak up about uncomfortable working conditions that may be causing or exacerbating a mental impairment, it may be in conjunction with addressing the employee's performance. Such conversations put both employees and employers on the defense and in awkward positions of assessing the true reasons for mistakes: an inherent inability to perform the essential job functions or a poor work environment.

Take the example of Ellen Gaube, a pharmacist at Day Kimball Hospital in Connecticut. Ms. Gaube sued her employer under the ADA (among other laws), complaining that poor air quality, a high level of noise, and an overly cool work environment intensified her preexisting depression, insomnia, and migraines.[85] She argued that these conditions affected her concentration and contributed to some of her errors at work.[86] Although Ms. Gaube ultimately lost her ADA claim, workplace wellness program designers can learn an important lesson from her case.[87] Specifically, addressing the work environment through a workplace safety and wellness program more proactively, before complaints or mistakes happen, can reduce the possibility of employee errors or complaints. Even if such errors or complaints still occur, the employer can communicate to the complaining employee with more confidence that it has acted proactively to minimize workplace stress hazards. Moreover, when it comes to mental impairments, many times employees do not openly discuss such impairments, for the reasons identified earlier. By using the reasonable accommodation requirement under the ADA to make the case for organizational improvements in workplace safety and wellness programs, workplace wellness program designers may by default address employee stress that might not otherwise come to

---

84 *Id.*
85 *Gaube v. Day Kimball Hosp.*, 2015 WL 1347000, at 2 (D. Conn. 2015).
86 *Id.*
87 *Id.* at 10 (dismissing plaintiff's ADA claim for failing to adequately allege the second and third elements of an ADA claim and failing to provide sufficient allegations through amending her complaint).

light. Such proactive efforts will do both employees and employers a favor.

Other Civil Rights Laws (Title VII, ADEA)

Similar to Title I of the ADA, the primary goal of other civil rights laws such as Title VII or the Age Discrimination in Employment Act (ADEA) is to prevent discrimination in employment of "protected classes." According to Title VII of the Civil Rights Act of 1964, these protected classes include a person's gender, race, ethnicity, national origin, and religion.[88] Under the ADEA, the protected class is persons who are age 40 or older.[89]

Recall that according to WHO, an employee's level of participation and control, perceived role in the organization, and interpersonal relationships with supervisors and employees, as well as the organization's overall culture, contribute to an employee's stress at work. Workplace wellness program designers can use civil rights laws to minimize these stress-related hazards. If an organization has not conducted recent or adequate training on **workplace bullying** or **workplace harassment**, the wellness program designer can point to the civil rights laws as a reason to include such training in the workplace wellness program.

Workplace bullying is pervasive. A 2007 survey conducted by Zogby and the Workplace Bullying Institute found that 37 percent of workers reported having been bullied at work; 13 percent reported that the bullying was occurring at the time of the survey, and 24 percent reported that bullying had occurred in the past.[90] When bullying is based on race, color, religion, sex (including pregnancy), national origin, age (40 or older), disability, or genetic information, it may constitute illegal harassment under civil rights laws such as Title VII, the ADEA, the ADA, or

---

88 42 U.S.C. § 2000e-2.
89 29 U.S.C. § 621 *et seq.*
90 Dianne Avery and Catherine Fisk, "Overview of the Law of Workplace Harassment," in *Litigating the Workplace Harassment Case* (American Bar Association 2010): 5, http://apps.americanbar.org/abastore/products/books/abstracts/5190452%20intro_abs.pdf.

GINA.[91] Harassment becomes unlawful when: (1) enduring the offensive conduct becomes a condition of continued employment; or (2) the conduct is severe or pervasive enough to create a work environment that a reasonable person would consider intimidating, hostile, or abusive.[92] Offensive conduct may include, but is not limited to, offensive jokes, slurs, epithets or name calling, physical assaults or threats, intimidation, ridicule or mockery, insults or put-downs, offensive objects or pictures, and interference with work performance.[93] Harassment can occur in a variety of circumstances, for example: (1) the harasser can be the victim's supervisor, a supervisor in another area, an agent of the employer, a coworker, or a nonemployee; (2) the victim does not have to be the person harassed, but can be anyone affected by the offensive conduct; (3) unlawful harassment may occur without economic injury to, or discharge of, the victim.[94]

Employers may be automatically liable for harassment by a supervisor that results in a negative employment action such as termination, failure to promote or hire, or loss of wages.[95] If the supervisor's harassment results in a hostile work environment, the employer can avoid liability only if it can prove that (1) it reasonably tried to prevent and promptly correct the harassing behavior; and (2) the employee unreasonably failed to take advantage of any preventive or corrective opportunities provided by the employer.[96] The employer will be liable for harassment by non-supervisory employees or nonemployees over whom it has control (e.g., independent contractors or customers on the premises), if it knew, or should have known, about the harassment and failed to take prompt and appropriate corrective action.[97]

Therefore, including workplace bullying and harassment training in workplace wellness programs will foster a culture that does not tolerate harassment of any kind, and create a mechanism by which the employer

---

91 "EEOC Harassment Fact Sheet," http://www.eeoc.gov/laws/types/harassment.cfm.
92 *Id.*
93 *Id.*
94 *Id.*
95 *Id.*
96 *Id.*
97 *Id.*

tries to prevent harassment from occurring. Such proactive steps can operate in favor of the employer should an employee accuse the employer of condoning workplace harassment. More importantly, however, encompassing workplace bullying and harassment training in a workplace wellness program will likely reduce the risk of civil rights claims and the prevalence of a stress-related hazard.

Mental Health Parity and Addiction Equity Act and the ACA

Workplace wellness programs that aim to tackle workplace stress and to help employees achieve a healthy mental state may turn to EAPs. As noted earlier, EAPs do not address organizational stressors, but they can offer a complementary method of addressing workplace stress. Employers that offer EAPs must be mindful of the requirements under the Mental Health Parity and Addiction Equity Act (MHPAEA) and the Affordable Care Act (ACA) to ensure that their programs are compliant.

A quick history lesson on the MHPAEA will help readers appreciate why the law exists. Long before the MHPAEA was passed, Congress tried to address the unequal coverage and treatment of mental health benefits in insurance. According to Mental Health America, an advocacy group addressing the needs of those living with mental illness and promoting the overall mental health of all Americans, health insurance plans have imposed barriers that limit access to needed behavioral health care for both mental and substance use disorders.[98] The group attributes this discrimination against mental health and substance abuse disorder treatment to a lack of understanding regarding mental health and deep-rooted stigma against those with mental health treatment needs.[99] The federal General Accounting Office (GAO) reports that health insurers have provided more limited mental health coverage primarily because of

---

[98] "Mental Health America Issue Brief: Parity," http://www.mentalhealthamerica.net/issues/issue-brief-parity.
[99] *Id.*

cost concerns.[100] These limitations took the form of limits on hospital days, outpatient office visits, and annual or lifetime dollar amounts.[101]

The first recognition that the United States needed to do more with regard to mental health issues came from President John F. Kennedy in 1961, when he called on the U.S. Civil Service Commission to require the Federal Employee Health Benefits Program (the health insurer for federal employees) to cover psychiatric illnesses at a level equivalent to general medical care.[102] This effort did not last.[103]

Not until 1996, when Congress passed the Mental Health Parity Act (MHPA), were new federal standards imposed on the mental health coverage offered under most employer group health plans.[104] Specifically, the MHPA prohibits employers with more than 50 employees from imposing annual or lifetime dollar limits on mental health coverage that are more restrictive than those imposed on medical and surgical coverage.[105] Nevertheless, a GAO survey two years after the passage of the MHPA found that although most employers complied with the new law, most employer health plans contained at least one other plan design feature that was more restrictive for mental health benefits than for medical and surgical benefits.[106]

The MHPAEA, passed in 2008, built upon the strides made by the MHPA by requiring a broader application of **parity** between mental health or substance use disorder benefits and medical/surgical benefits. This time, the law required parity with regard to financial requirements (such as deductibles, co-payments, coinsurance, and other out-of-pocket expenses) as well as treatment limitations (such as frequency of treatment, number of visits, number of treatment days, prior authorization requirements, and network adequacy).[107] The law does not require employers to offer any mental health or substance use disorder benefits (though they

100 *Mental Health Parity Act: Despite New Federal Standards, Mental Health Benefits Remain Limited* (U.S. General Accounting Office (GAO) Report HEHS-00-95, May 2000): 3, http://www.gao.gov/assets/240/230309.pdf.
101 *Id.*
102 "Mental Health America Issue Brief, Parity."
103 *Id.*
104 *Mental Health Parity Act: Despite New Federal Standards*, at 3.
105 *Id.* at 3.
106 *Id.* at 5.
107 78 Fed. Reg. 68240–68246 (November 13, 2013); *see also* "Mental Health America Issue Brief, Parity."

may be required under the ACA), but to the extent that an employer plan does offer such benefits, the plan must meet the parity requirements.[108] The MHPAEA does not apply to all health plans; Medicare, traditional fee-for-service Medicaid, small employer plans that were created before March 23, 2010 and satisfy certain requirements to be "grandfathered" under the ACA, retiree-only plans, and Tricare plans are not covered by the MHPAEA.[109] The ACA expanded MHPAEA's requirements, however, to the small group (ACA non-grandfathered) and individual markets.[110]

How Does the MHPAEA Affect EAPs?

The MHPAEA does not apply to certain EAPs that qualify as excepted benefits, as explained below, or are not offered under (nor otherwise constitute) a group health plan. An EAP that is offered under (or itself is considered) a group health plan, and does not qualify as an excepted benefit, must be designed in a manner that meets parity requirements as between the group health plan's mental health/substance use disorder and medical/surgical benefits.

Excepted Benefits Issue

EAPs are exempt from MHPAEA requirements if they qualify as **excepted benefits**. Excepted benefits are generally exempt from health reform requirements added by the Health Insurance Portability and Accountability Act, as well as from the ACA.[111] In addition, eligibility for excepted benefits still permits an individual to obtain a premium tax credit under the ACA if an individual chooses to enroll in coverage under a health plan through an insurance exchange.[112]

There are four categories of excepted benefits. The first category includes benefits that are generally not health coverage, such as automobile insurance, liability insurance, workers' compensation, and accidental

---

108 "Mental Health America Issue Brief, Parity."
109 *Id.*; *see also* SAMHSA, "Implementation of the Mental Health Parity Addiction Equity Act (MHPAEA)," http://www.samhsa.gov/health-financing/implementation-mental-health-parity-addiction-equity-act.
110 78 Fed. Reg. 68240 (November 13, 2013).
111 IRC §§ 9831(b), (c), 9832(c); 26 C.F.R. § 54.9831-1(c);79 Fed. Reg. 59130 (October 1, 2014).
112 79 Fed. Reg. at 59130; 26 U.S.C. §§ 36B(c)(2), 5000A(f)(3).

death and dismemberment coverage.[113] The benefits in this category are excepted from HIPAA and ACA compliance with insurance market reforms, such as first-dollar coverage of preventive services, no annual limits, and premium rating limits.[114] In contrast, the benefits in the second, third, and fourth categories are types of health coverage but are excepted only if certain conditions are met.[115]

The second category of excepted benefits is limited excepted benefits, which may include limited-scope vision or dental benefits, and benefits for long-term care, nursing home care, home health care, or community-based care, as well as "other similar, limited benefits as are specified in regulations."[116] The third category of excepted benefits, referred to as "noncoordinated excepted benefits," includes both coverage for only a specified disease (such as cancer-only policies), and hospital indemnity or other fixed indemnity insurance.[117] The fourth category is supplemental excepted benefits, which must be coverage supplemental to Medicare coverage or veteran's healthcare benefits, or similar coverage that is supplemental to a group health plan.[118] For the second category, to qualify as excepted benefits, the coverage must be provided under a separate policy, certificate, or contract of insurance, or must not be deemed an "integral part" of a larger group health plan.[119] For the third and fourth categories, to qualify as excepted benefits, the coverage must be provided under a separate policy, certificate, or contract of insurance in all cases.[120]

EAPs can fall within the fourth category of excepted benefits: benefits supplemental to group health plan coverage. However, to qualify as excepted benefits and therefore be exempt from complying with ACA insurance market reforms and MHPAEA requirements, the EAP must meet four criteria. First, the EAP must not provide significant benefits in the nature of medical care, taking into account the amount, scope, and

---

113 IRC § 9832(c)(1).
114 IRC § 9831(b).
115 IRC §§ 9831(c), 9832(c)(2)-(4).
116 IRC § 9832(c)(2).
117 IRC § 9832(c)(3).
118 IRC § 9832(c)(4).
119 IRC § 9831(c)(1).
120 IRC § 9831(c)(1).

duration of covered services.[121] For example, an EAP that provides only limited, short-term outpatient counseling for substance use disorder services (without covering inpatient, residential, partial residential, or intensive outpatient care) without requiring prior authorization or review for medical necessity does not provide significant benefits in the nature of medical care.[122] EAPs that provide disease management services, such as laboratory testing, counseling, and prescription drugs for individuals with chronic conditions such as diabetes, do provide significant benefits in the nature of medical care and therefore would fail to qualify as excepted benefits.[123]

Second, the EAP must not be coordinated with group health plan benefits.[124] That is, participants in the group health plan must not be required to use and exhaust benefits under the EAP (making the EAP a gatekeeper) before an individual is eligible for group health plan benefits.[125] Also, EAP participation must not depend upon group health plan participation.[126] However, the EAP may be financed by the group health plan.[127]

Third, to qualify as excepted benefits, the EAP may not require employee premiums or contributions as a condition of participation in the EAP.[128] Fourth and finally, the EAP may not impose any cost-sharing requirements.[129]

EAPs that meet these four criteria are exempt from meeting HIPAA, ACA, and MHPAEA requirements such as the prohibition against annual dollar limits, the required coverage or preventive care services without cost-sharing, and mental health parity requirements.[130] Also, eligibility for an EAP that qualifies as an excepted benefit, in and of itself, will not

---

121 26 C.F.R. § 54.9831-1(c)(3)(vi)(A).
122 79 Fed. Reg. 59133 (October 1, 2014).
123 *Id.*
124 26 C.F.R. § 54.9831-1(c)(3)(vi)(B).
125 *Id.*
126 *Id.*
127 79 Fed. Reg. 59134 (October 1, 2014).
128 26 C.F.R. § 54.9831-1(c)(3)(vi)(C).
129 26 C.F.R. § 54.9831-1(c)(3)(vi)(D).
130 79 Fed. Reg. 59132 (October 1, 2014).

preclude an employee from qualifying for premium tax credits through the ACA insurance exchanges.[131]

Parity Issue

To the extent that an EAP constitutes (or is offered under) a group health plan and is not an excepted benefit, the MHPAEA requirements will apply.[132] For example, if the group health plan requires employees to use EAP services as a starting point for mental health services before accessing treatment services outside the EAP, this requirement must have parity with medical/surgical benefits.[133] Hence, if the employer's group health plan did not require employees with medical or surgical needs to first exhaust benefits offered through the EAP (or a similar program) before accessing treatment services outside the wellness program, such a requirement likely would violate the MPHAEA. To illustrate, the federal Departments of Labor, Treasury, and Health and Human Services offer this example in the final MHPAEA rules:

> Example: An employee maintains both a major medical plan and an EAP. The EAP provides, among other benefits, a limited number of mental health or substance use disorder counseling sessions. Participants are eligible for mental health or substance use disorder benefits under the major medical plan only after exhausting the counseling sessions provided by the EAP. No similar exhaustion requirement applies with respect to medical/surgical benefits provided under the major medical plan.
>
> Conclusion: In this example, limiting eligibility for mental health and substance use disorder benefits only after EAP benefits are exhausted is a nonquantitative treatment limitation subject to the

---

131 *Id.* Employees with incomes between 100 percent and 400 percent of the federal poverty level qualify for premium tax credits through the health insurance exchanges if their employer does not offer minimum essential coverage that is both affordable and of minimum value. Because excepted benefits are exempt from the ACA requirements, such as qualifying as minimum essential coverage and the employer penalty for failing to offer such coverage to employees, the employer's EAP offering would not hinder the employee's ability to obtain such tax credits on the exchange. *See* IRC §§ 36B (eligibility for premium tax credit), 4980H (employer penalty provision), and 5000A(f)(3) (excepted benefits are not "minimum essential coverage").
132 78 Fed. Reg. 68240, 68251 (November 13, 2013).
133 *Id.*

parity requirements. Because no comparable requirement applies to medical/surgical benefits, the requirement may not be applied to mental health or substance use disorder benefits.[134]

Conclusion

Workplace wellness programs that incorporate OSHA, workers' compensation, ADA, and civil rights requirements and considerations may not only achieve greater compliance with those laws, but may also create an environment that reduces factors identified by WHO as inducing workplace anxiety and stress. Offering EAPs alone often does not address stress and anxiety factors in a holistic manner. However, EAPs can be useful behavioral health components of a wellness program. It is important for wellness professionals and organizations to understand which laws, such as the MHPHEA and the ACA, apply to the EAP so that they can ensure compliance of that portion of the wellness program.

RULE THE RULES

Key Points in Chapter 8

1. Costs associated with workplace stress are monumental. One study estimated that mental health disorders cost U.S. employers $317.5 billion, compared to $310 billion for occupational injury and illness.
2. Costs associated with workplace stress come from workers' compensation claims, short- and long-term disability, presenteeism, and absenteeism.
3. Although employers have ranked stress as the primary workforce issue, only 15 percent identify it as a top priority of their health and productivity programs.

---

134 78 Fed. Reg. 68273, Example 6 (November 13, 2013).

4. Comprehensive workplace wellness programs utilize two approaches to address workplace stress: (a) individual (e.g., providing EAP programs, stress management workshops, physical activity programs, programs for employees and managers to enhance their problem-solving and communication skills), and (b) organizational (e.g., assessing environmental risks and establishing policies and procedures to create a healthy work environment and culture).

5. There are several federal laws that, when properly applied in the design of workplace wellness programs, can facilitate the creation of a positive organizational culture by reducing workplace stress. These include OSHA, ADA, Title VII of the Civil Rights Act, ADEA, MHPAEA, and ACA.

6. Implementing programs to address workplace stress may also help reduce workers' compensation claims. Workers' compensation laws (state laws) are relevant when an employee experiences a physical injury while working or psychological harm due to work-related stress.

7. The OSHA general duty clause (a requirement covering private employers) can be used by workplace wellness professionals to help justify the need for creating and implementing a comprehensive wellness program. OSHA guidelines, such as those addressing workplace violence prevention, can be used to enhance the overall safety and health program.

8. Under the ADA, a disability can include mental health disorders such as anxiety and depression. Reducing stress hazards may help prevent ADA claims involving mental health disorders, as well as addressing employer obligations under the ADAAA.

9. Workplace bullying and harassment can constitute violations of civil rights laws. However, these types of violations, and the stress-related hazards they create, can be minimized through bullying and harassment training for employees as part of a comprehensive wellness program.

10. The MHPAEA, passed by Congress in 2008, requires parity between mental health or substance abuse disorder benefits and

medical/surgical benefits with regard to (a) financial requirements (e.g., deductibles, co-payments) and (b) treatment limitations (e.g., frequency of treatment, number of visits).

11. There are some limited exemptions from MHPAEA, but the ACA generally expanded MHPAEA requirements to include small and individual markets.

12. If the MHPAEA applies to an EAP because it is considered a group health plan and not an excepted benefit, then EAP services under the group health plan must meet parity requirements.

Study Questions

1. Describe the prevalence and adverse consequences of stress and mental illness on both employees and employers.

2. Give examples of individual and organizational approaches that can address workplace stress and mental illness.

3. Describe what is meant by the "no-fault" aspect of workers' compensation laws and the types of injuries that are covered by workers' compensation.

4. Identify the stress-related hazards, as defined by WHO, that were present in each of the following cases: *Harper, Cox, Lucke, Dietz,* and *Hynes.*

5. For each of the following federal laws, describe preventive law strategies that workplace wellness professionals can help develop and implement to be compliant with the laws and to help create a more stress-free work environment.
   A. OSHA
   B. ADA
   C. Title VII of the Civil Rights Act
   D. ADEA

6. Define *parity* with regard to financial requirements and treatment limitations under the MHPAEA.

7. Describe the four categories of excepted benefits and the likely category in which EAPs would be exempt from MHPAEA requirements.

8. Explain the implications of an EAP that does not meet one of the excepted benefits.

Key Terms

employee assistance program
  (EAP)
excepted benefits
mental health disorders
occupational stress
parity

presenteeism
psychological injury
stress-related hazards
workplace bullying
workplace harassment

9

Data Privacy: The Web We Have Weaved

Learning Objectives

After reading this chapter, workplace wellness professionals will be able to:
1. Discuss the origins and meaning of U.S. privacy laws.
2. Understand and appreciate the tremendous growth in data collection in both health care and workplace wellness programs.
3. Describe how medical technologies have led to various challenges in keeping personal data private and secure.
4. Explain the potential benefits and dangers regarding the use of Big Data in workplace wellness programs.
5. Describe the major privacy and/or security regulations in the following laws and why it is important to apply them in workplace wellness programs: HIPAA, ADA, GINA, FTCA, FCRA, and GLBA.
6. Make a good case for following the HIPAA privacy and security regulations even if the workplace wellness program is not required to do so because it does not qualify as a group health plan.
7. Describe legal cases in which plaintiffs claimed that privacy and/or security laws were violated, and the lessons learned from these cases for workplace wellness programs.
8. Develop and implement preventive law strategies into the design and delivery of wellness programs that are reflective of the many privacy and security laws applicable to workplace wellness programs.

The real danger is the gradual erosion of individual liberties through automation, integration, and interconnection of many small, separate record-keeping systems, each of which alone may seem innocuous, even benevolent, and wholly justifiable.

—Anonymous[1]

Fundamentally, privacy is about having control over how information flows.

—Danah Boyd[2]

Introduction

Data is the new money.[3] Data, whether it be personal information data, financial data, or health data, is coveted by a wide variety of people and organizations that want to use data for marketing, research, benchmarking, monitoring progress, product development, and yet-to-be discovered uses. These uses are possible in the current era of **Big Data**.

The era of Big Data is also the Wild West when it comes to privacy and security of that data.[4] Indeed, the concept of preserving or advancing privacy and security in the era of Big Data is anathema to some hard-core enthusiasts. For those enthusiasts, unfettered innovation in data collection, processing, and sharing is more valuable than protecting data privacy.[5] To oppose innovation in the name of privacy is taboo. Some even contend that privacy is dead.[6]

---

1 Cited in U.S. Privacy Protection Study Commission, Personal Privacy in an Information Society (1977) available at http://epic.org/privacy/ppsc1977report.
U.S. Privacy Study Commission (1977).
2 "Making Sense of Privacy and Publicity," SXSW, Austin, TX (March 13, 2010).
3 Beth Kutscher, "Competition Heats Up for Patient-Generated Data," *Modern Healthcare* (November 12, 2015), www.modernhealthcare.com/article20151112/NEWS/151119993?template.
4 Chris Jay Hoofnagle, "Reflections on the NC JOLT Symposium: The Privacy Self-Regulation Race to the Bottom," N.C. J. of L. & Tech. 5, no. 2 (Spring 2004): 213; *see also* Jay Hancock, "Workplace Wellness Programs Put Employee Privacy at Risk," *Kaiser Health News* (September 30, 2015), http://khn.org/news/workplace-wellness-programs-put-employee-privacy-at-risk/.
5 Julie E. Cohen, "What Privacy Is For," *Harvard L. Rev.* 126 (2013): 1904, 1920 ("The need to incentivize innovation is offered as the justification for strengthening proprietary control of intellectual goods and as the justification for regulating information networks lightly (if at all)").
6 Jacob Morgan, "Privacy Is Completely and Utterly Dead, and We Killed It," *Forbes* (August 19, 2014), http://www.forbes.com/sites/jacobmorgan/2014/08/19/privacy-is-completely-and-utterly-dead-and-we-killed-it/#1639e8d2dfbd (stating that we have reached a point, in today's world of Facebook, iPhones, Twitter, Google searches, and other online access points, that privacy is pretty much a lost cause).

Yet, even in our world of mass sharing of personal information through social media, smartphones, search engines, music, movie and video downloads, fitness trackers, and other forms of the **Internet of Things**,[7] there is a scholarly contingent holding that privacy not only still has meaning, but is also necessary and worth fighting for. Ignoring or dismissing privacy risks ignoring or dismissing a natural human need, as well as law. To help readers appreciate the virtue of privacy, this chapter discusses the origins and meaning of privacy law in the United States. We then explore the growth in data collection in both the healthcare and wellness spheres, and how those spheres are starting to merge when it comes to data. The chapter also examines how individuals and organizations may misuse the vast quantity of personal data and how current laws aim to prohibit such misuse. The chapter ends with some reflections and tips for wellness professionals to consider when collecting data through workplace wellness programs. By adopting programs that value privacy, wellness professionals and organizations will not only be respecting privacy law, but will also gain greater trust from program participants and help stop the erosion of a basic human right.

Origins and Importance of a Right to Privacy

Some legal scholars argue that a **right to privacy** is a natural instinct, deriving from **natural law**.[8] Rights derived from natural law are immutable, absolute, and belong to every human, whether in the state of nature or in society.[9] Thus, individuals possess a right to privacy simply

---

7 The *Internet of Things* or *IoT* refers to the ability of everyday objects to connect to the Internet and send and receive data. It includes, for example, Internet-connected cameras that allow you to post pictures online with a single click; home automations systems that turn on your front porch light when you leave work; and bracelets that share with your friends how far you have biked or run during the day. Federal Trade Commission Staff Report, *Internet of Things: Privacy and Security in a Connected World* (January 2015): i, https://www.ftc.gov/system/files/documents/reports/federal-trade-commission-staff-report-november-2013-workshop-entitled-internet-things-privacy/150127iotrpt.pdf.
8 Anita L. Allen, "The Natural Origins of the American Right to Privacy: Natural Law, Slavery, and the Right to Privacy Tort," *Fordham L. Rev.* 81 (2012):1187, 1197–1198.
9 *Id.* at 1198.

by virtue of being human, a right that unwanted intrusions, publications, and stolen identities can offend.[10]

Under this natural law theory, the right to privacy is always present, regardless of what the written law says. Legal scholars have explained why the right to privacy is so vital to human existence by emphasizing the human need for self-actualization and growth. According to these scholars, humans possess an "autonomous core," an essential self that is identifiable after the "residue of influence has been subtracted."[11] Lack of privacy means reduced opportunity and scope for "self-making."[12] If one is constantly being surveilled and characterized, there is less time and opportunity to exploit environmental serendipity—the unexpected encounters and juxtapositions that open new pathways for emergent subjectivity to explore.[13] Moreover, privacy is what permits the self to develop based on what one experiences in one's social environment. In other words, privacy gives individuals the breathing room to develop and flourish.[14]

Moreover, citizens who are subject to pervasive surveillance and shaping by powerful commercial and political interests will increasingly lack the ability to form and pursue meaningful agendas for human flourishing.[15] They will lose the ability to think critically and instead perceive the world through the lenses that society creates for us.[16] The ability to practice citizenship, such as voting and public debate, is defined in part by the practices that existing institutions encourage, permit, and foreclose.[17] Privacy enables individuals to develop critical perspectives on the world around them.[18]

Other legal scholars have characterized respect for our own privacy and that of others as an ethical virtue and hold that practicing reserve and modesty are positive character traits.[19] In this sense, privacy is both a duty and a right.[20] "Our duty of privacy to ourselves asks that we take

---

10 *Id.* at 1200.
11 Cohen, "What Privacy Is For," at 1907.
12 *Id.* at 1911.
13 *Id.* at 1910.
14 *Id.* at 1911.
15 *Id.* at 1912.
16 *Id.* at 1913.
17 *Id.* at 1912.
18 *Id.* at 1906.
19 Allen, "The Natural Origins of the American Right to Privacy," at 1211.
20 *Id.*

into account the way in which our own characters, personalities, and life enterprises could be adversely affected by decisions to flaunt, expose, and share rather than to reserve, conceal, and keep."[21] Interfering with someone's privacy deprives that person of control over his or her reputation and the freedom to enjoy a life of reserve outside the public gaze.[22] Privacy, then, is a cornerstone of freedom and it is something that a just society would not deny.[23]

Even without this innate concept of privacy, there are dozens of federal and state laws that make up a patchwork of privacy protection in the United States. Thus, in addition to a natural law concept of privacy, there are enforceable legal rights to privacy even though the U.S. Constitution fails to use the actual word *privacy* anywhere.[24] Legal scholars often point to a *Harvard Law Review* article from 1890 as the origin of the legal right to privacy. Samuel Warren and Louis Brandeis wrote the article, "The Right to Privacy," in response to the invention of portable cameras. In the article they noted that "[r]ecent inventions and business methods call attention to the next step which must be taken for the protection of the person, and for securing to the individual ... the right to be let alone .... [N]umerous mechanical devices threaten to make good the prediction that what is whispered in the closet shall be proclaimed from the house-tops."[25]

Several decades later, in 1928, Justice Brandeis drew from his law review article in his dissenting opinion in *Olmstead v. United States,* stating that the Founders had "conferred, as against the government, the right to be let alone—the most comprehensive of rights and the right most favored by civilized men."[26] Then, in the 1960s, the United States Supreme Court rendered two decisions recognizing the right to privacy under the First and Fourth Amendments to the Constitution. In *Gris-*

---

21 *Id.*
22 Allen, "The Natural Origins of the American Right to Privacy," at 1212.
23 *Id.* at 1209.
24 *Id.* at 1212 (noting that the word *privacy* "does not appear in the U.S. Constitution," but "rich conceptions of privacy are implicit in any plausible renderings of the Bill of Rights").
25 White House Report, *Big Data: Seizing Opportunities, Preserving Values* (May 2014): 15 https://www.whitehouse.gov/sites/default/files/docs/big_data_privacy_report_may_1_2014.pdf (citing Samuel Warren and Louis Brandeis, "The Right to Privacy," *Harvard L. Rev.* 4 (1890): 193, 195) [hereinafter "Big Data Report"].
26 *Id.* at 16, citing *Olmstead v. United States,* 277 U.S. 438, 478 (1928).

wold v. Connecticut, the Supreme Court found a right of privacy in the First and Fourteenth Amendments to the U.S. Constitution that protects the marital relationship, overturning a Connecticut law that prohibited individuals from using contraceptives.[27] In *Katz v. United States*, the Supreme Court identified a right to privacy protected by the Fourth Amendment to the U.S. Constitution.[28] In that case, police recorded telephone conversations that Charles Katz had in a public telephone booth.[29] The Court stated that the Fourth Amendment protects people, not places, and that what a person knowingly exposes to the public, even in his own home or office, is not a subject of Fourth Amendment protection.[30] However, what a person seeks to preserve as private, even in an area accessible to the public, may be constitutionally protected.[31]

Both *Griswold* and *Katz* stand for protection against unwarranted governmental intrusion into a person's private matters. Those cases recognized an implicit right to privacy within the Bill of Rights; it is the right to privacy that make the express guarantees of the Bill of Rights meaningful.[32] Thus, the Supreme Court viewed the right to privacy as fundamental to a free society and worthy of protection against government intrusion.

Furthermore, the law also protects an individual's right to privacy from intrusion by other private citizens. Civil courts began to recognize an "invasion of privacy" tort after the 1934 *Restatement (First) of Torts* recognized an unreasonable and serious **invasion of privacy** as a basis upon which to sue someone.[33] Courts in most states recognize privacy as a complex of four potential torts, as shown in Table 9.1.[34]

---

27 *Griswold v. Connecticut*, 381 U.S. 479, 483 (1965) (stating that the First Amendment has a penumbra where privacy is protected from governmental intrusion).
28 *Katz v. United States*, 389 U.S. 347 (1967).
29 *Id.* at 348.
30 *Id.* at 351.
31 *Id.*
32 Allen, "The Natural Origins of the American Right to Privacy," at 1191; *see also Griswold*, 381 U.S. at 483 ("The right of 'association,' like the right of belief, is more than the right to attend a meeting; it includes the right to express one's attitudes or philosophies by membership in a group or by affiliation with it or by other lawful means. Association in that context is a form of expression of opinion; and while it is not expressly included in the First Amendment its existence is necessary in making the express guarantees fully meaningful.").
33 Big Data Report, *supra* note 25, at 16.
34 *Id.*

	Tort
1	Intrusion upon a person's seclusion or solitude, or into his/her private affairs.
2	Public disclosure of embarrassing private facts about an individual.
3	Publicity placing someone in a false light in the public eye.
4	Appropriation of someone's likeness for the advantage of another.

Table 9.1   Complex of Four Potential Torts for Invasion of Privacy Civil Action

Some contemporary critics argue that the "complex of four" torts does not sufficiently recognize privacy issues arising from the extensive collection, use, and disclosure of personal information by businesses in the modern marketplace.[35] Others suggest that automated processing should in fact ease privacy concerns, because it uses computers operated under precise controls to perform tasks that used to be handled by people.[36] Whether the complex of four torts as well as the patchwork of federal and state laws and guidance discussed later in this chapter is sufficient to protect privacy amid the growing industry of personal data collection is in question. The world of Big Data and data collection continues to evolve at meteoric speed, and wellness professionals and organizations are part of that evolution whether they realize it or not. It is imperative that the wellness industry understand its role in the Big Data world and appreciate the value of privacy in that world, in order for the industry to foster credibility and trust in the eyes of the consumer.

Growth of Data Collection in Health and Wellness and Beyond

Since the beginning of the 21st century, there has been a push to digitize health information. The federal government kick-started the effort to build an electronic health information highway with the Health

---

35 Id.
36 Big Data Report, *supra* note 25 at 16–17.

Insurance Portability and Accountability Act (HIPAA) in 1996. Title II, Subtitle F of that law is entitled "Administrative Simplification," the purpose of which it states as follows:

> It is the purpose of this subtitle to improve the Medicare program under title XVIII of the Social Security Act, the Medicaid program under title XIX of such Act, and the efficiency and effectiveness of the healthcare system, by encouraging the development of a health information system through the establishment of standards and requirements for the electronic transmission of certain health information.[37]

Thus, the aim of the administrative simplification portion of HIPAA was to establish electronic transmission of certain health information.[38] To do this, HIPAA required the Secretary of the Department of Health and Human Services (DHHS) to adopt standards for transactions, and data elements for such transactions, to enable health information to be exchanged electronically. The law required DHHS to focus on transactions involving:

- Health claims or equivalent encounter information
- Health claims attachments
- Enrollment and disenrollment in a health plan
- Eligibility for a health plan
- Healthcare payment and remittance advice
- Health plan premium payments
- First report of injury
- Health claim status
- Referral certification and authorization[39]

These transactions predominantly involved insurance-related transactions with traditional healthcare providers such as physicians and

---

37 Pub. L. No. 104–191, tit. II, subtit. F, § 261.
38 Id. at § 262; see also 45 C.F.R. pts. 160, 162, and 164.
39 Pub. L. No. 104–191, tit. II, subtit. F, § 262; 42 U.S.C. § 1320d-2.

hospitals. Health information collected by the wellness industry was not the original focus, but with the broad definition of **healthcare information** and *health care*, as discussed later in this chapter, HIPAA privacy and security regulation can encompass that industry as well.

Market forces responded to the sweeping declaration of HIPAA to electronically transmit and exchange health information with the growth of **electronic health records (EHRs), health information exchanges (HIEs), interoperability efforts,** and **personalized health information (PHI).**

EHRs, HIEs, and Interoperability Efforts

EHRs can facilitate the collection, storage, and sharing of comprehensive real-time information that enables healthcare providers to make informed decisions with their patients.[40] They can also help improve population health by serving as a tool for the medical community to find unexpected increases in diseases within a community.[41] Two important uses that may be relevant to the wellness industry include providing individuals and healthcare providers with access to medical history, diagnoses, medications, immunization dates, allergies, radiology images, and laboratory test results at the point of care, as well as increasing organization, accuracy, and use of patient information.[42]

In the first years of the 21st century, the adoption of EHRs by physicians and hospitals moved slowly.[43] Congress accelerated the adoption of EHRs through the Health Information Technology for Economic and Clinical Health Act (HITECH) as part of the American Recovery and Reinvestment Act (ARRA) of 2009.[44] HITECH did just that, increasing hospital adoption of EHR systems by 47 percent between 2009 and 2013 and by 26 percent for physicians in that same time period.[45] As of June 2014, 75 percent (403,000+) of the nation's eligible professionals

---

40 DHHS Office of the National Coordinator for Health Information Technology Report to Congress, "Update on the Adoption of Health Information Technology and Related Efforts to Facilitate the Electronic Use and Exchange of Health Information" (October 2014): 9, https://www.healthit.gov/sites/default/files/rtc_adoption_and_exchange9302014.pdf.
41 *Id.* at 9.
42 *Id.* at 11.
43 *Id.*
44 *Id.*
45 *Id.*

and 92 percent (4,500+) of eligible hospitals and critical access hospitals had received incentive payments under HITECH to adopt meaningful use of certified EHR technology.[46] The EHR incentive program not only provides financial rewards for adopting EHR technology, such as up to $44,000 in financial assistance from the Medicare program to physician practices that adopt meaningful use of that technology, but starting in 2015, it also imposes financial penalties on providers who do not adopt and demonstrate such use.[47]

According to DHHS, the next phase of EHR adoption will move beyond getting everyone wired, to focusing on the outcomes that technology helps providers achieve and rewarding them for those outcomes.[48] DHHS also wants to connect smartphone apps, analytic tools, and plug-in technology with other electronic health information so that all relevant health information can support patient care.[49] In a related effort, DHHS is prioritizing interoperability between health information technologies to ensure continuity of care between providers and help patients engage in their own care.[50]

These initiatives are being spurred by a number of factors. First, in early 2015 DHHS set a goal to have 50 percent of Medicare payments by 2018 linked to getting better results for patients, providing better care and spending healthcare dollars more wisely.[51] Second, the Medicare Access and CHIP Reauthorization Act of 2015 (MACRA) requires DHHS to consider quality, cost, and clinical practice improvement activities in calculating how it determines Medicare physician payments.[52]

46 *Id.* at 913.
47 *Id.* at 13; *see also* HealthIT.gov, "EHR Incentive Payment Timeline," https://www.healthit.gov/providers-professionals/ehr-incentive-payment-timeline; Centers for Medicare and Medicaid Services, "Medicare and Medicaid EHR Incentive Program Basics," https://www.cms.gov/regulations-and-guidance/legislation/ehrincentiveprograms/basics.html (noting that starting in 2015, the payment reduction starts at 1 percent and increases each year that an eligible professional does not demonstrate meaningful use, to a maximum of 5 percent).
48 Andy Slavitt and Karen DeSalvo, "EHR Incentive Programs: Where We Go Next," The CMS Blog (January 19, 2016), https://blog.cms.gov/2016/01/19/ehr-incentive-programs-where-we-go-next/.
49 *Id.*
50 *Id.*
51 *Id.*
52 *Id.*

To effectively accomplish **value-based care**, which can be defined as better health at lower cost, care coordination is essential. Effective care coordination requires meaningful exchange of health information, not just the collection of that information. As noted earlier, one of DHHS's goals is to achieve interoperability of health information technology. The first phase of this interoperability goal has been labeled *health information exchange* or *HIE*. Electronic HIE allows different types of healthcare providers to appropriately access and securely share a patient's vital medical information electronically.[53] Although HIE helps with coordination of care among different providers, it does not readily loop in health information from outside the traditional health system. Therefore, information collected through wellness programs or at other venues and times outside the traditional healthcare system has not been shared during this initial phase of HIE.[54] Thus, in the next six years, the federal Office of the National Coordinator for Health Information Technology (ONC) aims to enhance interoperability by allowing individuals, care providers, and public health departments to send, receive, find, and use an expanded set of health information across the care continuum to support team-based care.[55] This goal will enable interoperability between medical devices, home-monitoring tools, and EHRs.[56]

Indeed, this is already happening. For example, IBM has created Watson Care Manager, a platform that integrates disparate types of clinical and individual data and applies cognitive analysis to draw out insights for care managers.[57] Patients can opt in to have IBM Watson Care Manager collect from wireless-enabled scales, wearable devices, other types of sensors, and from assessments delivered to the patient's device, such as an Apple Watch.[58] The data collected is fed back into the IBM Watson Health

---

53 HealthIT.gov, "What Is HIE?," https://www.healthit.gov/providers-professionals/health-information-exchange/what-hie.

54 Office of National Coordinator for Health Information Technology, *Connecting Health and Care for the Nation: A 10-Year Vision to Achieve an Interoperable Health IT Infrastructure* (2014): 4, https://www.healthit.gov/sites/default/files/ONC10yearInteroperabilityConceptPaper.pdf.

55 *Id.* at 7.

56 *Id.*

57 IBM, "News Release: IBM Watson Health Cloud Capabilities Expand" (September 10, 2015), https://www-03.ibm.com/press/us/en/pressrelease/47624.wss.

58 *Id.*

Cloud, which analyzes the data over time and helps care managers decide which interventions are working and what care management options the patient may need in the future.[59] The ability of IBM's Watson Care Manager to connect health data from a myriad of sources may allow a care manager to notice that an individual has walked only a small percentage of the number of steps he usually does, or that a patient has had significant weight change in a given week.[60]

In addition to IBM, other companies such as Welltok and Validic have built a business model of creating a single entry point for providers, insurers, and employers to access a wealth of patient data from different data sources.[61] Welltok's CafeWell Concierge app becomes knowledgeable about a user's health status, available benefits, preferences, and behaviors, and can then deliver highly personalized and actionable recommendations.[62] The app can also integrate the information from a person's benefits plan with personalized health data, such as from a wearable fitness tracker (which may track a person's preferred foods, steps taken, or hours slept in a day).[63]

Personalized Health Information

Effective care coordination must also recognize and address an individual's specific health needs. As noted earlier, there are a number of platforms that are already connecting the data collected from different sources, such as wearable technology and mobile device applications (apps). The EHR and HIE infrastructure provides the backbone for sharing personalized health information from genetic tests, wearables, health apps, and other monitoring technology.

The federal government has done its part to spark an interest in investing in personalized health information by creating its **Precision Medicine**

---

59 *Id.*
60 Jon Asplund, "How Watson Might Empower Health Care Consumers," *Hospitals & Health Networks Magazine* (November 17, 2015), http://www.hhnmag.com/articles/6725-how-watson-might-empower-health-care-consumers.
61 Kutscher, "Competition Heats Up for Patient-Generated Health Data," *supra* note 3.
62 Welltok Blog, "IBM and Welltok Transform Benefit and Health Management for Employees" (November 12, 2015), http://blog.welltok.com/ibm-and-welltok-transform-benefit-and-health-management-for-employees.
63 *Id.*

Initiative or PMI. Announced by President Barack Obama in January 2015 during his State of the Union address, the PMI aims to cure diseases like cancer and diabetes and to give all of us access to the personalized information we need to keep ourselves and our families healthier.[64] PMI seeks to maximize effectiveness in disease treatment and prevention by taking into account individual variability in genes, environment, and lifestyle.[65] The PMI will establish a cohort of 1 million volunteers who will provide information about their genetics, environment, behavior, and lifestyle that will, it is hoped, lead to more accurate diagnoses, more rational disease prevention strategies, better treatment selection, and the development of new therapies.[66] Through the use of mobile health technologies, such as phones, wearables, and in-home devices, the PMI program will be able to longitudinally measure changes in activity, sleep behavior, nutrition, and/or social interactions, which may provide new insight into the development of certain diseases as well as responses to therapies.[67]

Private companies are also jumping on the personalized medicine bandwagon. Newtopia, a Canadian-based corporate wellness vendor, performs genetic screening and psychosocial assessments to capture personal health datasets about employees' risk for diabetes, heart disease, stroke, and other health risks.[68] Newtopia uses the datasets, including DNA markers, to develop individualized plans that aim to maximize health-based outcomes.[69] Companies like Newtopia are hoping that if workers are more aware of their risk factors, including genetic risk factors, they will be more motivated to take steps to improve their health.

Finally, mobile device technology is becoming ubiquitous. In the United States, 91 percent of adults have a mobile phone and 64 percent have a smartphone.[70] Every smartphone has a unique number that serves as an

---

64 PMI Working Group, *The Precision Medicine Initiative Cohort Program—Building a Research Foundation for 21st Century Medicine* (September 17, 2015): 1, http://www.nih.gov/sites/default/files/research-training/initiatives/pmi/pmi-working-group-report-20150917-2.pdf [hereinafter "PMI Report"].
65 *Id.*
66 PMI Report at 6.
67 *Id.* at 16.
68 Tom Murphy, "Genetic Testing Moves into World of Employee Health," Associated Press (April 28, 2015), http://www.washingtontimes.com/news/2015/apr/28/genetic-testing-moves-into-world-of-employee-healt/; *see also* https://www.newtopia.com/approach/#personalization.
69 Murphy, "Genetic Testing Moves into World of Employee Health."
70 PMI Report at 8.

identifier (unique ID), which allows companies to gather information and create profiles of cell phone users for advertisers.[71] Unique IDs pose serious privacy risks, as they are extremely difficult or impossible to delete and can be linked to other information, including the users' location.[72]

Many medical technologies that were traditionally found only in a clinical setting are now mobile, home-based, and/or consumer-operated, such as blood pressure devices, home defibrillators, and heart rate monitors.[73] Wearable devices, such as fitness trackers, smart watches, smart clothing, and other devices, are becoming so popular that researchers are predicting the growth rate of these devices to outpace the growth rate of smartphone and tablet use.[74] About 21 percent of U.S. consumers already own a fitness tracker; about 10 percent of those owners actually wear the device daily.[75] Many workplace wellness programs incorporate wearable technology into the program. For example, according to a survey of Wisconsin employers, 30 percent of those surveyed stated that wearable trackers were part of their 2015 wellness program.[76] A national survey by Mercer found that 24 percent of companies with 500 or more employees encourage employees to track their activity with a wearable device.[77] Another group estimates that 40 to 50 percent of employers with a wellness program use trackers.[78]

---

71 Jamie Lynn Flaherty, "Digital Diagnosis: Privacy and the Regulation of Mobile Phone Health Applications," 40 *Am. J. L. & Med.* 416 (2014): 431.

72 *Id.*

73 PMI Report at 8.

74 Brier Dudley, "Fitness Gadgets Raise Privacy Concerns Under New Health Insurance Rules," *Seattle Times* (February 10, 2014), http://www.seattletimes.com/business/fitness-gadgets-raise-privacy-concerns-under-new-health-insurance-rules/; *see also* Lisa Nagele-Piazza, "Employer Wellness Plans May Raise Data Collection Issues," *Bloomberg BNA* (March 21, 2016), http://www.bna.com/employer-wellness-plans-n57982069107/.

75 Jonah Comstock, "PwC: 1 in 5 Americans Own a Wearable; 1 in 10 Wears Them Daily," *MobiHealth News* (October 21, 2014), http://mobihealthnews.com/37543/pwc-1-in-5-americans-owns-a-wearable-1-in-10-wears-them-daily; *see also* Al Sacco, "Fitness Trackers Are Changing Online Privacy—and It's Time to Pay Attention," *CIO* (August 14, 2014) (citing the Pew Research Center's Internet & American Life Project), http://www.cio.com/article/2465142/wearable-technology/fitness-trackers-are-changing-online-privacy-and-its-time-to-pay-attention.html.

76 Wellness Council of Wisconsin, "January 2015 Member Poll Results: Is Wisconsin Stepping into Wearable Trackers?" (2015).

77 Roberto Michel, "Keeping Health on Track with Wearables," *Madison Magazine* (March 23, 2016), http://www.channel3000.com/madison-magazine/business-city-life/keeping-health-on-track-with-wearables/38584138.

78 Patience Haggin, "As Wearables in Workplace Spread, So Do Legal Concerns," *Wall St. J.* (March 13, 2016), http://www.wsj.com/articles/as-wearables-in-workplace-spread-so-do-legal-concerns-1457921550.

Wearables can sync up with smartphones and other software platforms, downloading data relating to the wearer's physical activity, heart rate, calories burned, sleep cycles, routes travelled, and height and weight details—as well as the person's email addresses, log-ins, passwords, and other credentials.[79] Similarly, healthcare apps that individuals download to their mobile devices capture highly sensitive medical information.[80] As of 2012, about 7 percent of American primary care physicians recommended health apps to their patients for purposes of providing medication reminders, monitoring a patient's health in real time, and transmitting information to caregivers.[81] The information collected by wearables and apps is then uploaded to the cloud for storage and analysis.[82]

The **cloud** is software and services that run on the Internet instead of a personal computer's hard drive or phone's memory.[83] Videos, photos, documents, games, medical information, and insurance claims reside ("live") in the cloud.[84] By virtue of living in the cloud, the information is available on any device with an Internet connection and accessible from anywhere.[85] This means that your personal data is stored in massive data centers around the world instead of on a device in your home, business, or hand.[86] Amazon, Google, Apple, Microsoft, and Facebook are among the biggest data center operators for consumer cloud services.[87] It is becoming increasingly difficult for both consumers and businesses to avoid using the cloud.[88]

79 Sacco, "Fitness Trackers Are Changing Online Privacy."

80 Alan Mozes, "Health Care Apps Often Offer Little Privacy Protection: Study," *HealthDay News* (March 9, 2016), http://consumer.healthday.com/health-technology-information-18/cellphone-health-news-729/healthcare-apps-offer-little-privacy-protection-708807.html.

81 *Id.*

82 *Id.*; *see also* Joseph J. Lazzarotti, "Wearables, Wellness and Privacy," *Nat'l. L. Rev.* (September 22, 2015), http://www.natlawreview.com/article/wearables-wellness-and-privacy.

83 David Goldman, "What Is the Cloud?," *CNN Money* (September 3, 2014), http://money.cnn.com/2014/09/03/technology/enterprise/what-is-the-cloud/.

84 *Id.*

85 *Id.*

86 *Id.*

87 *Id.*

88 *Id.*

Big Data

All this collection and sharing of data from multiple technologies within the cloud has coalesced into the era of Big Data. According to one source, *Big Data* is shorthand for the combination of a technology and a process.[89] The technology consists of information-processing hardware capable of sifting, sorting, and interrogating vast quantities of data in very short time periods.[90] The process involves mining the data for patterns, distilling the patterns into predictive analytics, and applying those analytics to new data.[91] "Together, the technology and the process comprise a technique for converting data flows into a particular, highly data-intensive type of knowledge."[92]

The sources and formats that contribute to Big Data continue to grow in variety and complexity.[93] As already noted, wearables contribute to Big Data. Other sources include the public web, social media, mobile applications, government records and databases, commercial databases, geospatial data, surveys, sensors, and radio-frequency identification (RFID) chips, among others.[94]

The information that is collected from this vast array of sources ends up in the hands of **data brokers** for collation and analysis. *Data brokers* are companies whose primary business is collecting personal information about consumers from a variety of sources and aggregating, analyzing, and sharing that information, or information derived from it, for purposes of marketing products, verifying an individual's identity, or detecting fraud.[95] Data brokers do not interact directly with consumers, so consumers often do not know what information is being collected about them, who is collecting it, or how the information is being used.[96]

---

89 Cohen, "What Privacy Is For," at 1920.
90 *Id.*
91 *Id.*
92 Cohen, "What Privacy Is For," at 1920–1921.
93 Big Data Report, *supra* note 25 at 5.
94 *Id.*
95 Federal Trade Commission, "Data Brokers: A Call for Transparency and Accountability" (May 2014): 3, https://www.ftc.gov/system/files/documents/reports/data-brokers-call-for-transparency-accountability-report-federal-trade-commission-may-2014/140527databrokerreport.pdf.
96 *Id.*

In 2014, the Federal Trade Commission (FTC) conducted a study of data brokers and found that data brokers provide the information they compile to clients for three primary purposes: (1) marketing products and services; (2) risk mitigation (such as verifying someone's identity and fraud detection); and (3) people search (e.g., finding old friends, tracking the activities of executives and competitors, researching a potential love interest, networking, or locating court records).[97] Selling data to various clients for these purposes earned the nine data brokers studied by the FTC $426 million in annual revenue in 2012.[98] The nine data brokers studied (with a brief description of their markets) were:

1. *Acxiom*—Provides consumer data and analytics for marketing campaigns and fraud detection. Its databases contain information about 700 million consumers worldwide, with more than 3,000 data segments for nearly every U.S. consumer.

2. *Corelogic*—Provides data and analytic services to businesses and government using property, consumer, and financial information. Its databases include more than 795 million historical property transactions, more than 93 million mortgage applications, and property-specific data covering more than 99 percent of U.S. residential properties.

3. *Datalogix*—Provides businesses with marketing data on almost every U.S. household and more than $1 trillion in consumer transactions.

4. *eBureau*—Provides predictive scoring and analytics services for marketers, financial services companies, online retailers, and others. It adds more than 3 billion new records each month.

5. *ID Analytics*—Provides analytics services designed principally to verify people's identities or to determine whether a transaction is likely fraudulent.

---

97 Federal Trade Commission, "Data Brokers: A Call for Transparency and Accountability," at 23.
98 *Id.*

6. *Intelius*—Provides businesses and consumers with background check and public record information.

7. *PeekYou*—Has patented technology that analyzes content from more than 60 social media sites, news sources, home pages, and blog platforms to provide clients with detailed consumer profiles.

8. *Rapleaf*—A data aggregator that has at least one data point associated with more than 80 percent of all U.S. consumer email addresses. Rapleaf supplements email lists with the email address owner's age, gender, marital status, and 30 other data points.

9. *Recorded Future*—Captures historical data on consumers and companies across the Internet and uses that information to predict future behavior of those consumers and companies.[99]

The FTC assembled a chart (see Table 9.2) that provides a snapshot of the main categories of data broker clients. In reference to this table, "alternative payment providers" are companies that provide consumers with alternative methods of payment rather than traditional methods such as checks or credit cards.[100] Consumer packaged goods manufacturers include companies that manufacture items that consumers use and have to replace frequently, such as food and beverages, apparel, and household products.[101] Technology companies include hardware companies, software companies, Internet companies, and other technology companies.[102] Finally, telecom companies include telephone, mobile, cable, and satellite television providers and other telecommunications companies.[103]

---

99 Federal Trade Commission, "Data Brokers: A Call for Transparency and Accountability," at 89.
100 *Id.* at 40.
101 *Id.*
102 *Id.*
103 *Id.*

	Direct Marketing	Online Marketing	Marketing Analytics	Identity Verification	Fraud Detection	People Search
Alternative payment providers				X	X	
Attorneys & investigators	X					
Automotive industry	X	X	X			
Consumer packaged goods manufacturers	X	X	X			
Other data brokers	X	X	X	X	X	
Educational institutions	X			X	X	
Energy/ Utilities	X					
Government entities	X		X	X	X	X
Hospitality, travel & entertainment	X	X	X			
Individual consumers						X
Insurance companies	X		X	X	X	
Lenders & financial services firms	X	X	X	X	X	X
Marketing & advertising firms	X	X	X	X	X	X
Media	X		X			X

Table 9.2   FTC's Main Categories of Data Broker Clients[104]

104 Federal Trade Commission, "Data Brokers: A Call for Transparency and Accountability," at 39–40.

	Direct Marketing	Online Marketing	Marketing Analytics	Identity Verification	Fraud Detection	People Search
Nonprofit entities & political campaigns	X	X		X	X	
Pharmaceutical firms	X		X			X
Real estate services	X				X	X
Retail companies	X	X	X	X	X	X
Technology companies	X	X	X			X
Telecom companies	X		X	X	X	

Table 9.2 *(continued)*

A diagram (see Figure 9.1) shows how personal information flows from the consumer to data broker clients. As one can imagine, the benefits of Big Data are countless. For marketers, small bits of data can be brought together to create a clear picture of a person to predict preferences or behaviors.[105] These detailed personal profiles and personalized experiences can deliver products and offers to precise segments of the population.[106] Consumers benefit from increased and innovative product offerings fueled by increased competition from small businesses that are able to connect with consumers they may not otherwise have been able to reach.[107] In the home, smart meters can enable energy providers to analyze consumer energy use, identify issues with home appliances, and enable consumers to be more energy conscious.[108] On the road, car sensors can notify drivers of dangerous road conditions, and software updates can occur wirelessly, obviating the need for a trip to the dealer.

---

105 Big Data Report, *supra* note 25 at 7.
106 *Id.*
107 Federal Trade Commission, "Data Brokers: A Call for Transparency and Accountability," at v.
108 FTC Staff Report, "Internet of Things: Privacy & Security in a Connected World" (January 2015): ii, https://www.ftc.gov/system/files/documents/reports/federal-trade-commission-staff-report-november-2013-workshop-entitled-internet-things-privacy/150127iotrpt.pdf.

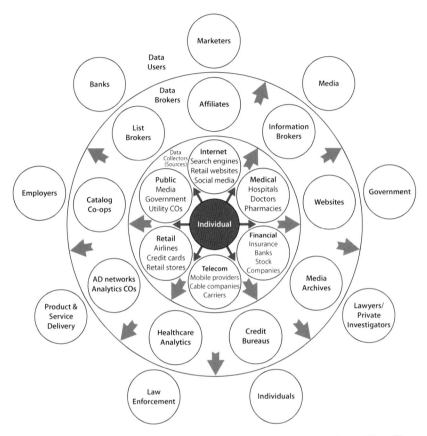

Figure 9.1   The Flow of Personal Information from the Consumer to Data Broker Clients[109]

On the health front, use of Big Data can help identify potential risk factors for disease, and manage that disease through prevention or active treatment.[110] As mentioned earlier, the PMI program aims to use the various data collected from its volunteers to better identify causes of disease and develop new therapies. Big Data can help connect the dots between isolated data points to obtain a fuller, clearer picture of barriers

109 Adapted from Federal Trade Commission, *Protecting Consumer Privacy in an Era of Rapid Change: Recommendations for Business and Policymakers* (report) (March 2012): 100, https://www.ftc.gov/sites/default/files/documents/reports/federal-trade-commission-report-protecting-consumer-privacy-era-rapid-change-recommendations/120326privacyreport.pdf.
110 *Id.* at ii.

and opportunities to improve individual and population health. Big Data can further motivate and inspire those individuals aiming to live healthier lives by providing them with information about products, services, and ideas that they may not otherwise be exposed to. Public and private insurers can use predictive analytics to flag likely instances of reimbursement fraud before claims are paid.[111]

Potential Dangers of Big Data

Despite all the advantages Big Data can provide, it does present certain dangers. One of the more nefarious dangers is the possibility of using Big Data for **redlining**. The term derives from the banking industry practice of drawing red lines around neighborhoods where they would not loan money.[112] Redlining became a potent tool of discrimination against African-Americans, Latinos, Asians, and Jews.[113] There are new worries that Big Data could be used to "digitally redline" unwanted groups, either as customers, employees, tenants, or recipients of credit.[114]

With regard to the collection and use of wellness data, one source wonders whether credit card companies could raise rates for employees whom wellness programs reveal to be couch potatoes, inferring that they are more likely to default.[115] Or, life insurers could deny coverage or raise prices based on unhealthy wellness results.[116] There is also a fear that employers may turn to productivity data to justify raises, promotions, and firings.[117] One legal scholar has surmised that once a critical mass of employees begins voluntarily exchanging private health information through fitness trackers, it is probable that employers will assume that those who refuse to do so have something to hide.[118] Failure to use

---

111 Big Data Report, *supra* note 25 at 6.
112 *Id.* at 53.
113 *Id.*
114 *Id.*
115 Hancock, "Workplace Wellness Programs Put Employee Privacy at Risk."
116 *Id.*
117 Haggin, "As Wearables in the Workplace Spread, So Do Legal Concerns."
118 Michelle M. Christovich, "Why Should We Care What Fitbit Shares?: A Proposed Statutory Solution to Protect Sensitive Personal Fitness Information," 38 *Hastings Comm. & Ent. L.J.* 91 (2016): 104.

a fitness tracker may lead to adverse employment consequences, a form of negative discrimination that is difficult to prove.[119]

A related danger is the possibility of using wellness data to "shame" individuals based on their health or fitness status.[120] Even in the absence of an adverse employment action, an environment where wellness data is used to shame employees could be construed as harassment, or at the very least create an unhealthy corporate culture.

Furthermore, with all the data that is accumulating about individuals, it is getting easier for data brokers to re-identify de-identified data.[121] Data brokers can integrate diverse data through what some analysts call the **mosaic effect**, whereby personally identifiable information can be derived or inferred from datasets that do not even include personal identifiers, thereby bringing into focus a picture of who an individual is and what he or she likes.[122] De-identified data might include blood pressure, cholesterol, drug use, and disease history.[123] Wellness professionals or organizations may believe that allowing the disclosure or sale of de-identified information protects the privacy of individuals. Yet, researchers have shown that de-identified information can be linked to the subject by combining it with voter lists, credit card records, and the multitude of other databases that exist and are growing.[124]

The world of Big Data also suffers from a lack of transparency. It is commercialized research that is not beholden to the checks and balances of research conducted in academic settings with oversight from an institutional review board.[125] Instead, research agendas and datasets are typically kept secret, as are the analytics that data brokers use. Consumers often do not even know who is using their data, much less when, where, and how their data is being used.[126] The activities of data brokers— acquiring a vast array of detailed, specific, and sometimes very sensitive information about consumers, analyzing that data to make inferences

---

119 *Id.*
120 Nagele-Piazza, "Employer Wellness Plans May Raise Data Collection Issues."
121 Big Data Report, *supra* note 25 at 8.
122 *Id.*
123 Hancock, "Workplace Wellness Programs Put Employee Privacy at Risk."
124 *Id.*
125 Cohen, "What Privacy Is For," at 1924–1926.
126 *Id.* at 1925.

about them, and then sharing it with clients in a range of industries—all take place behind the scenes, without consumers' knowledge.[127] Companies can buy, from any number of data brokers, lists of individuals in America who are afflicted with a particular disease or condition, including mental health and substance abuse conditions.[128] Companies that have consumer data, such as retailers, are finding that the data about their customers may be just as valuable, if not more valuable, than the actual product or service they sell to individuals.[129]

Along with collection, storage, and disclosure of massive amounts of personal information comes the increased risk of **data breaches.** In 2015, there were 253 healthcare data breaches that resulted in the loss of more than 112 million records.[130] Thirty-eight percent of those breaches were reported to the HHS Office of Civil Rights as "Unauthorized Access/Disclosure."[131] Ninety percent of the top 10 breaches were reported as a "Hacking/IT Incident."[132] Another top category was "theft," which constituted 29 percent of all breaches.[133] This means that for many breaches, the culprit was a hacker or a thief. Because health data is so valuable and ubiquitous, as one observes from the success of data brokers and the increasing presence of electronic health data, such data is becoming more vulnerable to attacks.

Although recent health data attacks have focused on health insurers and providers, wellness programs that use and disclose health information are not immune. Indeed, an employee for a wellness program vendor fell victim to a theft of an unencrypted, nonpassword-protected flash drive.[134] That flash drive contained the personal information of about

---

127 Federal Trade Commission, "Data Brokers: A Call for Transparency and Accountability," at vii.
128 Steve Kroft, "The Data Brokers: Selling Your Personal Information," CBS News transcript (March 9, 2014), http://www.cbsnews.com/news/the-data-brokers-selling-your-personal-information/.
129 Id.
130 Dan Munro, "Data Breaches in Healthcare Totaled Over 112 Million Records in 2015," Forbes (December 31, 2015), http://www.forbes.com/sites/danmunro/2015/12/31/data-breaches-in-healthcare-total-over-112-million-records-in-2015/#2e8e36cf7fd5.
131 Id.
132 Id.
133 Id.
134 Joanne Wojcik, "Milwaukee Sues Over Wellness-Program Data Theft," Modern Healthcare (December 27, 2013), http://www.modernhealthcare.com/article/20131227/INFO/312279994.

9,000 city employees, and their spouses and domestic partners, who were participating in their employer's wellness program.[135]

The business of hacking into systems containing health data is also taking a more sinister turn with the proliferation of *ransomware*, a virus that computer hackers use to shut down computer systems until a ransom is paid. During one month in 2016, five healthcare organizations reported being hit by such computer viruses.[136] The virus may be deployed through an email attachment.[137] When opened by an unwitting email recipient, the virus launches other software that moves through an infected computer system, scrambling computer files with impenetrable encryption, then posts a demand that the victim pay a ransom to the hackers in order to regain access to its own files.[138] In 2012, it was estimated that ransomware was yielding hackers $33,000 per day.[139] Some fear that attacks on medical devices may be next, leaving people without access to life-saving devices such as infusion pumps until a ransom is paid.[140] Wellness devices and programs, with their wealth of data, may also be vulnerable. Indeed, the faculty at Penn State expressed a fear that the information they were asked to disclose through a health assessment could be vulnerable to online hackers.[141]

Finally, on a more philosophical level, in the world of Big Data, people are becoming less mysterious and more subject to labels and false assumptions. This is because the techniques of Big Data subject individuals to predictive judgments about their preferences.[142] Users of Big Data, such as retailers, marketers, and other commercial entities, use Big Data to shape and produce an individual's preferences.[143] According to one

---

135 *Id.*
136 Joseph Conn, "U.S., Canada Issue Ransomware Warning for Hospitals After Three Hit in a Week," *Modern Healthcare* (April 4, 2016), http://www.modernhealthcare.com/article/20160404/ NEWS/160409962.
137 Joseph Conn, "Ransomware Scare: Will Hospitals Pay for Protection?," *Modern Healthcare* (April 11, 2016), http://www.modernhealthcare.com/article/20160409/MAGAZINE/304099988.
138 *Id.*
139 *Id.*
140 *Id.*
141 Mike Dawson, "Penn State Faculty Senate Debates Wellness Plan as University Defends Steps Taken," *Centre Daily Times* (September 30, 2013), http://www.centredaily.com/news/local/education/ penn-state/article42827487.html.
142 Cohen, "What Privacy Is For," at 1925.
143 *Id.* at 1925.

legal scholar, shaping a person's preferences so that they become more commercially predictable undermines human innovation.[144] This scholar contends that the human innovative drive is unpredictable and robust, and needs serendipity and privacy to thrive.[145] Human innovation—both the likelihood that it will occur and the substance of it—is at risk when privacy is squeezed to the margins and when the pathways of serendipity are disrupted and rearranged to serve more linear, commercial imperatives.[146]

Privacy should not be cast as the spoiler of Big Data progress.[147] To remain healthy, society must see value in both data processing and privacy.[148] Losing the mystery of humanity erodes one's willingness to take chances, be surprised, and grow.

The Regulation of Privacy

There are a number of laws that aim to protect individual privacy, including the privacy and security rules under the Health Insurance Portability and Accountability Act (HIPAA), the Americans with Disabilities Act (ADA), the Genetic Information Nondiscrimination Act (GINA), the Federal Trade Commission Act (FTCA), the Gramm-Leach-Bliley Act (GLBA), and the Fair Credit Reporting Act (FCRA). The pertinent parts of each of these federal laws are summarized in this section. There are also guidelines or "best practices" set forth by the federal government, such as Fair Information Practice Principles (FIPPs), that rely on self-regulation. There are also numerous state laws that protect privacy, both generally and with regard to specific types of information. For example, Wisconsin has statutes that protect the privacy of patient healthcare records,[149] mental health treatment records,[150] and HIV test results.[151] There is also a general privacy statute that provides individuals with a private cause of action for "invasions of privacy." The statute is

144 *Id.* at 1926–1927.
145 *Id.* at 1927.
146 *Id.* at 1927.
147 *Id.* at 1926.
148 *Id.* at 1927.
149 Wis. Stat. § 146.82.
150 Wis. Stat. § 51.30.
151 Wis. Stat. § 252.15(3m).

interpreted in accordance with the common law right to privacy and defines an *invasion of privacy* to include:

- Intrusion upon the privacy of another of a nature that is highly offensive to a reasonable person, in a place that a reasonable person would consider private or in a manner that could qualify as trespassing;
- Using for advertising or commercial purposes the picture of another person without their consent;
- Publicizing the private life of another in a manner highly offensive to a reasonable person when no public interest in the matter exists.[152]

Although a state-by-state recital and analysis of relevant privacy laws is beyond the scope of this book, it is critical that wellness professionals and organizations familiarize themselves with the privacy laws in each state in which they do business.

Despite these various federal and state laws to protect privacy, there are significant gaps in privacy regulation that leave vast amounts of information unprotected. Privacy laws are not keeping up with the incredibly fast developments in health information technology. To remain trustworthy in the eyes of wellness program participants, wellness professionals and organizations must fill in those regulatory gaps whenever possible. First, though, it is important to know the boundaries of the current federal regulatory landscape concerning the privacy of data collected by wellness professionals and organizations.

HIPAA

Recall that HIPAA's Administrative Simplification provision aimed to regulate the electronic transmission of certain "health information." The law defined *health information* as information, whether oral or recorded

---

[152] Wis. Stat. § 995.50.

in any form or medium, that: (a) is created or received by a healthcare provider, health plan, public health authority, employer, life insurer, school or university, or healthcare clearinghouse; and (b) relates to the past, present, or future physical or mental health or condition of an individual, the provision of health care to an individual, or the past, present, or future payment for the provision of health care to an individual.[153] That definition is broad enough to include much of the information collected and used by workplace wellness programs.

However, when HHS developed the HIPAA privacy and security regulations, effective in 2003 and 2005, respectively, it limited the application of those regulations to **protected health information (PHI)** used or disclosed by HIPAA "covered entities."[154] Later, under the Health Information Technology for Economic and Clinical Health Act (HITECH) of 2009, HHS expanded compliance with the HIPAA security rule and portions of the privacy rule to "business associates."[155]

Covered entities include health plans, healthcare clearinghouses, and healthcare providers that transmit any health information in electronic form in connection with a covered transaction.[156] **Business associates** are persons who are not employees of a covered entity but provide services to a covered entity that requires use or disclosure of PHI.[157] Covered entities may be a business associate of another covered entity.[158] Business associates include persons who offer a personal health record to one or more individuals on behalf of a covered entity as well as subcontractors that create, receive, maintain, or transmit PHI on behalf of the business associate.[159] Notably, a plan sponsor (often the employer) of a group health plan is not a business associate of the group health plan (such as the insurance issuer or HMO) if the requirements under

153 Pub. L. No. 104-191, tit. II, subtit. F, § 262; *see also* 45 C.F.R. § 160.103 (definition of *health information*).
154 45 C.F.R. § 164.502; *see also* 78 Fed. Reg. 5566, 5569 (January 25, 2013), https://www.gpo.gov/fdsys/pkg/FR-2013-01-25/pdf/2013-01073.pdf.
155 Pub. L. No. 111-5, § 13404 (42 U.S.C. § 17934).
156 *Id.*
157 45 C.F.R. § 160.103 (definition of *business associate*).
158 *Id.*
159 *Id.*

45 C.F.R. § 164.504(f) are met.[160] Also, the privacy regulations exclude health information, including genetic information, in "employment records held by an employer in its role as employer" from the definition of PHI.[161]

Generally speaking, the **HIPAA Privacy Rule** "requires covered entities to have safeguards in place to ensure the privacy of protected health information, sets forth the circumstances under which covered entities may use or disclose an individual's protected health information, and gives individuals rights with respect to their protected health information, including rights to examine and obtain a copy of their health records and to request corrections. Covered entities that engage business associates to work on their behalf must have contracts or other arrangements in place with their business associates to ensure that the business associates safeguard protected health information, and use and disclose the information only as permitted or required by the Privacy Rule."[162] That includes PHI maintained in electronic formats.[163] The Privacy Rule regulations are found at 45 C.F.R. Part 164, Subpart E.

The Security Rule regulations are found at 45 C.F.R. Part 160 and Subparts A and C of Part 164. According to HHS, the **HIPAA Security Rule** "establishes national standards to protect individuals' electronic protected health information that is created, received, used, or maintained by a covered entity."[164] As already noted, HITECH expanded compliance with the Security Rule to business associates. The Security Rule requires covered entities and business associates to implement appropriate administrative, physical, and technical safeguards to ensure the confidentiality, integrity, and security of electronic protected health

---

160 *Id.* Those requirements include, for example, amending the plan documents to establish the permitted and required uses and disclosures of information by the plan sponsor, requiring the plan sponsor to certify that it will not use or further disclose the information other than as permitted by the plan documents or as required by law and not use or disclose the information for employment-related actions and decisions.

161 *Id.* at § 160.103.

162 45 C.F.R. pt. 160; subpts. A and E of pt. 164; 78 Fed. Reg. 5566 (Jan. 25, 2013) (supplementary information).

163 45 C.F.R. pt. 160; subpts. A and E of pt. 164; 78 Fed. Reg. 5566 (Jan. 25, 2013) (supplementary information).

164 HHS, "The Security Rule," http://www.hhs.gov/hipaa/for-professionals/security/.

information.[165] Unlike the Privacy Rule, which applies to PHI in any format, the Security Rule does not apply to PHI that is transmitted orally or in paper form; it applies only to electronic PHI ("e-PHI").[166]

The administrative, physical, and technical safeguards that covered entities and business associates must implement under the Security Rule aim to do the following:

1. Ensure the confidentiality, integrity, and availability of all e-PHI that the covered entity or business associate creates, receives, maintains, or transmits.
2. Protect against any reasonably anticipated threats or hazards to the security or integrity of such information.
3. Protect against any reasonably anticipated uses or disclosures of such information that are not permitted or required under the Privacy Rule.
4. Ensure compliance with the Security Rule by the covered entity or business associate's workforce.[167]

The **HIPAA Breach Notification Rule** requires covered entities to notify individuals whose **unsecured PHI** is breached, as well as the Secretary of Health and Human Services and the media under certain methods and circumstances.[168] Business associates have a duty to notify the covered entity of a breach.[169] *Breach* means the acquisition, access, use, or disclosure of PHI in a manner not permitted by the HIPAA Privacy Rule which compromises the security or privacy of the PHI. *Unsecured PHI* is PHI that is not rendered unusable, unreadable, or indecipherable to unauthorized persons through the use of a technology or methodology specified by the Secretary of Health and Human Services.[170]

---

165 HHS, "Summary of the HIPAA Security Rule," http://www.hhs.gov/hipaa/for-professionals/security/laws-regulations/.
166 *Id.*
167 45 C.F.R. § 164.306.
168 45 C.F.R. § Åò 164.400 *et seq.*
169 45 C.F.R. § 164.410.
170 45 C.F.R. § 164.402.

This refers to electronic PHI that is not encrypted or hard-copy PHI that is not destroyed.[171]

Not all inadvertent disclosures constitute a breach. For example, unintentional access or use of PHI by a workforce member acting under the authority of a covered entity or a business associate, if such access or use was made in good faith and within that person's scope of authority, does not constitute a breach so long as the PHI is not further used or disclosed in violation of HIPAA.[172] A disclosure of PHI by a person who is otherwise authorized to access the PHI at a covered entity or business associate to another person authorized to access the PHI is not a breach.[173] Disclosures to unauthorized persons who are not reasonably likely to retain the information disclosed also do not constitute breaches under the HIPAA Breach Notification Rule.[174]

Compliance with the HIPAA Privacy and Security Rules requires covered entities and business associates to expend a lot of resources. A sample, but not exhaustive, list of the various requirements imposed by the Privacy and Security Rules follows.

For covered entities:

- Create and implement HIPAA Privacy, Security, and Breach Notification policies and procedures
- Appoint HIPAA privacy and security officials
- Create and distribute a notice of privacy practices
- Create and distribute patient authorizations
- Create and enter into business associate agreements (BAAs)
- Adhere to minimum necessary standards
- Adhere to breach standards
- Adhere to plan sponsor disclosure standards

---

171 U.S. Dep't of Health and Human Services, *Guidance to Render Unsecured Protected Health Information Unusable, Unreadable, or Indecipherable to Unauthorized Individuals*, http://www.hhs.gov/hipaa/for-professionals/breach-notification/guidance/index.html.
172 45 C.F.R. § 164.402.
173 *Id.*
174 *Id.*

Business associates should:

- Comply with the BAA requirements
- Implement applicable HIPAA privacy, security, and breach notification policies and procedures
- Enter into a BAA with their subcontractors
- Cooperate with government investigations into HIPAA compliance
- Designate a security official and (for best practice) a privacy official
- Notify covered entities of breaches

One other important point to note about HIPAA and its relationship to various state privacy laws is that HIPAA sets a floor of protection for PHI. If a state law is "more stringent" than HIPAA, the state law governs.[175] A *more stringent state law* is one that is more protective of a person's privacy by being more restrictive in allowing PHI uses or disclosures, or one that permits greater rights of access to or amendment of a person's own PHI.[176]

HIPAA Privacy and Security in the Workplace Wellness Context

According to the U.S. Department of Health and Human Services (DHHS) Office of Civil Rights (OCR), the federal agency with oversight over HIPAA compliance, whether HIPAA privacy and security rules apply to workplace wellness programs depends on the way those programs are structured.[177] According to OCR, workplace wellness programs that are part of a group health plan are subject to HIPAA because the group health plan qualifies as a HIPAA-covered entity.[178] A wellness vendor for such a wellness program would be subject to HIPAA as a business associate. HIPAA places restrictions on the sharing of PHI

---

175 45 C.F.R. § 160.203(b).
176 45 C.F.R. § 160.201.
177 DHHS Office of Civil Rights Guidance, HIPAA Privacy and Security and Workplace Wellness Programs, https://www.hhs.gov/hipaa/for-professionals/privacy/workplace-wellness/ (last visited January 6, 2017).
178 *Id.*

between the group health plan and employer sponsor of the plan.[179] Often, the employer as plan sponsor will be involved in administering certain aspects of the group health plan, which may include administering wellness program benefits (such as distributing incentives) offered through the plan.[180] Where this is the case and absent written authorization from the individual to disclose the information, the group health plan may provide the employer as plan sponsor with access to the PHI necessary to perform its plan administration functions. This disclosure to the plan sponsor may happen only if the employer amends its plan documents to indicate the following:

- That any agents to whom the employer provides PHI agree to the same use and disclosure restrictions and conditions that apply to the employer.
- That the employer will not use or disclose the PHI for employment-related actions and decisions or in connection with any other benefit or employee benefit plan of the employer.
- That the employer will report to the group health plan any use or disclosure of the PHI that is inconsistent with uses or disclosures provided for of which it becomes aware.
- That it will make available PHI in accordance with HIPAA's individual access rule at 45 C.F.R. § 164.524.
- That the employer will make available PHI for amendment and incorporate any amendments to PHI in accordance with 45 C.F.R. § 164.526.
- That the employer will make available the information required to provide an accounting of disclosures in accordance with 45 C.F.R. § 164.528.
- That the employer will make its internal practices, books, and records relating to the use and disclosures of PHI received from the group health plan available to the HHS Secretary for purposes of determining HIPAA compliance by the group health plan.

---

179 *Id.*
180 *Id.*

- That the employer will return or destroy, if feasible, all PHI received from the group health plan when no longer needed for the purpose for which the disclosure was made. If return or destruction is not feasible, the employer should state that it will limit further uses and disclosures to those purposes that make the return or destruction of the PHI infeasible.

- That the employer will ensure adequate separation between the group health plan and the employer plan sponsor. To do this, the employer's plan documents should describe those persons, employees, or classes of employers who will be given access to PHI. The plan documents should state that those employees with PHI access will be limited to plan administration functions that the employer plan sponsor performs for the group health plan.

- Finally, the plan documents should provide an effective mechanism for resolving any issues of noncompliance by persons with PHI access.[181]

If the employer as plan sponsor does not perform plan administration functions on behalf of the group health plan, access to PHI by the plan sponsor without written authorization of the individual is more circumscribed.[182] In these cases, group health plans may disclose to the plan sponsor only:

- Information on which individuals are participating in the group health plan or enrolled in the health insurance issuer or HMO offered by the plan; and/or

- Summary health information if requested for purposes of modifying the plan or obtaining premium bids for coverage under the plan.[183]

According to OCR, if a workplace wellness program is offered by an employer directly and not as part of a group health plan, the health information that is

181 DHHS Office of Civil Rights Guidance, HIPAA Privacy and Security and Workplace Wellness Programs, *supra* note 177; *see also* 45 C.F.R. § 164.504(f).
182 *Id.*
183 *Id.*

collected from employees by the employer is not protected by HIPAA privacy and security rules.[184] However, this blanket statement by OCR does not account for the possibility that a workplace wellness program itself might qualify as a group health plan if the wellness program provides "medical care" (see Chapter 3). If the wellness program offers lifestyle improvement activities only, such as exercise or nutrition activities not tied to any specific, diagnosed disease improvement for an employee, then non-group health plan wellness programs would not be subject to HIPAA privacy and security rules. Recall from Chapter 3 that lifestyle improvement activities do not qualify as medical care, which is a key ingredient for constituting a group health plan. Regardless of the technical accuracy of OCR's statement that HIPAA never applies to wellness programs offered directly by employers, the statement is important from an enforcement perspective. Because OCR is the enforcement agency for HIPAA privacy and security compliance, its views on when HIPAA applies in certain situations is important when determining compliance risk. Also, regardless of whether a wellness program is part of a group health plan, an employee's health information that is legitimately part of the employee's employment record, is not protected by HIPAA.[185]

Group health plans wellness programs subject to the HIPAA Privacy Rule may have to obtain an employee's written authorization in accordance with the HIPAA authorization provision before disclosing PHI to an employer.[186] An authorization may be necessary even if the disclosure to the employer is otherwise permissible under the ADA, such as for making employee disability accommodations.[187]

Obtaining an employee's HIPAA-compliant written authorization may also be necessary for some wellness professionals who need PHI from a participant's healthcare provider. Wellness professionals such as dietitians and exercise physiologists may need to obtain medical information from an employee's healthcare provider in order to safely and effectively design and deliver a proper program. This is especially true

---

184 *Id.*
185 45 C.F.R. § 160.103 (definition of PHI excludes employment records held by a covered entity in its role as an employer).
186 81 Fed. Reg. 31142 (May 17, 2016); *see also* 45 C.F.R. § 164.508(c).
187 81 Fed. Reg. 31142 (May 17, 2016).

for employees who have diagnosed medical conditions and are taking certain medications. For example, it is important for an exercise professional to obtain from the employee's healthcare provider (e.g., physician, physical therapist, occupational therapist) any specific exercise recommendations and/or contraindications the professional should follow given the employee's medical condition(s). The exercise professional may also request the results of a graded exercise test (GXT) or blood pressure records, for example, of an employee who indicated hypertension on his or her pre-activity screening device. For an employee with hypertension, the exercise professional may want to send blood pressure records (e.g., a log of blood pressure readings taken by the exercise professional before, during, and after exercise) periodically to the employee's physician to keep the physician abreast of the employee's progress. In either case— whether the exercise professional is requesting medical information from a healthcare provider or sending medical information to a healthcare provider—the exercise professional should have the employee sign a HIPAA-compliant authorization. An example of such a form is available elsewhere.[188] This two-way communication between exercise professionals and healthcare providers is becoming more evident given the Exercise is Medicine (EIM) initiative, which is discussed in Chapter 11.

Even when HIPAA does apply in the workplace wellness context, protections of PHI privacy may be weakening under the accelerating development of Big Data. For example, subcontractors that receive PHI from business associates must agree to limit further use or disclosure of the PHI to the purpose for which it was disclosed to the subcontractor.[189] Given the growing capabilities of Big Data, the purposes for which PHI may be disclosed from a covered entity to downstream entities are both vast and vague. For example, a purpose for the disclosure may be for data analytics. Data analytics in the world of Big Data and data brokers has a much different meaning, and much greater potential for abuse,

---

188 *See, e.g.*, HIPAA Collaborative of Wisconsin, "Wisconsin Authorization Form," http://hipaacow.org/resources/hipaa-cow-documents/privacy-security/; *see also* JoAnn M. Eickhoff-Shemek, David L. Herbert, and Daniel P. Connaughton, *Risk Management for Health/Fitness Professionals: Legal Issues and Strategies* (Baltimore, MD: Lippincott Williams & Wilkins, 2009): 166.
189 45 C.F.R. § 164.504(e)(4)(B)(ii)(B)(1).

than it did in 2003 and 2005 when HHS first required compliance with the Privacy and Security Rules. Absent a contractual provision by the covered entity prohibiting certain uses and disclosures of PHI, HIPAA privacy rules could technically permit downstream entities to use and disclose PHI for data analytics purposes, such as consumer profiling, that have proliferated since the time HHS drafted the HIPAA Privacy and Security Rules.

Another HIPAA compliance loophole involves **de-identified PHI**. *De-identified PHI* is data that does not identify an individual and for which there is no reasonable basis to believe that the information can be used to identify an individual.[190] HIPAA privacy rules do not protect de-identified PHI.[191] Given the escalating and mysterious power of Big Data, what may seem like de-identified data—and therefore safe for a covered entity or business associate to sell, use, and/or disclose—may still be very valuable to a data broker or other downstream entity. Data brokers may still be able to combine that de-identified data with other data to identify an individual. Moreover, if de-identified PHI is re-identified, HIPAA only requires covered entities to comply with the HIPAA Privacy Rule with regard to that re-identified information, not business associates or other downstream entities (unless those business associates or downstream entities are contractually bound by a covered entity to protect re-identified information).[192]

ADA

The ADA also has privacy protections for employees who work for employers with at least 15 employees.[193] ADA § 102(d)(3)(B) applies to information obtained through permissible medical examinations of prospective or current employees.[194] Recall from Chapter 4 that the ADA

---

190 45 C.F.R. § 164.514(a).
191 45 C.F.R. § 164.502(d).
192 45 C.F.R. § 164.502(d)(2)(ii).
193 29 C.F.R. § 1630.2(e) (definition of *employer*).
194 29 C.F.R. § 1630.14.

permits "voluntary" medical examinations, and the final ADA rules now give some definition of what might constitute "voluntary" when a wellness program offers financial incentives for participating in a health assessment or biometric screening. Medical information collected through a voluntary or other permissible medical exam must be kept in a separate medical file and is treated as a confidential medical record.[195] Information within such files may be disclosed only in limited circumstances. For example, managers and supervisors may be informed of work restrictions on duties of an employee or necessary accommodations.[196] A medical condition identified through a medical examination may also be revealed to first aid or safety personnel providing treatment, or government officials who are conducting investigations of compliance.[197] In most other cases, however, the medical information collected by an employer, such as through a health assessment or a biometric screen, must be kept confidential, in a file separate from the employee's other employment information, and not used for any discriminatory purposes.[198]

According to the EEOC, information may be confidential even if it contains no medical diagnosis or treatment course and even if it is not generated by a healthcare professional.[199] For example, an employee's request for a reasonable accommodation would be considered medical information subject to the ADA's confidentiality requirements. However, it is important to note that employees and applicants currently engaging in the illegal use of drugs are not covered by the ADA when an employer acts on the basis of such use.[200] Tests for illegal drugs are not subject to the ADA's restrictions on medical examinations (e.g., the medical examinations do not have to be voluntary).[201] Employers may hold illegal drug

---

195 *Id.*
196 *Id.*
197 *Id.*
198 *Id.*
199 EEOC, "Facts about the Americans with Disabilities Act," https://www.eeoc.gov/eeoc/publications/fs-ada.cfm.
200 *Id.*
201 *Id.*

users and alcoholics to the same performance standards as other employees.[202]

As discussed in Chapter 4, the ADA rules require wellness programs to provide participating employees with a written notice that clearly and understandably explains what medical information the program will obtain, how that information will be used, who will receive it, and the restrictions on its disclosure.[203] The notice should also describe methods the employer uses to prevent improper disclosure of medical information.[204]

The final ADA rule also adds a new subsection that limits disclosure of medical information collected through a wellness program to an employer sponsor of the program. Wellness programs must disclose employee health information in aggregate terms that are not reasonably likely to identify an individual employee, except as necessary to administer the wellness program or as otherwise permitted by the ADA.[205] This is similar to what HIPAA already requires for group health plan wellness programs, as discussed earlier. The EEOC states that a wellness program that is part of a group health plan likely will be able to comply with ADA health information disclosure standards by complying with the HIPAA privacy rule.[206] The EEOC expects both employers and administrators of wellness programs to ensure compliance with the ADA's disclosure limitation.[207]

The final ADA rules also prohibit employers from requiring employees to agree to the sale, exchange, sharing, transfer, or other disclosure of medical information, except to the extent permitted by the ADA to carry out specific activities related to the wellness program, as a condition for participating in a wellness program or receiving a wellness program incentive.[208] Similarly, employers may not require employees to waive confidentiality protections available under the ADA as a condition for participating in a wellness program or receiving a wellness program

202 Id.
203 81 Fed. Reg. 31126, 31134 (May 17, 2016).
204 Id.
205 29 C.F.R. § 1630.14(4)(iii); 81 Fed. Reg. 31126, 31142 (May 17, 2016).
206 81 Fed. Reg. 31126, 31142 (May 17, 2016).
207 81 Fed. Reg. 31126, 31142 (May 17, 2016).
208 29 C.F.R. § 1630.14(d)(4)(iv).

incentive. As alluded to earlier, complying with this requirement may become more challenging in the world of Big Data. Employers and wellness vendors may sell or share de-identified information that could later be re-identified. It will be interesting to see whether anyone attempts to argue that the sale of de-identified information that is later re-identified violates this provision of the ADA (as well as a similar provision under GINA, discussed below).

In the guidance to the ADA final rule, the EEOC declares that employers and wellness providers must take steps to protect the confidentiality of employee medical information provided through a wellness program.[209] The EEOC recognizes that some of these protections may be required by law (such as those discussed above under the ADA and HIPAA). But, other protections may be "best practices." Hence, the EEOC expects employers and wellness vendors to adopt best practices when it comes to collecting, storing and disclosing employee health information. One best practice may be for the employer or wellness vendor to adopt many of the HIPAA privacy and security standards. At a minimum, the EEOC mentions that it is critical for employers and wellness providers to train all individuals who handle medical information about the requirements of the ADA and, as applicable, HIPAA's privacy, security and breach requirements, and any other privacy laws. The EEOC also expects employers and wellness providers to have clear privacy policies and procedures related to the collection, storage, and disclosure of medical information. Such policies and procedures should include disciplinary procedures of employees and vendors who breach employee health information confidentiality. The policies and procedures should also prohibit individuals who make employment-related decisions, such as hiring, termination, or discipline, from handling employee medical information. To help prevent inappropriate use of employee health information by the employer's decision-makers, the EEOC guidance recommends using a third-party vendor that maintains strict confidentiality and data security procedures. If an employer uses a third-party vendor, the EEOC encourages the employer to familiarize

209 81 Fed. Reg. 31126, 31142 (May 17, 2016).

itself with the vendor's privacy policies to ensure the confidentiality of medical information. If an employer does not use a third-party vendor and instead administers its own wellness program, the employer should have adequate firewalls in place to prevent unintended disclosure. If individuals who handle medical information obtained through a wellness program also act as decision-makers (which may be the case for a small employer that administers its own wellness program), they may not use the information to discriminate on the basis of disability in violation of the ADA.

Employers and wellness providers should guard against unauthorized access to online systems and other technology through use of encryption for medical information stored electronically.[210] The EEOC expects employers and wellness vendors to report breaches of confidentiality to affected employees immediately and to thoroughly investigate such breaches.[211]

GINA

GINA Title II requires employers that possess genetic information in writing about an employee to "maintain such information on forms and in medical files (including where the information exists in electronic forms and files) that are separate from personnel files and treat such information as a confidential medical record."[212] However, employers may keep genetic information in the same file "in which it maintains confidential medical information" subject to the Americans with Disabilities Act."[213] Genetic information that an employer receives orally need not be reduced to writing, but such oral information may not be disclosed except as otherwise permitted by GINA.[214]

---

210 *Id.*
211 *Id.*
212 29 C.F.R. § 1635.9(a)(1).
213 29 C.F.R. § 1635.9(a)(2).
214 29 C.F.R. § 1635.9(a)(3).

Employers may not disclose genetic information except in the following, limited circumstances:

1. To the employee or individual about whom the information pertains upon receipt of the employee's or individual's written request
2. To an occupational or other health researcher if the research is conducted in compliance with the regulations and protections provided for under 45 C.F.R. Part 46
3. In response to a court order, except that the employer may disclose only the genetic information expressly authorized by such order; and if the court order was secured without the knowledge of the employee or individual to whom the information refers, the employer shall inform the employee or individual of the court order and any genetic information that was disclosed pursuant to the order
4. To government officials investigating compliance with GINA if the information is relevant to the investigation
5. To the extent the disclosure is made in support of an employee's compliance with the certification provisions of § 103 of the Family and Medical Leave Act (29 U.S.C. § 2613) or such requirements under state family and medical leave laws
6. To a federal, state, or local public health agency only with regard to information about the manifestation of a disease or disorder that concerns a contagious disease that presents an imminent hazard of death or life-threatening illness, provided that the individual whose family member is the subject of the disclosure is notified of the disclosure[215]

To the extent that genetic information qualifies as PHI (e.g., is used or disclosed by a HIPAA-covered entity or business associate), HIPAA privacy and security protections would apply.[216]

---

215 29 C.F.R. § 1635.9(b).
216 29 C.F.R. § 1635.9(c).

The final GINA rules also prohibit employers from conditioning participation in a wellness program on, or providing any reward to an employee, spouse, or other covered dependent in exchange for, their agreement permitting the sale, exchange, sharing, transfer, or other disclosure of genetic information, including information about the manifestation of disease or disorder of an employee's family member.[217] Thus, it is very important for wellness program providers and purchasers to ensure that their agreements do not permit the downstream sale of genetic information, which includes current health status information of an employee's family member.

The GINA rule states that before a spouse provides health information as part of a health assessment or biometric screen, the spouse must provide prior, knowing, voluntary, and written authorization.[218] GINA already requires such authorization from employees when providing genetic information.[219] The preamble to the final rule reminds employers of this existing duty to obtain prior authorization when seeking genetic information. This reminder seeks to ensure that spouses who agree to provide information about their current or past health status when participating in a health assessment or biometric screen also provide such authorization. The authorization form that the spouse signs must describe the confidentiality protections and restrictions on the disclosure of genetic information.[220] Specifically, the authorization must contain the following elements:

1. It must be written so that the individual providing the genetic information is reasonably likely to understand it
2. It must describe the type of genetic information that the group health plan plans to obtain and the general purpose for which the plan will use that information
3. It must describe the restrictions on disclosure of the genetic information

---

217 29 C.F.R. § 1635.8(b)(2)(iv).
218 29 C.F.R. § 1635.8(b)(2)(iii).
219 *See* 42 U.S.C. § 2000ff-1(b)(2)(B).
220 81 Fed. Reg. 31143, 31155, n. 47 (May 17, 2016).

4. It must state that individually identifiable genetic information will be provided only to the individual (or family member if the family member is receiving genetic services) and the licensed healthcare professionals or board-certified genetic counselors involved in providing such services

5. It must state that managers, supervisors, or others who make employment decisions, or anyone else in the workplace, will not have access to the genetic information

6. It must state that any individually identifiable genetic information provided as part of a voluntary wellness program is only available for purposes of such services and is not disclosed to the employer except in aggregate terms that do not disclose the identity of specific individuals[221]

The employee does not have to sign an authorization for the spouse to provide information about the spouse's current or past health status.[222]

FTCA

The Federal Trade Commission (FTC) is an independent U.S. law enforcement agency charged with protecting consumers and enhancing competition across broad sectors of the economy.[223] The FTC's primary legal authority comes from § 5 of the FTC Act (FTCA), which prohibits unfair or deceptive practices in the marketplace.[224] The legal standards for unfairness and deception are independent of each other.[225] Depending on

---

221 *Id.*
222 81 Fed. Reg. at 31155.
223 FTC, "FTC 2014 Privacy and Data Security Update," https://www.ftc.gov/system/files/documents/reports/privacy-data-security-update-2014/privacydatasecurityupdate_2014.pdf.
224 *Id.*
225 FTC, *Federal Reserve Consumer Compliance Handbook, Federal Trade Commission Act Section 5: Unfair or Deceptive Acts or Practices*, https://www.federalreserve.gov/boarddocs/supmanual/cch/ftca.pdf. It should be noted that agencies that regulate the financial industry apply the same legal standards as the FTC with regard to determining whether an act or practice is unfair or deceptive. *See, e.g., FDIC Compliance Examination Manual, Federal Trade Commission Act Section 5 Unfair or Deceptive Acts or Practices* (November 2015), at VII-1.2, https://www.fdic.gov/regulations/compliance/manual/7/VII-1.1.pdf.

the facts, an act or practice may be unfair, deceptive, or both.[226] An act or practice is unfair when it:

- Causes or is likely to cause substantial injury to consumers,
- Cannot be reasonably avoided by consumers, and
- Is not outweighed by countervailing benefits to consumers or to competition.[227]

Public policy, as established by statute, regulation, or judicial decisions, may be considered with all other evidence in determining whether an act or practice is unfair.[228] An act or practice is deceptive when:

- A representation, omission, or practice misleads or is likely to mislead the consumer,
- A consumer's interpretation of the representation, omission, or practice is considered reasonable under the circumstances; and
- The misleading representation, omission, or practice is material.[229]

The FTC's enforcement authority extends over most companies doing business in the United States.[230] Some exceptions from the FTCA include banks, air carriers, and companies subject to the Packers and Stockyards Act.[231] Given the limited number of exceptions, the FTCA would cover most employers and wellness companies.

The FTC uses FTCA § 5 to protect consumer data privacy and security. Indeed, the FTC has brought enforcement actions addressing a wide range of privacy issues, including spam, social networking, behavioral

---

226 FTC, *Federal Reserve Consumer Compliance Handbook, Federal Trade Commission Act Section 5: Unfair or Deceptive Acts or Practices.*
227 *Id.*
228 *Id.*
229 *Id.*
230 15 U.S.C. § 45(a).
231 *Id.*

advertising, pretexting, spyware, peer-to-peer file sharing, and mobile technology uses.[232] Here are some fairly recent enforcement examples:

- PaymentsMD, LLC, an online billing portal, and its chief executive officer, failed to adequately inform consumers that the company would seek highly detailed medical information from pharmacies, medical labs, and insurance companies.[233] According to the complaint, the authorization language included a statement that "health records related to your treatment may be used or disclosed pursuant to this Authorization."[234] However, the FTC found that the website design made the statement hard to read and easy to skip over by having the consumer click on a single check box that preceded all of the authorizations.[235] The FTC found the acts and practices by PaymentsMD, LLC, to be deceptive and in violation of 15 U.S.C. § 45(a).

- The FTC complained about GMR Transcription Services and its owners for failing to provide reasonable and appropriate security measures to protect personal information uploaded to the company's services by its customers. GMR contracted with independent typists as well as another company based in India to transcribe both medical and nonmedical audio files. GMR customers include university students and faculty, other corporations, government agencies, and healthcare providers and hospitals. Customers log into GMR's website and upload audio files to a leased server located on GMR's computer network. Although GMR had a privacy policy that required transcriptionists to sign a confidentiality agreement, indicated that uploaded personal information is highly secure and not divulged to anyone, and advertised that it was HIPAA compliant, the FTC found such statements to be deceptive. Specifically, the FTC asserted that GMR and its owners failed to

232 "FTC 2014 Privacy and Data Security Update," https://www.ftc.gov/system/files/documents/reports/privacy-data-security-update-2014/privacydatasecurityupdate_2014.pdf.
233 Id.
234 In re PaymentsMD, LLC, Complaint, Dkt. No. C-4505, ¶ 9 (Fed. Trade Comm. Jan. 27, 2015), https://www.ftc.gov/system/files/documents/cases/150206paymentsmdcmpt.pdf.
235 Id.

require typists to adopt and implement security measures, such as installing antivirus applications, or confirm that they had done so. The FTC also stated that GMR failed to adequately verify that the medical transcription company based in India used encryption and typist authentication methods before granting typists access to the files. GMR also did not request or review the medical transcription company's security practices. The FTC discovered that all of the medical transcript files were publicly available and were accessed using a search engine. Consumers would have no way of independently discovering GMR's security failures.[236]

- The FTC alleged that Genelink, Inc., and Foru International violated the FTCA in two ways. First, the companies deceived consumers by advertising that a cheek-swab DNA test would allow them to provide customized dietary supplements and skincare products that mitigate or compensate for an individual's genetic disadvantages. The FTC found those claims to be untrue and lacking in scientific proof. The FTC also accused the companies of failing to employ reasonable and appropriate measures to prevent unauthorized access to consumers' personal information. The companies used third parties to receive, process, or maintain customers' personal information, and the companies stored the personal information on their corporate network. The companies had a privacy policy stating that they send personal customer information to third-party subcontractors and agents. The privacy policy further stated that the third parties did not have the right to use the personal customer information beyond what was necessary to assist the companies and fulfill customer orders. The companies entered into contracts with these third parties requiring them to maintain the confidentiality and security of the personal customer information and restricting them from using such information in any way not expressly authorized by the companies. Nevertheless, despite having this privacy policy, the FTC found that the companies failed

---

236 *In re GMR Transcription Servs., Inc., Complaint*, Dkt. No. C-4482 (Fed. Trade Comm., August 14, 2014), https://www.ftc.gov/system/files/documents/cases/140821gmrcmpt.pdf.

to protect the security of consumers' personal information. They failed to contractually require that the third parties implement and maintain appropriate safeguards for consumers' personal information. The companies did not provide reasonable oversight of the third parties by requiring them to implement simple, low-cost, and readily available defenses to protect the personal information. Some of the specific security failures included:

- Maintaining consumers' personal information, including names, addresses, email addresses, telephone numbers, dates of birth, social security numbers, and bank account numbers in clear text
- Providing company employees, regardless of business need, with access to consumers' complete personal information
- Providing third-party service providers with access to consumers' complete personal information (rather than, for example, to fictitious datasets) to develop new applications
- Failing to perform assessments to identify reasonably foreseeable risks to the security, integrity, and confidentiality of consumers' personal information on the respondents' network
- Providing a service provider, which needed only certain categories of information for its business purposes, with access to consumers' complete personal information
- Not using readily available security measures to limit wireless access to their network

Because of the discrepancies in what the companies claimed, both in terms of the success of their products and in their data security, the FTC alleged that the companies' acts and practices were unfair, deceptive, and in violation of the FTCA.[237]

Workplace Wellness Lessons to Be Learned from FTCA Cases

Although many workplace wellness programs may not be subject to HIPAA privacy and security protections, the FTC has prosecuted cases

---

237 *In re Genelink, Inc. & Foru International Corp. Complaint*, Dkt. No. C-4456 (Fed. Trade Comm. May 8, 2014), https://www.ftc.gov/system/files/documents/cases/140512genelinkcmpt.pdf.

against companies for failing to implement HIPAA-like privacy and security policies and procedures. Whether a vendor or employer operates the wellness program, to the extent that the program collects personal information from employees, the vendor or employer should create and implement robust privacy and security policies and procedures and ensure that its downstream subcontractors do the same. As seen from the preceding FTCA cases, having a privacy policy is not enough. In fact, having a privacy policy stating that personal information is handled with care and is protected, but in practice doing little to follow through on that promise, could be deemed unfair and deceptive under the FTCA.

FTC Breach Notification Rule

Since February 22, 2010, the FTC has been enforcing its Health Breach Notification Rule.[238] The FTC implemented that rule, found at 16 C.F.R. Part 318, as part of the American Recovery and Reinvestment Act of 2009, the same law that created the HITECH Act.[239] Indeed, the requirements of the FTC Health Breach Notification Rule are similar to the HIPAA Breach Notification Rule, which stemmed from HITECH and governs covered entities and business associates.

The FTC Health Breach Notification Rule imposes notification duties on (1) vendors of **personal health records (PHRs)**; (2) PHR-related entities; and (3) third-party service providers for PHR vendors or PHR-related entities in the event of a security breach involving PHR identifiable health information.[240] The rule defines *PHR* as an electronic record of personally identifiable health information on an individual that can be drawn from multiple sources and that is managed, shared, and controlled by or primarily for the individual.[241] A *PHR vendor* is an entity, other than a HIPAA-covered entity or business associate, that offers or

---

238 Federal Trade Commission Tips and Advice, "Health Breach Notification Rule" (August 2009), https://www.ftc.gov/tips-advice/business-center/guidance/health-breach-notification-rule.
239 16 C.F.R. § 318.1.
240 16 C.F.R. § 318.3.
241 16 C.F.R. § 318.2.

maintains a PHR.[242] A *PHR-related entity* is an entity, other than a HIPAA-covered entity or business associate, that:

- Offers products or services through the website of a PHR vendor
- Offers products or services through the websites of HIPAA-covered entities that offer individuals' PHRs
- Accesses information in a PHR or sends information to a PHR[243]

A *third-party service provider* is an entity that:

- Provides services to a PHR vendor in connection with the offering or maintenance of a PHR or to a PHR-related entity in connection with a product or service offered by that entity; and
- Accesses, maintains, retains, modifies, records, stores, destroys, or otherwise holds, uses, or discloses unsecured PHR identifiable health information as a result of such services[244]

The FTC rule does not apply to businesses or organizations that are covered under the HIPAA rule.[245] Thus, wellness professionals or organizations that are not otherwise covered by the HIPAA Privacy and Security Rules may be covered by the FTC Health Breach Notification Rule. Specifically, if a wellness professional or organization has a website that allows people to maintain their medical information online or provides applications for personal health records (e.g., a device that allows people to upload readings from a blood pressure cuff or pedometer into their PHR), the FTC Health Breach Notification Rule applies.[246] PHR vendors and PHR-related entities that experience a breach of unsecured PHR-identifiable information must notify both the individuals whose information was acquired by an unauthorized person as the result of the security breach and the FTC.[247] The timing of the FTC notice depends on the

---

242 *Id.*
243 *Id.*
244 *Id.*
245 Federal Trade Commission Tips and Advice, "Health Breach Notification Rule."
246 *Id.*
247 16 C.F.R. § 318.3(a).

number of individuals whose unsecured PHR-identifiable information was breached. If the breach involves 500 or more individuals, the FTC must be notified within 10 business days following the date of discovery of the breach.[248] If the breach involves fewer than 500 individuals, the PHR vendor or PHR-related entity should maintain a log of any such breach and submit the log annually to the FTC no later than 60 calendar days following the end of the calendar year.[249] PHR vendors and PHR-related entities provide the FTC notice through the FTC website.[250]

In addition, if a breach involves 500 or more residents of a state or jurisdiction, PHR vendors and PHR-related entities must notify prominent media outlets serving that state or jurisdiction.[251] Regarding timing, issuance of the individual and media notices must occur as soon as possible, but no later than 60 calendar days after the discovery of the breach.[252]

Like the HIPAA Breach Notice Rule, the FTC Health Breach Notification Rule dictates how PHR entities must deliver the notice and what the notice must contain. PHR entities may send the notice by first-class mail to the individual's last known address or, if the individual has indicated a preference to receive notice by email, then by email. The rule provides alternatives if either of those options fails to notify individuals. The notice must include the following information:

- A brief description of what happened, including the date of the breach and the date the breach was discovered (if known)
- A description of the types of unsecured PHR-identifiable health information that were involved in the breach (such as full name, Social Security number, date of birth, home address, account number, or disability code)
- Steps individuals should take to protect themselves from potential harm resulting from the breach

248 16 C.F.R. § 318.5(c).
249 Id.
250 Id.
251 16 C.F.R. § 318.5(b).
252 16 C.F.R. § 318.4(a).

- A brief description of what the entity that suffered the breach is doing to investigate the breach, to mitigate harm, and to protect against any further breaches
- Contact procedures for individuals to ask questions or learn additional information, which shall include a toll-free telephone number, an email address, website, or postal address.[253]

Third-party service providers that discover a breach of security must provide notice of the breach to the PHR vendor or PHR-related entity, depending on the circumstances, and obtain an acknowledgment from the PHR vendor or PHR-related entity that the notice was received.[254] The notice must include the identity of each customer of the vendor or PHR-related entity whose unsecured PHR-identifiable information has been, or is reasonably believed to have been, acquired during the breach.[255] To help third-party service providers comply with this requirement, PHR vendors and PHR-related entities must notify each third-party service provider of its status as a PHR vendor or PHR-related entity and that it is subject to the FTC Health Breach Notification Rule.[256] Third-party service providers must notify the PHR vendor or PHR-related entity of a breach without unreasonable delay, but no later than 60 calendar days after the discovery of the breach.[257]

Note that the duty to notify the various entities of a breach pertains to *unsecured* **PHR-identifiable information** only. The rule defines *unsecured* to mean PHR-identifiable information that is not protected through encryption or destruction.[258] Thus, if a wellness professional or organization is subject to the FTC Health Breach Notification Rule and the PHR-identifiable information subject to the unauthorized acquisition is either encrypted or destroyed, the notice requirements would not apply.

253 16 C.F.R. § 318.6.
254 16 C.F.R. § 318.3(b).
255 *Id.*
256 *Id.*
257 16 C.F.R. § 318.4(a).
258 16 C.F.R. § 318.2; *see also* "FTC Facts for Business: Complying with the FTC's Health Breach Notification Rule" (April 2010): 3, https://www.ftc.gov/system/files/documents/plain-language/bus56-complying-ftcs-health-breach-notification-rule.pdf.

What Does This Mean for Workplace Wellness?

If a wellness professional or organization interacts with PHRs on some level, such as exchanging or uploading health information to or with a PHR through mobile or other applications, or offers a PHR product, that professional or organization could be subject to the FTC Health Breach Notification Rule. To avoid the notification requirements under the rule, the wellness professional or organization should create and implement policies and procedures to ensure that any health information collected, stored, or transmitted is encrypted. Doing so would make the information secured and therefore exempt from the notification requirement. In addition, creating and implementing policies and procedures to reduce the risk of a breach are also advisable. Wellness professionals and organizations could use the HIPAA Privacy and Security Rules as guides for creating and implementing such policies and procedures, even if those HIPAA rules do not apply to them. The HIPAA Privacy and Security Rules can provide useful approaches to managing the privacy and security of health information.

FCRA

The Fair Credit Reporting Act (FCRA), enacted in 1970, serves three main purposes:

1. To prevent the misuse of sensitive consumer information by limiting recipients to those who have a legitimate need for it
2. To improve the accuracy and integrity of consumer reports
3. To promote the efficiency of the nation's banking and consumer credit systems[259]

Before FCRA, the business of collecting information about consumers and selling reports based on that information was largely unregulated.[260] There was no requirement that the information about consumers be

---

259 FTC, *40 Years of Experience with the Fair Credit Reporting Act*, at 1 (July 2011).
260 Marc S. Roth and Charles Washburn, "Data Brokers Face Blurring Lines, Increased Regulatory Risks," *Bloomberg BNA* (August 22, 2012), www.bna.com/data-brokers-face-blurring-lines/.

accurate. Community leaders learned that inaccurate information can lead to unfair denials of loans, jobs, apartments, and other things.[261] There was no obligation to inform consumers that someone had used a report in a transaction, so the consumer would be unaware that inaccurate information may have been the reason behind the denial.[262] There was also no limit on the purposes for which someone could obtain a consumer report, raising significant privacy concerns.[263] The FCRA attempted to address these abuses. Congress has amended FCRA several times since 1970, with major changes adopted in 1996 and 2003, and most recently in 2010 pursuant to the Dodd-Frank Wall Street Reform and Consumer Protection Act.[264]

The FCRA regulates the practices of **consumer reporting agencies (CRAs)** that collect and compile consumer information into consumer reports for use by credit grantors, insurance companies, employers, landlords, and other entities in making eligibility decisions affecting consumers.[265] It also regulates "furnishers of information" to CRAs and users of consumer reports. Generally, information in consumer reports includes a consumer's credit history and payment patterns, as well as demographic and identifying information and public record information (e.g., arrests, judgments, and bankruptcies).[266] The FCRA defines **consumer report** more broadly. Under § 603(d)(1) of the FCRA, *consumer report* means:

> Any written, oral, or other communication of any information by a consumer reporting agency bearing on a consumer's credit worthiness, credit standing, credit capacity, character, general reputation, personal characteristics, or mode of living which is used or expected to be used or collected in whole or in part for the purpose of serving as a factor in establishing the consumer's eligibility for (A) credit or insurance to be used primarily for personal,

---

261 *Id.*
262 *Id.*
263 *Id.*
264 *Id.*
265 FTC, *40 Years of Experience with the Fair Credit Reporting Act*, at 1; *see also* 15 U.S.C. §§ 1681 *et seq.*, also cited as §§ 601–629 of the Consumer Credit Protection Act; *see also* 15 U.S.C. § 1681s-2 (furnishers of information) and 15 U.S.C. § 1681m.
266 FTC, *40 Years of Experience with the Fair Credit Reporting Act*, at 1.

family, or household purposes; (B) employment purposes; or (C) any other purpose authorized under section 604.[267]

Thus, any information about a consumer's character, reputation, or personal characteristics (such as health or physical fitness characteristics) could be part of a consumer report. Importantly, for information to be considered a consumer report, it must be used or expected to be used to determine eligibility for one of the stated purposes in the definition, such as for employment or credit purposes.[268] A report used for "employment purposes" means a report used for the purpose of evaluating a consumer for employment, promotion, reassignment, or retention as an employee.[269]

The FCRA defines *consumer reporting agency* as "any person which, for monetary fees, dues, or on a cooperative nonprofit basis, regularly engages in whole or in part in the practice of assembling or evaluating consumer credit information or other information on consumers for the purpose of furnishing consumer reports to third parties, and which uses any means or facility of interstate commerce for the purpose of preparing or furnishing consumer reports."[270] It is important to note that the terms *consumer report* and *consumer reporting agency* are defined in a mutually dependent manner and must be construed together.[271] Thus, an entity is not a CRA if it provides information that is not for one of the purposes identified in the definition of *consumer report*.[272] For example, an information services company that generates reports that are solely for target marketing purposes would not constitute a CRA subject to the FCRA.[273]

If an entity is a CRA, however, FCRA imposes a number of obligations on it. CRAs must:

1. Establish procedures to ensure that they report consumer information only to those with a legitimate purpose for it (such as for

---

267 15 U.S.C. § 1681a.
268 FTC, *40 Years of Experience with the Fair Credit Reporting Act*, at 20.
269 15 U.S.C. § 1681a(h).
270 15 U.S.C. § 1681a(f).
271 FTC, *40 Years of Experience with the Fair Credit Reporting Act*, at 28.
272 *Id.*
273 Roth and Washburn, "Data Brokers Face Blurring Lines."

insurance underwriting, credit transactions, or employment purposes)[274]

2. Take certain actions relating to identity theft[275]
3. Avoid furnishing obsolete adverse information in certain consumer reports[276]
4. Adopt reasonable procedures to assure privacy and accuracy of consumer reports[277]
5. Provide only limited disclosures to governmental agencies except in cases involving counterintelligence and counterterrorism[278]
6. Provide consumers certain disclosures, upon request, at no cost or for a reasonable charge[279]
7. Follow certain procedures if a consumer disputes the completeness or accuracy of any item of information contained in his or her file[280]
8. Follow certain procedures in reporting public record information for employment purposes or when reporting adverse information other than public record information in investigative consumer reports[281]

The FTC, one of the agencies that enforces the FCRA (the other being the Consumer Financial Protection Bureau [CFPB]), has expressed concern about data brokers falling outside FCRA's requirements or, if they do fall within FCRA, violating its provisions.[282] In a 2012 case, the FTC alleged that data broker Spokeo collected information about consumers from hundreds of online and offline sources, including social media networks, other data brokers, and other sources.[283] Spokeo used the information to create consumer profiles that identified specific individuals

---

274 FCRA § 604.
275 FCRA §§ 605A, 605B.
276 FCRA §§ 605, 607(a).
277 FCRA §§ 604, 607(a), 607(b).
278 FCRA §§ 625–626.
279 FCRA §§ 609, 610, 612.
280 FCRA § 611.
281 FCRA §§ 613, 614.
282 Roth and Washburn, "Data Brokers Face Blurring Lines."
283 *United States v. Spokeo, Inc.*, Complaint 12-CV-05001 (C.D. Cal. June 7, 2012), https://www.ftc.gov/sites/default/files/documents/cases/2012/06/120612spokeocmpt.pdf.

and displayed identifying information like the individual's physical address, telephone number, marital status, age range, or email address.[284] The consumer profile also contained information about a person's hobbies, ethnicity, religion, participation on social networking sites, and economic health status.[285] Spokeo sold the profiles through paid subscriptions to businesses, including entities operating in human resources, background screening, and recruiting.[286] These entities would use the profiles in determining whether to interview a job candidate or hire a candidate after an interview.[287]

In 2010, Spokeo changed its website "Terms of Service" to state that it was not a CRA and that consumers may not use the company's website or information for FCRA-covered purposes.[288] However, Spokeo failed to revoke access to or otherwise ensure that existing users, including human resource subscribers, did not use the company's website or information for FCRA-covered purposes.[289]

The FTC concluded that Spokeo's consumer profiles constituted consumer reports as defined by FCRA because the information in those profiles related to a consumer's character, general reputation, personal characteristics, or mode of living.[290] Moreover, the profiles were used, or were expected to be used, in whole or in part, as a factor in determining the consumer's eligibility for employment.[291] Because Spokeo provided consumer reports for a fee, and because those reports were used or expected to be used for employment purposes (a FCRA-related purpose), the FTC considered Spokeo a CRA.[292]

The FTC alleged that, despite Spokeo's proclamation on its website that it was not a CRA, in practice it was a CRA.[293] Because it was a CRA, the FCRA required it to maintain reasonable procedures to limit

---

284 *Id.* at ¶ 9.
285 *Id.*
286 *Id.*
287 *Spokeo* at ¶ 10.
288 *Id.* at ¶ 11.
289 *Id.*
290 *Spokeo* at ¶ 12.
291 *Id.*
292 *Spokeo* at ¶ 13.
293 *Id.*

the furnishing of consumer reports to the purposes specified under FCRA.[294] According to the FTC, Spokeo did not have these procedures, such as requiring prospective users of the information to identify themselves to Spokeo, certify the purpose for which they sought information, and certify that the user would not use the information for any other purpose.[295] The FTC also accused Spokeo of not verifying the identity of or purpose for which the information is sought by each new prospective user of the information.[296] The FTC alleged that Spokeo did not provide a notice to users of consumer reports.[297] The user notice provides users of consumer reports with important information regarding their obligations under FCRA, including the obligation of the user to provide a notice to consumers who are the subject of an adverse action (e.g., denial of employment) based in whole or in part on information contained in the consumer report.[298] Spokeo agreed to settle the FTC's charges by entering into a consent decree that included payment of an $800,000 civil penalty, various injunctive provisions, and a ban on further violations of FCRA.[299]

The FTC has also sent warning letters to mobile application marketers suggesting that their background screening apps may violate FCRA.[300] The letters warned the app developers that if they have reason to believe that the background reports they provide are being used for screening regarding employment, housing, credit, or other similar purposes, they must comply with FCRA.[301] The important lesson from these FTC actions is that any company that regularly collects and markets consumer data for a fee and has any reason to believe that such data is to be used for employment, housing, credit, or insurance purposes may be subject to FCRA as a CRA.

---

294 *Spokeo* at ¶ 14.
295 *Id.*
296 *Spokeo* at ¶¶ 14 and 17.
297 *Id.* at 16.
298 *Id.*
299 FTC, "Press Release, Spokeo to Pay $800,000 to Settle FTC Charges" (June 12, 2012), https://www.ftc.gov/news-events/press-releases/2012/06/spokeo-pay-800000-settle-ftc-charges-company-allegedly-marketed.
300 Roth and Washburn, "Data Brokers Face Blurring Lines."
301 *Id.*

In addition to CRAs, **furnishers of information**, as defined by FCRA, also have obligations under FCRA. Generally, persons may furnish information concerning their transactions and experiences with consumers to CRAs, and CRAs may gather information, without consumers' permission and over their objection.[302] However, the information furnished must be accurate. Persons who regularly and in the ordinary course of business furnish information to one or more CRAs about the person's transactions or experiences with any consumer must promptly notify the CRA if the furnisher of information determines that the information furnished is incomplete or inaccurate.[303] Furnishers of information must provide anything needed to make the information complete and accurate.[304] This obligation applies even when a furnisher no longer has a contractual relationship with the CRA to which it originally furnished the information.[305]

Furnishers of information must also not furnish information to CRAs if the furnisher knows or has reasonable cause to believe that the information is inaccurate.[306] However, if a furnisher clearly and conspicuously specifies an address where consumers can send disputes concerning the accuracy of information about them, the furnisher can rely on that dispute process as the means of determining whether the information is inaccurate.[307] If a consumer disputes the information, the furnisher of information must notify the CRA of such dispute and investigate the dispute.[308] Furnishers of information must also have procedures for responding to notice by a CRA of identity theft.[309]

Furnishers of medical information have an added duty to notify CRAs of their status as a medical information furnisher.[310] Furnishers of medical information are persons whose primary business is providing medical services, products, or devices, or the person's agent or assignee,

---

302 FTC, *40 Years of Experience with the Fair Credit Reporting Act*, at 92.
303 FCRA § 623(a)(2).
304 FTC, *40 Years of Experience with the Fair Credit Reporting Act*, at 92.
305 *Id.*
306 FCRA § 623(a)(1)(A).
307 FCRA § 623(a)(1)(C).
308 FCRA §§ 623(a)(3), 623(b).
309 FCRA § 623(a)(6).
310 FCRA § 623(a)(9).

who furnish information to a CRA on a consumer.[311] Providing this notice to CRAs will enable the CRA to comply with its duties regarding the reporting of medical information. Specifically, the FCRA prohibits CRAs from furnishing medical information in consumer reports without consumer consent, unless the information being furnished pertains to medical debts and the information is coded to avoid identifying the provider and nature of the transaction.[312] Also, FCRA requires parties who receive medical information to keep such information confidential.[313] FCRA defines **medical information** as "information or data, whether oral or recorded, in any form or medium, created by or derived from a healthcare provider or the consumer, that relates to: a) the past, present, or future physical, mental or behavioral health or condition of an individual; b) the provision of health care to an individual; or c) the payment for the provision of health care to an individual."[314]

If a user of consumer reports takes any adverse action with respect to any consumer based in whole or in part on information contained in a consumer report, that user must provide the consumer with notice of the adverse action.[315] The notice, which can be oral, written, or electronic, must provide the name, address, and telephone number of the CRA that furnished the report.[316] The notice must also include a statement that the CRA did not make the adverse action decision and therefore is unable to provide the consumer with the specific reasons why the adverse action was taken.[317] FCRA requires the user to notify consumers of their right to obtain a free copy of the consumer report from the CRA and their right to dispute the accuracy or completeness of any information in the consumer report furnished by the CRA.[318] Finally, CRAs should provide a notice to users and furnishers of information about their various responsibilities under FCRA.[319]

---

311 *Id.*
312 FCRA § 604(g).
313 *Id.*
314 FCRA § 603(ii)(1).
315 FCRA § 615.
316 FCRA § 615(a)(3).
317 *Id.*
318 FCRA § 615(a)(4).
319 FCRA § 607(d).

What Does FCRA Mean for Workplace Wellness?

Because employers do not typically use wellness program information for purposes of employee hiring, promotion, reassignment, or retention, and because such uses would in most cases violate the ADA, it is unlikely that wellness organizations would qualify as CRAs under FCRA. A more likely situation in which FCRA would apply in the workplace wellness context is when wellness organizations, such as those that provide wearable technology or health apps, furnish information to data brokers. The data brokers may qualify as CRAs. Wellness companies whose primary business is providing disease management services or medical products or devices would be furnishers of medical information if they report information to a CRA. FCRA dictates that such wellness companies must notify the CRA of their medical information furnisher status. As illustrated in the *Spokeo* case, however, it may not be clear whether the data broker is a CRA. Even if the data broker indicates that it is not a CRA subject to FCRA, in practice it might be subject to FCRA, as the FTC found in *Spokeo*.

As a result, if a wellness organization collects consumer information that is eventually disclosed to data brokers, the wellness organization may want to comply with FCRA standards just as a precaution. These standards are good practices regardless of whether FCRA applies, such as ensuring that the information is accurate and specifying an address where consumers can send disputes concerning the accuracy of information about them. If the wellness organization collects health information, the organization may want to inform the data broker that it is a furnisher of medical information. If the wellness organization discloses consumer information to a data broker for use in target marketing purposes only, the FCRA obligations would not apply. Nevertheless, some employees may frown upon use of their data for such purposes. Wellness professionals and companies who are concerned about protecting an employee's right to privacy and instilling employee confidence in the wellness program can incorporate the spirit of FCRA into their programs. For example, the wellness organization could prohibit, through contract, any downstream entities from using employee information for targeted marketing or any other unnecessary purpose unless the employee consents to such use. Regardless of whether FCRA applies to a wellness organization, adopting that law's standards of data accuracy, giving consumers an opportunity to correct their information, and requiring consumer consent before using their medical information can reduce risk and increase consumer confidence in a wellness program.

GLBA

Congress created the Gramm-Leach-Bliley Act (GLBA) through Public Law No. 106-102 on November 12, 1999. Congress wrote that the policy behind GLBA is to require financial institutions to respect the privacy of their customers and to protect the security and confidentiality of those customers' nonpublic personal information.[320] Congress charged the following federal and state agencies with establishing appropriate standards for the financial institutions within those agencies' jurisdiction relating to administrative, technical, and physical safeguards:

- Federal Deposit Insurance Corporation (FDIC) (banks)
- National Credit Union Administration (federally insured credit unions and their subsidiaries)
- Securities and Exchange Commission (SEC) (broker/dealer, investment companies, and advisors)
- State insurance authorities (insurance industry)
- FTC (any other financial institution or other person not subject to the jurisdiction of any agency or authority previously listed)[321]

As noted, the law applies to **financial institutions**, which are institutions engaged in **financial activity** business.[322] Relevant financial activities for the health and wellness industry include:

1. Lending, exchanging, transferring, investing for others, or safeguarding money or securities; or

---

320 15 U.S.C. § 6801.
321 15 U.S.C. §§ 6801, 6805(a).
322 15 U.S.C. § 6809(3).

2. Insuring, guaranteeing, or indemnifying against loss, harm, damage, illness, disability, or death, or providing and issuing annuities, and acting as principal, agent, or broker for purposes of the foregoing, in any state. Insurers are subject to these rules, and they often offer wellness programs.[323]

Arguably, health providers that offer a significant number of long-term payment programs that charge interest could fall within the first category in the preceding list.[324] More importantly for the wellness industry, however, is that the second category in the list covers health insurers. Many health insurers offer workplace wellness programs. As a result, workplace wellness programs offered through a health insurer may receive privacy notices under both HIPAA and GLBA.[325]

Organizations that are subject to the GLBA have a number of obligations with regard to **nonpublic personal information** of the organization's customers. *Nonpublic personal information* means personally identifiable financial information:

- Provided by a consumer to a financial institution
- Resulting from any transaction with the consumer or any service performed for the consumer; or
- Otherwise obtained by the financial institution[326]

The term does not include publicly available information,[327] but it does include any list, description, or other grouping of consumers that is derived using any nonpublic personal information other than publicly available information.[328] In the insurance context, personally identifiable

---

323 15 U.S.C. § 6809; Bank Holding Company Act § 4(k)(4).
324 *See, e.g.,* Privacy Rights Clearinghouse, *Medical Information Covered by Laws Other than HIPAA* (California Medical Privacy Act Fact Sheet C8, March 2013), https://www.privacyrights.org/medical-information-covered-by-laws-other-than-HIPAA.
325 *See, e.g.,* "CIGNA Gramm-Leach-Bliley Privacy Notice for CIGNA Policyholders" (noting that the notice designed to comply with GLBA is separate from the notice designed to comply with HIPAA and making reference to disclosing nonpublic personal information for supporting or improving CIGNA programs or services such as its wellness programs).
326 15 U.S.C. § 6809(4).
327 *Id.*
328 *Id.*

financial information includes information a consumer provides to an insurer to obtain an insurance product or service from the insurer.[329] It also includes information about a consumer resulting from a transaction involving an insurance product or service.[330] So, names, account numbers, Social Security numbers, the fact that an individual is a customer of the financial institution, and other information insurers require to obtain products or services from them would be covered under the GLBA.[331]

The three primary obligations for financial institutions to meet under the GLBA are: (1) providing a privacy notice to consumers that describes what information the company collects about its customers, with whom it shares the information, and how it protects or safeguards the information; (2) providing customers with the right to opt out of having their information shared with certain third parties; and (3) limiting how a financial institution can use or redisclose the nonpublic personal information.[332]

In particular, the law regulates use and disclosure of nonpublic personal information by financial institutions to nonaffiliated third parties. A **nonaffiliated third party** is any entity that is not an affiliate of, or related by common ownership, or affiliated by corporate control with, the financial institution, but does not include a joint employee of such institution.[333] Generally, a financial institution may not disclose nonpublic personal information to a nonaffiliated third party unless the financial institution first provides the consumer with a notice about the disclosure and an opportunity for the consumer to opt out of the disclosure.[334] However, a financial institution may provide nonpublic personal information to a nonaffiliated third party without notice or opt-out in order to perform services for or functions on behalf of the financial institution, including marketing of the financial institution's own products

---

329 *See, e.g.*, Wis. Admin. Code § INS 25.04(22).
330 *Id.*
331 FTC, "In Brief: The Financial Privacy Requirements of the Gramm-Leach-Bliley Act" (July 2002), https://www.ftc.gov/system/files/documents/plain-language/bus53-brief-financial-privacy-requirements-gramm-leach-bliley-act.pdf.
332 *Id.*
333 15 U.S.C. § 6809(5).
334 15 U.S.C. § 6802(a) and (b).

or services.[335] To do so, though, the financial institution must fully disclose the provision of such information and enter into a contractual agreement with the third party that requires the third party to maintain the confidentiality of such information.[336]

Financial institutions that fall within the FTC's jurisdiction (such as healthcare providers that have long-term payment programs with interest) must also abide by the GLBA Safeguards Rule or data security rule. This rule requires financial institutions to develop, implement, and maintain a written comprehensive information security program.[337] The goals of such a security program are to:

1. Insure the security and confidentiality of customer information (including information in both paper and electronic form that is handled or maintained by the financial institution or an affiliated entity)
2. Protect against any anticipated threats or hazards to the security or integrity of such information
3. Protect against unauthorized access to or use of such information that could result in substantial harm or inconvenience to any customer[338]

Required components of the GLBA data security program include the following:

- Designate an employee or employees to coordinate the security program.
- Conduct a risk assessment to identify foreseeable internal and external risks to the security, confidentiality, and integrity of customer information that could result in unauthorized disclosure, misuse, alteration, destruction, or other compromise of the

---

335 15 U.S.C. § 6802(b)(2).
336 *Id.*
337 16 C.F.R. § 314.1.
338 16 C.F.R. § 314.3.

information. The risk assessment should consider risks in the following areas:

- Employee training and management
- Information systems, including network and software design, as well as information processing, storage, transmission, and disposal
- Detection, prevention, and response to attacks, intrusions, or other systems failures.

- Design and implement information safeguards to control the risks the financial institution identifies through the risk assessment, and regularly test or otherwise monitor the effectiveness of the safeguards' key controls, systems, and procedures.
- Oversee service providers, by:
  - Taking reasonable steps to select and retain service providers that are capable of maintaining appropriate safeguards for the customer information at issue; and
  - Requiring service providers by contract to implement and maintain such safeguards.
- Evaluate and adjust the financial institution's security program in light of the results of the required testing and monitoring or for any other reason that has a material impact on the information security program.[339]

What Does GLBA Mean for Workplace Wellness?

Because most wellness professionals and organizations that may be subject to GLBA requirements may fall within the insurer umbrella, those professionals and organizations should consult their state insurance laws to determine and understand their specific obligations under the law. Wellness professionals and organizations that work for or with health insurers should be aware of GLBA requirements and create and implement privacy and security policies and procedures to facilitate compliance with that law.

---

339 16 C.F.R. § 314.4.

Best Practices and Self-Regulation

Many of today's privacy laws are founded on the **Fair Information Practice Principles**, or FIPPs.[340] For example, FIPPs served as the basis for the Privacy Act of 1974, which regulates the federal government's maintenance, collection, use, and dissemination of personal information in systems of records.[341]

At their core, the FIPPs articulate basic protections for handling personal data.[342] These protections include notice, choice, access, accuracy, data minimization, security, and accountability.[343] Specifically, the FIPPs protect an individual's right to know what data is being collected about him or her and how it is used.[344] FIPPs protections also address an individual's right to object to some uses and to correct inaccurate information.[345] Under the FIPPs, organizations that collect information have an obligation to ensure that the data is reliable and kept secure.[346]

The FIPPs form a common thread through the various privacy laws discussed in this chapter, as well as self-regulation proposals by the government. The FTC has taken a leading role in shaping and encouraging self-regulation of data privacy and security by stakeholders.[347] Specifically, the FTC has convened roundtables of stakeholders to identify best practices in personal information processing.[348] It has also created a **Privacy Framework** and encourages companies that collect and use consumer data to adopt the best practices outlined in that framework.[349] The FTC intends the framework to assist Congress as it considers privacy

---

340 Big Data Report, *supra* note 25, at 17.
341 *Id.*
342 *Id.*
343 Federal Trade Commission, "Staff Report, Internet of Things: Privacy and Security in a Connected World" (January 2015): i, https://www.ftc.gov/system/files/documents/reports/federal-trade-commission-staff-report-november-2013-workshop-entitled-internet-things-privacy/150127iotrpt.pdf.
344 Big Data Report at 17.
345 *Id.*
346 *Id.*
347 Cohen, "What Privacy Is For," at 1928.
348 *Id.*
349 FTC Report, "Protecting Consumer Privacy in an Era of Rapid Change: Recommendations for Business and Policymakers" (March 2012): vii, https://www.ftc.gov/sites/default/files/documents/reports/federal-trade-commission-report-protecting-consumer-privacy-era-rapid-change-recommendations/120326privacyreport.pdf.

legislation.[350] The FTC does not intend the framework to serve as a basis for law enforcement actions or regulations under laws currently enforced by it.[351]

The framework offers the following principles:

1. **Privacy By Design**
   a. Companies should promote consumer privacy throughout their organizations and at every stage of the development of their products and services.
   b. Companies should maintain comprehensive data management procedures throughout the life cycle of their products and services.

2. **Simplified Consumer Choice**
   a. Practices that do not require choice. Companies do not need to provide choice before collecting and using consumer data for practices that are consistent with the context of the transaction or the company's relationship with the consumer, or are required or specifically authorized by law.
   b. Companies should provide consumer choice for other practices. For practices requiring choice, companies should offer the choice at a time and in a context in which the consumer is making a decision about his or her data. Companies should obtain affirmative express consent before (1) using consumer data in a materially different manner than claimed when the data was collected; or (2) collecting sensitive data for certain purposes.

3. **Transparency**
   a. Privacy notices should be clearer, shorter, and more standardized to enable better comprehension and comparison of privacy practices.
   b. Companies should provide reasonable access to the consumer data they maintain; the extent of access should be proportionate to the sensitivity of the data and the nature of its use.

---

350 *Id.*
351 *Id.*

c. All stakeholders should expand their efforts to educate con-
    sumers about commercial data privacy practices.[352]

The FTC also continues to work with the data collection industry on
improving:

- The ability of consumers to not be tracked by browser vendors
- Mobile privacy disclosures
- Consumer access to information held by data brokers
- Privacy efforts by Internet service providers (ISPs), operating sys-
  tems, browsers, and social media
- The enforceability of self-regulatory codes as well as the FTC
  Act.[353]

The Precision Medicine Initiative has also created Privacy and Trust Principles. These Principles cover governance; transparency; respecting participant preferences; participant empowerment through access to information,
data sharing, access, and use; and data quality and integrity.[354]

Despite the good intentions and enthusiasm for self-regulation by the
government and data collection industry, there are valid criticisms of self-
regulation. For some, self-regulation consisting of control of information
flows via notice and choice insufficiently protects privacy, because it lacks
transparency.[355] Effective privacy protection requires regulatory inquiry
about information processing activity and must include strategies for
exposing information processing to adequate public scrutiny.[356]

Others contend that consumers have privacy fatigue and fail to use
opt-out procedures or take time to understand privacy options.[357] For
example, under the self-regulatory regime adopted by advertisers and ad
networks, many online behavioral ads include a standardized icon

---

352 FTC Report, "Protecting Consumer Privacy in an Era of Rapid Change," at vii–viii.
353 Id. at viii–ix.
354 The White House, *Precision Medicine Initiative: Privacy and Trust Principles* (November 9, 2015),
https://www.whitehouse.gov/sites/default/files/microsites/finalpmiprivacyandtrustprinciples.pdf.
355 Cohen, "What Privacy Is For," at 1931 (2013).
356 Id.
357 Big Data Report, *supra* note 25 at 17.

Figure 9.2   Standardized Icon Used in Online Advertising

(see Figure 9.2), which indicates that information is being collected for purposes of behavioral ad targeting, and links to a page where the consumer can opt out of such collection.[358]

According to the online advertising industry, this icon has appeared on ads billions of times, but only a tiny fraction of users access this feature or understand its meaning.[359] In addition to consumers having privacy fatigue from seeing numerous privacy policies and settings, some believe that online privacy tools are hidden or too difficult for users to navigate.[360] Others surmise that consumers simply are not bothered by personalized ads when they enjoy a robust selection of free content, products, and services.[361] As a result of this lack of consumer participation in protecting their own privacy, self-regulation may be insufficient to protect the larger societal value of privacy.

One legal scholar has analogized privacy self-regulation to the attempts at self-regulation by the food and drug industry in the early 20th century.[362] During that era, manufacturers of food and drugs profited from the sale of adulterated and mislabeled products, as well as through the marketing of sometimes dangerous "patent medicines."[363] They would bottle ordinary tap water, color it with dye, and sell it as a cancer cure.[364] They would market miracle medicines for children that

---

358 *Id.*
359 *Id.*
360 *Id.*
361 *Id.*
362 Hoofnagle, "Reflections on the NC JOLT Symposium," *supra* note 4.
363 *Id.* at 213.
364 *Id.* at 214.

were in fact opium.[365] Real honeycombs would be combined with laboratory-created glucose to create "natural honey."[366]

Self-regulation resulted in a race to the bottom by shielding companies from accountability.[367] Honest companies were unable to compete with those manufacturers that could cut costs by mislabeling or misrepresenting the contents of food.[368] Such manufacturers rejected the idea of federal law that would require food and drugs to be safe and pure, or even laws that required notice of product ingredients.[369]

This legal scholar points out that just as the laissez-faire approach did not work for the food and drug industry, so it will not work for protecting data privacy and security. Unlike the food and drug industry, where the products can be tested for adulteration, privacy-invasive practices are opaque—and are kept that way deliberately.[370] Regulating the data collection industry may shine a light on data collection and use practices, but it may also result in unexpected benefits. Regulating the food and drug industry provided individuals with the freedom to purchase any food or other product without assuming unreasonable risks.[371] Regulating the data collection industry may give individuals the freedom to share information without putting their privacy and security at risk. Some may view government-imposed regulation as paternalistic and infringing upon enterprise rights. Nevertheless, such regulation may also liberate consumers from unwarranted and unwanted intrusion and create a respect for individuality.

Finding the Right Balance for Wellness

What is at stake for the wellness industry is its credibility with the wellness program participant. As consumers become more aware of Big Data, its goldmine status, its lack of transparency, and its potential for

---

365 *Id.*
366 *Id.*
367 Hoofnagle, "Reflections on the NC JOLT Symposium," *supra* note 4 at 215.
368 *Id.* at 213.
369 *Id.* at 215.
370 *Id.* at 215.
371 *Id.* at 216.

misusing personal information, they may become more dubious of data collection efforts. Consumers may begin to doubt the claims by wellness professionals and companies that they are in the business to improve health. To avoid acquiring such a reputation, it is imperative that wellness professionals and companies adopt strong privacy values and make those values a selling point for their products and services.

An example of good intentions gone wrong occurred with the City of Houston's wellness program. In 2015, when the City of Houston told city workers that they would pay more for health insurance premiums unless they participated in the city's wellness program, many employees jumped on board. Through health risk assessment forms, those employees who participated were required to disclose sensitive health and other data to a wellness vendor hired to manage the program.[372] Signing the authorization form granted authorization for the vendor to pass data to third parties and to post personal information in areas "reviewable to the public."[373] Once the worker unions found out, the city was pressured to change its wellness program vendors to ones with stronger privacy policies.[374]

One may wonder whether the City of Houston might have experienced a different outcome had it required strict privacy and security standards of its wellness vendor, or if the wellness vendor had made data privacy and security a priority. Wellness companies that adopt transparent data collection practices that demonstrate concern for data privacy and security may more easily win the hearts and minds of wellness program participants. A starting point for wellness companies would be to adopt the HIPAA privacy and security standards, even if the company is not subject to HIPAA. Companies should also adopt the self-regulatory standards developed by the FTC regarding collection of consumer data. Specifically, wellness companies should aim to be leaders in data collection transparency; respect for participant preferences; participant empowerment through access to information, data sharing, access, and use; and data quality and integrity. Doing so will not only mitigate any risk of violating privacy or security laws, but will also give consumers

---

372 Hancock, "Workplace Wellness Programs Put Employee Privacy at Risk," *supra* note 4.
373 *Id.*
374 *Id.*

confidence in the wellness program and may increase their willingness to participate.

Other ideas to help wellness professionals and companies achieve data privacy and security compliance are provided in the checklist in the "Key Points" section.

RULE THE RULES

Key Points in Chapter 9

For this chapter, the key points are summarized in the following Compliance Checklist. Developing and implementing each of these recommendations will help ensure compliance with the many privacy and security laws that apply to workplace wellness programs.

Compliance Checklist

- Keep employee health data separate from other personnel records.
- If you are an employer, avoid using employee health data to make adverse employment decisions.
- Use vendors to collect health data, so as to create a firewall between the employee data and the employer to prevent inappropriate use of data.
- In accordance with the ADA and GINA rules, provide a notice and authorization to employee and spouse participants before collecting their medical or genetic information.
- Share only aggregate health information with employers, unless an exception under HIPAA or the ADA applies.
- Group health plan wellness programs should not disclose PHI to an employer unless the employer has certified that it has amended its plan documents in accordance with the provisions in the HIPAA privacy rule.
- Revise business associate agreements to prohibit downstream entities from using PHI for "data analytics." Be very specific about the purposes for which the downstream entities can use data.

- Verify that wellness vendors have a privacy policy and adhere to it.
- Read the privacy policies of data collectors and ask questions if their data use and disclosure policies are unclear or create discomfort.
- Implement robust privacy and security practices, such as encryption, minimum necessary use and disclosure practices, security risk assessments, and wireless access limits, and ensure that such privacy and security practices are implemented by downstream entities.
- Seek to understand the web of information sharing that occurs when employee health data is collected. Does the wellness vendor work with labs, app publishers, fitness device makers, gyms, or rewards companies? If so, review the privacy and security policies of each of those downstream vendors.
- Draft privacy policies that minimize the sharing of data, such as discouraging the sharing of health and wellness information on social media sites.
- Review data collection service agreements to determine whether employee health data is being shared.
- Restrict the sharing of health data by vendors and other downstream entities to the sole purpose of administering the wellness program and the purpose for which it was disclosed (i.e., to improve health). At the very least, restrict downstream entities that receive de-identified data from re-identifying it.
- Review and amend business associate agreements to restrict use of data, including de-identified data.
- Implement applicable privacy and security policies and procedures, even if you are not subject to HIPAA, to garner trust in your wellness program.
- As part of your privacy and security policies and procedures, ensure that any electronic health information is secure both while "at rest" and while in transmission. This includes encrypting any data storage devices such as flash drives, mobile devices, or laptop computers. Consult with information technology professionals who can help you conduct a security risk assessment regarding your data.

- Communicate to wellness program participants that you take the privacy and security of their personal information seriously and have taken all necessary steps to protect it.
- Adopt the FTC's Privacy Framework Principles as part of your privacy and security policies and procedures and inform employees and clients of that adoption.
- Follow through on your commitment to protect the privacy and security of wellness program participant information by monitoring compliance with privacy and security policies and procedures.

Study Questions

1. Describe what is meant by a "right to privacy" and the application of that right to achieving the goals of workplace wellness programs.
2. Describe examples of how Big Data has expanded in recent years and the potential benefits and dangers of its use in workplace wellness programs.
3. Prepare a list of the major requirements with regard to PHI for both covered entities and business associates under the HIPAA Privacy and Security Rules.
4. For each of the following laws, describe the major privacy and/ or security requirements that are applicable or potentially applicable to workplace wellness programs: ADA, GINA, FTCA, FCRA, and GLBA.
5. Given the failures in the FTCA cases, explain why workplace wellness employers and vendors should create not only a privacy and security policy, but also specific privacy and security procedures to ensure that its downstream subcontractors do the same.
6. Explain why it is good idea for workplace wellness programs to comply with the HIPAA privacy and security regulations even if the program does not qualify as a group health plan.

7. Prepare a list of items to be included in a wellness vendor contract that describes the vendor's obligations with regard to the privacy and security of employee health data.
8. Develop a list of key points that could be included in a rationale statement to help convince decision-makers that it is essential to comply with privacy and security laws.

Key Terms

Big Data
business associate
cloud
consumer report
consumer reporting agency (CSR)
covered entity
data breach
data broker
de-identified PHI
electronic health records (EHRs)
fair information practice
 principles (FIPPs)
financial activity
financial institution
furnishers of information
furnishers of medical
 information
healthcare information
health information exchange
 (HIE)
HIPAA Breach Notification Rule
HIPAA Privacy Rule

HIPAA Security Rule
Internet of Things
interoperability efforts
invasion of privacy
medical information
mosaic effect
natural law
nonaffiliated third party
nonpublic personal information
personal health records (PHRs)
personalized health information
Precision Medicine Initiative
 (PMI)
privacy framework
protected health information
 (PHI)
redlining
right to privacy
unsecured PHI
unsecured PHR identifiable
 information
value-based care

10

Moving Wellness to mHealth: A World of Heavier (FDA) Regulation

Learning Objectives

After reading this chapter, workplace wellness professionals will be able to:

1. Understand mobile health (mHealth) and wellness technologies and their interface with users through applications (apps) downloaded onto devices such as smartphones and tablet computers.
2. Define *medical device* as described in the 1976 Medical Device Amendments, which also expanded the regulatory authority of the FDA over such devices.
3. Describe the three classes of medical devices that are subject to Food and Drug Administration (FDA) regulation.
4. Detail how the FDA guidance statements distinguish between mHealth and wellness technologies.
5. Describe the types of mobile medical apps that are subject to FDA regulatory oversight.
6. Describe the types of mobile apps over which the FDA has enforcement discretion.
7. List quality practices recommended by the FDA for manufacturers of all mobile apps that may meet the definition of a medical device.
8. Describe the types of apps that the FDA has concluded are not medical devices and are not subject to FDA regulatory requirements.
9. Describe the requirements in the FDA guidance statement for low-risk wellness devices and the types of products that are considered low-risk wellness devices.
10. Utilize a decision algorithm to determine if a general wellness product (including a mobile app) qualifies as a low-risk wellness device, which would not be subject to FDA regulation.

The Creative Destruction of Medicine—it's the future!

—Stephen Colbert

*Today, there are numerous non-traditional health service providers—
Nike, Fitbit, Microsoft, Qualcomm—moving quickly into this space.
And with health-related services like Asthmapolis or [Massive
Health's] The Eatery sitting on an iPhone or Android screen beside
Twitter, YouTube, or Facebook applications, the boundaries between
lifestyle and life-care are blurring, perhaps even fading away.*

—Fabio Sergio, Executive Creative Director, Frog Design

Introduction

Companies that have made their mark in the wellness industry are beginning to move into the development of clinical technology. In 2016, Fitbit
publicized a push to transform itself into a "digital health company"
that relies less on consumers and more on the healthcare industry.[1] Other
companies seem to be jumping on that bandwagon as well.[2] According
to Fitbit's CEO, the goal is for Fitbit gadgets to monitor blood pressure
and blood sugar, and even diagnose disease.[3]

Stepping into the world of diagnosis and treatment of disease, however, comes with a steep regulatory price. The rules that govern workplace wellness pale in comparison to the rules that govern medical care.
Because insurance often pays for medical care, including government
insurance like Medicare and Medicaid, healthcare providers must navigate copious amounts of reimbursement rules both at the federal and
state levels. There are also malpractice and professional licensing issues
that weigh heavily in everyday practice. There are rules that govern with
whom providers may collaborate or employ, with whom they can share

---

1 Selina Wang, "Fitbit's Move into Medical Gadgets Risks Attracting FDA Scrutiny," *Bloomberg Technology* (April 15, 2016), http://www.bloomberg.com/news/articles/2016-04-15/fitbit-s-move-into-medical-
gadgets-risks-attracting-fda-scrutiny.
2 *Id.*
3 *Id.*

information (and how they can share that information), with whom they can share or waive fees for services, the meeting of quality standards, information submission requirements, information retention requirements, and more.

The company Theranos provides a recent example of a high-tech startup falling prey to the staggering amount of regulation in health care. Theranos developed a laboratory test, which it claimed could detect hundreds of diseases, but required only one drop of blood and cost a fraction of what a conventional laboratory would charge for those tests.[4] Theranos began offering tests to the public in late 2013 and opened 42 blood-drawing wellness centers in Arizona, 2 in California, and 1 in Pennsylvania.[5] Most other blood-drawing centers are in Walgreens drugstores.[6] The Centers for Medicare and Medicaid Services (CMS) sent a letter to Theranos on March 18, 2016, proposing sanctions against its leaders and taking away federal licensing for its laboratory facilities for continued failure to correct major problems with testing accuracy and competence.[7] For example, Theranos failed to properly hire and train qualified people to run the testing machines; allowed unlicensed workers to review patient test results; failed to follow manufacturers' instructions on equipment; and did not have a proper, written protocol in place to calibrate the machines to maintain accuracy.[8] Indeed, in July 2016, CMS banned Theranos's CEO from owning or operating a medical laboratory for at least two years.[9] The company also faces a fine of $10,000 for every day it is out of compliance.[10]

---

4 John Carreyrou, "Hot Startup Theranos Has Struggled with Its Blood-Test Technology," *Wall St. J.* (October 16, 2015), http://www.wsj.com/articles/theranos-has-struggled-with-blood-tests-1444881901; Reed Abelson and Andrew Pollack, "Theranos Under Federal Criminal Investigation, Adding to Its Woes," *New York Times* (April 18, 2016); Sarah Buhr, "Theranos Under Criminal Investigation," *Techcrunch* (April 18, 2016), http://techcrunch.com/2016/04/18/theranos-under-criminal-investigation-by-the-sec-and-u-s-attorneys-office/.
5 Carreyrou, "Hot Startup Theranos Has Struggled."
6 *Id.*
7 Sarah Buhr, "Regulators Plan to Revoke Theranos' Federal License and Ban Founder Elizabeth Holmes," *Techcrunch* (April 13, 2016), http://techcrunch.com/2016/04/13/regulators-plan-to-revoke-theranos-federal-license-and-ban-founder-elizabeth-holmes/; CMS, "Letter to Sunil Dhawan, Elizabeth Homes and Ramesh Balwani, Regarding CLIA Number 05D2025714" (March 18, 2016), http://online.wsj.com/public/resources/documents/cms20160412.pdf.
8 Buhr, "Regulators Plan to Revoke Theranos' Federal License."
9 Andrew Pollack, "Elizabeth Holmes of Theranos Is Barred from Running Lab for 2 Years," *New York Times* (July 8, 2016), http://www.nytimes.com/2016/07/09/business/theranos-elizabeth-holmes-ban.html?_r=0.
10 *Id.*

Of particular concern for wellness companies interested in developing technological devices or tools to market to the healthcare industry, there is also the specter of regulation by the Food and Drug Administration (FDA). This prospect of FDA regulation is the focus of this chapter. Part of this technological revolution in medical care is known as **mobile health** or **mHealth:** the use of mobile communications devices such as smartphones and tablet computers for health or medical purposes, usually for diagnosis, treatment, or simply well-being and maintenance.[11] Most mobile health technologies interface with users through applications (apps) downloaded onto iPhones, iPads, or Android or Windows devices, for example.[12] One aspiration of mHealth and other healthcare technology is to decentralize, demystify, and democratize medicine, shifting the locus of care away from expensive institutions like hospitals and toward individual patients.[13] The push for medical clinicians to incorporate mHealth into their practices is increasing.[14]

As noted earlier, along with this increased interest by healthcare providers in mHealth and other wellness technology comes an increased likelihood of becoming subject to FDA regulation. The goal behind FDA regulation is consumer safety. On September 25, 2013, and again on February 9, 2015, the FDA issued guidance for the mHealth industry.[15] The FDA also issued draft guidance for the wellness industry regarding low-risk devices on January 20, 2015.[16] None of these guidance documents has the force of law,[17] but they provide wellness professionals and organizations with insight into how the FDA views certain health technologies in relation to the Food, Drug, and Cosmetic Act (FDCA).

---

11 Nathan Cortez, "The Mobile Health Revolution," 47 *U.C.Davis L. Rev.* 1173 (2013–2014): 1176.

12 *Id.* at 1176.

13 *Id.* at 1197.

14 Natalie R. Bilbrough, "The FDA, Congress, and Mobile Health Apps: Lessons from DSHEA and the Regulation of Dietary Supplements," 74 *Md. L. Rev.* 921 (2014–2015): 929.

15 FDA, *Mobile Medical Applications Guidance for Industry and Food and Drug Administration Staff* (February 9, 2015), http://www.fda.gov/downloads/MedicalDevices/.../UCM263366.pdf.

16 FDA, *General Wellness: Policy for Low Risk Devices Draft Guidance for Industry and Food and Drug Administration Staff* (January 20, 2015), http://www.fda.gov/downloads/medicaldevices/deviceregulationandguidance/guidancedocuments/ucm429674.pdf.

17 *See, e.g.,* FDA, *Mobile Medical Applications Guidance for Industry and Food and Drug Administration Staff,* at 5 (noting that FDA's guidance documents, including the mHealth guidance, do not establish legally enforceable responsibilities).

After briefly describing the FDCA as applied to medical devices, this chapter summarizes the FDA guidance for mHealth and low-risk wellness devices. The decision algorithm provided by the FDA in the wellness device guidance appears at the end of this chapter, to help readers determine whether a device must comply with the FDCA.

The FDCA and Regulation of Medical Devices

Congress created the FDA in 1906 to govern therapeutic drugs.[18] At that time, medical devices were not thought to be appropriate candidates for federal regulation because very few products existed for prolonged application for the human body.[19] The 1938 Food, Drug and Cosmetic Act expanded the FDA's authority to include the regulation of medical devices.[20] However, the FDA did not have authority to require the manufacturer of any device to prove the safety, much less the effectiveness, of its product.[21] With the introduction of highly sophisticated medical technologies in the 1960s, the FDA began to push for stronger regulatory authority over medical devices.[22] After almost a decade of debate on the proper regulatory systems, in 1976, Congress amended the FDCA with the Medical Device Amendments (MDA). These amendments broadly defined a **medical device** as follows:

> An instrument, apparatus, implement, machine, contrivance, implant, in vitro reagent, or other similar or related article, including any component, part, or accessory, which is ... intended for use in the diagnosis of disease or other conditions, or in the cure, mitigation, treatment or prevention of disease ... or intended to affect the structure or function of the body.[23]

18 Stephen McInerney, "Can You Diagnose Me Now? A Proposal to Modify the FDA's Regulation of Smartphone Mobile Health Applications with a Pre-Market Notification and Application Database Program," 48 *U. Mich. J.L. Reform* 1073 (2014–2015): 1084.
19 *Id.*
20 *Id.*
21 *Id.*
22 McInerney, "Can You Diagnose Me Now?," at 1084–1085.
23 *Id.* at 1085–1086 (citing 21 U.S.C. § 321(h) (2012)).

Thus, an important consideration in whether a device is subject to FDA medical device regulation is determination of the device's "intended use." To determine the intended use, the FDA looks at a product's labeling claims, advertising matter, or oral or written statements by manufacturers or their representatives.[24] Generally, products, including software, are considered medical devices if they are intended for a medical purpose.[25]

If a product is considered a medical device, the manufacturer must comply with certain FDA regulatory requirements. These requirements include:

- **Establishment registration**—Manufacturers (both domestic and foreign) and initial distributors (importers) of medical devices must register their establishments with the FDA. All establishment registrations must be submitted electronically unless a waiver has been granted by the FDA. All registration information must be verified annually between October 1 and December 31 of each year. In addition to registration, foreign manufacturers must also designate a U.S. Agent. Beginning October 1, 2007, most establishments are required to pay an establishment registration fee.[26]
- **Medical device listing**—Manufacturers must list their devices with the FDA. Establishments required to list their devices include:
    1. Manufacturers
    2. Contract manufacturers that commercially distribute the device
    3. Contract sterilizers that commercially distribute the device
    4. Repackagers and relabelers
    5. Specification developers
    6. Reprocessors of single-use devices
    7. Remanufacturers

24 *Id.* at 1086 (noting that the regulatory language for medical devices and drugs is identical, but that the level of regulation is much less strict for most devices).
25 *Id.*
26 U.S. Food and Drug Administration, "Overview of Device Regulation: Fact Sheet" (August 14, 2015) http://www.fda.gov/MedicalDevices/DeviceRegulationandGuidance/Overview/ (citing 21 C.F.R. pt. 807).

8. Manufacturers of accessories and components sold directly to the end user

9. U.S. manufacturers of "export only" devices[27]

-   **Premarket Notification 510(k), unless exempt, or premarket approval (PMA)**—If your device requires the submission of a Premarket Notification 510(k), you cannot commercially distribute the device until you receive a letter of substantial equivalence from the FDA authorizing you to do so. A 510(k) must demonstrate that the device is substantially equivalent to one legally in commercial distribution in the United States: (1) before May 28, 1976; or (2) to a device that has been determined by FDA to be substantially equivalent. The FDA may charge a fee for medical device Premarket Notification 510(k) reviews. A small business may pay a reduced fee. The application fee applies to Traditional, Abbreviated, and Special 510(k)s. The payment of a premarket review fee is not related in any way to FDA's final decision on a submission. Most Class I devices and some Class II devices are exempt from the Premarket Notification 510(k) submission.[28]

Products requiring PMAs are Class III devices (high-risk devices that pose a significant risk of illness or injury), or devices found not substantially equivalent to Class I and II predicates through the 510(k) process. The PMA process is more involved and includes the submission of clinical data to support claims made for the device. Medical device user fees apply to original PMAs and certain types of PMA supplements. Small businesses are eligible for reduced or waived fees.[29] See the discussion later in this section on the three different classes of devices under FDA regulation.

-   **Investigational device exemption (IDE) for clinical studies**—An investigational device exemption (IDE) allows the investigational device to be used in a clinical study in order to collect the safety

---

27 *Id.*
28 *Id.* (citing 21 C.F.R. pt. 807, subpt. E).
29 *Id.* (citing 21 C.F.R. pt. 814).

and effectiveness data required to support a PMA application or a Premarket Notification 510(k) submission to the FDA. Clinical studies with devices of significant risk must be approved by the FDA and by an institutional review board (IRB) before the study can begin. Studies with devices of nonsignificant risk must be approved by an IRB only before the study can begin.[30]

- **Quality system (QS) regulation**—The quality system regulation includes requirements related to the methods used in, and the facilities and controls used for: designing, purchasing, manufacturing, packaging, labeling, storing, installing, and servicing of medical devices. Manufacturing facilities undergo FDA inspections to assure compliance with the QS requirements.[31]
- **Labeling requirements**—Labeling includes labels on the device as well as descriptive and informational literature that accompanies the device.[32]
- **Medical device reporting (MDR)**—Incidents in which a device may have caused or contributed to a death or serious injury must to be reported to the FDA under the Medical Device Reporting program. In addition, certain malfunctions must also be reported. The MDR regulation is a mechanism for the FDA and manufacturers to identify and monitor significant adverse events involving medical devices. The goals of the regulation are to detect and correct problems in a timely manner.[33]

As described earlier, the FDA regulates three different classes of medical devices.[34] Under this classification system, the FDA determines the amount of premarket and postmarket regulation required by the FDCA.[35] The higher the classification, the more scrutiny the device receives.[36] The three classes of medical devices are:

---

30 *Id.* (citing 21 C.F.R. pt. 812).
31 *Id.* (citing 21 C.F.R. pt. 820).
32 *Id.* (citing 21 C.F.R. pt. 801).
33 *Id.* (citing 21 C.F.R. pt. 803).
34 McInerney, "Can You Diagnose Me Now?," at 1086.
35 *Id.*
36 Cortez, "The Mobile Health Revolution," at 1201.

- Class I devices: Have the least regulation and generally do not require any premarket review by the FDA. Examples of Class I devices include elastic bandages and examination gloves.[37]
- Class II devices: Have "moderate risk" and are subject to a relatively cursory premarket notification, known as a 510(k) notice, which the FDA generally accepts.[38] In addition, Class II devices undergo special controls such as performance standards, postmarket surveillance, patient registries, special labeling requirements, and premarket data requirements and guidelines.[39] Examples of Class II devices include x-ray machines, powered wheelchairs, and acupuncture needles.[40]
- Class III devices: High-risk devices; these generally require premarket approval.[41] Premarket approval is a complex and expensive process that obligates the manufacturer to submit clinical data proving the device's safety and effectiveness.[42] The approval process takes more than five months, on average, even if a device is simply a newer version of an already approved device (i.e., a 510(k) clearance).[43] Therapeutic drugs must go through a similar approval process.[44] Examples of Class III devices include implantable pacemaker pulse generators and endosseous implants.[45]

The FDCA also gives the FDA the authority to set good manufacturing practice requirements for medical devices; to ban worthless and dangerous products from the market; and to require notification, replacement, or refund by makers of defective products.[46]

With regard to software, the FDA has long considered software products to meet the definition of a *device* when the software is intended for

---

37 *Id.* at 1201.
38 *Id.* at 1201–1202.
39 McInerney, "Can You Diagnose Me Now?," at 1087; *see also* Cortez, "The Mobile Health Revolution," at 1201.
40 McInerney, "Can You Diagnose Me Now?," at 1087.
41 *Id.*
42 *Id.*
43 Adam Candeub, "Digital Medicine, the FDA, and the First Amendment," 49 GA. L. REV. 933 (2014–2015): 944.
44 McInerney, "Can You Diagnose Me Now?," at 1087.
45 *Id.*
46 *Id.* (citing Medical Device Amendments of 1976, Pub. L. No. 94-295, § 518).

use in diagnosing and treating diseases and other conditions.[47] Although the FDA views software products as within the FDCA purview, the FDA announced that it would exercise **enforcement discretion** over many types of **low-risk software,** such as software that merely provides information.[48] *Enforcement discretion* means that the FDCA applies to the device and the FDA has legal authority to enforce regulations, but it chooses not to enforce those regulations.[49] The take-away regarding FDA regulation of devices is that if the device is intended to diagnose or treat a disease or condition, it is likely that it will be subject to FDA regulation.

Guidance for Mobile Medical Apps and Low-Risk Wellness Devices

The FDCA grants the FDA authority to issue regulations, and also allows interested parties to request a public hearing as part of the rule-making process.[50] The FDCA also includes residual rulemaking authority to address matters not specifically covered by the formal rulemaking provision.[51] This allows the FDA to conduct notice-and-comment procedures for the promulgation of rules.[52] This "informal" rulemaking procedure avoids the burdensome hearing procedure required with formal rulemaking.[53] Yet, even informal rulemaking has become lengthy and difficult for the FDA.[54] As a result, the FDA has resorted to issuing "guidance," offering the FDA a convenient shortcut for communicating its expectations to regulated entities.[55] The guidance process is not without critics, however. A primary criticism is that these informal announcements operate as de facto rules without the normal procedural safeguards

---

47 McInerney, "Can You Diagnose Me Now?," at 1087–1088.
48 *Id.* at 1088.
49 *Id.*
50 Lars Noah, "Governance by the Backdoor: Administrative Law(lessness?) at the FDA," 93 NEB. L. REV. 89 (2014–2015): 94; 21 U.S.C. § 371(e).
51 Noah, "Governance by the Backdoor," at 94–95; 21 U.S.C. § 371(a).
52 Noah, "Governance by the Backdoor," at 94–95.
53 *Id.* at 95.
54 *Id.* at 95.
55 *Id.* at 97.

that allow for public comment and review.[56] Despite this criticism, the FDA has recently issued guidance documents for both mobile medical apps and low-risk wellness devices.

Mobile Medical Apps Guidance

The FDA updated its original guidance relating to mobile medical applications on February 9, 2015.[57] The guidance defines **mobile medical app** as a software application that can be run on a smartphone, tablet, or other portable computer, or a web-based software platform tailored to a mobile platform but executed on a server, that meets the definition of *device* in § 201(h) of the FDCA and is intended either: (a) to be used as an accessory to a regulated medical device; or (b) to transform a mobile platform into a regulated medical device.[58] Generally, if a mobile app is intended for use in performing a medical device function (i.e., for diagnosis of disease or other conditions, or the cure, mitigation, treatment, or prevention of disease), it is a medical device, regardless of the platform on which it is run.[59] Recall that the FDA looks at a product's labeling claims, advertising materials, and oral or written statements by manufacturers or their representatives to determine a device's intended use.[60]

The key for wellness professionals and organizations is to determine whether a mobile app constitutes a mobile *medical* app or just a **mobile app**. If the latter, the FDA will exercise enforcement discretion, which (as noted earlier) means that the FDA chooses not to enforce compliance of those apps under the FDCA.[61] If the app is a mobile "medical" app, then the FDA will apply its regulatory oversight over those apps.[62] See Table 10.1 for the apps the FDA considers to be mobile "medical" apps subject to its oversight.[63] Mobile apps over which the FDA intends to exercise enforcement discretion are listed in Table 10.2.[64]

---

56 *Id.*
57 FDA, *Mobile Medical Applications Guidance for Industry and Food and Drug Administration Staff* (February 9, 2015), http://www.fda.gov/downloads/MedicalDevices/.../UCM263366.pdf.
58 *Id.* at 7.
59 *Id.* at 8.
60 *Id.* at 8.
61 *Id.* at 13.
62 *Id.* at 13.
63 *Id.* at 14–15.
64 *Id.* at 16–18, 23.

Type of Mobile Medical App	Examples	Must Comply With:
Apps that are an extension of one or more medical devices by connecting to such devices for purposes of controlling the devices or for use in active patient monitoring or analysis of medical device data.	• Display of medical images directly from a picture archiving and communication system (PACS) server • Remote display of data from bedside monitors • Apps that provide the ability to control inflation and deflation of blood pressure cuff • Apps that control delivery of insulin on insulin pump by transmitting control signals to the pump from the mobile platform	Regulations applicable to the connected medical device.
Apps that transform the mobile platform into a regulated medical device by using attachments, display screens, or sensors or by including functionalities similar to those of currently regulated medical devices.	• Blood glucose strip reader attached to a mobile platform to function as glucose meter • Attachment of electrocardio-graph electrodes to mobile platform to measure, store, and display ECG signals • App that uses built-in accel-erometer on a mobile plat-form to collect motion information for monitoring sleep apnea • App that uses sensors (inter-nal and external) on a mobile platform for creating elec-tronic stethoscope function • App that displays radiologi-cal images for diagnosis	The device classification associated with the transformed platform.
Apps that become a regulated medical device (software) by performing patient-specific analysis and providing patient-specific diagnosis or treatment recommendations.	• Apps that use patient-specific parameters and calculate dosage or create a dosage plan for radiation therapy • Computer-aided detection (CAD) software image-pro-cessing software • Radiation therapy treatment planning software	The FDA encourages manufacturers of these types of apps to contact the FDA to discuss what, if any, regulatory requirements may apply.

Table 10.1   Mobile Medical Apps with FDA Regulatory Oversight

Type of Mobile App	Examples
Apps that provide or facilitate supplemental clinical care, by coaching or prompting, to help patients manage their health in their daily environment.	• Apps that coach patients with conditions such as cardiovascular disease, hypertension, diabetes, or obesity, and promote strategies for maintaining a healthy weight, getting optimal nutrition, exercising, managing salt intake, or adhering to predetermined medication dosing schedules by simple prompting. • Apps that use video and video games to motivate patients to do their physical therapy exercises at home. • Apps that provide periodic educational information, reminders, or motivational guidance to smokers trying to quit, patients recovering from addiction, or pregnant women. • Apps that help patients with diagnosed psychiatric conditions (e.g., PTSD, depression, anxiety, OCD) maintain their behavioral coping skills by providing a "Skill of the Day" behavioral technique or audio messages that the user can access when experiencing increased anxiety. • Apps that prompt users to enter which herb and drug they would like to take concurrently, and then provide information about whether interactions have been seen in the literature and a summary of what type of interaction was reported. • Apps that use patient characteristics such as age, sex, and behavioral risk factors to provide patient-specific screening, counseling, and preventive recommendations from well-known and established authorities.
Apps that provide patients with simple tools to organize and track their health information.	Apps that provide simple tools for patients with specific conditions or chronic disease, such as: • Obesity • Anorexia • Arthritis • Diabetes • Heart disease to log, track, or trend their events or measurements (e.g., blood pressure measurements, drug intake times, diet, daily routine or emotional state) and share this information with their healthcare provider as part of a disease-management plan.
Apps that provide easy access to information related to patients' health conditions or treatments (beyond providing an electronic "copy" of a medical reference).	• Apps that use a patient's diagnosis to provide a clinician with best-practice treatment guidelines for common illnesses or conditions such as the flu. • Apps that are drug-drug interaction or drug-allergy lookup tools.

Table 10.2   Mobile Apps with FDA Enforcement Discretion

Type of Mobile App	Examples
Apps that are specifically marketed to help patients document, show, or communicate to providers potential medical conditions.	• Apps that serve as videoconferencing portals specifically intended for medical use and to enhance communications between patients, healthcare providers, and caregivers. • Apps specifically intended for medical uses that utilize a mobile device's built-in camera or a connected camera for purposes of documenting or transmitting pictures (e.g., photos of a patient's skin lesions or wounds) to supplement or augment what would otherwise be a verbal description in a consultation with a healthcare provider or between providers.
Apps that perform simple calculations routinely used in clinical practice.	Medical calculators for: • Body mass index (BMI) • Total body water/Urea volume of distribution • Mean arterial pressure • Glasgow Coma Scale score • APGAR score • NIH Stroke Scale • Delivery date estimator
Apps that enable individuals to interact with PHR or EHR systems.	Apps that allow patients to gain electronic access to health information stored in a personal health record or electronic health record system.
Apps that meet the definition of medical device data systems.	Apps intended to transfer, store, convert format, and display medical device data, without controlling or altering the functions or parameters of any connected medical device. These apps include those that are used as a secondary display for a regulated medical device when these apps are not intended to provide primary diagnosis, help make treatment decisions, or be used in connection with active patient monitoring.

Table 10.2 Mobile Apps with FDA Enforcement Discretion (*continued*)

Regardless of whether a medical device is subject to FDA enforcement authority or is one to which the FDA applies enforcement discretion, the FDA strongly recommends that manufacturers of all mobile apps that may meet the definition of a medical device follow the **Quality System regulation** in the design and development of those apps.[65] This regulation includes good manufacturing practices.[66] A partial list of these practices includes:

1. Having a quality policy
2. Conducting quality audits
3. Having sufficient personnel with the necessary education, background, training, and experience to ensure a quality device
4. Having design controls to ensure that specified design requirements are met
5. Having production and process controls
6. Having procedures to ensure that devices are routinely calibrated, inspected, checked, and maintained
7. Having procedures to handle products that do not conform to specified requirements
8. Creating and maintaining a device history record.[67]

In addition to mobile apps that the FDA considers medical devices (and either applies its enforcement authority or does not), there is a third category of mobile apps that the FDA concludes are not medical devices at all and therefore are not subject to regulatory requirements under the FDCA.[68] Examples of these types of apps are listed in Table 10.3.

---

65 FDA, *Mobile Medical Applications Guidance for Industry and Food and Drug Administration Staff*, at 13.
66 *Id.*
67 21 C.F.R. pt. 820.
68 FDA, *Mobile Medical Applications Guidance for Industry and Food and Drug Administration Staff*, at 20.

Type of Mobile App	Examples
Apps intended to provide access to electronic "copies" (e.g., e-books, audio books) of medical textbooks or other reference materials with generic text search capabilities. Not intended for use in diagnosis, cure, mitigation, treatment, or prevention of disease.	• Medical dictionaries • Electronic copies of medical textbooks or literature articles such as the *Physician's Desk Reference* or *Diagnostic and Statistical Manual of Mental Disorders* • Library of clinical descriptions for diseases and conditions • Encyclopedia of first-aid or emergency care information • Medical abbreviations and definitions • Translations of medical terms across multiple languages
Apps intended for healthcare providers to use as educational tools for medical training or to reinforce training previously received.	• Medical flash cards with medical images, pictures, graphs • Question/Answer quiz apps • Interactive anatomy diagrams or videos • Surgical training videos • Medical board certification or recertification preparation apps • Games that simulate various cardiac arrest scenarios to train health professionals in advanced CPR skills
Apps intended for general patient education and to facilitate patient access to commonly used reference information.	• Portals for healthcare providers to distribute educational information (e.g., interactive diagrams, useful links and resources) to their patients regarding their disease, treatment, or upcoming procedure • Guides for patients to ask appropriate questions to physicians relevant to particular disease, condition, or concern • Information apps about gluten-free food products or restaurants • Apps that match patients with appropriate clinical trials and facilitate communication between patient and clinical trial investigator • Tutorials or training videos on how to administer first aid or CPR • Apps that allow users to input pill shape, color, or imprint and displays pictures and names of pills that match the description • Apps that find the closest medical facilities and doctors to user's location • Apps that provide lists of emergency hotlines and physician/nurse advice lines • Apps that provide and compare costs of drugs and medical products at pharmacies in the user's location

Table 10.3   Apps That Are *Not* Medical Devices, with No FDA Regulatory Requirements[69]

---

69 *Id.* at 20–22.

Type of Mobile App	Examples
Apps that automate general office operations in a healthcare setting and are not intended for use in the diagnosis, cure, mitigation, treatment, or prevention of disease.	• Apps that determine billing codes • Apps that enable insurance claims data collection and processing • Apps that analyze insurance claims for fraud or abuse • Apps that perform medical business accounting functions • Apps that generate reminders for scheduled medical appointments • Apps that help patients track, review, and pay medical bills online • Apps that manage shifts for doctors • Apps that manage or schedule hospital rooms or bed spaces • Apps that provide wait times and electronic check-in for hospital emergency room or urgent care facilities • Apps that allow healthcare providers or staff to process payments • Apps that track or perform patient satisfaction surveys after a clinical encounter
Apps that are generic aids or general-purpose products that are not specifically intended for medical purposes.	• Apps that use the mobile platform as a magnifying glass • Apps that use the mobile platform for recording audio, note-taking, replaying audio with amplification • Apps that allow patients or healthcare providers to interact through email, web-based platforms, or video • Apps that provide maps and turn-by-turn directions to medical facilities (and other locations) • Apps that allow healthcare providers to communicate in a secure and protected method

Table 10.3 Apps That Are *Not* Medical Devices, with No FDA Regulatory Requirements (*continued*)

Guidance for Low-Risk Wellness Devices

In addition to mobile apps, wellness professionals and organizations may develop or encounter other products that the FDA considers to present "low risk" to consumer safety. The FDA released its final guidance regarding **low-risk wellness devices** on July 29, 2016.[70] According to the FDA, low-risk products generally promote a healthy lifestyle and meet the

---

70 FDA, *General Wellness: Policy for Low Risk Devices, Guidance for Industry and Food and Drug Administration Staff* (July 29, 2016), http://www.fda.gov/downloads/medicaldevices/deviceregulationandguidance/guidancedocuments/ucm429674.pdf.

following two factors: (1) are intended for only general wellness use; and (2) present a very low risk to users' safety.[71]

Intended for General Wellness Only

The FDA defines a *general wellness product* to be one that meets one of the following criteria: (1) has an intended use that relates to maintaining or encouraging a general state of health or a healthy activity; or (2) an intended use claim that associates the role of healthy lifestyle with helping to reduce the risk or impact of certain chronic diseases or conditions and where it is well understood and accepted that healthy lifestyle choices may play an important role in health outcomes for the disease or condition.[72]

Importantly, the first category of general wellness product does not make any reference to diseases or conditions. To fall within this category, the general wellness product may relate to:

- Weight management
- Physical fitness, including products intended for recreational use
- Relaxation or stress management
- Mental acuity
- Self-esteem (e.g., devices with a cosmetic function that make claims related only to self-esteem)
- Sleep management
- Sexual function[73]

In contrast, products that relate to the following would not qualify as general wellness products (and therefore could be subject to FDA regulation):

- The treatment or diagnosis of obesity
- The treatment of an eating disorder
- The treatment of anxiety

---

71 *Id.* at 1–2.
72 *Id.* at 2–3.
73 *Id.* at 3.

- A computer game that will diagnose or treat autism
- The treatment of muscle atrophy or erectile dysfunction
- The restoration of a structure or function impaired due to a disease (e.g., a claim that a prosthetic device enables amputees to play basketball)[74]

The second category of general wellness products is comprised of two subcategories: (1) intended uses to promote, track, and/or encourage choices, which, as part of a healthy lifestyle, may help to reduce the risk of certain chronic diseases or conditions; and (2) intended uses to promote, track, and/or encourage choices which, as a part of a healthy lifestyle, may help living well with certain chronic diseases or conditions.[75] Both subcategories of disease-related wellness products should only make claims about healthy lifestyle choices reducing the risk of chronic disease or a medical condition if those claims are generally accepted and described in peer-reviewed scientific publications.[76] For example, it is generally accepted that a healthy lifestyle reduces the risk of or helps better manage heart disease, high blood pressure, and type 2 diabetes.[77]

Presents a Very Low Risk to User's Safety
In addition to being intended for general wellness, in order for a product to qualify as a low-risk wellness device, the product must also not present inherent risks to a user's safety.[78] The FDA considers a product to present an inherent risk to a user's safety if the product:

- Is invasive
- Is implanted
- Involves an intervention or technology that may pose a risk to a user's or other persons' safety if specific regulatory controls are not applied, such as risks from lasers or radiation exposure[79]

---

74 *Id.* at 4.
75 *Id.* at 4.
76 *Id.*
77 *Id.*
78 FDA, *General Wellness: Policy for Low Risk Devices*, at 5.
79 *Id.* at 5.

Examples of such products include:

- Sunlamp products promoted for tanning purposes (exposure to ultraviolet radiation creates an increased risk of skin cancer).
- Implants promoted for improved self-image or enhanced sexual function (creates an increased risk of rupture or adverse reaction to implant materials, as well as from the implantation procedure).
- A laser product that claims to improve confidence in the user's appearance by rejuvenating the skin (laser technology presents a risk of skin and eye burns and presents usability considerations that may be addressed with labeling and other device controls).
- A neurostimulation product that claims to improve memory, due to the risks to a user's safety from electrical stimulation.
- A product that claims to enhance a user's athletic performance by providing suggestions based on the results of relative lactic acid testing, when the product uses venipuncture to obtain the blood samples needed for testing. This is an invasive product because it obtains blood samples by piercing the skin, which may pose a risk of infection transmission.[80]

Another way to determine whether a wellness device qualifies as low risk is to investigate whether the FDA already regulates products of the same type as the product in question.[81] Wellness professionals and organizations may visit the FDA website at http://www.accessdata.fda.gov/scripts/cdrh/cfdocs/cfpcd/classification.cfm to search for similar products that the FDA might already regulate.

However, a product that qualifies as a low-risk wellness device is not subject to FDA regulation. The FDA does not intend to examine these low-risk products to determine whether they are "medical devices" subject to the FDCA or, if they are devices, whether they are in compliance with the FDCA.[82]

---

80 *Id.* at 6.
81 *Id.* at 5.
82 *Id.* at 2.

Putting It Together

Given these "first category" and "second category" descriptions of general wellness products, it appears that wearable technology (e.g., Fitbit, Jawbone) devices that track data such as exercise and dietary behavior would be considered low-risk wellness devices and therefore not subject to any FDA regulatory requirements. They also present a very low risk to the user's safety as described later. However, if this technology changes in the future (e.g., becomes a medical device that is intended to diagnose and treat a disease), it would become subject to FDA regulations. Therefore, workplace wellness programs that provide wearable technology for their employees may not need to be concerned with these FDA regulations at the moment, but may need to comply with FDA laws as technology changes and moves more into clinical applications. Of course, wellness programs that use information-collecting devices must still address compliance with privacy, confidentiality, and security regulations, as described in Chapter 9.

Wellness professionals and organizations may wonder how the FDA *Guidance for Mobile Apps* and *Guidance for Low Risk Wellness Devices* relate to one another. Mobile apps can be a type of low-risk wellness device, as shown in the diagram in Figure 10.1.

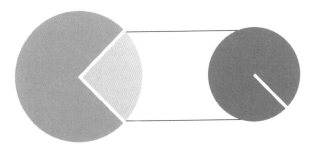

■ Other, such as exercise equipment, audio recordings, video games, software programs

■ Mobile Apps

Figure 10.1   Types of Low-Risk Wellness Devices

So, a wellness professional or organization that uses a mobile app as part of a wellness program should refer first to the low-risk wellness device decision algorithm (following). If after applying the algorithm the wellness professional concludes that the mobile app does not qualify as a general wellness product, then the wellness professional should consult the *Mobile Medical Applications Guidance* to determine whether the FDCA applies to the app.

Decision Algorithm for General Wellness Products[83]

A1. Does the product have an intended use that relates to maintaining or encouraging a general state of health or a healthy activity?

Does the product only involve claims about sustaining or offering general improvement to functions associated with a general state of health that do not make any reference to diseases or conditions? Claims in this category include weight management, physical fitness, relaxation or stress management, mental acuity, self-esteem, sleep management, or sexual function.

Yes   ☐   Go to A3.
No   ☐   Go to A2.

A2. Does the product have an intended use that relates the role of healthy lifestyle in helping to reduce the risk or impact of certain chronic diseases or conditions? Does intended use include a claim relating to a disease or medical condition? *(In answering this question, the following two questions must be considered together.)*

a. Does the product have an intended use that relates to sustaining or offering general improvement to functions associated with a general state of health while making reference to diseases or conditions, and where it is well understood and accepted that healthy lifestyle choices may play an important role in health outcomes for the disease or condition?

---

83 *Id.* at 9–10.

AND

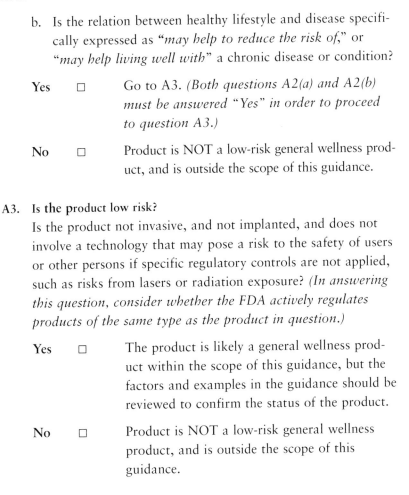

b. Is the relation between healthy lifestyle and disease specifically expressed as *"may help to reduce the risk of,"* or *"may help living well with"* a chronic disease or condition?

Yes   ☐   Go to A3. *(Both questions A2(a) and A2(b) must be answered "Yes" in order to proceed to question A3.)*

No   ☐   Product is NOT a low-risk general wellness product, and is outside the scope of this guidance.

A3. **Is the product low risk?**
Is the product not invasive, and not implanted, and does not involve a technology that may pose a risk to the safety of users or other persons if specific regulatory controls are not applied, such as risks from lasers or radiation exposure? *(In answering this question, consider whether the FDA actively regulates products of the same type as the product in question.)*

Yes   ☐   The product is likely a general wellness product within the scope of this guidance, but the factors and examples in the guidance should be reviewed to confirm the status of the product.

No   ☐   Product is NOT a low-risk general wellness product, and is outside the scope of this guidance.

RULE THE RULES

Key Points in Chapter 10

1. The increased interest and growth in mobile health (mHealth) and wellness technologies have led to FDA regulation of these technologies.

2. The Food, Drug and Cosmetic Act (FDCA) expanded the FDA's authority to include regulation of medical devices.

3. The FDA regulates three classifications of medical devices. The higher the classification, the more scrutiny the device receives.

4. The FDA issued guidance statements for both the mHealth industry and the wellness industry in 2015.

5. Software products that meet the definition of a medical device (e.g., a mobile medical app that is intended to be used to diagnose and treat disease) are subject to regulatory oversight by the FDA.

6. Low-risk software (e.g., a mobile app that merely provides information) is subject to FDA enforcement discretion.

7. The FDA has identified specific mobile apps that are not medical devices and thus are not subject to regulatory requirements.

8. The FDA strongly recommends that manufacturers of all mobile apps that may meet the definition of medical device follow the Quality System regulation, which includes quality manufacturing practices.

9. The FDA has provided guidance for low-risk wellness devices (including mobile apps) that meet two factors: (a) are intended for general wellness use only, and (b) present a very low risk to the user's safety. If the device meets these two factors, it is not subject to FDA regulation.

10. A decision algorithm can be used to determine if a wellness product qualifies as a general wellness product.

Study Questions

1. Describe the purposes of the federal government's regulation of mobile health (mHealth) and wellness technologies.

2. Regarding the Medical Amendments Act, describe how it defined *medical device* and the regulatory authority the Act gave to the FDA.

3. List and describe the three different classes of medical devices, including software if intended for medical purposes.

4. Explain the differences between *mobile medical app* and *mobile app* with regard to FDA regulation.

5. Give examples of the types of apps that the FDA has concluded are not medical apps at all and therefore are not subject to regulatory requirements.

6. Regarding the FDA guidance for low-risk wellness devices, list and describe the factors that must be met for the wellness device not to be subject to FDA regulation.

7. For a wellness device (including software) used by employees in your workplace wellness program, use the decision algorithm to determine if the device qualifies as a low-risk wellness device.

Key Terms

enforcement discretion

low-risk software

low-risk wellness device

medical device

mobile app

mobile health (mHealth)

mobile medical app

Quality System Regulation

11

What's Next for Workplace Wellness?

Learning Objectives

After reading this chapter, workplace wellness professionals will be able to:

1. Understand the distinctions between the healthcare and wellness industries.
2. Describe the need for the healthcare and wellness industries to work together toward a common goal to improve population health.
3. Explain how employee engagement strategies in wellness programs can be used in health care to enhance patient engagement.
4. Describe the purposes of the National Prevention Strategy of the ACA and how workplace wellness professionals can help lead efforts to improve the health of communities.
5. Summarize various ACA provisions that provide opportunities to enhance the integration of health care and public health.
6. Develop and implement ACA initiatives such as (a) offering wellness services to accountable care organizations, (b) providing annual wellness visits for physician clinics, and (c) assisting the health insurance community in complying with the Quality Improvement Strategy.
7. Understand the concept of precision wellness and the need for cultural competence and compliance training, as well as efforts to increase diversity among wellness professionals.
8. List the many advances that have occurred in workplace wellness.

9. List the many benefits of a collaborative effort to address compliance training and the development of standards and guidelines and describe how these benefits can advance the profession.
10. Describe the need for compliance training and the development of standards and guidelines related to workplace wellness laws and practice.

If you can dream it, you can do it.

—Walt Disney

You can't solve a problem on the same level that it was created. You have to rise above it to the next level.

—Albert Einstein

Introduction

To achieve the goal of improving population health, workplace wellness professionals and organizations should embrace, and arguably lead, three initiatives. First, workplace wellness professionals and organizations should apply their skills and knowledge to the larger community, including the healthcare community. The Affordable Care Act (ACA) has provided a number of programs to help wellness professionals and organizations bridge the divide that currently exists between health care and wellness. Second, they should adopt a precision wellness approach and use the purpose of the Civil Rights laws as a model for inclusion. To help accomplish this initiative, there must be greater emphasis on compliance in workplace wellness education. Compliance training relates to the third initiative, which is for the workplace wellness industry to establish compliance standards and ethical guidelines which will enhance the opportunities to achieve well-being.

Bridging the Divide Between Wellness and Health Care

Currently, the United States views the healthcare and wellness industries separately. As far as spending, 97 percent of national health expenditures goes to healthcare services, with only 3 percent going to prevention.[1] Yet, despite this disparity, the biggest determinants of health are not medical care or even genetics, but rather behaviors and environmental factors.[2] In the United States, the primary causes of premature adult deaths are related to unhealthy behaviors such as tobacco use (18.1 percent) and poor diet and lack of physical activity (15.2 percent).[3] By 2020, the World Health Organization predicts that two-thirds of all disease worldwide will be the result of lifestyle choices.[4]

The distinction between health care and wellness also exists in the way health professionals practice and are trained. For the most part, the medical field focuses on providing health care, while wellness care, such as lifestyle changes, is left to those in the wellness industry. For example, according to one 2015 survey, only 30 percent of U.S. health professionals provided exercise counseling during the previous 12 months.[5] Barriers include lack of time, compensation, knowledge, and resources.[6] Moreover, most training of physicians, social workers, psychologists, and physician assistants does not include wellness topics such as physical activity, nutrition, and stress management.[7] However, one initiative, **Exercise Is Medicine (EIM)**, provides guidance for physicians and other healthcare providers to help their patients engage in a regular exercise program. The vision of this collaborative effort between healthcare providers and exercise professionals and organizations is to:

- Have healthcare providers assess every patient's level of physical activity at every clinic visit
- Determine if the patient is meeting the U.S. National Physical Activity Guidelines

1 Joe Alper, "Population Health Implications of the Affordable Care Act: Workshop Summary," from Institute of Medicine and Board on Population Health and Public Health Practice, *Roundtable on Population Health Improvement* (Washington, DC: National Academies Press, 2014): 6, http://www.nap.edu/catalog.php?record_id=18546.
2 *Id.*
3 Rani Polak, Rachel M. Pojednic, and Edward M. Phillips, "Lifestyle Medicine Education," *Am. J. of Lifestyle Med.* 9, no. 5 (September 2015): 361, http://www.ncbi.nlm.nih.gov/pmc/articles/PMC4561845/pdf/10.1177_1559827615580307.pdf.
4 *Id.*
5 *Id.*
6 *Id.*
7 Polak, Pojednic, and Phillips, "Lifestyle Medicine Education," at 363.

- Provide each patient with brief counseling to help him or her meet the guidelines and/or refer the patient to either healthcare or community-based resources for further physical activity (PA) counseling[8]

The wellness community should encourage more widespread adoption of the EIM initiative. See the sidebar for more information regarding EIM at the worksite.

"EIM seeks to support ... innovative worksite wellness programs and concepts by providing an additional level of infrastructure to promote physical activity to employees. Many large employers have onsite healthcare professionals to provide yearly physicals and acute health services for their employees. EIM calls upon worksite healthcare professionals to:

- Assess the physical activity levels of all patients that they see
- Provide information and education on the importance of regular physical activity
- Give a basic exercise prescription (as appropriate)
- Refer employees to existing programs or fitness facilities located at the worksite
- Maintain close communication with onsite exercise professionals about the activity levels of inactive employees"

Note: EIM encourages healthcare providers to refer their patients to EIM-credentialed exercise professionals. For example, EIM Level II requires a bachelor's degree in exercise science/exercise physiology/kinesiology, and Level III requires a master's degree in exercise science/exercise physiology/kinesiology or a bachelor's degree in exercise science/exercise physiology/kinesiology plus 4,000 hours of clinical exercise experience. Both levels also require an accredited certification that requires a degree to be eligible to sit for the examination. Healthcare providers can reduce their liability risk when referring their patients to an exercise professional by making sure the exercise professional is qualified and competent and has the necessary knowledge and skills to meet the needs of their patients. See Chapter 6 for more on this topic of qualifications and competence of exercise professionals.

---

8 "What Is Exercise Is Medicine®—A Global Health Initiative" (2016), http://www.exerciseismedicine. org/support_page.php/about/.

Even the law and insurance distinguish between wellness and health care. Within the category of prevention, there is prevention that includes disease management or other "medical care" and prevention that includes "self-improvement" wellness initiatives. Costs of **self-improvement wellness care**, such as expenses incurred for physical activity, or stress or weight management, are not reimbursable by Medicare, Medicaid, or most private insurance plans,[9] nor are such expenses excludable from one's taxable income.[10] Traditionally, the government and insurance companies have not provided financial incentives for individuals to adopt self-improvement wellness activities, even though such activities are preventive in nature and in the long run can improve health outcomes and reduce healthcare costs.

The separation between health care and wellness is beginning to shrink, however. Health care is undergoing a transformation, arguably due more to need than desire. To achieve substantial and lasting improvements in population health, all the stakeholders of the health and wellness industries must act in a concerted effort and align around the common goal of improving **population health**.[11] Spurred by a societal need to control healthcare costs and improve the health of the nation, the dominance of traditional health service delivery models is slowly eroding. Recent exposés by *Time Magazine* and Consumer Reports stirred debate on the exorbitant price of health care in the United States and questioned why the bills are so high and value so low when compared to other developed countries.[12] For example, the average cost of an employer family health plan increased from $6,438 in 2000 to $16,351 by 2013.[13] Yet, despite having the highest

---

9 *See, e.g.*, Medicare.gov, "Your Medicare Coverage: Gym Memberships & Fitness Programs," http://www.medicare.gov/coverage/fitness-programs.html (stating that original Medicare does not cover gym memberships); Sandra Boodman, "Few Insurers Provide Coverage for Weight Loss Treatment," *Kaiser Health News* (September 21, 2010), http://kaiserhealthnews.org/news/obesity-coverage/.
10 IRC § 213(d) (definition of *medical care*); IRS Publication 502 (prohibiting tax deductions for health club memberships or weight loss programs if used for improving well-being only), http://www.irs.gov/publications/p502/ar02.html.
11 Committee on Integrating Primary Care and Public Health and Institute of Medicine, *Primary Care and Public Health: Exploring Integration to Improve Population Health* (Washington, DC: National Academies Press, 2012): 1, http://www.nap.edu/read/13381/chapter/2.
12 Steven Brill, "Why Medical Bills Are Killing Us," *Time* (February 26, 2013), http://www.uta.edu/faculty/story/2311/Misc/2013,2,26,MedicalCostsDemandAndGreed.pdf; "Why Is Healthcare So Expensive?," *Consumer Reports* (September 2014), http://www.consumerreports.org/cro/magazine/2014/11/it-is-time-to-get-mad-about-the-outrageous-cost-of-health-care/index.htm.
13 Consumer Reports, "Why Is Healthcare So Expensive?"

per-capita health costs in the world, out of 11 developed countries, the United States ranked fifth in quality and worst for infant mortality.[14] It also did the worst job of preventing deaths from treatable conditions, such as strokes, diabetes, high blood pressure, and certain treatable cancers.[15]

To help address this current lack of healthcare value, **traditional healthcare models** led by hospitals and medical groups are being eclipsed by innovative well-being models spearheaded by the technology, retail, and wellness sectors. These sectors are developing convenient ways to personalize health and wellness and to share that personalized health data across the community to a wider variety of people and organizations that can help individuals achieve their health and wellness goals, and ultimately avoid using the expensive healthcare system.

In essence, these sectors are embracing the idea of improving population health by engaging the population one individual at a time. Some in the workplace wellness industry, such as Dr. Vic Strecher, have described this effort as finding a person's "purpose" for achieving an optimal life.[16] Each sector, including the worksite wellness industry, must now take its efforts one step further and begin seeing itself as integral not only to improving employee health, but also to communities at large. Indeed, as pointed out by the Robert Wood Johnson Foundation, there is a link between an unhealthy workforce and unhealthy communities.[17] Employees who go home to unhealthy neighborhoods undermine workplace health promotion efforts.[18] By moving beyond the workplace and into the community, wellness professionals and organizations can have a greater impact on reducing risk factors such as obesity or smoking, which can lead to a more productive workforce that misses fewer days of work and incurs lower healthcare expenditures.[19]

The workplace wellness industry in particular is uniquely positioned to lead the effort in engaging community members in their own health improvement. Maximizing **employee engagement** is a topic frequently

14 Id.
15 Id.
16 Victor J. Strecher, On Purpose (Ann Arbor, MI: Dung Beetle Press, 2013): 213.
17 Robert Wood Johnson Foundation, "Issue Brief: Why Healthy Communities Matter to Business" (May 2016): 3, http://www.rwjf.org/content/dam/farm/reports/issue_briefs/2016/rwjf428899.
18 Id.
19 Id.

addressed by the workplace wellness industry, because better employee engagement leads to more successful workplace wellness programs.[20] **Patient engagement** in the healthcare industry, however, is a relatively new concept. As noted by one scholar, lip service may be paid to the principle of involving patients, such as handing out general information leaflets or inviting patients to attend meetings, but there is no real effort to respond to patients' concerns.[21] That is due in part to current delivery systems, which limit patients' involvement by failing to routinely provide people with details of their own clinical results and conditions and other important clinical data.[22]

In other words, the current healthcare system does not reward medical providers for engaging patients. Interventions that address nonmedical determinants of health, such as home visits, education, service-enriched housing, workforce training, healthy eating, and exercise exist outside the scope of the traditional healthcare payment system.[23] As workplace wellness industry scholars are aware, effective strategies of employee engagement can turn a wellness program from a superficial activity into a meaningful benefit.[24] Similarly, to truly engage patients, the healthcare paradigm must shift from asking "What is the matter?" to "What matters to you?"[25] Wellness professionals such as health educators, health coaches, fitness and nutrition professionals, and others who identify with the wellness industry are well positioned to lead health care down that road.

The Impact of the ACA Provisions

There are a number of **ACA provisions** that can facilitate the convergence between health care and wellness. For example, the ACA created the National Prevention Council, which is tasked with creating a

---

20 Soeren Mattke et al., *Workplace Wellness Programs Study Final Report* (Rand Health, 2013): 133, http://www.nexgenhce.com/images/RAND_Wellness_Study_-_May_2013.pdf.
21 Jeremy Laurance et al., "Patient Engagement: Four Case Studies That Highlight the Potential for Improved Health Outcomes and Reduced Costs," *Health Affairs* 33, no. 9 (September 2014): 1628.
22 *Id.*
23 Ian Galloway, "Using Pay-for-Success to Increase Investment in the Nonmedical Determinants of Health," *Health Affairs* 33, no. 11 (November 2014): 1897.
24 *See, e.g.*, Rosie Ward, "Engagement in Wellness Programs: Separating Fact from Fiction," Salveo Partners Blog (September 5, 2014), https://salveopartners.com/engagement-wellness-programs-separating-fact-fiction/.
25 Laurance et al., "Patient Engagement," at 1628.

National Prevention Strategy to realize the benefits of prevention for all Americans' health.[26] Part of that strategy is to enhance coordination and integration of clinical, behavioral, and complementary health strategies and to promote self-improvement care.[27] Recently, the Centers for Disease Control and Prevention (CDC) and the Health Resources and Services Administration (HRSA) created a chart identifying the various ACA provisions that the CDC and HRSA could leverage to better integrate primary care and public health.[28] Wellness industry stakeholders should consider using many of these same ACA provisions to apply their skills beyond the workplace. See Table 11.1 for these ACA provisions and HRSA/CDC opportunities. To the extent these ACA provisions are impacted by the new presidential team in 2017, wellness industry stakeholders could advocate for the same or similar provisions in replacement legislation.

As mentioned earlier, wellness professionals may leverage a number of these ACA initiatives, as well as others not identified in the chart, to move beyond the workplace. For example, wellness professionals and organizations should explore potential involvement with **accountable care organizations (ACOs)**. According to CMS, ACOs are groups of doctors, hospitals, and other healthcare providers who come together voluntarily to give coordinated high-quality care to their patients.[29] Under the Medicare ACO programs, such as the Medicare Shared Savings Program (MSSP), when the ACO succeeds both in delivering high-quality care and spending healthcare dollars more wisely, it will share in the savings it achieves for the Medicare program.

One way in which wellness professionals and organizations could get involved in ACOs is to offer wellness services to ACO patients. The MSSP law allows ACOs to provide patients with "in-kind items or services"

---

26 National Prevention Council, *National Prevention Strategy* (June 2011), at 6.
27 *Id.* at 20.
28 Institute of Medicine, "Summary," in *Primary Care and Public Health: Exploring Integration to Improve Population Health* (Washington, DC: National Academies Press, 2012); doi:10.17226/13381, http://www.nap.edu/download/13381#.
29 Centers for Medicare and Medicaid Services, "Accountable Care Organizations (ACOs) Fact Sheet" (January 6, 2015), https://www.cms.gov/Medicare/Medicare-Fee-for-Service-Payment/ACO/index.html?redirect=/Aco/.

Affordable Care Act Provision	HRSA and CDC Opportunities
Community Transformation Grants (ACA §§ 4002 and 4201) The provision authorizes and funds community transformation grants to improve community health activities and outcomes.	• Given that Community Transformation Grants can be viewed as the public health counterpart to the Centers for Medicare & Medicaid Services (CMS) Innovation Center (CMMI) pilots, HRSA and CDC should be aware of the communities where both of these programs are involved. • As community resources for wellness improve through the Transformation Grant system, it may be possible to encourage state and local health department recipients to develop linkages with primary care providers as a central focus of their program planning. • CDC could also begin to link those resources to CMMI pilots, which must be able to link their patients and physician practices with community resources.
Community Health Needs Assessments (ACA § 9007) The provision amends the Internal Revenue Code by adding new § 501(r), "additional requirements for certain hospitals." The new requirements apply to all facilities licensed as hospitals and organizations recognized by the Treasury Secretary as hospitals and spell out new obligations for all hospitals seeking federal tax-exempt status.	• HRSA and CDC could engage with community hospitals and national hospital associations to develop approaches to hospital community benefit planning, as well as to promote a joint approach to the selection of interventions and implementation strategies to address identified problems (for example, the extension of primary care services into nontraditional settings; the formation of collaboratives among community primary care providers and local public health and other agencies; and community health promotion activities involving diet, exercise, and injury risk reduction, as well as other population-level interventions).

Table 11.1   ACA Provisions and HRSA/CDC Opportunities

Affordable Care Act Provision	HRSA and CDC Opportunities
Medicaid Preventive Services (ACA §§ 4106 and 2001) (ACA § 4108) The provision gives states the option to improve coverage of clinical preventive services for traditional eligibility groups, as well as Medicaid benchmark coverage for newly eligible persons, redefined to parallel the Act's definition of essential health benefits, which includes coverage for preventive services. It also provides Medicaid incentives for prevention of chronic diseases.	• Primary care providers and public health departments could become participating Medicaid providers and collaborate in designing programs to furnish preventive services to adult and child populations. • HRSA and CDC could collaborate with CMS on the development of joint guidance regarding coverage of preventive services. Such guidance might explain both the required and optional preventive service provisions of the law, as well as federal financing incentives for coverage of those services. Such guidance also might describe best practices in making preventive services more accessible to Medicaid beneficiaries through the use of expanded managed care provider networks and out-of-network coverage in nontraditional locations such as schools, public housing, and workplace sites; qualification criteria for participating providers; recruitment of providers; measurement of quality performance; and assessment of impact on population health. • HRSA and CDC have a crucial role to play in the implementation of state demonstrations, particularly in outreach to community providers to enlist them as active participants in such demonstrations, training and technical support to state Medicaid agencies, outreach to public health departments and health centers in demonstration states, and collaboration with CMS on the development of outcome standards and scalability criteria.

Table 11.1   (continued)

Affordable Care Act Provision	HRSA and CDC Opportunities
Community Health Centers (ACA § 5601) The provision expands funding for health centers.	• An imperative for HRSA is to preserve and strengthen the role of health centers as core safety-net providers of clinical care and prevention in the communities they serve. Incentives could be built into funding for these centers to promote activities and linkages with local public health departments and encourage community engagement and partnerships for community-based prevention. • Outreach campaigns to promote clinical preventive services in underserved communities, as well as initiatives aimed at improving the quality of primary care for populations with serious and chronic health conditions, could focus on how to improve the performance of health centers.
National Prevention, Health Promotion and Public Health Council and the National Prevention Strategy (ACA § 4001) The provision creates the National Prevention, Health Promotion and Public Health Council to create a collaborative national strategy to address health in the nation.	• HRSA and CDC could use the Council as a mechanism for working with other agencies around the integration of primary care and public health.
CMS Innovation Center (CMMI) (ACA § 3021) The provision establishes CMMI to develop, conduct, and evaluate pilots for improving quality, efficiency, and patient health outcomes in both the Medicare and Medicaid programs, with an emphasis on dual enrollees.	• HRSA and CDC could engage with CMMI in the implementation of its community health innovation program to develop models that would leverage clinical care to achieve a broader impact on population health. • In the CMMI provisions of the ACA and elsewhere in the Act, a major thrust of healthcare reform is attention to dually eligible Medicare/Medicaid beneficiaries. HRSA and CDC could develop an initiative aimed at improving the health and health care of this population.

Table 11.1 *(continued)*

Affordable Care Act Provision	HRSA and CDC Opportunities
Accountable care organizations (ACOs) (ACA § 3022) The provision authorizes the Secretary of the Department of Health and Human Services (HHS) to enter into agreements with ACOs on a shared savings basis to improve the quality of patient care and health outcomes and increase efficiency.	• HRSA could encourage health centers to form ACOs and link with public health departments in this endeavor. • HRSA and CDC could develop models of collaboration between public health departments and ACOs that include safety-net providers. Such models might emphasize the role of public health in needs assessment, performance measurement and improvement, health promotion, and patient engagement, all of which are central elements of ACOs.
Patient-centered medical homes (ACA § 3502) The provision authorizes state Medicaid programs to establish medical homes for Medicaid beneficiaries with chronic health conditions, and authorizes the Secretary of HHS to award grants for the establishment of health teams to support primary care.	• HRSA and CDC could collaborate on further development of the medical home model and its team-based approach to care and encourage the inclusion of local public health departments in that model. • HRSA and CDC could provide technical support to state Medicaid agencies seeking to pursue the medical home model, imparting best practices in the design and development of a medical home that is comprehensive, efficient in care delivery, and patient-/family-centered. This support could also be expanded to include the development of performance measurement tools for measuring progress in these areas. • HRSA and CDC could develop a sustainable model for the medical home in Medicare and Medicaid that encourages inclusion of local public health departments, supports multiple population types, and can be translated for private health insurance as well.

Table 11.1 (continued)

Affordable Care Act Provision	HRSA and CDC Opportunities
Primary Care Extension Program (ACA § 5405) The provision authorizes the Agency for Healthcare Research and Quality (AHRQ) to award competitive grants to states for the establishment of Primary Care Extension Programs to improve the delivery of primary care and community health.	• HRSA and CDC could work with AHRQ to ensure that Primary Care Extension Programs include a public health orientation and integrate community health issues into practice- and clinic-based primary care improvement activities. • HRSA and CDC, working jointly with AHRQ, could seek collaboration with CMMI to fund Primary Care Extension Program models for which there is evidence for improving personal and population health.
National Health Service Corps (ACA § 5207) The provision expands funding for the National Health Service Corps.	• HRSA and CDC could collaborate in prioritizing the recruitment and placement of National Health Service Corps resources and developing linkages with existing Epidemic Intelligence Service (EIS) officers placed in state and local health departments.
Teaching Health Centers (ACA § 5508) The provision authorizes and funds the establishment of and ongoing operational support for teaching health centers, which must be community-based.	• HRSA could work with teaching health centers to adopt the patient-centered medical home curriculum and ensure that any curriculum used to train residents includes strong community and public health components—ideally with residents working on projects that concretely promote primary care-public health integration. • HRSA and CDC could work with the centers on training programs that would be aimed at producing competency to work in community health teams, given the emphasis placed on teams under the ACA.

Table 11.1   *(continued)*

if there is a reasonable connection between the items and services and the patient's medical care and the items or services are preventive care items or services or advance a clinical goal for the patient.[30] Thus, for example, an ACO may offer its patients free health coaching, disease management, and/or fitness or nutrition services, to help keep its patients on track to completing clinical goals or preventing further medical conditions. Patients who adhere to these preventive measures should save the ACO money, which means an increase in the potential for shared savings. ACOs should be willing to use this legal provision in the MSSP program to invest in wellness items and services for the ACO's patients.

Another ACA provision of which wellness professionals can take advantage is the **annual wellness visit (AWV)** for Medicare beneficiaries. The AWV includes the establishment of, or update to, the individual's medical and family history, and measurement of his or her height, weight, body-mass index or waist circumference, and blood pressure, with the goal of health promotion and disease detection and fostering the coordination of the screening and preventive services that may already be covered and paid for by Medicare.[31] Medical professionals such as health educators, registered dietitians, nutrition professionals, or other licensed practitioners may provide the AWV under the direct supervision of a physician.[32] Thus, the law permits many wellness professionals to provide AWVs for a physician clinic. Indeed, one primary care physician wrote about his positive experience with adding a health educator to his practice to conduct the AWVs.[33] In that clinic, the health educator promoted the AWVs with patient outreach and education.[34] Then, when patients came in for the AWV, she would spend 45 minutes

---

30 42 C.F.R. § 425.304(a)(2).
31 CMS, "Annual Wellness Visit (AWV), Including Personalized Prevention Plan Services (PPPS)," *MLN Matters* No. MM7079 (March 2, 2016), https://www.cms.gov/Outreach-and-Education/Medicare-Learning-Network-MLN/MLNMattersArticles/downloads/mm7079.pdf (citing ACA § 4103 and 42 C.F.R. §§ 411.15(a)(1) and 411.15(k)(15)).
32 *Id.* Direct supervision in the office setting means the physician must be present in the office suite and immediately available to furnish assistance and direction throughout the performance of the procedure. It does not mean that the physician must be present in the room when the procedure is performed. 42 C.F.R. § 410.32(b)(3)(ii).
33 M. Lee Chambliss et al., "Adding Health Education Specialists to Your Practice," *Family Practice Management* (March/April 2014): 10, http://www.aafp.org/fpm/2014/0300/p10.html.
34 *Id.* at 11–12.

to an hour with the patient conducting the different measures and working on education and personal motivation.[35]

Not only did the clinic raise enough revenue from the Medicare reimbursement rate for the AWV to pay for the health educator,[36] it also added what some are calling the "blockbuster drug" of the century: patient engagement.[37] Studies have shown that patient engagement improves patients' health and reduces healthcare use and costs.[38] It can also have a positive impact on health outcomes, medication adherence, and rates of hospital admission.[39] Yet, to play an active role in their own health care, patients need information and motivation.[40] Wellness professionals are well suited to provide information and motivation to patients about their health. More medical providers should take advantage of the AWV and the skills of wellness professionals as a mechanism to engage patients in their own health. To make this happen, wellness professionals must reach out to the medical community and educate them on how wellness professionals can help improve patient outcomes and reduce overall healthcare costs.

In addition to reaching out to the medical community, wellness professionals and organizations should also reach out to the health insurance community to help them comply with another ACA provision that took effect in the fall of 2016: the **Quality Improvement Strategy (QIS)**. The ACA requires health plans that have participated in the federal insurance "Marketplace" or "Exchange" for two consecutive years to implement a QIS that offers incentives to providers or health plan enrollees with the aim of improving health.[41] As part of the QIS, health plans must include at least one of the following:

1. Activities for improving health outcomes
2. Activities to prevent hospital readmissions

---

35 *Id.*

36 Chambliss et al., "Adding Health Education Specialists to Your Practice," at 14.

37 Laurance et al., "Patient Engagement," at 16–27.

38 *Id.*

39 *Id.*

40 Laurance et al., "Patient Engagement," at 16–28.

41 Health Insurance Marketplace, *Quality Improvement Strategy: Technical Guidance and User Guide for the 2017 Coverage Year* (November 5, 2015): 6, https://www.cms.gov/Medicare/Quality-Initiatives-Patient-Assessment-Instruments/QualityInitiativesGenInfo/Downloads/QIS-Technical-Guidance-and-User-Guide.pdf (citing ACA § 1311(g)).

3. Activities to improve patient safety and reduce medical errors
4. Activities for wellness and health promotion; and/or
5. Activities to reduce health and healthcare disparities.[42]

Plans must link these activities to an incentive.[43] For providers, the incentive may be a higher level of payment or a bonus payment awarded when the provider meets certain quality performance targets.[44] Alternatively, the plan may give the provider resources, such as physician practice transformation and clinical support. Plans may decide to incentivize enrollees through a monetary reduction of what an enrollee pays for premiums and other out-of-pocket costs (e.g., co-payments or coinsurance).[45] Plans could provide these rewards to enrollees as a result of the enrollee making certain choices or exhibiting healthy behaviors, such as seeking preventive services, seeking high-value providers, or accessing nutritional counseling.[46]

One of the eligible activities health plans can implement are wellness and health promotion activities. Examples of these types of activities include smoking cessation, weight management, stress management, healthy lifestyle support, and diabetes prevention.[47] To administer these activities to health plan enrollees, health plans should hire or contract with wellness professionals and organizations. Wellness professionals and organizations can use this ACA provision to move beyond the workplace by connecting with health plans and showing those plans how the wellness industry can help them meet the QIS requirement.

These are just some examples of how wellness professionals and organizations can use the ACA to apply their knowledge and skills in venues outside the workplace. Over the years, the workplace wellness industry has produced valuable research, tools, and skilled professionals to engage people in their health and well-being. The health industry could benefit from the knowledge and resources of the workplace wellness industry. It may be up to the workplace wellness industry to lead the integration

---

42 *Id.* at 6 (emphasis added).
43 *Id.* at 7.
44 *Id.*
45 *Id.*
46 *Id.*
47 Health Insurance Marketplace, *Quality Improvement Strategy*, at 8.

effort by learning about ACA opportunities, thinking creatively about collaborating with other sectors, and communicating the common goal of improving health.

Precision Wellness

It is no secret that workplace wellness has its critics.[48] Critics question whether wellness programs truly reduce employer health costs.[49] Yet, part of the problem with evaluating the effectiveness of wellness programs is that there is no statutory, regulatory, or uniform definition of the term *wellness program*.[50] Similarly, there is no uniform definition of *wellness*. Indeed, people may disagree on whether someone is experiencing wellness in his or her life.

The truth is, it may be impossible to define wellness, and in turn, a wellness program. Just as the healthcare industry is adopting a precision medicine model to enhance the effectiveness of health care, as discussed in Chapter 9, workplace wellness may have to move further toward a **precision wellness model**. In fact, the authors argue that it must move in that direction if workplace wellness desires to remain relevant to and trustworthy for its beneficiaries. Precision wellness demands adoption of a more diverse view of what constitutes health and wellness. Adhering to typical stereotypes will no longer suffice.

According to a national study, people who encountered the threat of being judged by negative stereotypes related to weight, age, race, gender, or social class in healthcare settings reported adverse health effects.[51] Specifically, the researchers found that those people were more likely to

---

48 *See, e.g.,* Al Lewis, Vik Khanna, and Shana Montrose, "Workplace Wellness Produces No Savings," Health Affairs Blog (November 25, 2014), http://healthaffairs.org/blog/2014/11/25/workplace-wellness-produces-no-savings/.
49 *Id.*
50 Bahaudin G. Mujtaba and Frank J. Cavico, "Corporate Wellness Programs: Implementation Challenges in the Modern American Workplace," *Int'l J. Health Pol'y & Mgmt.* 1, no. 3 (2013): 193–199, http://www.ncbi.nlm.nih.gov/pmc/articles/PMC3937880/pdf/ijhpm-1-193.pdf.
51 University of Southern California, "Healthcare: How Stereotypes Hurt: Stereotypes in Health Care Environment Can Mean Poorer Health Outcomes," *ScienceDaily* (2014), www.sciencedaily.com/releases/2015/10/151020091344.htm.

have hypertension, to be depressed, and to rate their own health more poorly.[52] They were also more distrustful of their doctors, felt dissatisfied with their care, and were less likely to use highly accessible preventive care, including the flu vaccine.[53] Although the researchers studied the healthcare industry, one could easily extrapolate the problem and the findings to the workplace wellness industry. Negative stereotypes regarding weight, age, race, gender, or social class in workplace wellness programs can reduce the efficacy of those programs. To address healthcare stereotype threats, the researchers recommend implementing policies that enhance medical school training in cultural competency and increasing the diversity of the healthcare workforce.[54] One possible training tool to help achieve this goal is a kit (a DVD and CD-ROM) produced by the American Medical Association (AMA) entitled "Working Together to End Racial and Ethnic Disparities One Physician at a Time."[55] The DVD features interviews with healthcare professionals and patients who have experienced disparities in health care firsthand; the CD-ROM covers components of healthcare disparities such as quality of care, trust and stereotyping, cultural competency, language barriers, and health literacy.

The workplace wellness industry should take similar action. In order to be more inclusive, workplace wellness professionals and organizations need training in cultural competency, and there should be more diversity in the industry's leadership.

Cultural Competency Training

For cultural competency, several government resources are available, such as the CDC and *Healthy People 2020* websites. Specific to worksite wellness programs, see "Addressing Diversity and Health Literacy at the Workplace," a chapter in *ACSM's Worksite Health Handbook.*[56]

---

52 *Id.*

53 *Id.*

54 *Id.*

55 American Medical Association, *Working Together to End Racial and Ethnic Disparities One Physician at a Time* (2005). DVD and CD-ROM.

56 Antronette K. Yancey, A. Janet Tomiyama, and Nicole R. Keith, "Addressing Diversity and Health Literacy at the Worksite," in *ACSM's Worksite Health Handbook*, ed. Nicolas P. Pronk (Champaign, IL: Human Kinetics, 2009): 214–223.

This ACSM handbook chapter provides an overview of diversity issues in workplace wellness programs, as well as potential solutions for workplace wellness professionals to address diversity issues in the design and delivery of programs.

Training in cultural competency and recognition of the importance of diversity can assist in the adoption of precision wellness by creating a deeper understanding and appreciation for individual needs and differences. Blaming and stereotyping often originate from personal dispositions or biases. Training in this area is especially important for wellness professionals. Research[57] has shown that exercise science students (both undergraduate and graduate) possess negative associations and bias toward obese individuals. Academic programs as well as continuing education efforts of professional organizations should address this bias in their educational programs, as well as other potential biases regarding age, ethnicity, physical competence, gender, and sexual orientation.[58]

In addition, part of the cultural competency in workplace wellness goal must include compliance training. The need for more comprehensive compliance training is discussed further later. However, for purposes of attaining greater diversity, the workplace wellness community could benefit from learning the law, particularly civil rights laws, which can serve as a useful guide in designing and implementing inclusive wellness programs. When used appropriately, the law can remind workplace wellness professionals and organizations that all persons, regardless of ability, gender, race, religion, or age, should be able to participate and enjoy the benefits of workplace wellness.

Diversity in Leadership

Diversity in what it means to be well is a byproduct of adopting a precision wellness initiative. In order to effectively embrace diversity, the workplace wellness industry must do a better job of reflecting that diversity in its leadership. Two examples of what that diversity might

---

57 Heather O. Chambliss, Carrie E. Finley, and Steven N. Blair, "Attitudes Toward Obese Individuals Among Exercise Science Students," *Med. & Sci. in Sports & Exercise* 36, no. 3 (March 2004): 468–474.
58 Deana Melton and Teresa Dail, "Preparing Students for a Diverse Workplace: Strategies to Improve Dispositions," *J. Phys. Educ., Recreation & Dance* 81, no. 9 (November/December 2010): 25–31, 46.

look like are two women who are shattering traditional notions of what it means to be physically fit and well.

Mirna Valerio[59]

Mirna is a 250-pound, African-American distance runner. Her BMI is 39.2. Yet, she is a marathoner, ultramarathoner, and trail runner. She is also accepting of her body and has learned that no matter how much she runs and how carefully she controls what she eats, her weight will not go below 240 pounds. Mirna is not alone. There are countless others who, despite exercising and following a high-quality diet, can only whittle their BMI to a certain point.[60] They need to live healthfully with the disease of obesity, rather than making themselves miserable trying to "cure" themselves of it.[61] Indeed, as Mirna's story shows, scales do not measure the presence or absence of health. Rather, weight is a combination of genetic, behavioral, environmental, and psychological factors, and varies tremendously from individual to individual.[62] Mirna's destruction of the traditional runner stereotype is inspiring others, who also may not fit that traditional stereotype, to run.[63]

Jessamyn Stanley[64]

Jessamyn is a 27-year-old African-American woman who describes herself as a "yoga enthusiast and fat femme."[65] She is also a yoga teacher who can do all types of yoga poses.[66] She has more than 40,000 Instagram followers who see photos of her doing the splits, a forearm stand, and downward dog.[67] She rejects the idea of trying to emulate the models featured in Western media.[68] Her message is resonating with women

---

59 John Brant, "Ultra: Is It Possible to Be Fat and Fit?," *Runner's World* (July 21, 2015), http://www.runnersworld.com/runners-stories/ultra.
60 *Id.*
61 *Id.*
62 *Id.*
63 *Id.*
64 Leigh Weingus, "How This Badass Yogi Is Teaching Women to Love Their Bodies," *Huffington Post* (May 29, 2015), http://www.huffingtonpost.com/2015/05/29/jessamyn-yoga-teacher_n_7471232.html.
65 *Id.*
66 *Id.*
67 *Id.*
68 *Id.*

all over the world.[69] They are hungry for yoga teachers with whom they can relate.[70]

The workplace wellness industry needs more role models like Mirna and Jessamyn. If those two women can inspire others to engage in healthy activities like running and yoga because they are more relatable, then workplace wellness must seek role models who represent the diversity of what it means to be fit and well. Using the principles of civil rights laws such as the ADA, Title VII, GINA, and HIPAA as a guide, the workplace wellness industry can proactively recruit role models who do not fit the traditional mold of a healthy individual. By moving away from blaming or stereotyping, more people may become engaged in their health and well-being. Also, as noted by one researcher, even small gains for individuals, when repeated across hundreds of millions of people, can translate into major advances in health.[71]

Compliance Training, Standards, and Guidance

A third direction the workplace wellness industry should take is to develop training and standards for workplace wellness compliance and guidelines on how to implement those standards. As discussed throughout this book, to be truly effective in compliance, one must adopt a preventive law approach. To successfully adopt a preventive law approach, one needs to fully understand and appreciate the legal landscape of workplace wellness programs. As noted in the preface to this book, this full understanding and appreciation can be accomplished by learning about the "What, Why, and How" of workplace wellness laws. See Figure 11.1.

A full understanding of and appreciation for workplace wellness laws are currently missing in the workplace wellness industry. Yet, before assessing what is missing in the industry, it is critical to first recognize what the industry has accomplished.

---

69 *Id.*
70 *Id.*
71 Laurance et al., "Patient Engagement," *supra* note 21, at 1627.

Figure 11.1   The What, Why, and How of Workplace Wellness Laws

Workplace Wellness Industry Accomplishments

The industry has made significant strides in establishing best practices and criteria needed for comprehensive workplace wellness programs, such as through the WELCOA Seven Benchmarks listed in Chapter 2 of this book, the Centers for Disease Control and Prevention (CDC) Scorecard,[72] and the Health Enhancement Research Organization (HERO) Scorecard.[73] These tools can help workplace wellness professionals assess the "comprehensiveness" of their program, and also help them identify evidence-based strategies to implement effective workplace wellness programs. As noted

---

72 Centers for Disease Control and Prevention, *The CDC Worksite Health ScoreCard: An Assessment Tool for Employers to Prevent Heart Disease, Stroke, and Related Health Conditions* (Atlanta: U.S. Department of Health and Human Services, 2014), http://www.cdc.gov/dhdsp/pubs/docs/hsc_manual.pdf.
73 HERO, "Health and Well-Being Best Practices Scorecard Fact Sheet" (2014), http://hero-health.org/scorecard/.

in Chapter 2, using these tools can create a solid foundation on which to build a workplace wellness program.

The workplace wellness industry has also established accreditation mechanisms and accredited programs to properly recognize and train workplace wellness programs and professionals. For example, the National Committee for Quality Assurance (NCQA) offers a Wellness and Health Promotion accreditation for workplace wellness programs. NCQA's program:

- **Assesses health plans and vendors that provide wellness services** using an evidence-based set of requirements to distinguish quality services
- **Comprehensively evaluates key areas of health promotion,** including how wellness programs are implemented in the workplace, how services such as coaching are provided to help participants develop skills to make healthy choices, and how individual health information is properly safeguarded
- **Uses standardized program measures** that allow employers to make informed comparisons when choosing among several wellness vendors[74]

This accreditation helps employers determine whether a wellness program offering meets certain criteria deemed by NCQA to be worthy of recognition.

There are also accredited academic programs throughout the United States for preparation of workplace wellness professionals. These academic programs are in health education, public health, exercise science, and health promotion and wellness. Professional organizations, such as the National Wellness Institute, WELCOA, and the International Association of Worksite Health Promotion, as well as many local workplace wellness councils, offer education, training, and certifications for workplace wellness professionals.

Finally, the workplace wellness industry has developed a plethora of textbooks, journals, articles, newsletters, websites, professional conferences,

---

74 NCQA, "Wellness and Health Promotion Accreditation Fact Sheet," http://www.ncqa.org/programs/accreditation/wellness-health-promotion-accreditation#sthash.H46GQGz0.dpuf.

and webinars that provide workplace wellness professionals with the knowledge and skills to be successful. For example, Dr. Michael O'Donnell has authored a comprehensive text entitled *Health Promotion in the Workplace* (4th ed.), which covers health promotion program management; theories of behavior change; and core components such as health assessments, fitness, nutrition, tobacco prevention, and employee assistance programs, as well as the importance of social relationships and organizational culture.[75]

Compliance Training, Standards, and Guidance: The Missing Link for Workplace Wellness

Despite the wealth of information available to workplace wellness professionals and organizations, none of these resources adequately addresses workplace wellness laws and regulations. For example, the CDC Scorecard briefly addresses the HIPAA/ACA incentive rules, but fails to address the myriad of data privacy and security concerns, tax issues, practitioner competency, workers' compensation concerns, regulatory oversight over laboratories or devices, contractual matters, or the role of civil rights laws in workplace wellness program design. Certainly some of the resources available to the workplace wellness industry address some legal compliance concerns, but the efforts are incomplete. For example, the NCQA accreditation for wellness programs has questions relating to whether the program protects the confidentiality of information of individuals and whether the program addresses the rights of individuals.[76] However, the accreditation program offers no guidance on what various laws may apply to the program, how the program can best comply with those laws, and why it is important to comply with those laws. Moreover, the accreditation program lacks comprehensiveness as to the types of laws that may apply to many workplace wellness programs, such as workers' compensation and Fair Labor Standards Act issues, civil rights issues beyond disability, and the legal issues raised by wearable technology and mHealth.

---

75 Journal of Health Promotion, "Health Promotion in the Workplace Fact Sheet," http://
healthpromotionjournal.com/index.php?com_route=pages&view=health-promotion-in-the-workplace.
76 NCQA, "Wellness and Health Promotion Accreditation Fact Sheet."

Because of these deficiencies, workplace wellness professionals and organizations are not receiving the education and training they need to properly comply with all the laws and regulations that apply to workplace wellness programs. As a result, current programming may not be as effective, sensitive, and inclusive as it could be with comprehensive compliance training, standards, and guidance. Workplace wellness compliance training can help professionals and organizations appreciate the different needs of individuals, the importance of adhering to the rules, and the risk involved when one does not adhere to the rules. This appreciation can lead to workplace wellness programs that are more sensitive to participant concerns and needs, which will undoubtedly increase the level of trust by participants in those programs. This book and its accompanying training curriculum are meant to be a start for that training effort.

It may also be helpful for workplace wellness leaders and organizations to work together to develop national standards and guidelines in workplace wellness compliance that could be incorporated into many of the existing workplace wellness resources referenced in this book. For example, workplace wellness organizations could collaborate to create a document that identifies compliance standards, guidelines, and maybe even a uniform code of ethics for all workplace wellness program professionals. The group could define *compliance standards* as the legal requirements that workplace wellness programs must meet to be considered a best-practice program. These standards could fill the gap that currently exists in the law, such as with data privacy.

As discussed in Chapter 9, there are many laws that could address data privacy in the workplace wellness context, but there are some gray areas. There may be some programs that are outside the purview of any of those data privacy laws. Those programs may rely on guidance by federal agencies, such as the Federal Trade Commission (FTC), but those guidelines may not apply or relate well to the unique issues faced by workplace wellness individuals and organizations. The collaborative group could assess each of those laws and form privacy and security standards that best-practice workplace wellness programs should follow, even though they may not be legally required to do so. The group could also produce standards that include a requirement to follow and become trained on the laws that impact workplace wellness programs.

One benefit of the industry creating its own standards is a reduction in the perceived need for external regulation and control.[77] As discussed in Chapter 4, government authorities such as the EEOC are taking a great interest in workplace wellness programs. If the workplace wellness industry invests the effort to construct compliance standards for its members, and those members adopt those standards, there may be less need for external regulators to police industry stakeholders.

The collaborative group could also create guidelines for the workplace wellness industry, which the group could define as recommendations on how to properly implement workplace wellness laws. Although some existing workplace wellness resources identify some of the laws that affect workplace wellness, there is a shortage of clear guidance on how best to implement and integrate those laws into workplace wellness programs. Just as the industry has created best practices in employee motivation, wellness program marketing and evaluation, the industry should also develop best practices for workplace wellness program compliance.

Finally, the collaborative group could include in its compliance document a "Code of Ethics" for wellness professionals. As noted earlier, many different professions and individuals identify themselves as part of the workplace wellness profession. There are a number of certification programs for the profession. However, there has not been a uniform code of ethics for those working in the field. Because of this diversity in the field, it may be helpful for the workplace wellness industry to create a set of ethical expectations for those working in the industry. The expectations could address areas such as collecting, handling, storing, and disclosing sensitive information; ensuring competency to perform activities; communicating effectively across different cultures; and prohibiting discrimination based on a program participant's various characteristics.

---

77 Susan Jacob, Dawn M. Decker, and Timothy S. Hartshorne, *Ethics and Law for School Psychologists*, 6th ed. (Hoboken, NJ: Wiley, 2011): 6.

Some of this collaborative work has already started. Wellness industry leaders Ryan Picarella, Al Lewis, Rosie Ward, and Jon Robison have created an industry Code of Conduct that sets minimum standards to help wellness programs meet employer and employee expectations.[78] The Code of Conduct that these leaders advocate wellness programs should adopt is as follows:

1. Programs Should Do No Harm. "Our organization resolves that its program should do no harm to employee health, corporate integrity or employee/employer finances. Instead we will endeavor to support employee well-being for our customers, their employees and all program constituents."

2. Employee Benefits and Harm Avoidance. "Our organization will recommend doing programs with/for employees rather than to them, and will focus on promoting well-being and avoiding bad health outcomes. Our choices and frequencies of screenings are consistent with the United States Preventive Services Task Force (USPSTF), CDC guidelines, and Choosing Wisely."

3. Respect for Corporate Integrity and Employee Privacy. "We will not share employee-identifiable data with employers and will ensure that all protected health information (PHI) adheres to HIPAA regulations and any other applicable laws."

4. Commitment to Valid Outcomes Measurement. "Our contractual language and outcomes reporting will be transparent and plausible. All research limitations (e.g., 'participants vs. non-participants' or the 'natural flow of risk' or ignoring dropouts) and methodology will be fully disclosed, sourced, and readily available."[79]

The benefits of a collaborative effort to develop compliance standards and guidelines are many. First, a collaborative effort by the existing

---

78 Rosie Ward, Ph.D., The Employee Health Program Code of Conduct: Programs Should Do No Harm, LinkedIn (August 12, 2016), https://www.linkedin.com/pulse/employee-health-program-code-conduct-programs-should-do-ward-ph-d-?trk=hp-feed-article-title-publish (last visited January 6, 2017).
79 Id.

workplace wellness groups will lead to stakeholder buy-in and support. Second, the very exercise of meeting among collaborators will provide a helpful "training" for those collaborators and will produce a document that can serve as a training resource for the industry, along with this book. Third, establishing and adhering to a compliance standard and guideline document can minimize legal liability for workplace wellness programs—something that most employers will appreciate. Fourth, as advocated throughout this book, adopting compliance standards and guidelines in workplace wellness programs will enhance the quality and effectiveness of those programs. Fifth, compliance standards and guidelines can address the previously discussed lack of cultural competency and diversity by ensuring that the standards account for the different needs and abilities of wellness program participants. Sixth, compliance standards and guidelines can increase the operational efficiency for workplace wellness professionals by taking out much of the guesswork on how to comply with workplace wellness program laws and regulations.

Finally, by adopting workplace wellness compliance standards and guidelines, the industry can enhance the reputation of both workplace wellness programs and the professionals who work within it. The public may see the existence of standards and guidelines in workplace wellness program compliance as a sign of maturity and a genuine concern to do right by employee health.

RULE THE RULES

Key Points in Chapter 11

1. There is a need for the healthcare and wellness industries to work together to achieve a common goal of improving population health.

2. Workplace wellness professionals who have excellent skills in obtaining employee engagement can provide assistance to enhance patient engagement in healthcare settings.

3. Workplace wellness professionals can lead various efforts, through the ACA's National Prevention Strategy and other ACA initiatives, to improve the health of communities.

4. Specific ACA healthcare initiatives that workplace wellness professionals can help develop and implement include (a) offering wellness services to accountable care organizations, (b) providing and conducting annual wellness visits for physician clinics, and (c) assisting the health insurance community in complying with the Quality Improvement Strategy.

5. There is a need for the workplace wellness to move toward a precision wellness model that includes cultural competency and compliance training for wellness professionals, and increases diversity among wellness professionals.

6. Although many accomplishments have been made in workplace wellness, there is a missing link among these accomplishments: the lack of and need for compliance training and the development of standards and guidelines that reflect the many workplace wellness laws. These needs can be addressed through a collaborative effort among wellness leaders and organizations.

7. Many positive outcomes can occur from such collaborative efforts: (a) reducing the need for external regulation, (b) providing resources for training of wellness staff and stakeholders, (c) enhancing the quality of programs and services, and (d) enhancing cultural competency and diversity.

Study Questions

1. Compare and contrast the healthcare and insurance industries with the wellness industry with regard to wellness care.

2. Describe how traditional healthcare models are slowly eroding and the opportunities this may provide for wellness professionals.

3. Describe ACA initiatives that workplace wellness professionals can assist with to enhance the health of communities.

4. Prepare a written document outlining how workplace wellness professionals can assist (a) healthcare providers to achieve ACS

initiatives involving ACOs and AWVs, and (b) health insurance providers to meet the ACA provisions of the QIS.

5. Explain how the experiences of Mirna Valerio and Jessamyn Stanley justify the need for a precision wellness model that involves training in cultural competency and diversity.

6. List the many accomplishments that have been achieved in the workplace wellness field and, for each, describe how the topic of workplace wellness laws and regulations could be included.

7. Describe the benefits that could result if national standards and guidelines addressing workplace wellness laws and regulations were made available to all workplace wellness stakeholders.

Key Terms

ACA provisions
accountable care organization (ACO)
annual wellness visit (AWV)
employee engagement
Exercise Is Medicine

patient engagement
population health
precision wellness model
Quality Improvement Strategy (QIS)
self-improvement wellness care
traditional healthcare models

Afterword

By Barbara J. Zabawa, JD, MPH

When I started the Center for Health and Wellness Law, LLC, in 2014, I set out to connect my passion for preventive health care with my interest in preventive law and skills as a lawyer. It was around that same time that the EEOC had two cases pending against Wisconsin employers for their workplace wellness programs. Being located in Wisconsin, I had great interest in those cases. I soon realized that there were little to no resources for workplace wellness professionals to learn about legal risks in designing workplace wellness programs. I found very few presentations and articles on the topic, and no books. In fact, I found no one in the legal community committed solely to understanding and helping the workplace wellness industry, particularly from the perspective of those creating and delivering the wellness items and services. My purpose was born.

I decided to write a book regarding workplace wellness law to demonstrate the wide array of laws that affect workplace wellness program design and implementation. As one can see from the number of legal topics covered in this book, the legal landscape is vast and extends way beyond the laws regarding financial incentives. However, this book does not cover every possible law that may affect or implicate workplace wellness programs. In particular, it does not address the numerous state and local laws that often play a role in workplace wellness program design and implementation. For example, it does not cover state laws that prohibit discrimination based on use of lawful products outside of work, such as tobacco or alcohol. Wisconsin, my home state, has such a law, and thus these considerations must be factored into any workplace wellness program design in Wisconsin. It would be a daunting task to adequately address all state and local laws in a single book. As a result, it is important for the reader to know that ruling the rules discussed in this book is not the end of the story. Workplace wellness professionals and organizations should also consult with local legal counsel to ensure that their programs comply with state and local laws.

Nevertheless, this book attempts to serve as a resource for workplace wellness professionals and organizations, to at least help them appreciate the assortment of different laws that affect workplace wellness programs. For those professionals who participate in the accompanying training curriculum, the book will provide foundational knowledge about workplace wellness program compliance. Armed with this knowledge, the professional can feel more confident about recognizing compliance red flags when designing or implementing workplace wellness programs.

The path to ruling the rules is to know what they are about and why they exist. Equipped with this knowledge, the wellness professional can use the rules purposefully in designing a wellness program. In fact, the wellness professional gains a deeper understanding of why rules exist and the people whom the rules aim to protect. Perhaps this knowledge will persuade wellness professionals and organizations to think more broadly and strive to implement programs that are more inclusive and sensitive to the diverse needs of the people they serve.

It is my goal to make the law more accessible so that it can serve as a guide rather than a burden. This book is the first step in that process. In the end, what matters is that people embrace well living. I hope wellness professionals and organizations use this book to design better programs that improve the lives of more people. I can think of no higher professional satisfaction.

Glossary

The following key terms are defined as used in this book. *Black's Law Dictionary* is cited for certain legal terms.

ACA provisions   Provisions of the Affordable Care Act (ACA) that can facilitate the convergence between health care and wellness.

accountable care organizations (ACOs)   Groups of doctors, hospitals, and other healthcare providers, who come together voluntarily to give coordinated, high-quality care to their patients and who are held accountable for those efforts.

accreditation   A credentialing method to reward organizations/ programs that meet certain standards established by the accrediting agency.

administrative law   Body of law created by administrative agencies in the form of rules, regulations, orders, and decisions to carry out regulatory powers and duties of such agencies. *Black's Law Dictionary* (6th ed., 1990): 46.

annual wellness visit (AWV)   An Affordable Care Act provision for Medicare beneficiaries that includes the establishment of, or update to, the individual's medical and family history, and measurement of his or her height, weight, body mass index or waist circumference, and blood pressure, with the goal of health promotion and disease detection and fostering the coordination of the screening and preventive services that may already be covered and paid for by Medicare.

appellate court   A court higher than the trial court to which a party in a civil case or the defendant in a criminal case can appeal the trial court's decision.

arbitration   A process of dispute resolution in which a neutral third party (arbitrator) renders a decision after a hearing at which both parties have an opportunity to be heard. Where arbitration is voluntary, the disputing parties select the arbitrator who has the power to render a binding decision. *Black's Law Dictionary* (6th ed., 1990): 105.

authorization form   The form required by the Genetic Information Nondiscrimination Act (GINA) that employees and spouses must sign before providing genetic information as part of a health risk assessment or biometric screen.

best practices   Practices developed by the workplace wellness community that can be used to develop a solid corporate culture that supports preventive law practice.

Big Data   Shorthand for the combination of a technology and a process. The technology consists of information-processing hardware capable of sifting, sorting, and interrogating vast quantities of data in very short time periods. The process involves mining the data for patterns, distilling the patterns into predictive analytics, and applying the analytics to new data. Together, the technology and the process comprise a technique for converting data flows into a particular, highly data-intensive type of knowledge.

biometric screening   The measurement of physical characteristics, such as height, weight, body mass index (BMI), blood pressure, blood cholesterol, blood glucose, and aerobic fitness, that can be done at the workplace and used as part of a workplace health assessment to benchmark and evaluate changes in employee health status over time.

breach of duty   One of the four essential elements of a negligence claim; the action or inaction by the defendant that the plaintiff alleges breached the defendant's duty.

business associate   Person who is not an employee of a HIPAA-covered entity but provides services to a covered entity that requires use or disclosure of protected health information (PHI). Under the HIPAA law, a business associate is defined as a person who, on behalf of a covered entity or an organized healthcare arrangement in which the covered entity participates, but other than in the capacity of a member of the workforce of such covered entity or arrangement, creates, receives, maintains, or transmits PHI for a function or activity regulated by the HIPAA administrative simplification rule, including claims processing or administration, data analysis, processing or administration, utilization review, quality assurance, patient safety activities, billing, benefit management, practice management and repricing; or provides, other than in the capacity of a member of the workforce of such covered entity, legal, actuarial, accounting, consulting, data aggregation, management, administrative, accreditation, or financial services to or for such covered entity, or to or for an organized healthcare arrangement in which the covered entity participates, where the provision of the service involves the disclosure of PHI from such covered entity or arrangement, or from another business associate of such covered entity or arrangement, to the person. 45 C.F.R. § 160.103.

case law   The aggregate of reported cases as forming a body of jurisprudence, or the law of a particular subject as evidenced or formed by the adjudged cases, in distinction to statutes and other sources of law. It includes the aggregate of reported cases that interpret statutes, regulations and constitutional provisions. *Black's Law Dictionary* (6th ed., 1990): 216.

causation   One of the four necessary elements of a negligence claim; the breach of duty by the defendant must have caused the harm suffered by the plaintiff.

certification   A type of credentialing method by which individuals or organizations must meet certain criteria, such as education and passage of an exam for individuals or (in the case of organizations) certain operational conditions, to earn the credential.

certiorari   A writ of common law origin issued by a superior to an inferior court requiring the inferior court to produce a certified record of a particular case tried therein. The writ is issued in order that the court issuing the writ may inspect the proceedings and determine whether there have been any irregularities. It is most commonly used to refer to the Supreme Court of the United States, which uses the writ of certiorari as a discretionary device to choose the cases it wishes to hear. *Black's Law Dictionary* (6th ed., 1990): 228. A petition asking the Supreme Court to hear a case.

civil law   Law concerned with civil or private rights and remedies, as contrasted with criminal laws. *Black's Law Dictionary* (6th ed., 1990): 246.

Deals with disputes between private parties (individuals, organizations, and businesses). Party 1 (plaintiff) hires a lawyer who files a lawsuit claiming that Party 2 (defendant) failed to carry out a legal duty that resulted in some type of harm to Party 1.

cloud Software and services that run on the Internet instead of a separate computer's hard drive or phone's memory.

common law A body of law that develops and derives through judicial decisions, as distinguished from legislative enactments. *Black's Law Dictionary* (6th ed., 1990): 276.

compensatory damages As opposed to punitive damages, compensatory damages compensate the plaintiff for the loss or harm caused; compensatory damages restore the injured party to the position he or she was in prior to the injury.

compliance program A program developed by a company to help the company comply with the law, which can also be used as a basis to practice preventive law.

consumer report Any written, oral, or other communication of any information by a consumer reporting agency bearing on a consumer's creditworthiness, credit standing, credit capacity, character, general reputation, personal characteristics, or mode of living which is used or expected to be used or collected in whole or in part for the purpose of serving as a factor in establishing the consumer's eligibility for (a) credit or insurance to be used primarily for personal, family, or household purposes; (b) employment purposes; or (c) any other purpose authorized under § 604 of the Fair Credit Reporting Act.

consumer reporting agency (CRA) Agency that collects and compiles consumer information into consumer reports for use by credit grantors, insurance companies, employers, landlords, and other entities in making eligibility decisions affecting consumers.

covered entity A term defined by the HIPAA privacy and security rules that refers to health plans, healthcare clearinghouses, and healthcare providers that transmit any health information in electronic form in connection with a covered transaction. 45 C.F.R. § 160.103.

criminal law   Law for the purpose of preventing harm to society. Criminal law (a) declares what conduct is criminal, and (b) prescribes the punishment to be imposed for such conduct. It includes the definition of specific offenses and general principles of liability. Substantive criminal laws are commonly codified into criminal or penal codes. *Black's Law Dictionary* (6th ed., 1990): 374. Deals with crimes against society (e.g., conduct that reflects a violation of a federal or state statute) and the punishment of the crime. The government files the case against the defendant accused of committing the crime.

curative law   As opposed to preventive law, the type of law which reflects the protection of people from others who may wrong them and in which one reacts to a legal disaster by hiring a lawyer with good "fighter skills" to come in and save the day in court.

data breach   Improper disclosure of or access to personal information that compromises the privacy or security of that data.

data broker   A company whose primary business is collecting personal information about consumers from a variety of sources and aggregating, analyzing, and sharing that information, or information derived from it, for purposes of marketing products, verifying an individual's identity, or detecting fraud.

defendant   Person in a lawsuit defending or denying the claim or the accused in a criminal case.

de-identified PHI   Data that does not disclose individually identifiable health information and regarding which there is no reasonable basis to believe that the information can be used to identify an individual.

de minimis fringe benefits   Benefits that are nontaxable because, considering their value and the frequency with which they are provided, they are so small as to make accounting for them unreasonable or impractical.

duty   One of the four elements of a negligence claim; the legal duty or standard of care owed by the defendant to the plaintiff.

electronic health records (EHRs)   Health records stored and managed electronically to facilitate the collection, storage, and sharing of comprehensive real-time information so that healthcare providers can make informed decisions with their patients.

employee assistance program (EAP) An employee benefit that may be part of a workplace wellness program and may include referral services and short-term substance use disorder or mental health counseling, as well as financial counseling and legal services.

employee engagement A topic frequently addressed by the workplace wellness industry because better employee engagement (interest and participation) in wellness programs leads to more successful programs.

employee welfare benefit plan A plan, fund, or program that is established or maintained by an employer for the purpose of providing for its participants or their beneficiaries, through the purchase of insurance or otherwise, (a) medical, surgical, or hospital care or benefits, or benefits in the event of sickness, accident, disability, death, or unemployment, or vacation benefits, apprenticeship or other training programs, or day care centers, scholarship funds, or prepaid legal services; or (b) any benefit described in § 302(c) of the Labor Management Relations Act of 1947 (other than pensions upon retirement or death, and insurance to provide such pensions).

enforcement discretion Situation in which the Food, Drug and Cosmetic Act (FDCA) applies to a device and the FDA has legal authority to enforce regulations, but it chooses not to enforce those regulations or exercise that authority.

Equal Employment Opportunity Commission (EEOC) The federal agency tasked with enforcing Title I of the Americans with Disabilities Act (ADA) and Title II of the Genetic Information Nondiscrimination Act (GINA).

excepted benefits Benefits generally exempt from health reform requirements added by HIPAA as well as the ACA. There are four categories of excepted benefits. The first category includes benefits that are generally not health coverage, such as automobile insurance, liability insurance, workers' compensation, and accidental death and dismemberment coverage. The second category is limited excepted benefits, which may include limited-scope vision or dental benefits, and benefits for long-term care, nursing home care, home health care, or community-based care. The third category, referred to as "noncoordinated excepted benefits," includes both coverage for only a specified disease (such as cancer-only policies), and hospital indemnity or other fixed-indemnity insurance. The fourth category is supplemental excepted benefits, which must be coverage supplemental to Medicare coverage or veteran's healthcare benefits, or similar coverage that is supplemental to a group health plan. For each category, the benefits must be provided under a separate policy, certificate, or contract for insurance.

exclusive benefit rule A rule under ERISA that requires employers to serve employee interests in terms of benefits offered.

Exercise Is Medicine An initiative that provides guidance for physicians and other healthcare providers to help their patients engage in regular exercise programs.

expert witness Witness whom the court considers to have special experience, knowledge, education, or training that qualifies him or her to offer testimony; in workplace wellness cases, such a witness is one who relies on safety standards, guidelines, and/or position papers published by professional organizations to help provide evidence of the duties one party owes to another in a lawsuit.

Fair Information Practice Principles (FIPPs) Principles that articulate basic protections for handling personal data; serve as the source of many of today's privacy laws.

family Individuals related to the employee by blood, marriage, or adoption.

family medical history Information about the manifestation of disease or disorder in family members of an individual.

financial activity Activities subject to the Gramm-Leach-Bliley Act (GLBA), such as lending, exchanging, transferring, investing, or safeguarding money or securities; or insuring, guaranteeing, or indemnifying against loss, harm, damage, illness, disability, or death; or providing and issuing annuities, and acting as principal, agent, or broker for purposes of the foregoing, in any state.

financial incentives   Offers often used as part of a workplace wellness program to promote or incentivize participation in the program; may include cash, cash equivalents (e.g., discounted gym memberships), and novelty items (e.g., t-shirts or gift cards).

financial institution   For purposes of the Gramm-Leach-Bliley Act (GLBA), an institution engaged in financial activity business. *See* financial activity.

furnishers of information   For purposes of the Fair Credit Reporting Act (FCRA), persons who regularly and in the ordinary course of business furnish information to one or more consumer reporting agencies about the persons' transactions or experiences with any consumer.

furnishers of medical information   For purposes of the Fair Credit Reporting Act (FCRA), persons whose primary business is providing medical services, products, or devices, or such a person's agent or assignee, who furnish information to a consumer reporting agency on a consumer.

genetic information   Data about (a) an individual's genetic tests; (b) the genetic tests of an individual's family members; and (c) the manifestation of a disease or disorder in the individual's family member (i.e., family medical history).

gross negligence   The intentional failure to perform a manifest duty in reckless disregard of the consequences as affecting the life or property of another. *Black's Law Dictionary* (6th ed., 1990): 1033.

group health plan   An employer-sponsored welfare benefit plan to the extent that the plan provides medical care to employees or their dependents directly or through insurance or otherwise.

harm   One of the four elements of a negligence claim; a plaintiff must suffer harm in the form of an injury (emotional or physical) or damage to property.

healthcare information   Information, whether oral or recorded in any form or medium, that (a) is created or received by a healthcare provider, health plan, public health authority, employer, life insurer, school or university, or healthcare clearinghouse; and (b) relates to the past, present, or future physical or mental health or condition of an individual, the provision of health care to an individual, or the past, present, or future payment for the provision of health care to an individual.

health-contingent wellness program   A type of wellness program under the HIPAA/ACA rules which is further divided into activity-only and outcomes-based programs; financial incentives thereunder are tied to achieving a health status goal, such as a certain weight or blood pressure (outcomes-based), or completing an activity that some individuals may be unable to do or have difficulty doing because of a health factor (activity-only), such as severe asthma, pregnancy, or a recent surgery.

health information exchanges (HIEs)   First phase of interoperability of electronic health information to help with care coordination; electronic HIEs allow different types of healthcare providers to appropriately access and securely share a patient's vital medical information electronically.

health risk assessment (HRA)   Can have different definitions. One definition, used by the state of Wisconsin, is a computer-based health-promotion tool consisting of a questionnaire; a biometric health screening to measure vital health statistics, including blood pressure, cholesterol, glucose, weight, and height; a formula for estimating health risks; an advice database; and a means to generate reports.

HIPAA Breach Notification Rule   Legal provision that requires certain responses by covered entities and business associates when a breach of unsecured PHI occurs. A *breach* is the acquisition, access, use, or disclosure of PHI in a manner not permitted under the HIPAA Privacy Rule which compromises the security or privacy of the PHI. 45 C.F.R. § 164.402.

HIPAA Privacy Rule   Requires covered entities to have safeguards in place to ensure the privacy of protected health information; sets forth the circumstances under which covered entities may use or disclose an individual's protected health information; and gives individuals rights with respect to their protected health information, including rights to examine and obtain a copy of their health records and to request corrections.

HIPAA Security Rule Establishes national standards to protect individuals' electronic protected health information that is created, received, used, or maintained by a covered entity.

income taxes Taxes on the annual profits arising from property, business pursuits, professions, trades, or offices, as well as on a person's income, wages, salary, commissions, emoluments, profits, and the like, or the excess thereof over a certain amount. Income taxes are the largest source of revenue for the United States government.

independent contractor One who renders services in the course of self-employment or occupation, and who follows the employer's desires only as to the results of the work.

inherent risks Risks that cause injuries because they are inseparable from the activity and harm suffered from them is no one's fault.

intentional tort (act) Tort or wrong perpetuated by one who intends to do that which the law has declared wrong as contrasted with negligence in which the tortfeasor fails to exercise that degree of care in doing what is otherwise permissible. *Black's Law Dictionary* (6th ed., 1990): 1489.

intermediate expenses Expenses that provide no benefit to the taxpayer other than to aid in the production of money.

Internal Revenue Code (IRC) § 213 An exception carved out from the general rule of IRC § 262 for medical care expenses; prohibits deductions for personal, living, or family expenses.

Internet of Things Name for the ability of everyday objects to connect to the Internet and send and receive data. It includes, for example, Internet-connected cameras that allow posting of pictures online with a single click; home automations systems that turn on front porch lights at a specified time; and bracelets that share with friends how far a person has biked or run during the day.

interoperability efforts A Department of Health and Human Services priority to connect smartphone apps, analytic tools, and plug-in technology with other electronic health information so that all relevant health information can support patient care.

invasion of privacy   A tort that includes intrusion upon a person's seclusion or solitude, or into his private affairs; public disclosure of embarrassing private facts about an individual; publicity placing someone in a false light in the public eye; or appropriation of someone's likeness for the advantage of another.

involuntary expenses   Expenses that take away from taxpayers' ability to build their material wealth.

job task analysis   An analysis that validates the performance domains, tasks, and associated knowledge and/or skills by conducting a survey of current certificants and/or individuals who provide services or perform a job consistent with the purpose of the credential.

laboratory   A facility that performs certain testing on human specimens to obtain information that can be used for the diagnosis, prevention, or treatment of any disease or impairment; or assesses the health of a human being; or performs procedures to determine, measure, or otherwise describe the presence or absence of various substances or organisms in a human body.

licensure   A type of credential that is decided by state governments, not by the federal government; the requirements for a license can vary from state to state.

low-risk software   Software over which the Food and Drug Administration (FDA) exercises enforcement discretion, such as software that merely provides information.

low-risk wellness device   Products that generally promote a healthy lifestyle and meet the following two factors: (a) are intended for only general wellness use; and (b) present a very low risk to users' safety.

manifestation of disease or disorder   A term used under GINA to mean that a person has been or could reasonably be diagnosed with a particular disease or disorder by a healthcare professional with appropriate training and expertise in the field of medicine involved.

medical care   Amounts paid for (a) the diagnosis, cure, mitigation, treatment, or prevention of disease, or amounts paid for the purpose of affecting any structure or function of the body; (b) transportation primarily for and essential to such medical care; and (c) insurance covering such medical care.

medical care expenses   Costs for something other than personal expenses; to constitute a medical care expense, an expenditure must be intermediate in nature, at most returning the taxpayer to a status quo, a whole position of good health; expenses for the diagnosis, prevention, or treatment of a specific defect.

medical device   A device regulated by the Food and Drug Administration (FDA) and defined as an instrument, apparatus, implement, machine, contrivance, implant, in vitro reagent, or other similar or related article, including any component, part, or accessory, which is intended for use in the diagnosis of disease or other conditions, or in the cure, mitigation, treatment, or prevention of disease, or which is intended to affect the structure or function of the body.

medical exam   A procedure or test that seeks information about an individual's physical or mental impairments or health.

medical information   For purposes of the Fair Credit Reporting Act (FCRA), information or data, whether oral or recorded, in any form or medium, created by or derived from a healthcare provider or the consumer, that relates to (a) the past, present, or future physical, mental, or behavioral health or condition of an individual; (b) the provision of health care to an individual; or (c) the payment for the provision of health care to an individual.

mental health disorders   Psychological or psychiatric disorders such as anxiety and depression; these problems cost U.S. employers $317.5 billion annually, compared to the $310 billion employers spend each year on occupational injury and illness generally.

mobile app   A software application for a mobile device over which the Food and Drug Administration (FDA) will or does exercise enforcement discretion.

mobile health (mHealth)   The use of mobile communications devices such as smartphones and tablet computers for health or medical purposes, usually for diagnosis, treatment, or simply well-being and maintenance.

mobile medical app   A software application that can be run on a smart-phone, tablet, or other portable computer, or a web-based software platform tailored to a mobile platform but executed on a server, which meets the definition of *device* in § 201(h) of the Food Drug and Cosmetic Act (FDCA) and is intended either (a) to be used as an accessory to a regulated medical device; or (b) to transform a mobile platform into a regulated medical device.

mosaic effect   A means by which personally identifiable information can be derived or inferred from datasets that do not even include personal identifiers, bringing into focus a picture of who an individual is and what he or she likes.

natural law   Rights that are immutable and absolute and belong to every human, whether in the state of nature or in society.

negligence (or negligent conduct)   Failing to do something (inaction or omission) that a reasonably prudent professional would have done under the circumstances, or doing something (improper action or commission) that a reasonably prudent professional would not have done under the circumstances.

nonaffiliated third party   For purposes of the Gramm-Leach-Bliley Act (GLBA), any entity that is not an affiliate of, or related by common ownership or affiliated by corporate control with, a specific financial institution; does not include a joint employee of such an institution.

nonpublic personal information   For purposes of the Gramm-Leach-Bliley Act (GLBA), personally identifiable financial information (a) provided by a consumer to a financial institution; (b) resulting from any transaction with the consumer or any service performed for the consumer; or (c) otherwise obtained by the financial institution.

occupational stress   Stress caused by participation in employment; a growing public health concern that increases the risk for depression and anxiety disorders.

parity   Equality between mental health or substance use disorder benefits and medical/surgical benefits.

participatory wellness program A type of workplace wellness program under the HIPAA/ACA rules in which a participant earns financial incentives by merely participating in the program.

patient engagement A relatively new concept in the healthcare industry that adopts the principle of involving patients in their own health care, including shifting the paradigm from "What is the matter?" to "What matters to you?"

Personal Health Investment Today (PHIT) Act A proposed act that would amend the Internal Revenue Code to allow a medical care tax deduction for up to $1,000 ($2,000 for a joint return or head of household) of qualified sports and fitness expenses, such as amounts paid for fitness facility memberships, physical exercise programs, and exercise equipment.

personal health records (PHRs) Electronic records of identifiable health information on an individual that can be drawn from multiple sources and that are managed, shared, and controlled by or primarily for the individual.

personalized health information Information and data that reflect an individual's specific health needs.

plaintiff A person who brings a legal action; the party who complains or sues in a civil action and is so named on the record.

population health As opposed to an individual's health, the health of the population being measured. For workplace wellness, includes the recognition that there is a link between an unhealthy workforce and unhealthy communities; to improve worker health, workplace wellness must look beyond individual behaviors and also look at the health of the worker's community.

Precision Medicine Initiative (PMI) Program announced by President Barack Obama in January 2015 during his State of the Union address. The PMI aims to cure diseases like cancer and diabetes and to give each person access to the personalized information needed to keep individuals and their families healthier. The PMI seeks to maximize effectiveness in disease treatment and prevention by taking into account individual variability in genes, environment, and lifestyle.

precision wellness model A model similar to the Precision Medicine Initiative, which aims to enhance wellness by taking into account an individual's unique traits and needs; such a model requires cultural competence and diversity regarding what it means to be well.

presenteeism The measurable extent to which health symptoms, conditions, and diseases adversely affect the work productivity of individuals who choose to remain at work.

preventive law As opposed to curative law, the type of law that facilitates human interaction and purpose and tries to prevent lawsuits. Preventive law requires creative thinking, timely planning, and purposeful execution to minimize legal risks; maximize legal rights; and optimize legal outcomes of transactions (deals), relationships (disputes), and opportunities (problems).

primary assumption of risk A defense in a lawsuit that can be very effective in getting the case dismissed, especially if the injury was due to inherent risks. The law does not allow individuals to recover monetary damages for an injury they received when voluntarily exposing themselves to a known and appreciated danger.

privacy framework A framework developed by the Federal Trade Commission (FTC) to assist Congress as it considers privacy legislation. The framework offers the following principles: (a) privacy by design; (b) simplified consumer choice; and (c) transparency.

professional standard of care The ethical or legal duty of a professional to exercise the level of care, diligence, and skill prescribed in the code of practice of his or her profession, or to behave as other professionals in the same discipline would in the same or similar circumstances.

protected health information (PHI) Individually identifiable health information, in any format, to which the Health Insurance Portability and Accountability Act of 1996 (HIPAA) privacy and security rules apply. Under HIPAA, *PHI* means individually identifiable health information that is transmitted by electronic media, maintained in electronic media, or transmitted or maintained in any other form or medium. 45 C.F.R. § 160.103.

psychological injury An injury that affects one's mental state and arises from a discrete, identifiable accident or from the effects of repetitive events, no one of which can be identified as causing the injury.

punitive damages Also known as *exemplary damages*; damages on an increased scale, awarded to the plaintiff over and above what will barely compensate him for his property loss, where the wrong done to him was aggravated by circumstances of violence, oppression, malice, fraud, or wanton and wicked conduct on the part of the defendant, and are intended to solace the plaintiff for mental anguish, laceration of his feelings, shame, degradation, or other aggravations of the original wrong, or else to punish the defendant for his evil behavior or to make an example of him. *Black's Law Dictionary* (6th ed., 1990): 390.

Quality Improvement Strategy (QIS) An Affordable Care Act provision, effective in Fall 2016, that requires health plans that have participated in the federal insurance "marketplace" or "exchange" for two consecutive years to implement a program that offers incentives to providers or health plan enrollees with the aim of improving health. The strategy can include activities for improving health outcomes; activities to prevent hospital readmissions; activities to improve patient safety and reduce medical errors; activities for wellness and health promotion; and/or activities to reduce health and healthcare disparities.

Quality System Regulation A regulation that the Food and Drug Administration (FDA) strongly recommends be followed by manufacturers of all mobile apps that may meet the definition of a medical device. This regulation includes practices such as having a quality policy; conducting quality audits; having sufficient personnel with the necessary education, background, training, and experience to ensure creation of a quality device; having design controls to ensure that specified design requirements are met; having production and process controls; having procedures to ensure that devices are routinely calibrated, inspected, checked, and maintained; having procedures to handle products that do not conform to specified requirements; and creating and maintaining a device history record.

reasonable accommodations An ADA provision that requires employers to provide employees with "reasonable accommodations," which may include modifications or adjustments to the work environment, to allow an employee with a disability to enjoy equal benefits and privileges of employment as are enjoyed by similarly situated employees without a disability.

reasonable alternative standard A standard requiring that health-contingent programs must offer ways to allow an individual to obtain the reward when, for that individual during that period, it is unreasonably difficult due to a medical condition or medically inadvisable to satisfy the initial standard.

redlining A form of discrimination; the term that derives from the banking industry practice of drawing red lines around neighborhoods where they would not loan money.

respondeat superior A legal doctrine in which an employer can be held liable for injury to person or property of another proximately resulting from the acts of an employee done within the scope of the employee's employment. *Black's Law Dictionary* (6th ed., 1990): 1312.

right to privacy A natural instinct, deriving from natural law, that resists unwanted intrusions, publications, and stolen identities.

risk management Preventive law strategies that can minimize legal liability exposures associated with tort and contract law.

safe harbor A provision within the ADA that allows an organization covered by the ADA, such as an employer with 15 or more employees, to administer the terms of a bona fide benefit plan based on underwriting risks, classifying risks, or administering risks.

scope of practice The procedures, actions, and processes that a health-care practitioner is permitted to undertake in keeping with the terms of the professional license. The scope of practice is limited to that which the law allows for specific education and experience, and specific demonstrated competency. Each jurisdiction has laws, licensing bodies, and regulations that describe requirements for education and training, and define scope of practice.

self-improvement wellness care Actions taken to improve one's sense of well-being and not necessarily to address any underlying health condition, such as physical activity or stress or weight management; expenses for self-improvement wellness care are not reimbursable by Medicare, Medicaid, or most private insurance plans.

stare decisis A Latin phrase meaning "to stand on decided cases"; a policy adopted by courts to stand by precedent and not to disturb a settled point. *Black's Law Dictionary* (6th ed., 1990): 1406.

Statute of Frauds The requirement that certain contracts must be in writing (e.g., the sale of goods, such as exercise equipment, that cost $500 or more).

statutory certification Certification that allows only professionals with specific credentials to use certain titles as set forth in the state statute.

statutory law A formal written enactment of a legislative body, whether federal, state, city, or county. An act of the legislature declaring, commanding, or prohibiting something. *Black's Law Dictionary* (6th ed., 1990): 1410.

stress-related hazards Work-related hazards identified by the World Health Organization that can induce or improve employee stress, depending on how an employer addresses them, such as job content, workload and work pace, work hours, participation and control, career development, employee's role in the organization, interpersonal relationships, organizational culture, and homework interface.

strict liability A concept applied by courts in product liability cases in which the seller is liable for any and all defective or hazardous products that unduly threaten a consumer's personal safety; sometimes referred to as "no fault" liability; it is not based on fault, but on public policy. Thus, a violation of a strict liability law means an automatic violation without consideration or examination of the violator's state of mind. *See, e.g., Black's Law Dictionary* (6th ed., 1990): 1422.

supportive organizational culture The type of culture in a business that increases the effectiveness of preventive law.

tax-deductible wellness benefits   Health coverage contributions, such as premium or other health plan cost-sharing reductions.

tax deductions   Indirect subsidies which are alternatives to budget outlays, credit assistance, or other instruments of public policy.

tax policy   A group contest in which powerful interests vigorously endeavor to rid themselves of present or proposed tax burdens.

therapeutic jurisprudence   The use of social science to study the extent to which a legal rule or practice promotes the psychological and physical well-being of the people it affects.

tort   A legal wrong committed upon the person or property independent of a contract. It may be either (1) a direct invasion of some legal right of the individual; (2) the infraction of some public duty by which special damage accrues to the individual; (3) the violation of some private obligation by which like damage accrues to the individual. *Black's Law Dictionary* (6th ed., 1990): 1489.

traditional health care models   Models led by providers, payers, government, and drug and device organizations; often focused on improving sick care, rather than on preventive care, and dominated by the fee-for-service payment system.

trial court   The court where legal cases begin and in which either a judge or a jury renders a decision in favor of one of the parties.

unenforceable contract   A contract that violates a statute or is against public policy.

unsecured PHI   For purposes of HIPAA, electronic PHI that is not protected through encryption or hard-copy PHI that is not destroyed.

unsecured PHR identifiable information   For purposes of the Federal Trade Commission Act (FTCA), personal health record (PHR) identifiable information that is not protected through encryption or destruction.

value-based care   The concept of better health at a lower cost.

values statement   A statement adopted by an organization that forms the foundation on which a compliance or preventive law program is based.

vendor   A seller of goods or services.

vicarious liability The imposition of liability on one person for the actionable conduct of another; *respondeat superior* is a type of vicarious liability.

voidable contract A contract that is missing one of the four elements of a valid contract: agreement, consideration, contractual capacity, and legality.

voluntary workplace wellness program A workplace wellness program in which employees do not feel coerced into participating; under the HIPAA/ACA, ADA, and GINA rules, a program will be considered voluntary if financial incentives offered through the program do not exceed 30 percent of the total cost of self-only coverage.

waiver A contract signed by an individual prior to participation in an activity that can absolve or protect potential defendants, such as fitness/wellness staff members and the facility, from their own "ordinary" negligence.

workplace bullying Repeated, health-harming mistreatment of one or more persons (the *targets*) by one or more perpetrators; abusive conduct that is threatening, humiliating, or intimidating.

workplace harassment Offensive conduct that becomes a condition of continued employment, or conduct that is severe or pervasive enough to create a work environment that a reasonable person would consider intimidating, hostile, or abusive; to be illegal under civil rights laws, the conduct must be based on race, color, religion, sex (including pregnancy), national origin, age (40 or older), disability, or genetic information.

Table of Cases

Index